OXFORD WORLD'S CLASSICS

GULLIVER'S TRAVELS

JONATHAN SWIFT (1667–1745) was born of English parents in Dublin, where he was educated at Trinity College, and in 1713 became Dean of St Patrick's Cathedral. While previously living in London, he had made friends with Pope, Gay, and Arbuthnot, formed with them the Scriblerus Club, and written propaganda for the Tory administration of another club member, Robert Harley. He had first made his mark as a satirist with *A Tale of a Tub* and *The Battle of the Books* (1704), and after his return to Dublin (1714) he used his genius for polemical satire to defend Ireland (i.e. Anglo-Irish Protestants) against exploitation by the English Whigs, most sensationally in *A Modest Proposal* (1729). Politics figured in *Gulliver's Travels* also, but only as a single element in a story of universal appeal, full of humour and excitement. Written when Swift was nearly 60, and first published in 1726, it at once became, quite literally, one of the world's classics.

PAUL TURNER is an Emeritus Fellow of Linacre College, Oxford, and has worked in several fields of Greek, Latin, and English literature. His publications include translations of Lucian, Ovid, and More's *Utopia*, an edition of Browning's *Men and Women*, and a critical biography of Tennyson.

OXFORD WORLD'S CLASSICS

*For almost 100 years Oxford World's Classics have brought
readers closer to the world's great literature. Now with over 700
titles—from the 4,000-year-old myths of Mesopotamia to the
twentieth century's greatest novels—the series makes available
celebrated as well as lesser-known writing.*

*The pocket-sized hardbacks of the early years contained
introductions by Virginia Woolf, T. S. Eliot, Graham Greene,
and other literary figures that enriched the experience of reading.
Today the series is recognized for its fine scholarship and
reliability in texts that span world literature, drama and poetry,
religion, philosophy and politics Each edition includes perceptive
commentary and essential background information to meet the
changing needs of readers.*

OXFORD WORLD'S CLASSICS

JONATHAN SWIFT

Gulliver's Travels

Edited with an Introduction and Notes by
PAUL TURNER

Oxford   New York

OXFORD UNIVERSITY PRESS

Oxford University Press, Great Clarendon Street, Oxford OX2 6DP

Oxford New York

Athens Auckland Bangkok Bogota Bombay Buenos Aires
Calcutta Cape Town Dar es Salaam Delhi Florence Hong Kong Istanbul
Karachi Kuala Lumpur Madras Madrid Melbourne Mexico City
Nairobi Paris Singapore Taipei Tokyo Toronto Warsaw

and associated companies in
Berlin Ibadan

Oxford is a trade mark of Oxford University Press

Introduction, Note on the Text,
Chronology, and Explanatory Notes © Paul Turner 1971, 1986
Select Bibliography © Paul Turner 1994

First published as a World's Classics paperback 1986
Reissued as an Oxford World's Classics paperback 1998

British Library Cataloguing in Publication Data
Data available

Library of Congress Cataloging in Publication Data
Data available
ISBN 0-19-283377-4

1 3 5 7 9 10 8 6 4 2

Printed in Great Britain by
Caledonian International Book Manufacturing Ltd.
Glasgow

CONTENTS

Abbreviations   vi
Introduction   ix
Note on the Text   xxvii
Select Bibliography   xxviii

A Chronology of Jonathan Swift   xxx
Advertisement   xxxii
A Letter from Captain Gulliver to his Cousin Sympson   xxxiii
The Publisher to the Reader   xxxvii

A VOYAGE TO LILLIPUT   3

A VOYAGE TO BROBDINGNAG   69

A VOYAGE TO LAPUTA,
   BALNIBARBI, LUGGNAGG,
   GLUBBDUBDRIB, AND JAPAN   141

A VOYAGE TO THE COUNTRY OF
   THE HOUYHNHNMS   211

Explanatory Notes   289

ABBREVIATIONS

AM	*Atlantic Monthly.*
Bacon	*Works of Francis Bacon*, ed. J. Spedding, R. L. Ellis, and D. D. Heath (1857–74).
Bonner	W. H. Bonner, *Captain William Dampier* (1934).
Buckley	M. W. Buckley, *FL* 270–8.
Case	A. E. Case, *Four Essays on GT* (1958).
Clark	P. O. Clark, 'A Gulliver Dictionary', *SP*, i (1953), 592–624.
Corr.	*Correspondence of JS*, ed. H. Williams (1965).
DRN	*De Rerum Natura.*
Eddy	W. A. Eddy, *GT: A Critical Study* (1963; repr. from 1923).
Ehrenpreis 1	I. Ehrenpreis, *MLN* lxx (1955), 95–100.
2	*PMLA* lxx (1955), 706–16.
3	*PMLA* lxxii (1957), 880–99.
4	*REL* iii, no. 3 (1962), 18–38.
5	*Swift: The Man, his Works, and the Age* (1962, 1967).
ELH	*Journal of English Literary History.*
ELN	*English Language Notes.*
ES	*English Studies.*
Exp.	*The Explicator.*
Firth	C. H. Firth, *Proceedings of the British Academy*, ix (1919), 237–59.
FL	*Fair Liberty Was All His Cry*, ed. A. N. Jeffares (1967).
Frantz	R. W. Frantz, *MP* xxix (1931), 49–57.
Gough	*GT*, ed. A. B. Gough (1956; repr. from 1915).
GT	*Gulliver's Travels.*
Histoire	Cyrano de Bergerac, *Histoire comique des états et empires de la lune et du soleil*, ed. P. L. Jacob (n.d.; *c.*1858).
HLQ	*Huntington Library Quarterly.*
JEGP	*Journal of English and Germanic Philology.*
JHI	*Journal of the History of Ideas.*

Journal	Swift, *Journal to Stella*, ed. H. Williams (1965).
JS	Jonathan Swift.
Kaempfer	E. Kaempfer, *History of Japan*, tr. J. G. Scheuchzer (1727).
Kelling	H. D. Kelling, *SP* xlviii (1951), 761–78.
Lucian	Lucian, *Satirical Sketches*, tr. P. Turner (1968, repr. 1990).
Lycurgus	Plutarch, *Life of Lycurgus*.
Memoirs	*Memoirs of Martinus Scriblerus*, ed. C. Kerby-Miller (1950).
MLN	*Modern Language Notes*.
MLR	*Modern Language Review*.
MLQ	*Modern Language Quarterly*.
Mogg	F. Mogg, *Scientific American*, clxxix (1948), 52–5.
MP	*Modern Philology*.
NM1	M. Nicolson and N. M. Mohler, in M. Nicolson, *Science and Imagination* (1962), 110–54.
NM2	M. Nicolson and N. M. Mohler, *Annals of Science*, ii (1937), 405–30.
NQ	*Notes and Queries*.
OED	*Oxford English Dictionary*.
PMLA	*Publications of the Modern Language Association of America*.
Poems	*Poems of JS*, ed. H. Williams (1958).
Pons	É. Pons, *Mélanges offerts à M. Abel Lefranc* (1936), 219–28.
PQ	*Philological Quarterly*.
Prose	*Prose Writings of JS*, ed. H. Davis (1959–66).
PTA	*PTRS Abridg'd and Dispos'd under General Heads*, vols. iv, v: 1700–20, ed. H. Jones (1721); vol. vi: 1719–33, ed. J. Eames and J. Martyn (1734).
PTRS	*Philosophical Transactions of the Royal Society*.
Quinlan	M. J. Quinlan, *PQ* xlvi (1967), 412–17.
Quintana	R. Quintana, *Mind and Art of JS* (1953; repr. from 1936).
Rabelais	Rabelais, *Gargantua and Pantagruel*, tr. J. M. Cohen (1955).
REL	*Review of English Literature*.
RES	*Review of English Studies*.

Scott	*Prose Works of JS*, ed. Temple Scott (1897–1908).
SN	*Satire Newsletter.*
SoR	*Southern Review.*
SP	*Studies in Philology.*
SR	*Sewanee Review.*
Thackeray	W. M. Thackeray, *English Humourists of the Eighteenth Century* (1853).
TLS	*Times Literary Supplement.*
TSE	*Tulane Studies in English.*
TSLL	*Texas Studies in Literature and Language.*
Utopia	Sir Thomas More, *Utopia*, tr. P. Turner (1965).
UTQ	*University of Toronto Quarterly.*
Voyages	*Dampier's Voyages*, ed. J. Masefield (1906).
Williams	*GT*, ed. H. Williams (1926).
ZAA	*Zeitschrift für Anglistik und Amerikanistik.*

INTRODUCTION

I

Gulliver's Travels is not one of those books which 'the reader admires and lays down, and forgets to take up again'.[1] It was a bestseller when it first came out in 1726, and people have been reading it for pleasure, not merely for profit, ever since. George Orwell read it first just before he was 8, re-read it at least half a dozen times during his short life, and found it 'impossible to grow tired of'. 'If I were to make a list', he wrote, 'of six books which were to be preserved when all others were destroyed, I would certainly put *Gulliver's Travels* among them.'[2]

One thing that makes the book rather hard to lay down is the excitement of the story. Only the flying island episode is real science fiction, but throughout the narrative Swift uses the science-fiction technique of describing fantastic events with so much circumstantial detail that they seem perfectly credible. Thus the reader becomes seriously involved in Gulliver's unlikely adventures. Will he, for instance, manage to bring off his one-man commando-raid on the Blefuscudian fleet—or will he stagger back blinded by a hail of arrows? It is quite a tense moment; but in the nick of time the resourceful hero puts on his spectacles, and we all breathe a sigh of relief.

Another obvious attraction of *Gulliver's Travels* is its humour, which is often far more hilarious than one would expect from an author of nearly 60. As Swift's friend Arbuthnot put it, 'Gulliver is a happy man that at his age can write such a merry work.'[3] Some of the jokes were too broad for Victorian taste, and as late as 1915 the Clarendon Press editor felt it necessary to omit them; but the modern reader

---

[1] Dr Johnson, *Lives of the Poets*, ed. G. B. Hill (1968), i. 183.
[2] *Shooting an Elephant* (1950), 78.
[3] *Corr.*, iii. 179.

is likely to find their Rabelaisian character quite congenial. Equally in line with modern trends is the occasional violence of the satire. Thackeray described Part IV as 'filthy in word, filthy in thought, furious, raging, obscene',[4] and Edmund Gosse thought that 'the horrible foulness of this satire on the Yahoos . . . banishes from decent households a fourth part'[5] of the book; but nowadays most people would agree that shock-tactics are a legitimate element in satiric technique, and that Swift's 'horrible foulness' is usually justified by his moral purpose.

The story, then, the humour, and the satire have as much appeal for our period as they had for the eighteenth century; and certain passages may have even more. The sapce-age reader should find a special interest in that artificial satellite, the Island of Laputa; and all the moral issues raised by nuclear weapons are implied in Gulliver's offer to the King of Brobdingnag of enough destructive power to 'destroy the whole Metropolis, if ever it should pretend to dispute his absolute Commands'. The thinking-machine devised by the Professor at Lagado is clearly a prototype of the computer; and one of his colleagues is equally up to date in proposing a system of reciprocal brain-transplants between political party-leaders. George Orwell saw the Houyhnhnm community as a totalitarian state, with the Yahoos playing the role of the Jews in Nazi Germany, and found in Part III 'an extraordinarily clear prevision of the spy-haunted "police state", with its endless heresy-hunts and treason-trials'.[6] Finally, the episode of the Struldbrugs poses a major problem which was not at all urgent in Swift's day, but, thanks to modern medicine, is becoming increasingly urgent in ours: the problem whether it is right to prolong life after the capacity to enjoy life has gone.

In these and similar passages *Gulliver's Travels* may well be said to have more topical interest today than when it was originally published.

---

[4] Thackeray, 40.
[5] *History of Eighteenth Century Literature* (1889), 161–2.
[6] *Shooting an Elephant*, 75, 68.

II

The first hint for writing the book probably came from the Scriblerus Club, a group of friends who got together in 1713 with a plan to satirize every form of idiocy displayed by intellectuals, in the person of an imaginary pedant and 'scribbler', Martinus Scriblerus. The Club consisted of Pope, Swift, Gay, Arbuthnot, Parnell, and the Earl of Oxford, and the idea was to ridicule the published works of their victims (e.g. Bentley's edition of Milton) by claiming that Scriblerus wrote them, and also to publish new satires (e.g. the *Peri Bathous*, 1728) under the name of Scriblerus. But the main project was to publish a biography of their hero, which finally came out in 1741, as *The Memoirs of Martinus Scriblerus*.

In chapter xvi of the *Memoirs* the travels of Martinus are briefly summarized in such terms as to identify them with the travels of Gulliver. This chapter was probably written between 1727 and 1729; but the idea of sending Scriblerus off on a series of imaginary journeys seems to have formed part of the Club's original plan, and Swift, who had always been fond of reading travel-books, was apparently given the job of writing this one. The question is how much actually got written about Martinus's travels, and what relation they bear to *Gulliver's Travels*.

According to a statement by Pope in about 1728, 'It was from a part of these memoirs that Dr. Swift took his first hints for Gulliver. There were pygmies in Schreibler's[7] travels and the projects of Laputa.'[8] On the strength of this it has been suggested that 'A Voyage to Lilliput' and 'A Voyage to Laputa' incorporate material written perhaps as early as 1714 for the travels of Scriblerus; but there is no conclusive evidence to support such a theory, and Pope's words appear to mean only that the basic conception of Lilliput and of Laputa was suggested by Club discussions of the Scriblerus biography.

It is fairly clear from Swift's correspondence that the real composition of *Gulliver's Travels* began around the end of 1720, and was finished in the autumn of 1725. Parts I and II

---

[7] Quasi-German for 'scribbler'

[8] J. Spence, *Observations, Anecdotes and Characters*, ed. J. M. Osborn (1966), i. 56.

were mainly written in 1721–2, Part IV in 1723, and Part III in 1724–5.

When he started writing this 'merry work', he had no reason to feel particularly merry. He had failed to obtain any Church preferment in England, and had been forced to accept a mere Deanery in Ireland, a country which he disliked. The Tory government for which he had worked had fallen, and his friends Oxford and Bolingbroke had been impeached by the Whigs. He was suffering from a chronic disease, Ménière's syndrome, which caused deafness and increasingly severe fits of giddiness. To the sense of living in exile, cut off from his friends, was added in 1721 the news that one of his best friends, Matthew Prior, was dead; and in 1724 his ill health was intensified by 'a cruel Disorder that kept me in Torture for a Week . . . the Learned call it the Haemorrhoides internae which with the attendance of Strangury, loss of Blood, water-gruel and no sleep require more of the Stoick than I am Master of, to support it'.[9]

He faced these troubles, however, with a more cheerful philosophy than Stoicism: 'I give all possible way to Amusements, because they preserve my Temper as Exercise does my Health, and without Health and good humor I had rather be a dog.'[10] 'When you are melancholy, read diverting or amusing books; it is my Receit, and seldom fails.'[11] 'I always expect tomorrow will be worse, but I enjoy today as well as I can. This is my philosophy . . .'[12] The rich comedy of *Gulliver's Travels* is doubtless a by-product of this courageous determination to keep his spirits up, whatever happened; and while he was writing the book, his spirits must have soared spontaneously, when he scored a resounding victory over Walpole and the Whig government, in the matter of 'Wood's half-pence'. Wood had been given a patent to supply copper coins to Ireland, on a scale that would have seriously damaged the Irish economy. Swift rallied Irish resistance to the scheme in his anonymous *Drapier's Letters* (1724), which were so effective

[9] *Corr.*, iii. 9.   [10] *Corr.*, ii. 430.
[11] *Corr.*, ii. 432.   [12] *Corr.*, ii. 449.

that Walpole was finally forced to recall Wood's patent, and 'the Drapier' became a national hero. The extent of his triumph is indicated by the story that when Walpole, several years later, issued an order for Swift's arrest, he was told that an army of at least ten thousand men would be needed to arrest the Dean of Ireland.[13]

This political success must have greatly increased Swift's confidence in the power of his pen, and his determination to publish *Gulliver's Travels*; but the problem was first how to find a publisher prepared to risk publishing a transparently anti-Whig satire, and secondly how to avoid prosecution himself. To solve these problems he now made a trip to England, taking his manuscript with him, and arrived in London by the middle of March 1726. He spent most of the next few months staying with Pope at Twickenham, and seeing other old friends of the Scriblerus Club. No doubt he showed them his manuscript, and they discussed plans for publishing it; perhaps he had it transcribed, so that his handwriting could not be used as evidence against him.

Finally, in August, secret negotiations were started with a London printer and bookseller called Benjamin Motte. 'Motte receiv'd the copy (he tells me),' wrote Pope to Swift later, 'he knew not from whence, nor from whom, dropp'd at his house in the dark from a Hackney-coach: by computing the time, I found it was after you left England, so for my part, I suspend judgment.'[14] The 'copy' was part of the manuscript of *Gulliver's Travels*, accompanied by a letter, evidently composed by Swift, but written in what looks like Gay's hand,[15] and signed by Gulliver's imaginary cousin Richard Sympson. The letter asked Motte if he would publish the book, for a fee of £200 to the author (i.e. Gulliver), who 'intends the profit for the use of poor Sea-men'.[16] Motte evidently recognized the market-value of the work—he may even have guessed who wrote it, since Motte was the business successor of Swift's old friend and publisher, Benjamin Tooke—and he agreed to publish within a month of receiving the complete manuscript

---

[13] T. Sheridan, *Life of Swift* (1784), 276–8.   [14] *Corr.*, iii. 181.
[15] H. Williams, *The Text of GT* (1952), 17.   [16] *Corr.*, iii. 153.

(though not to pay the £200 quite so soon). The book came out on 28 October 1726.

By this time Swift was back in Ireland, He had not been able to correct the proofs himself, and when he saw a published copy, he found that Motte had not only allowed a large number of misprints to stand, but had deliberately altered the text of several passages,[17] cutting out or toning down the satire which he thought too dangerously outspoken. Swift was naturally annoyed that his work should be 'mangled and murdered'[18] in this way, and, presumably at his request, his friend Charles Ford wrote to Motte pointing out the misprints and protesting at the alterations.[19] Motte corrected most of the misprints in his next edition, but the prudential changes in the text were retained until 1735, when *Gulliver's Travels* was reprinted in Dublin by George Faulkner, as volume iii of Swift's *Works*.

Scholars have disagreed about the reliability of Faulkner's text; but the evidence seems to suggest that this edition was published with Swift's permission and under his general supervision, and that its text, which incorporates most of the *corrigenda* noted by Ford in Motte's first edition, is the nearest we can get to Swift's original manuscript, and to his final intentions for the book.[20] The text printed here, prepared by Herbert Davis, is based on Faulkner's 1735 edition.

Whatever the faults of his text, Motte's 1726 edition was an enormous success. The first impression sold out in a week; within three weeks ten thousand copies had been sold, and within two years the book had been translated twice into French, once into Dutch, and once into German. On 17 November Gay wrote to Swift:

About ten days ago a Book was publish'd here of the Travels of one Gulliver, which hath been the conversation of the whole town ever since ... nothing is more diverting than to hear the different opinions people give of it, though all agree in liking it extreamly. 'Tis generally said that you are the Author, but I am told, the Bookseller

---

[17] The most important changes are pointed out in the Explanatory Notes.
[18] *Corr.*, iv. 198. Cf. *Corr.*, iii. 189–90.   [19] *Corr.*, iii. 194–5.
[20] For opposing views of Faulkner's text, see Case, 1–49, and H. Williams, *The Text of GT* (1952).

declares he knows not from what hand it came. From the highest to the lowest it is universally read, from the Cabinet-council to the Nursery.[21]

Swift's friends shared in his triumph: for a while his correspondence was full of joking allusions to the book, and to the fiction that Swift had nothing to do with it. One such letter from Mrs Howard provoked the reply:

Madam,

When I received your Letter I thought it the most unaccountable one I ever saw in my Life, and was not able to comprehend three words of it together. The Perverseness of your Lines astonished me, which tended downwards to the right on one Page, and upward in the two others. This I thought impossible to be done by any Person who did not squint with both Eyes; an Infirmity I never observed in you. However, one thing I was pleased with, that after you had writ me *down*, you repented, and writ me *up*. But I continued four days at a loss for your meaning, till a Bookseller sent me the Travells of one Cap^tn Gulliver, who proved a very good Explainer, although at the same time, I thought it hard to be forced to read a Book of seven hundred Pages in order to understand a Letter of fifty lines . . .[22]

He was evidently in very good spirits—even when, several weeks later, one of his 'Houyhnhnms' bit his little finger.[23]

III

Gulliver's Travels starts like a novel, and in relating the adventures of a realistically conceived central character it obviously resembles the novels of Defoe, especially *Robinson Crusoe*, published seven years before. The adventures, however, soon become too fantastic for a novel, and the characterization of Gulliver is not always of central importance.

A closer definition would be to call the book a parody of a traveller's tale. This ancient genre goes back to Lucian's *True History* (2nd century AD), a riotous take-off of the travellers' tales current in classical times. Lucian goes off on a voyage of

[21] *Corr.*, iii. 182.
[22] *Corr.*, iii. 187. Cf. the comment on Lilliputian handwriting (p. 45).
[23] *Corr.*, iii. 196.

discovery across the Atlantic, and has a series of humorously incredible experiences (such as being blown up to the moon, and living for nearly two years inside a whale). That is the basic pattern of *Gulliver's Travels,* which borrows several details from Lucian;[24] but Swift is more concerned to parody the genuine travellers' tales of his own period, particularly those of the pirate and explorer William Dampier.

The mock-traveller's tale had been adapted by Sir Thomas More to serve as an introduction to his *Utopia* (1516), and *Gulliver's Travels* has clear connections with the Utopian romance. Chapter 6 of Part I, for instance, describes Lilliputian arrangements in Utopian terms, and the whole account of the Houyhnhnms seems to oscillate between a Utopia and a mock-Utopia.

Since More, several works had been written in the Lucianic genre, notably by Rabelais and Cyrano de Bergerac. The fourth and fifth books of Rabelais, written about 1547, describe the travels of Panurge and Pantagruel in search of the Oracle of the Bottle. On their way they visit various fantastic countries which allegorically satirize contemporary clerics, politicians, and academics. Swift uses a rather similar technique, and in particular his mockery of scientists in Laputa and Lagado corresponds with that of Rabelais in the Kingdom of Entelechy.[25]

In his *Histoire comique de la lune* (1657) Cyrano visits the moon, and finds it inhabited by giants. Like Gulliver in Brobdingnag, Cyrano is put on show as a freak, thrown into the company of a dwarf—who turns out to be the astronaut-hero of Bishop Godwin's *The Man in the Moon* (1638)—and becomes emotionally involved with a young giantess.

In using the Lucianic mock-traveller's tale, then, as a vehicle for Utopian speculation and contemporary satire, Swift was doing nothing new. What made his book unique was the complexity of its texture. *Gulliver's Travels* is as funny as a Lucianic parody; but it also has the excitement of a real traveller's tale, like the *Voyages* of Dampier, or of a realistic

---

[24] The most important parallels with previous authors are indicated in the Explanatory Notes.

[25] Bk. V, ch. xix–xxii (Rabelais, 645–53).

novel like *Robinson Crusoe*. Like Rabelais, Swift expresses through a light-hearted narrative much serious criticism of his contemporaries; but he also expresses certain profound thoughts about human life in general, which transcend his own age, and are still relevant in ours.

IV

The criticism of contemporaries is chiefly related to either politics or science. To understand the political satire we must remember that from 1710 to 1714 Swift had acted as Public Relations Officer for the Tory administration of Robert Harley (later Earl of Oxford) and Henry St John (later Viscount Bolingbroke). As editor of the *Examiner* he had written weekly articles attacking Whig policies and personalities, and defending Tory ones; and in his most influential pamphlet, *The Conduct of the Allies* (1711), he had argued in favour of the Tory plan to end the long War of the Spanish Succession, thus preparing his public to welcome the Treaty of Utrecht (1713).

In 1714 Queen Anne had died, and the Tory government had fallen. Once back in power, the Whigs had started a witch-hunt against their predecessors, setting up a Committee of Secrecy (1715) to investigate their conduct over the Peace, and charging Oxford and Bolingbroke with high treason. Bolingbroke had avoided trial by escaping to France, Oxford had been tried and imprisoned, and in 1722 Swift's friend Atterbury had also been tried and imprisoned for alleged complicity in a Jacobite plot. Meanwhile, Swift himself had been living in danger of prosecution for his public contributions to the Tory cause.

All these political events are the subject of mocking allusions in *Gulliver's Travels*. Gulliver's experiences in Lilliput partly allegorize those of Bolingbroke and Oxford around 1714. Gulliver has ended the war with Blefuscu (France) by a naval victory (the occupation of the French naval base at Dunkirk). By an irregular method (Bolingbroke's secret negotiations with the French) he has extinguished a dangerous fire (ended the War of the Spanish Succession), for which he deserves the nation's gratitude. Instead, he finds, himself impeached for a technical illegality, and for allowing the Blefuscudians too easy terms (one charge against Bolingbroke was enabling 'the French King, so exhausted and vanquished as he had been . . . to carry his designs by a peace glorious to him'[26]). The search of Gulliver's pockets obliquely ridicules the investigations of the Whig Committee of Secrecy; and Bolingbroke's flight to France is implicitly justified by the circumstances of Gulliver's escape to Blefuscu.

The anti-Gulliver cabal in Lilliput represents the Whigs. Skyresh Bolgolam is probably the Earl of Nottingham, a Tory who supported the Whigs in 1711; Flimnap is Walpole, and the 'King's cushion' that saves Flimnap's life when he falls from the tightrope is the Duchess of Kendal, who used her influence as a mistress of George I to restore Walpole to office in 1721 after he had been forced to resign in 1717.

King George favoured the Whigs, so he figures as the treacherous Emperor of Lilliput, the tyrannical King of Laputa, and as the subject of several passing gibes.[27] Queen Anne had favoured the Tories, but she was also the 'Royal Prude'[28] who had been shocked by Swift's *Tale of a Tub* (1704), and had therefore refused to give him a bishopric. She may be the model for the Lilliputian Empress, who at first smiles 'very graciously' at Gulliver through a window, but then bitterly resents his method of saving her wing of the palace.[29]

The passage in Part III, Chapter 6, about methods of 'discovering Plots and Conspiracies against the Government' is aimed chiefly at the trial of Atterbury; and the account (which neither Motte nor Faulkner dared to print) of the rebellion in Lindalino[30] is a transparent allegory of Swift's victory over Wood and Walpole. In this affair Swift had reason to disapprove not only of the 'King's cushion', who had helped Wood

---

[26] *Historical Register*, ii (1724), 2–3; Case, 131.

[27] e.g. p. 88, ll. 18–20.   [28] *Poems*, i. 193.

[29] There may also be a reference to Queen Anne's dislike of Oxford's drunken behaviour (Case, 76).

[30] pp. 170–1.

to get his patent, but also of Sir Isaac Newton, who, as Comptroller of the Mint, had reported favourably on Wood's coins, though an assay made in Ireland showed that many of them were seriously under weight.[31] Hence several unkind references to Newton, such as Aristotle's comment on the *Principia Mathematica*:

new Systems of Nature were but new Fashions, which would vary in every Age; and even those who pretend to demonstrate them from Mathematical Principles, would flourish but a short Period of Time, and be out of Vogue when that was determined.[32]

From politically motivated satire on Newton's theory of gravitation we may pass to other satire on contemporary science, for which the motive is rather less obvious. One reason why Swift laughed at scientists was doubtless that he found their activities inherently comic. For this attitude he had good literary precedents, such as the passage in the *Clouds* of Aristophanes where Socrates carefully measures the jumping range of a flea and discusses whether a gnat hums through its mouth or its anus.[33] Rabelais shows much the same attitude when he lists the projects of scientists in the kingdom of Entelechy (e.g. extracting farts from a dead donkey).[34] Sir Nicholas Gimcrack is a figure of fun in Shadwell's *The Virtuoso* (1676) simply because he is interested in dissecting lobsters and studying 'the nature of ants, flies, humble-bees, ear-wigs, millepedes, hog's-lice, maggots, mites in a cheese, tadpoles, worms, newts, spiders, and all the noble products of the sun'.[35] The moral of such satire is suggested when another character calls Sir Nicholas 'One who has broken his brains about the nature of maggots, who has studied these twenty years to find out the several sorts of spiders, and never cares for understanding mankind'.[36] Swift would probably have agreed that 'The proper Study of Mankind is Man',[37] and that scientific research on lower forms of life was self-evidently silly.

[31] H. Davis (ed.), *Drapier's Letters* (1935), 205–8.   [32] p. 198.
[33] ll. 144–52; 156–64.   [34] Rabelais, 651.
[35] II. ii. 288–90; III. iii. 1–5.   [36] I. ii. 11–13.
[37] Pope, *Essay on Man*, ii. 2.

Another element in Swift's attitude to science is the demand for practical results implied by this comment on the agricultural experiments in Balnibarbi.

I made bold to ask my Conductor, that he would be pleased to explain to me what could be meant by so many busy Heads, Hands and Faces, both in the Streets and the Fields, because I could not discover any good Effects they produced; but on the contrary, I never knew a Soil so unhappily cultivated, Houses so ill contrived and ruinous, or a People whose Countenances and Habit expressed so much Misery and Want.[38]

Most of the idiotic projects pursued in the Academy of Lagado were modelled on actual research carried out by members of the Royal Society.[39] As a matter of fact, the aims of this Society, like those of its inspirer, Bacon, were eminently utilitarian: it certainly envisaged the end of scientific knowledge as 'the relief of man's estate',[40] and it had already made important advances in applied science. To take only one example, Pepys was quite right in predicting (1666) that some Royal Society experiments in blood-transfusion might ultimately prove 'of mighty use to man's health'.[41]

Here Swift, perhaps, did not look far enough into the future—or did he? Of course he could not foresee the horrors of nuclear, chemical, or biological warfare, nor of the modern scientist's plans for genetic engineering; but perhaps he vaguely sensed the kind of 'brave new world' that science was liable to produce. A hint of such a presentiment may be found in the ambition of the Universal Artist to propagate a 'Breed of naked Sheep all over the Kingdom'. A clearer indication is the immediate result of Laputian technology: that the inhabitants of Balnibarbi may at any moment be deprived 'of the Benefit of the Sun and the Rain, and consequently' afflicted with 'Dearth and Diseases'.[42] If it is true that Swift made fun of scientists, because he dimly realized the potential dangers of science, this aspect of his satire deserves to be taken very seriously.

[38] p. 174.
[39] The original sources are given in the Explanatory Notes.
[40] Bacon, iii. 294.   [41] *Diary*, ed. H. B. Wheatley (1913), vi. 60–1.
[42] pp. 182, 170.

V

The most valuable element, however, in the content of *Gulliver's Travels* is the general comment that it makes on human life. This comment is expressed by viewing humanity from four different standpoints. The first is that of a physically superior being, who sees mankind as ridiculously small. The second is that of a physically inferior being, who sees mankind as grotesquely large. The third is the standpoint of common sense, from which the vast majority of mankind appear crazy and wicked. The fourth is that of a rational animal, which sees the whole human race as irrational and bestial.

As Gulliver progresses through this series of world-views, his own character and attitudes change. And here Swift raises the question: how should an intelligent and sensitive individual react to increasing knowledge of human nature?

Let us take the four views, one by one, noting what judgements emerge; then examine Gulliver's development throughout the book, and decide what this implies.

In Part I the human race is viewed in miniature, and at first seems rather charming; but the tiny creatures soon turn out to be treacherous and cruel. They are ready to sacrifice all humane feeling, whether towards Gulliver or the Blefuscudians, to their own petty ambitions. The moral of Lilliput is later made explicit by the King of Brobdingnag, apropos of ordinary human beings:

he observed, how contemptible a Thing was human Grandeur, which could be mimicked by such diminutive Insects as I: and yet, said he, I dare engage, those Creatures have their Titles and Distinctions of Honour; they contrive little Nests and Burrows, that they call Houses and Cities; they make a Figure in Dress and Equipage; they love, they fight, they dispute, they cheat, they betray.[43]

In Part II the human race appears coarse and callous. Gulliver is revolted by the Brobdingnagians' huge bodies, by their smell, their table-manners, and their physical habits. He is caused great pain by the thoughtlessness of the first the man who picks him up, and worked almost to death by the

[43] p. 98.

farmer, whose chief interest is money. Even the King and Queen show a certain lack of imagination in the jokes that they make about Gulliver's experiences with the monkey, and with giant flies. This general insensitivity extends to the Brobdingnagians' treatment of one another. The horrifying description of the beggars in Lorbrulgrud shows this people's inadequate social conscience, and the account of the execution stresses the barbarity of their penal system.

A few individuals, however, display lovable or admirable qualities. Glumdalclitch is unfailingly kind and considerate; and the King of Brobdingnag is humane enough to be shocked by European warfare. He acts, as we have seen, as an extension of the Part I viewpoint: he judges, as a superior being, the moral shortcomings of the 'little odious Vermin'[44] described to him by Gulliver.

In Part III Gulliver views human behaviour through the eyes of common sense, and sees the gift of reason everywhere misused, either for playing futile intellectual games, or for unscrupulously exploiting other people. In Glubbdubdrib he reads in human history the depressing lesson that crime does pay, and that human nature is becoming worse and worse. In Luggnagg he finds the lesson confirmed, first by the example of a cruel tyranny, and secondly by the Struldbrugs, who illustrate not only the general miseries of human life, but in particular the constant tendency of human beings to take advantage of one another. The harsh legislation against these wretched Immortals is justified because 'Otherwise, as Avarice is the necessary Consequent of old Age, those Immortals would in time become Proprietors of the whole Nation, and Engross the Civil Power; which, for want of Abilities to manage, must end in the Ruin of the Publick.'[45]

The last touch in this gloomy picture of human life is the contrast between the pagan Japanese and the Christian Dutch. 'Nominal Christianity', as Swift elsewhere calls it,[46] is accompanied by more wanton malice than nominal paganism.

In Part IV human beings, viewed by those rational animals,

---

[44] p. 126.   [45] p. 215.   [46] *Prose*, ii. 28.

the Houyhnhnms, appear as Yahoos, dirty, greedy, vicious, lecherous, and stupid. The Europeans described by Gulliver to his master are exactly like the Yahoos, except that they are more intelligent; but this only makes them worse, since, as his master puts it, 'when a Creature pretending to Reason, could be capable of such Enormities, he dreaded lest the Corruption of that Faculty might be worse than Brutality itself'.[47] As in Part III Christians behave more spitefully than pagans, so in Part IV 'civilized' men behave more disgustingly than animals.

From each of these four viewpoints the human race presents an unattractive picture; but the pictures are not identical (compare Glumdalclitch with the young female Yahoo who interrupts Gulliver's bathe), nor does any one picture claim to be complete. In each case Swift is saying: 'Consider human beings from *this* point of view, and *this* is what they will look like.' He does not say 'This is what human beings are.' To choose a trivial illustration: in Part I human beings have 'the fairest Complexion in the World', in Part II their complexions are 'rough and coarse, and ill coloured'.[48] Neither of these statements about human skin is offered as absolutely true.

The relativity of the pictures is particularly important to remember, when we come to Part IV. The Houyhnhnm view represents one aspect of humanity, but not the only one. The Houyhnhnms themselves are often meant to be admirable, sometimes to be absurd. To eighteenth-century man the horse was primarily a convenient means of transport, and it was an instructive paradox to imagine this convenience passing judgement on its employers. A twentieth-century satirist might achieve a similar effect by imagining a world governed by cars. To a ruling class of efficient internal-combustion engines, human behaviour would doubtless seem highly irrational; but such a fantasy would not imply that a car is better than a man.

The four pictures form a series, in which the view grows gradually darker; that is, they represent stages in Gulliver's

[47] p. 251.   [48] p. 82.

disillusionment. This brings us back to Swift's question: granted that, as one gets older, one learns more and more to the discredit of human nature, how should one react? The obvious reaction is to become a misanthrope, increasingly obsessed by what is wrong with people. That is what Gulliver does. He starts out as a cheerful, innocent character, who expects the best from everybody, and is genuinely surprised by the treachery that he meets in Lilliput: he ends by regarding human society as a mere assortment of 'Gibers, Censurers, Backbiters, Pick-pockets, Highwaymen, House-breakers, Attorneys, Bawds, Buffoons, Gamesters, Politicians, Wits, Spleneticks, tedious Talkers, Controvertists, Ravishers, Murderers, Robbers, Virtuoso's'.[49] The random arrangement of the list is clearly intended to suggest that Gulliver has lost all sense of proportion.

The last few chapters of the book show him becoming more and more unbalanced. By a number of small clues dropped into the text, the reader is given to understand that Gulliver is going too far, that his devotion to the Houyhnhnms is becoming an obsession, and his misanthropy a joke. Finally he turns into a figure of almost pure farce, who habitually stops up his nose with 'Rue, Lavender, or Tobacco-Leaves'[50] (except, presumably, when he is drinking in the horsy smell of his groom[51]).

In the person of Gulliver, the misanthropic satirist is mercilessly satirized; and the climax of the process comes in his final diatribe. After demonstrating in detail his sense of superiority to the whole human race, he concludes by denouncing the pride of others in a sentence that neatly illustrates his own: 'and therefore I entreat those who have any tincture of this absurd Vice, that they will not presume to appear in my Sight'.[52]

Swift, like Gulliver, found his fellow-men unsatisfactory; but he reacted rather differently. Gulliver becomes so obsessed with the generic faults of mankind, that he cannot appreciate the virtues of individuals. Swift never made this mistake. As he wrote to Pope, just after finishing *Gulliver's Travels*:

        [49] p. 284.   [50] p. 304.
        [51] p. 298.   [52] p. 305.

I have ever hated all Nations professions and Communityes, and all my love is towards individualls; for instance, I hate the tribe of Lawyers, but I love Councellor such a one, Judge such a one; . . . so with Physicians (I will not Speak of my own Trade), Soldiers, English, Scotch, French, and the rest, but principally I hate and detest that animal called man, although I hartily love John, Peter, Thomas and so forth.[53]

How heartily he loved his friends is clear from all his letters as this time, and especially from his reaction to the news of Arbuthnot's illness: 'O, if the World had but a dozen Arbuthnetts in it I would burn my Travels.'[54]

Gulliver weighs human beings in the balance of pure reason, and finds them wanting. He therefore feels 'Hatred, Disgust and Contempt' for his wife and family, who have (indeed somewhat irrationally) welcomed him home 'with great . . . Joy'.[55] Swift is prepared to be more tolerant, because he does not expect people to be rational: 'I tell you after all that I do not hate Mankind, it is vous autres who hate them because you would have them reasonable Animals, and are Angry for being disappointed. I have always rejected that Definition[56] and made another of my own.'[57] This new definition, he tells Pope, is the basis of *Gulliver's Travels*:

I have got Materials Towards a Treatis proving the falsity of that Definition *animal rationale* [a rational animal]; and to show it should be only *rationis capax* [capable of reason]. Upon this great foundation of Misanthropy (though not Timons manner) the whole building of my Travells is erected . . .[58]

The example of Gulliver, who becomes a misanthrope in Timon's manner, not Swift's, is designed to teach the opposite attitude, tolerance.

In recognizing the influence on human behaviour of irrational animal instinct, Swift was in line with modern psychology; but to understand his thought in its context, we must remember that he was not a modern psychologist, but an eighteenth-century clergyman. The moral of *Gulliver's Travels*,

[53] *Corr.*, iii. 103 (punctuation regularized to make the meaning clear).
[54] *Corr.*, iii. 104.   [55] p. 298.
[56] See first note to p. 213.   [57] *Corr.*, iii. 118.
[58] *Corr.*, iii. 103.

though doubtless based on practical experience, was theoreti-
cally linked with Christian theology. The Yahoos, for instance,
are described in much the same terms as theologians used to
describe the sinfulness of the flesh; and Part IV may be partly
interpreted as a vindication of the doctrine of Original Sin, in
reply to such optimistic philosophers as Shaftesbury and
Hutcheson, who argued for the natural goodness of man.

More interesting, perhaps, is the link with Christian ethics.
If Gulliver's self-betraying sermon against pride is a variation
on the theme 'Why beholdest thou the mote that is in thy
brother's eye, but considerest not the beam that is in thine
own eye?',[59] the episode of Don Pedro[60] clearly echoes the
parable of the Good Samaritan.[61] When the rational
Houyhnhnms have 'passed by on the other side', and expelled Gulliver from their country almost as callously as the
mutineers expelled him from the ship, he suddenly meets a
personification of real Christian charity. The contrast between Houyhnhnm indifference and Christian loving-kind-
ness, between Gulliver's sour misanthropy and Don Pedro's
patient philanthropy, cannot be fortuitous. The two men are
obviously meant to represent two different ways of reacting to
human frailty: 'the judicious Reader'[62] is left to make his
choice between Timon and the Good Samaritan.

[59] Matt. 7: 3   [60] pp. 295–7.
[61] Luke 10: 33–7.   [62] p. 301.

NOTE ON THE TEXT

THE text of *Gulliver's Travels* given here is taken from volume xi of Herbert Davis's edition of Swift's *Prose Writings* (1965 reprint). It is based on volume iii of George Faulkner's Dublin edition of Swift's *Works* (1735). For reasons summarized in the Introduction (pp. xv–xvi), this text of 1735 seems to have come far closer to what Swift originally wrote than the first edition of 1726, and also to have contained revisions representing his last ideas for the book.

SELECT BIBLIOGRAPHY

For books published up to 1980 see R. H. Rodino, *Swift Studies 1965–1980: An Annotated Bibliography* (New York, 1984). Of these, and more recent books, the following may be found most useful:

1. *Swift*

EHRENPREIS, IRVIN, *Swift: The Man, his Works, and the Age* (3 vols.; London, 1962–83).

WILLIAMS, KATHLEEN (ed.), *Swift: The Critical Heritage* (London, 1970).

DONOGHUE, DENIS (ed.), *Jonathan Swift: A Critical Anthology* (Harmondsworth, 1971).

RAWSON, C. J. (ed.), *Gulliver and the Gentle Reader: Studies in Swift and our Time* (London, 1973).

WARD, DAVID, *Jonathan Swift: An Introductory Essay* (London, 1973).

PROBYN, CLIVE T. (ed.), *The Art of Jonathan Swift* (London, 1978).

STEELE, PETER, *Jonathan Swift: Preacher and Jester* (Oxford, 1978).

FABRICANT, CAROLE, *Swift's Landscape* (Baltimore, 1982).

REILLY, PATRICK, *Jonathan Swift: The Brave Desponder* (Manchester, 1982).

RAWSON, CLAUDE (ed.), *The Character of Swift's Satire: A Revised Focus* (Newark, NJ, 1983).

ZIMMERMANN, EVERETT, *Swift's Narrative Satires: Author and Authority* (Ithaca, NY, 1983).

DOWNIE, J. A., *Jonathan Swift: Political Writer* (London, 1984).

ROSS, ANGUS, and WOOLLEY, DAVID (eds.), *Jonathan Swift* (Oxford Authors; Oxford, 1984).

NOKES, DAVID, *Jonathan Swift, a Hypocrite Reversed: A Critical Biography* (Oxford, 1985).

WOOD, NIGEL, *Swift* (Harvester New Readings; Brighton, 1986).

KELLY, ANN CLINE, *Swift and the English Language* (Philadelphia, 1988).

FISCHER, I. I., REAL, H. J., and WOOLLEY, J. (eds.), *Swift and his Contexts* (New York, 1989).

FLYNN, CAROL HOULIHAN, *The Body in Swift and Defoe* (Cambridge, 1990).

EILON, DANIEL, *Faction's Fictions: Ideological Closure in Swift's Satire* (Newark, NJ, 1991).

McMINN, JOSEPH, *Jonathan Swift: A Literary Life* (London, 1991).

2. *Gulliver's Travels*

LOCK, F. P., *The Politics of 'Gulliver's Travels'* (Oxford, 1980).

HAMMOND BREAN, *Gulliver's Travels* (Open Guides to Literature; Milton Keynes, 1988).

SMITH, FREDERIK N. (ed.), *The Genres of Gulliver's Travels* (Newark, NJ, 1990).

ERSKINE-HILL, HOWARD, *Swift: Gulliver's Travels* (Landmarks of World Literature; Cambridge, 1993).

A CHRONOLOGY OF
JONATHAN SWIFT

1667   Born in Dublin, of English parents, 30 November.

1673–82   At Kilkenny Grammar School.

1682–9   At Trinity College, Dublin (BA, 1686).

1689   Visited mother at Leicester; became secretary to Sir William Temple at Moor Park, Surrey, where he met Esther Johnson (Stella), then aged 8.

1690   Returned to Ireland.

1691–4   At Moor Park.

1692   MA, Oxford.

1694   Returned to Dublin.

1695   Ordained priest; became rector of Kilroot, near Belfast; proposed to Jane Waring (Varina).

1696–9   At Moor Park.

1699   Temple died. Swift went to Dublin as chaplain to Earl of Berkeley.

1700   Became vicar of Laracor, and prebendary of St Patrick's Cathedral, Dublin.

1701   Visited London. Stella settled in Dublin.

1702   DD, Trinity College, Dublin.

1704   *A Tale of a Tub* and *The Battle of the Books*.

1707–9   In London, negotiating for improvement in financial position of the Irish clergy; prolonged attack of chronic disease (Ménière's syndrome) causing giddiness and deafness; became intimate with Esther Vanhomrigh (Vanessa), then aged about 20; *Bickerstaff Papers*.

1709   Returned to Ireland.

1710–14   Resident in London; *Journal to Stella* (letters to Esther Johnson in Ireland); wrote Tory propaganda for administration of Harley (Earl of Oxford) and St John (Viscount Bolingbroke); made friends with Atterbury. Arbuthnot, Pope, Gay.

1710–11   Edited *Examiner*.

1711   *Argument against Abolishing Christianity; Conduct of the Allies*.

1713	Installed as dean of St Patrick's Cathedral, Dublin (June); returned to London (September); Pope proposed plan for Scriblerus Club.
1714	Queen Anne died; Tory Government fell; Swift returned to Dublin; Vanessa followed him.
1720	*Proposal for the Universal Use of Irish Manufacture.*
1723	Vanessa died.
1724	*Drapier's Letters.*
1726	Visited England (March–August); saw Pope, Gay, Arbuthnot, Bolingbroke; arranged for publication of *Gulliver's Travels* (28 October); *Cadenus and Vanessa.*
1727	Final visit to England (April–September).
1728	Stella died.
1729	*A Modest Proposal.*
1735	*Works* published by Faulkner in Dublin (including corrected edition of *Gulliver's Travels*).
1738	Increasing ill health and loss of memory.
1742	Outbreak of boils, followed by inflammation of left eye, led to brain injury causing aphasia. Put under guardianship as of 'unsound mind and memory'.
1745	Died 19 October, leaving about £11,000 to found a hospital for the insane.

ADVERTISEMENT*

MR SYMPSON'S *Letter to Captain* Gulliver,* *prefixed to this Volume, will make a long Advertisement unnecessary. Those Interpolations* complained of by the Captain, were made by a Person since deceased, on whose Judgement the Publisher relyed to make any Alterations that might be thought necessary. But, this Person, not rightly comprehending the Scheme of the Author, nor able to imitate his plain simple Style, thought fit among many other Alterations and Insertions, to compliment the Memory* of her late Majesty, by saying,* That she governed without a Chief Minister. *We are assured, that the Copy sent to the Bookseller in* London, *was a Transcript of the Original, which Original being in the Possession of a very worthy Gentleman* in* London, *and a most intimate Friend of the Authors; after he had bought the Book in Sheets, and compared it with the Originals, bound it up with blank Leaves, and made those Corrections, which the Reader will find in our Edition. For, the same Gentleman did us the Favour to let us transcribe his Corrections.*

A LETTER FROM
CAPT. GULLIVER,
TO HIS COUSIN SYMPSON*

I HOPE you will be ready to own publickly, whenever you shall be called to it, that by your great and frequent Urgency you prevailed on me to publish a very loose and uncorrect Account of my Travels; with Direction to hire some young Gentlemen of either University to put them in Order, and correct the Style, as my Cousin *Dampier** did by my Advice, in his Book called, *A Voyage round the World*. But I do not remember I gave you Power to consent, that any thing should be omitted, and much less that any thing should be inserted: Therefore, as to the latter, I do here renounce every thing of that Kind; particularly a Paragraph* about her Majesty the late Queen *Anne*, of most pious and glorious Memory; although I did reverence and esteem her more than any of human Species. But you, or your Interpolator, ought to have considered, that as it was not my Inclination, so was it not decent to praise any Animal of our Composition* before my Master *Houyhnhnm*:* And besides, the Fact was altogether false; for to my Knowledge, being in *England* during some Part of her Majesty's Reign, she did govern by a chief Minister; nay, even by two successively; the first whereof was the Lord of *Godolphin*, and the second the Lord of *Oxford*; so that you have made me *say the thing that was not*.* Likewise, in the Account of the Academy of Projectors, and several Passages of my Discourse to my Master *Houyhnhnm*, you have either omitted some material Circumstances, or minced or changed them in such a Manner, that I do hardly know mine own Work.* When I formerly hinted to you something of this in a Letter, you were pleased to answer, that you were afraid of giving Offence; that People in Power were very watchful over the Press; and apt not only to interpret, but to punish every thing which looked like an *Inuendo* (as I think you called it.) But pray, how could that which I spoke so many Years ago, and at above five Thousand Leagues distance, in another Reign, be applyed to any of the *Yahoos*,* who now are said to govern the Herd; especially, at a time when I little thought on or feared the Unhappiness of living under them. Have not I the most Reason to complain, when I see these very *Yahoos* carried by *Houyhnhnms* in a Vehicle, as if these* were Brutes, and those the rational Creatures? And, indeed, to avoid so monstrous and detestable a Sight, was one principal Motive of my Retirement hither.*

Thus much I thought proper to tell you in Relation to your self, and to the Trust I reposed in you.

I do in the next Place complain of my own great Want of Judgment, in being prevailed upon by the Intreaties and false Reasonings of you and some others, very much against mine own Opinion, to suffer my Travels to be published. Pray bring to your Mind how often I desired you to consider, when you insisted on the Motive of *publick Good*; that the *Yahoos* were a Species of Animals utterly incapable of Amendment by Precepts or Examples: And so it hath proved; for instead of seeing a full Stop put to all Abuses and Corruptions, at least in this little Island, as I had Reason to expect: Behold, after above six Months Warning, I cannot learn that my Book hath produced one single Effect according to mine Intentions: I desired you would let me know by a Letter, when Party and Faction were extinguished; Judges learned and upright; Pleaders honest and modest, with some Tincture of common Sense; and *Smithfield** blazing with Pyramids of Law-Books; the young Nobility's Education entirely changed; the Physicians banished; the Female *Yahoos* abounding in Virtue, Honour, Truth and good Sense: Courts and Levees of great Ministers thoroughly weeded and swept; Wit, Merit and Learning rewarded; all Disgracers of the Press in Prose and Verse, condemned to eat nothing but their own Cotten,* and quench their Thirst with their own Ink. These, and a Thousand other Reformations, I firmly counted upon by your Encouragement; as indeed they were plainly deducible from the Precepts delivered in my Book, And, it must be owned, that seven Months were a sufficient Time to correct every Vice and Folly to which *Yahoos* are subject; if their Natures had been capable of the least Disposition to Virtue or Wisdom: Yet so far have you been from answering mine Expectation in any of your Letters; that on the contrary, you are loading our Carrier every Week with Libels,* and Keys,* and Reflections, and Memoirs, and Second Parts;* wherein I see myself accused of reflecting upon great States-Folk; of degrading human Nature, (for so they have still the Confidence to stile it) and of abusing the Female Sex. I find likewise, that the Writers of those Bundles are not agreed among themselves; for some of them will not allow me to be Author of mine own Travels; and others make me Author of Books to which I am wholly a Stranger.

I find likewise, that your Printer hath been so careless as to confound the Times,* and mistake the Dates of my several Voyages and Returns; neither assigning the true Year, or the true Month, or Day of the Month: And I hear the original Manuscript is all destroyed,* since the Publication of my Book. Neither have I any Copy left; however, I have sent you some Corrections, which you may insert, if there should be a second Edition: And yet I cannot stand to them,* but shall leave that Matter to my judicious and candid Readers, to adjust it as they please.

I hear some of our Sea-*Yahoos* find Fault with my Sea-Language, as not proper in many Parts, nor now in Use.* I cannot help it. In my first Voyages, while I was young, I was instructed by the oldest Mariners, and learned to speak as they did. But I have since found that the Sea-*Yahoos* are apt, like the Land ones, to become new fangled in their Words; which the latter change every Year; insomuch, as I remember upon each Return to mine own Country, their old Dialect was so altered, that I could hardly understand the new. And I observe, when any *Yahoo* comes from *London* out of Curiosity to visit me at mine own House, we neither of us are able to deliver our Conceptions* in a Manner intelligible to the other.

If the Censure of *Yahoos* could any Way affect me, I should have great Reason to complain, that some of them are so bold as to think my Book of Travels a meer Fiction out of mine own Brain; and have gone as far as to drop Hints, that the

Houyhnhnms and *Yahoos* have no more Existence than the Inhabitants of *Utopia.**

Indeed I must confess, that as to the People of *Lilliput, Brobdingrag,* (for so the Word should have been spelt, and not erroneously *Brobdingnag*) and *Laputa;* I have never yet heard of any *Yahoo* so presumptuous as to dispute their Being, or the Facts I have related concerning them: because the Truth immediately strikes every Reader with Conviction.* And, is there less Probability in my Account of the *Houyhnhnms* or *Yahoos,* when it is manifest as to the latter, there are so many Thousands in this City, who only differ from their Brother Brutes in *Houyhnhnmland,* because they use a Sort of *Jabber,* and do not go naked. I wrote for their Amendment, and not their Approbation. The united Praise of the whole Race would be of less Consequence to me, than the neighing of those two degenerate *Houyhnhnms* I keep in my Stable; because, from these, degenerate as they are, I still improve in some Virtues, without any Mixture of Vice.

Do these miserable Animals* presume to think that I am so far degenerated as to defend my Veracity; *Yahoo* as I am, it is well known through all *Houyhnhnmland,* that by the Instructions and Example of my illustrious Master, I was able in the Compass of two Years (although I confess with the utmost Difficulty) to remove that infernal Habit of Lying, Shuffling, Deceiving, and Equivocating, so deeply rooted in the very Souls of all my Species; especially the *Europeans.*

I have other Complaints to make upon this vexatious Occasion; but I forbear troubling myself or you any further. I must freely confess, that since my last Return, some corruptions of my *Yahoo* Nature have revived in me by Conversing with a few of your Species, and particularly those of mine own Family, by an unavoidable Necessity; else I should never have attempted so absurd a Project as that of reforming the *Yahoo* Race in this Kingdom; but, I have now done with all such visionary Schemes for ever.

2 *April* 1727

THE PUBLISHER TO
THE READER*

xxxvii   The Publisher to the Reader

THE AUTHOR of these Travels, Mr *Lemuel Gulliver*, is my antient and intimate Friend; there is likewise some Relation between us by the Mother's Side. About three Years ago Mr *Gulliver* growing weary of the Concourse of curious People coming to him at his House in *Redriff*,* made a small Purchase of Land, with a convenient House, near *Newark*, in *Nottingham-shire*, his native Country; where he now lives retired, yet in good Esteem among his Neighbours.

Although Mr *Gulliver* was born in *Nottinghamshire*, where his Father dwelt, yet I have heard him say, his Family came from *Oxfordshire*; to confirm which, I have observed in the Church-Yard at *Banbury*,* in that County, several Tombs and Monuments of the *Gullivers*.

Before he quitted *Redriff*, he left the Custody of the following Papers in my Hands, with the Liberty to dispose of them as I should think fit. I have carefully perused them three Times: The Style is very plain and simple; and the only Fault I find is, that the Author, after the Manner of Travellers, is a little too circumstantial. There is an Air of Truth apparent through the whole; and indeed the Author was so distinguished for his Veracity,* that it became a Sort of Proverb among his Neighbours at *Redriff*, when any one affirmed a Thing, to say, it was as true as if Mr *Gulliver* had spoke it.

By the Advice of several worthy Persons, to whom, with the Author's Permission, I communicated these Papers, I now venture to send them into the World; hoping they may be, at least for some time, a better Entertainment to our young Noblemen, than the common Scribbles of Politicks and Party.

This Volume would have been at least twice as large,* if I had not made bold to strike out innumerable Passages relating to the Winds and Tides, as well as to the Variations and Bearings in the several Voyages; together with the minute Descriptions of the Management of the Ship in Storms, in the Style of Sailors: Likewise the Account of the Longitudes and

Latitudes; wherein I have Reason to apprehend that Mr *Gulliver* may be a little dissatisfied: But I was resolved to fit the Work as much as possible to the general Capacity of Readers. However, if my own Ignorance in Sea-Affairs shall have led me to commit some Mistakes, I alone am answerable for them: And if any Traveller hath a Curiosity to see the whole Work at large, as it came from the Hand of the Author, I will be ready to gratify him.

As for any further Particulars relating to the Author, the Reader will receive Satisfaction from the first Pages of the Book.

Richard Sympson

CAPTAIN LEMUEL GULLIVER OF REDRIFF ÆTAT SUÆ LVIII.

Sturt & Sheppard Sc.

Compositum jus, fasque animi, sanctosque recessus
Mentis, et incoctum generoso pectus honesto.

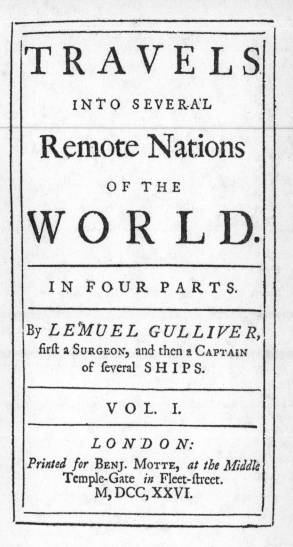

TRAVELS

INTO SEVERAL

Remote Nations

OF THE

WORLD.

IN FOUR PARTS.

By *LEMUEL GULLIVER,*
firſt a SURGEON, and then a CAPTAIN
of ſeveral SHIPS.

VOL. I.

LONDON:
Printed for BENJ. MOTTE, *at the Middle*
Temple-Gate *in* Fleet-ſtreet.
M, DCC, XXVI.

IN FOUR PARTS.

PART ONE

A Voyage to Lilliput*

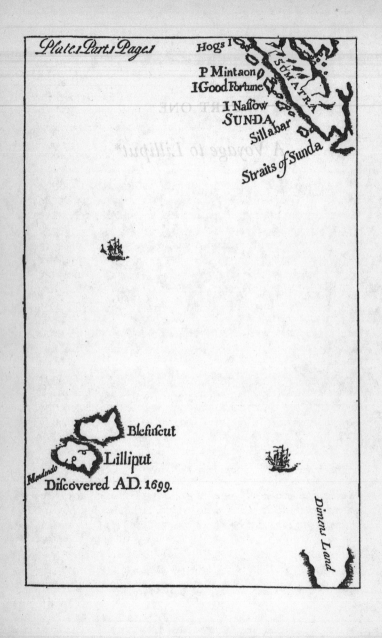

Plate.1 Part.1 Page.1

Hogs I

P Mintaon
I Good Fortune

I Naſſow
SUNDA
Sillabar

SUMATRA

Straits of Sunda

Blefuscut

Lilliput

Mendendo

Diſcovered A.D. 1699.

Dinens Land

CHAPTER ONE

The Author giveth some Account of himself and Family; his first Inducements to travel. He is shipwrecked, and swims for his Life; gets safe on shoar in the Country of Lilliput; *is made a Prisoner, and carried up the Country.*

MY FATHER had a small Estate in *Nottinghamshire*; I was the Third of five Sons. He sent me to *Emanuel-College* in *Cambridge,** at Fourteen* Years old, where I resided three Years, and applied my self close to my Studies: But the Charge of maintaining me (although I had a very scanty Allowance) being too great for a narrow Fortune; I was bound Apprentice to Mr *James Bates,* an eminent Surgeon in *London,* with whom I continued four Years; and my Father now and then sending me small Sums of Money, I laid them out in learning Navigation, and other Parts of the Mathematicks, useful to those who intend to travel, as I always believed it would be some time or other my Fortune to do. When I left Mr *Bates,* I went down to my Father; where, by the Assistance of him and my Uncle *John,* and some other Relations, I got Forty Pounds, and a Promise of Thirty Pounds a Year to maintain me at *Leyden:** There I studied Physick two Years and seven Months, knowing it would be useful in long Voyages.

Soon after my Return from *Leyden,* I was recommended by my good Master Mr *Bates,* to be Surgeon to the *Swallow,** Captain *Abraham Pannell* Commander; with whom I continued three Years and a half, making a Voyage or two into the *Levant,* and some other Parts. When I came back, I resolved to settle in *London,* to which Mr *Bates,* my Master, encouraged me; and by him I was recommended to several Patients. I took Part of a small House in the *Old Jury*; and being advised to alter my Condition, I married Mrs *Mary Burton,* second Daughter to Mr *Edmond Burton,* Hosier, in *Newgate-street,* with whom I received four Hundred Pounds for a Portion.*

But, my good Master *Bates* dying in two Years after, and I having few Friends, my Business began to fail; for my Conscience would not suffer me to imitate the bad Practice of too many among my Brethren. Having therefore consulted with my Wife, and some of my Acquaintance, I determined to go again to Sea. I was Surgeon successively in two Ships, and made several Voyages, for six Years, to the *East* and *West-Indies*; by which I got some Addition to my Fortune. My Hours of Leisure I spent in reading the best Authors, ancient and modern; being always provided with a good Number of Books; and when I was ashore, in observing the Manners and Dispositions of the People, as well as learning their Language; wherein I had a great Facility by the Strength of my Memory.

The last of these Voyages not proving very fortunate, I grew weary of the Sea, and intended to stay at home with my Wife and Family. I removed from the *Old Jury* to *Fetter-Lane*, and from thence to *Wapping*, hoping to get Business among the Sailors; but it would not turn to account. After three Years Expectation that things would mend, I accepted an advantageous Offer from Captain *William Prichard*, Master of the *Antelope*, who was making a Voyage to the *South-Sea*. We set sail from *Bristol*, *May* 4th, 1699,* and our Voyage at first was very prosperous.

It would not be proper for some Reasons, to trouble the Reader* with the Particulars of our Adventures in those Seas: Let it suffice to inform him, that in our Passage from thence to the *East-Indies*, we were driven by a violent Storm to the North-West of *Van Diemen*'s Land.* By an Observation, we found ourselves in the Latitude of 30 Degrees 2 Minutes South. Twelve of our Crew were dead by immoderate Labour, and ill Food: the rest were in a very weak Condition. On the fifth of *November*, which was the beginning of Summer in those Parts, the Weather being very hazy, the Seamen spyed a Rock, within half a Cable's length* of the Ship; but the Wind was so strong, that we were driven directly upon it, and immediately split. Six of the Crew, of whom I was one, having let down the Boat into the Sea, made a Shift* to get clear of the Ship, and the Rock. We rowed by my Computation, about three Leagues, till we were able to work no longer, being already spent with Labour while we were in the Ship. We therefore trusted ourselves to the Mercy of the Waves; and in about half an Hour the Boat was overset by a sudden Flurry from the North. What became of my Companions in the Boat, as well as of those who escaped on the Rock, or were left in the Vessel, I cannot tell; but conclude they were all lost. For my own Part, I swam as Fortune directed me, and was pushed forward by Wind and Tide. I often let my Legs drop, and could feel no Bottom: But when I was almost gone, and able to struggle no longer, I found myself within my Depth; and by this Time the Storm was much abated. The Declivity was so small, that I walked near a Mile before I got to the Shore, which I conjectured was about Eight o'Clock in the Evening. I then advanced forward near half a Mile, but could not discover any Sign of Houses or Inhabitants; at least I was in so weak a Condition, that I did not observe them. I was extremely tired, and with that, and the Heat of the Weather, and about half a Pint of Brandy that I drank as I left the Ship, I found my self much inclined to sleep. I lay down on the Grass, which was very short and soft; where I slept sounder than ever I remember to have done in my Life, and as I reckoned, above Nine Hours; for when I awaked,* it was just Day-light. I attempted to rise, but was not able to stir: For as I happened to lie on my Back, I found my Arms and Legs were strongly fastened on each Side to the Ground; and my Hair, which was long and thick, tied down in the same Manner. I likewise felt several slender Ligatures across my Body, from my Armpits to my Thighs. I could only look upwards; the Sun began to grow hot, and the Light offended mine Eyes. I heard a confused Noise about me, but in the Posture I lay, could see nothing except the Sky. In a little time I felt something alive moving on my left Leg, which advancing gently forward over my Breast, came almost up to my Chin; when bending mine Eyes downwards as much as I could, I perceived it to be a human Creature not six Inches high,* with a Bow and Arrow in his Hands, and a Quiver at his Back. In the mean time, I felt at least Forty more of the same Kind (as I conjectured) following the first. I was in the utmost Astonishment, and roared so loud, that they all ran back in a Fright; and some of them, as

I was afterwards told, were hurt with the Falls they got by leaping from my Sides upon the Ground. However, they soon returned; and one of them, who ventured so far as to get a full Sight of my Face, lifting up his Hands and Eyes by way of Admiration,* cryed out in a shrill, but distinct Voice,* *Hekinah Degul:* The others repeated the same Words several times, but I then knew not what they meant. I lay all this while, as the Reader may believe, in great Uneasiness: At length, struggling to get loose, I had the Fortune to break the Strings, and wrench out the Pegs that fastened my left Arm to the Ground; for, by lifting it up to my Face, I discovered the Methods they had taken to bind me; and, at the same time, with a violent Pull, which gave me excessive Pain, I a little loosened the Strings that tied down my Hair on the left Side; so that I was just able to turn my Head about two Inches. But the Creatures ran off a second time, before I could seize them; whereupon there was a great Shout in a very shrill Accent; and after it ceased, I heard one of them cry aloud, *Tolgo Phonac;** when in an Instant I felt above an Hundred Arrows discharged on my left Hand, which pricked me like so many Needles; and besides, they shot another Flight into the Air, as we do Bombs* in *Europe;* whereof many, I suppose, fell on my Body, (though I felt them not) and some on my Face, which I immediately covered with my left Hand. When this Shower of Arrows was over, I fell a groaning with Grief and Pain; and then striving again to get loose, they discharged another Volly larger than the first; and some of them attempted with Spears to stick me in the Sides; but, by good Luck, I had on me a Buff Jerkin,* which they could not pierce. I thought it the most prudent Method to lie still; and my Design was to continue so till Night, when my left Hand being already loose, I could easily free myself: And as for the Inhabitants, I had Reason to believe I might be a Match for the greatest Armies they could bring against me, if they were all of the same Size with him that I saw. But Fortune disposed otherwise of me. When the People observed I was quiet, they discharged no more Arrows: But by the Noise increasing, I knew their Numbers were greater; and about four Yards from me, over-against my right Ear, I heard a Knocking for above an Hour, like People at work; when turning my Head that Way, as well as the Pegs and Strings would permit me, I saw a Stage erected about a Foot and a half from the Ground, capable of holding four of the Inhabitants, with two or three Ladders to mount it: From whence one of them, who seemed to be a Person of Quality, made me a long Speech, whereof I understood not one Syllable. But I should have mentioned, that before the principal Person began his Oration, he cryed out three times *Langro Dehul san:** (these Words and the former were afterwards repeated and explained to me.) Whereupon immediately about fifty of the Inhabitants came, and cut the Strings that fastened the left side of my Head, which gave me the Liberty of turning it to the right, and of observing the Person and Gesture of him who was to speak. He appeared to be of a middle Age, and taller than any of the other three who attended him; whereof one was a Page, who held up his Train, and seemed to be somewhat longer than my middle Finger; the other two stood one on each side to support him. He acted every part of an Orator; and I could observe many Periods of Threatnings, and others of Promises, Pity and Kindness. I answered in a few Words, but in the most submissive Manner, lifting up my left Hand and both mine Eyes to the Sun, as calling him for a Witness; and being almost famished with Hunger, having not eaten a Morsel for some Hours before I left the Ship, I found the Demands of Nature so strong upon me, that I could not forbear shewing my Impatience (perhaps against the strict Rules of Decency) by putting my Finger frequently on my Mouth, to signify that I wanted Food. The *Hurgo* (for so they call a great Lord, as I afterwards learnt) understood me very well: He descended from the Stage, and commanded that several Ladders should be applied to my Sides, on which above an hundred of the Inhabitants mounted, and walked towards my Mouth, laden with Baskets full of Meat, which had been provided, and sent thither by the Kings's Orders upon the first Intelligence he received of me. I observed there was the Flesh of several Animals, but could not distinguish them by the Taste. There were Shoulders, Legs, and Loins shaped like those of Mutton, and very well dressed, but smaller than the Wings of a Lark. I eat them by two or three at a Mouthful; and took three Loaves at a time, about the bigness of Musket Bullets. They supplyed me as fast as they could, shewing a thousand Marks of Wonder and Astonishment at my Bulk and Appetite. I then made another Sign that I wanted Drink. They found by my eating that a small Quantity would not suffice me; and being a most ingenious People, they slung up with great Dexterity one of their largest Hogsheads; then rolled it towards my Hand, and beat out the Top; I drank it off at a Draught, which I might well do, for it hardly held half a Pint,* and tasted like a small Wine of *Burgundy*, but much more delicious. They brought me a second Hogshead, which I drank in the same Manner, and made Signs for more, but they had none to give me. When I had performed these Wonders, they shouted for Joy, and danced upon my Breast, repeating several times as they did at first, *Hekinah Degul*. They made me a Sign that I should throw down the two Hogsheads, but first warned the People below to stand out of the Way, crying aloud, *Borach Mivola*;* and when they saw the Vessels in the Air, there was an universal Shout of *Hekinah Degul*. I confess I was often tempted, while they were passing backwards and forwards on my Body, to seize Forty or Fifty of the first that came in my Reach, and dash them against the Ground. But the Remembrance of what I had felt, which probably might not be the worst they could do; and the Promise of Honour I made them, for so I interpreted my submissive Behaviour, soon drove out those Imaginations. Besides, I now considered my self as bound by the Laws of Hospitality to a Peple who had treated me with so much Expence and Magnificence. However, in my Thoughts I could not sufficiently wonder at the Intrepidity of these diminutive Mortals, who durst venture to mount and walk on my Body, while one of my Hands was at Liberty, without trembling at the very Sight of so prodigious a Creature as I must appear to them. After some time, when they observed that I made no more Demands for Meat, there appeared before me a Person of high Rank from his Imperial Majesty. His Excellency having mounted on the Small of my Right Leg, advanced forwards up to my Face, with about a Dozen of his

Retinue; And producing his Credentials under the Signet Royal, which he applied close to mine Eyes, spoke about ten Minutes, without any Signs of Anger, but with a kind of determinate* Resolution; often pointing forwards, which, as I afterwards found was towards the Capital City, about half a Mile distant, whither it was agreed by his Majesty in Council that I must be conveyed. I answered in few Words, but to no Purpose, and made a Sign with my Hand that was loose, putting it to the other, (but over his Excellency's Head, for Fear of hurting him or his Train) and then to my own Head and Body, to signify that I desired my Liberty. It appeared that he understood me well enough; for he shook his Head by way of Disapprobation, and held his Hand in a Posture to shew that I must be carried as a Prisoner. However, he made other Signs to let me understand that I should have Meat and Drink enough, and very good Treatment. Whereupon I once more thought of attempting to break my Bonds; but again, when I felt the Smart of their Arrows upon my Face and Hands, which were all in Blisters, and many of the Darts still sticking in them; and observing likewise that the Number of my Enemies encreased; I gave Tokens to let them know that they might do with me what they pleased. Upon this, the *Hurgo* and his Train withdrew, with much Civility and chearful Countenances. Soon after I heard a general Shout, with frequent Repetitions of the Words, *Peplom Selan,** and I felt great Numbers of the People on my Left Side relaxing the Cords to such a Degree, that I was able to turn upon my Right, and to ease my self with making Water; which I very plentifully did, to the great Astonishment of the People, who conjecturing by my Motions what I was going to do, immediately opened to the right and left on that Side, to avoid the Torrent which fell with such Noise and Violence from me. But before this, they had dawbed my Face and both my Hands with a sort of Ointment very pleasant to the Smell, which in a few Minutes removed all the Smart of their Arrows. These Circumstances, added to the Refreshment I had received by their Victuals and Drink, which were very nourishing, disposed me to sleep. I slept about eight Hours as I was afterwards assured; and it was no Wonder; for the Physicians, by the Emperor's Order, had mingled a sleeping Potion in the Hogsheads of Wine.

It seems that upon the first Moment I was discovered sleeping on the Ground after my Landing, the Emperor had early Notice of it by an Express;* and determined in Council that I should be tyed in the Manner I have related (which was done in the Night while I slept) that Plenty of Meat and Drink should be sent to me, and a Machine prepared to carry me to the Capital City.

This Resolution perhaps may appear very bold and dangerous, and I am confident would not be imitated by any Prince in *Europe* on the like Occasion; however, in my Opinion it was extremely Prudent as well as Generous. For supposing these People had endeavoured to kill me with their Spears and Arrows while I was asleep; I should certainly have awaked with the first Sense of Smart, which might so far have rouzed my Rage and Strength, as to enable me to break the Strings wherewith I was tyed; after which, as they were not able to make Resistance, so they could expect no Mercy.

These People are most excellent Mathematicians, and arrived to a great Perfection in Mechanicks by the Countenance and Encouragement of the Emperor, who is a renowned Patron of Learning. This Prince hath several Machines fixed on Wheels for the Carriage of Trees and other great Weights. He often buildeth his largest Men of War, whereof some are Nine Foot long, in the Woods where the Timber grows, and has them carried on these Engines* three or four Hundred Yards to the Sea. Five Hundred Carpenters and Engineers were immediately set at work to prepare the greatest Engine they had. It was a Frame of Wood raised three Inches from the Ground, about seven Foot long and four wide, moving upon twenty-two Wheels. The Shout I heard, was upon the Arrival of this Engine, which, it seems, set out in four Hours after my Landing. It was brought parallel to me as I lay. But the principal Difficulty was to raise and place me in this Vehicle. Eighty Poles, each of one Foot high, were erected for this Purpose, and very strong Cords of the bigness of Packthread were fastened by Hooks to many Bandages, which the Workmen had girt round my Neck, my Hands, my Body, and my Legs. Nine Hundred of the strongest Men were employed to draw up these Cords by many Pullies fastned on the Poles; and thus in less than three Hours, I was raised and slung into the Engine, and there tyed fast. All this I was told; for while the whole Operation was performing, I lay in a profound Sleep, by the Force of that soporiferous Medicine infused into my Liquor. Fifteen hundred of the Emperor's largest Horses, each about four Inches and a half* high, were employed to draw me towards the Metropolis, which, as I said, was half a Mile distant.

About four Hours after we began our Journey, I awaked by a very ridiculous Accident; for the Carriage being stopt a while to adjust something that was out of Order, two or three of the young Natives had the Curiosity to see how I looked when I was asleep; they climbed up into the Engine, and advancing very softly to my Face, one of them, an Officer in the Guards, put the sharp End of his Half-Pike* a good way up into my left Nostril, which tickled my Nose like a Straw, and made me sneeze violently: Whereupon they stole off unperceived; and it was three Weeks before I knew the Cause of my awaking so suddenly. We made a long March the remaining Part of the Day, and rested at Night with Five Hundred Guards on each Side of me, half with Torches, and half with Bows and Arrows, ready to shoot me if I should offer to stir. The next Morning at Sun-rise we continued our March, and arrived within two Hundred Yards of the City-Gates about Noon. The Emperor, and all his Court, came out to meet us; but his great Officers would by no means suffer his Majesty to endanger his Person by mounting on my Body.

At the Place where the Carriage stopt, there stood an ancient Temple,* esteemed to be the largest in the whole Kingdom; which having been polluted some Years before by an unnatural Murder, was, according to the Zeal of those People, looked upon as Prophane, and therefore had been applied to common Use, and all the Ornaments and Furniture carried away. In this Edifice it was determined I should lodge. The great Gate fronting to the North was about four Foot high, and almost two Foot wide, through which I could easily creep. On each Side of the Gate was a small Window not above six Inches from the Ground: Into that on the Left Side, the King's Smiths conveyed fourscore and eleven Chains, like those that hang to a Lady's Watch in *Europe*, and almost as large, which were locked to my Left Leg with six and thirty Padlocks. Over against this Temple, on the other Side of the great Highway, at twenty Foot Distance, there was a Turret at least five Foot high. Here the Emperor ascended with many principal Lords of his Court, to have an Opportunity of viewing me, as I was told, for I could not see them. It was reckoned that above an hundred thousand Inhabitants came out of the Town upon the same Errand; and in spight of my Guards, I believe there could not be fewer than ten thousand, at several Times, who mounted upon my Body by the Help of Ladders. But a Proclamation was soon issued to forbid it, upon Pain of Death. When the Workmen found it was impossible for me to break loose, they cut all the Strings that bound me; whereupon I rose up with as melancholly a Disposition as ever I had in my Life. But the Noise and Astonishment of the People at seeing me rise and walk, are not to be expressed. The Chains that held my left Leg were about two Yards long, and gave me not only the Liberty of walking backwards and forwards in a Semicircle; but being fixed within four Inches of the Gate, allowed me to creep in, and lie at my full Length in the Temple.

CHAPTER TWO

The Emperor of Lilliput, *attended by several of the Nobility, comes to see the Author in his Confinement. The Emperor's Person and Habit described. Learned Men appointed to teach the Author their Language. He gains Favour by his mild Disposition. His Pockets are searched, and his Sword and Pistols taken from him.*

WHEN I found myself on my Feet, I looked about me, and must confess I never beheld a more entertaining Prospect. The Country round appeared like a continued Garden; and the inclosed Fields, which were generally Forty Foot square, resembled so many Beds of Flowers. These Fields were intermingled with Woods of half a Stang,* and the tallest Trees, as I could judge, appeared to be seven Foot high. I viewed the Town on my left Hand, which looked like the painted Scene of a City in a Theatre.

I had been for some Hours extremely pressed by the Necessities of Nature; which was no Wonder, it being almost two Days since I had last disburthened myself. I was under great Difficulties between Urgency and Shame. The best Expedient I could think on, was to creep into my House, which I accordingly did; and shutting the Gate after me, I went as far as the Length of my Chain would suffer; and discharged my Body of that uneasy Load. But this was the only Time I was ever guilty of so uncleanly an Action; for which I cannot but hope the candid Reader will give some allowance, after he hath maturely and impartially considered my Case, and the Distress I was in. From this Time my constant Practice was, as soon as I rose, to perform that Business in open Air, at the full Extent of my Chain; and due Care was taken every Morning before Company came, that the offensive Matter should be carried off in Wheel-barrows, by two Servants appointed for that Purpose. I would not have dwelt so long upon a Circumstance, that perhaps at first Sight may appear not very momentous; if I had not thought it necessary to justify my

Character in Point of Cleanliness to the World; which I am told, some of my Maligners* have been pleased, upon this and other Occasions, to call in Question.

When this Adventure was at an End, I came back out of my House, having Occasion for fresh Air. The Emperor was already descended from the Tower, and advancing on Horseback towards me, which had like to have cost* him dear; for the Beast, although very well trained, yet wholly unused to such a Sight, which appeared as if a Mountain moved before him, reared up on his hinder Feet: But that Prince, who is an excellent Horseman, kept his Seat, until his Attendants ran in, and held the Bridle, while his Majesty had Time to dismount. When he alighted, he surveyed me round with great Admiration, but kept beyond the Length of my Chains. He ordered his Cooks and Butlers, who were already prepared, to give me Victuals and Drink, which they pushed forward in a sort of Vehicles* upon Wheels until I could reach them. I took those Vehicles, and soon emptied them all; twenty of them were filled with Meat, and ten with Liquor; each of the former afforded me two or three good Mouthfuls, and I emptied the Liquor of ten Vessels, which was contained in earthen Vials, into one Vehicle, drinking it off at a Draught; and so I did with the rest. The Empress, and young Princes of the Blood,* of both Sexes, attended by many Ladies, sate at some Distance in their Chairs; but upon the Accident that happened to the Emperor's Horse, they alighted, and came near his Person; which I am now going to describe. He is taller* by almost the Breadth of my Nail, than any of his Court; which alone is enough to strike an Awe into the Beholders. His Features* are strong and masculine, with an *Austrian* Lip,* and arched Nose, his Complexion olive, his Countenance* erect, his Body and Limbs well proportioned, all his Motions graceful, and his Deportment majestick. He was then past his Prime,* being twenty-eight Years and three Quarters old, of which he had reigned about seven,* in great Felicity, and generally victorious. For the better Convenience of beholding him, I lay on my Side, so that my Face was parallel to his, and he stood but three Yards off: However, I have had him since many Times in my Hand, and therefore cannot be deceived in the Description. His Dress was very plain and simple, the Fashion of it between the *Asiatick* and the *European*; but he had on his Head a light Helmet of Gold, adorned with Jewels, and a Plume on the Crest. He held his Sword drawn in his Hand, to defend himself, if I should happen to break loose; it was almost three Inches long, the Hilt and Scabbard were Gold enriched with Diamonds. His Voice was shrill, but very clear and articulate, and I could distinctly hear it when I stood up. The Ladies and Courtiers were all most magnificently clad, so that the Spot they stood upon seemed to resemble a Petticoat spread on the Ground, embroidered with Figures of Gold and Silver. His Imperial Majesty spoke often to me, and I returned Answers, but neither of us could understand a Syllable. There were several of his Priests and Lawyers present (as I conjectured by their Habits) who were commanded to address themselves to me, and I spoke to them in as many Languages as I had the least Smattering of, which were *High* and *Low Dutch*,* *Latin, French, Spanish, Italian,* and *Lingua Franca*;* but all to no purpose. After about two Hours the Court retired, and I was left with a strong Guard, to prevent the Impertinence, and probably the Malice of the Rabble,* who were very impatient to croud about me as near as they durst; and some of them had the Impudence to shoot their Arrows at me as I sate on the Ground by the Door of my House; whereof one very narrowly missed my left Eye. But the Colonel ordered six of the Ring-leaders to be seized, and thought no Punishment so proper as to deliver them bound into my Hands, which some of his Soldiers accordingly did, pushing them forwards with the But-ends of their Pikes into my Reach: I took them all in my right Hand, put five of them into my Coat-pocket; and as to the sixth, I made a Countenance as if I would eat him alive. The poor Man squalled terribly, and the Colonel and his Officers were in much Pain, especially when they saw me take out my Penknife: But I soon put them out of Fear; for, looking mildly, and immediately cutting the Strings he was bound with, I set him gently on the Ground, and away he ran. I treated the rest in the same Manner, taking them one by one out of my Pocket; and I observed, both the Soldiers and People were highly obliged at this Mark of my Clemency, which was represented very much to my Advantage at Court.

Towards Night I got with some Difficulty into my House, where I lay on the Ground, and continued to do so about a Fortnight; during which time the Emperor gave Orders to have a Bed prepared for me. Six Hundred Beds* of the common Measure were brought in Carriages, and worked up in my House; an Hundred and Fifty of their Beds sown together made up the Breadth and Length, and these were four double,* which however kept me but very indifferently from the Hardness of the Floor, that was of smooth Stone. By the same Computation they provided me with Sheets, Blankets, and Coverlets, tolerable enough for one who had been so long enured to Hardships as I.

As the News of my Arrival spread through the Kingdom, it brought prodigious Numbers of rich, idle, and curious People to see me; so that the Villages were almost emptied, and great Neglect of Tillage and Household Affairs must have ensued, if his Imperial Majesty had not provided by several Proclamations and Orders of State against this Inconveniency. He directed that those, who had already beheld me, should return home, and not presume to come within fifty Yards of my House, without Licence from Court; whereby the Secretaries of State got considerable Fees.

In the mean time, the Emperor held frequent Councils to debate what Course should be taken with me; and I was afterwards assured by a particular Friend, a Person of great Quality, who was as much in the *Secret* as any; that the Court was under many Difficulties concerning me. They apprehended my breaking loose; that my Diet would be very expensive, and might cause a Famine. Sometimes they determined to starve me, or at least to shoot me in the Face and Hands with poisoned Arrows, which would soon dispatch me: But again they considered, that the Stench of so large a Carcase might produce a Plague in the Metropolis, and probably spread through the whole Kingdom. In the midst of these Consultations, several Officers of the Army went to the Door of the great Council-Chamber; and two of them being admitted, gave an Account of my Behaviour to the six Criminals above-mentioned; which made so favourable an Impression in the Breast of his Majesty, and the whole Board, in my Behalf, that an Imperial Commission was issued out, obliging all the Villages nine hundred Yards round the City to deliver in every Morning six Beeves,* forty Sheep, and other Victuals for my Sustenance; together with a proportionable Quantity of Bread and Wine, and other Liquors: For the due Payment of which his Majesty gave Assignments upon* his Treasury. For this Prince lives chiefly upon his own Demesnes;* seldom, except upon great Occasions raising any Subsidies* upon his Subjects, who are bound to attend him in his Wars at their own Expence. An Establishment was also made of Six Hundred Persons to be my Domesticks, who had Board-Wages allowed for their Maintenance, and Tents built for them very conveniently on each side of my Door. It was likewise ordered, that three hundred Taylors should make me a Suit of Cloaths after the Fashion of the Country: That, six of his Majesty's greatest Scholars should be employed to instruct me in their Language: and, lastly, that the Emperor's Horses, and those of the Nobility, and Troops of Guards, should be exercised in my Sight, to accustom themselves to me. All these Orders were duly put in Execution; and in about three Weeks I made a great Progress in Learning their Language; during which Time, the Emperor frequently honoured me with his Visits, and was pleased to assist my Masters in teaching me. We began already to converse together in some Sort; and the first Words I learnt, were to express my Desire, that he would please to give me my Liberty; which I every Day repeated on my Knees. His Answer, as I could apprehend, was, that this must be a Work of Time, not to be thought on without the Advice of his Council; and that first I must *Lumos Kelmin pesso desmar lon Emposo*;* that is, *Swear a Peace with him and his Kingdom*. However, that I should be used with all Kindness; and he advised me to acquire by my Patience and discreet Behaviour, the Good opinion of himself and his Subjects. He desired I would not take ill, if he gave Orders to certain proper Officers to search me; for probably I might carry about me several Weapons,* which must needs be dangerous Things, if they answered the Bulk of so prodigious a Person.

I said, his Majesty should be satisfied, for I was ready to strip my self, and turn up my Pockets before him. This I delivered, part in Words and part in Signs. He replied, that by the Laws of the Kingdom, I must be searched by two of his Officers: That he knew this could not be done without my Consent and Assistance; that he had so good an Opinion of my Generosity and Justice, as to trust their Persons in my Hands: That whatever they took from me should be returned when I left the Country, or paid for at the Rate which I would set upon them. I took up the two Officers in my Hands, put them first into my Coat-Pockets, and then into every other Pocket about me, except my two Fobs, and another secret Pocket which I had no Mind should be searched, wherein I had some little Necessaries of no Consequence to any but my self. In one of my Fobs there was a Silver Watch, and in the other a small Quantity of Gold in a Purse. These Gentlemen, having Pen, Ink, and Paper about them, made an exact Inventory of every thing they saw, and when they had done, desired I would set them down, that they might deliver it to the Emperor. This Inventory I afterwards translated into *English*, and is Word for Word as follows.

IMPRIMIS,* In the right Coat-Pocket of the *Great Man Mountain* (for so I interpret the Words *Quinbus Flestrin**) after the strictest Search, we found only one great Piece of coarse Cloth, large enough to be a Foot-Cloth* for your Majesty's chief Room of State. In the left Pocket, we saw a huge Silver Chest, with a Cover of the same Metal, which we, the Searchers, were not able to lift. We desired it should be opened; and one of us stepping into it, found himself up to the mid Leg in a sort of Dust, some part whereof flying up to our Faces, set us both a sneezing for several Times together. In his right Waistcoat-Pocket, we found a prodigious Bundle of thin white Substances, folded one above another, about the Bigness of three Men, tied with a strong Cable, and marked with Black Figures; which we humbly conceive to be Writings, every Letter almost half as large as the Palm of our Hands. In the left there was a sort of Engine, from the Back of which were extended twenty long Poles, resembling the Pallisado's before your Majesty's Court; wherewith we conjecture the

Man Mountain combs his Head; for we did not always trouble him with Questions, because we found it a great Difficulty to make him understand us. In the large Pocket on the right Side of his middle Cover, (so I translate the word *Ranfu-Lo,** by which they meant my Breeches) we saw a hollow Pillar of Iron, about the Length of a Man, fastened to a strong Piece of Timber, larger than the Pillar; and upon one side of the Pillar were huge Pieces of Iron sticking out, cut into strange Figures; which we know not what to make of. In the left Pocket, another Engine of the same kind. In the smaller Pocket on the right Side, were several round flat Pieces of white and red Metal,* of different Bulk: Some of the white, which seemed to be Silver, were so large and heavy, that my Comrade and I could hardly lift them. In the left Pocket were two black Pillars irregularly shaped: we could not, without Difficulty, reach the Top of them as we stood at the Bottom of his Pocket: One of them was covered, and seemed all of a Piece; but at the upper End of the other, there appeared a white round Substance, about twice the bigness of our Heads. Within end of these was inclosed a prodigious Plate of Steel; which, by our Orders, we obliged him to shew us, because we apprehended they might be dangerous Engines. He took them out of their Cases, and told us, that in his own Country his Practice was to shave his Beard with one of these, and to cut his Meat with the other. There were two Pockets which we could not enter: These he called his Fobs; they were two large Slits cut into the Top of his middle Cover, but squeezed close by the pressure of his Belly. Out of the right Fob hung a great Silver Chain, with a wonderful kind of Engine at the Bottom. We directed him to draw out whatever was at the End of that Chain; which appeared to be a Globe, half Silver, and half of some transparent Metal: for on the transparent Side we saw certain strange Figures circularly drawn, and thought we could touch them, until we found our Fingers stopped with that lucid Substance. He put this Engine to our Ears, which made an incessant Noise like that of a Water-Mill. And we conjecture it is either some unknown Animal, or the God that he worships: But we are more inclined to the latter Opinion, because he assured us (if we understood him right, for he expressed himself very imperfectly) that he seldom did any Thing without consulting it. He called it his Oracle, and said it pointed out the Time for every Action of his Life. From the left Fob he took out a Net almost large enough for a Fisherman, but contrived to open and shut like a Purse, and served him for the same Use: We found therein several massy Pieces of yellow Metal, which if they be real Gold, must be of immense Value.

HAVING thus, in Obedience to your Majesty's Commands, diligently searched all his Pockets; we observed a Girdle about his Waist made of the Hyde of some prodigious Animal; from which, on the left Side, hung a Sword of the Length of five Men; and on the right, a Bag or Pouch divided into two Cells; each Cell capable of holding three of your Majesty's Subjects. In one of these Cells were several Globes or Balls of a most ponderous Metal, about the Bigness of our Heads, and required a strong Hand to lift them: The other Cell contained a Heap of certain black Grains, but of no great Bulk or Weight, for we could hold above fifty of them in the Palms of our Hands.

THIS is an exact Inventory of what we found about the Body of the *Man Mountain*; who used us with great Civility, and due Respect to your Majesty's Commission. Signed and Sealed on the fourth Day of the eighty ninth Moon of your Majesty's auspicious Reign.

*Clefren Frelock, Marsi Frelock.**

When this Inventory was read over to the Emperor, he directed me to deliver up the several Particulars. He first called for my Scymiter, which I took out, Scabbard and all. In the mean time he ordered three thousand of his choicest Troops, who then attended him, to surround me at a Distance, with their Bows and Arrows just ready to discharge: But I did not observe it; for mine Eyes were wholly fixed upon his Majesty. He then desired me to draw my Scymiter, which, although it had got some Rust by the Sea-Water, was in most Parts exceeding bright. I did so, and immediately all the Troops gave a Shout between Terror and Surprize; for the Sun shone clear, and the Reflexion dazzled their Eyes, as I waved the Scymiter to and fro in my Hand. His Majesty, who is a most magnanimous Prince, was less daunted than I could expect; he ordered me to return in into the Scabbard, and cast it on the Ground as gently as I could, about six Foot from the End of my Chain. The next Thing he demanded was one of the hollow Iron Pillars, by which he meant my Pocket-Pistols. I drew it out, and at his Desire, as well as I could, expressed to him the Use of it, and charging it only with Powder, which by the Closeness* of my Pouch, happened to escape wetting in the Sea, (an Inconvenience that all prudent Mariners take special Care to provide against) I first cautioned the Emperor not to be afraid; and then I let it off in the Air. The Astonishment here was much greater than at the Sight of my Scymiter. Hundreds fell down as if they had been struck dead; and even the Emperor, although he stood his Ground, could not recover himself in some time. I delivered up both my Pistols in the same Manner as I had done my Scymiter, and then my Pouch of Powder and Bullets; begging him that the former might be kept from Fire; for it would kindle with the smallest Spark, and blow up his Imperial Palace into the Air. I likewise delivered up my Watch, which the Emperor was very curious to see; and commanded two of his tallest Yeomen of the Guards to bear it on a Pole upon their Shoulders, as Dray-men in *England* do a Barrel of Ale. He was amazed at the continual Noise it made, and the Motion of the Minute-hand, which he could easily discern; for their Sight is much more acute than ours: He asked the Opinions of his learned Men about him, which were various and remote, as the Reader may well imagine without my repeating; although indeed I could not very perfectly understand them. I then gave up my Silver and Copper Money, my Purse with nine large Pieces of Gold, and some smaller ones; my Knife and Razor, my Comb and Silver Snuff-Box, my Handkerchief and Journal Book. My Scymiter, Pistols, and Pouch, were conveyed in Carriages to his Majesty's Stores; but the rest of my Goods were returned me.

I had, as I before observed, one private Pocket which escaped their Search, wherein there was a Pair of Spectacles (which I sometimes use for the Weakness of mine Eyes), a Pocket Perspective,* and several other little Conveniences;

which being of no Consequence to the Emperor, I did not
think my self bound in Honour to discover; and I apprehended they might be lost or spoiled if I ventured them out of
my Possession.

CHAPTER THREE

The Author diverts the Emperor and his Nobility of both Sexes, in a very uncommon Manner. The Diversions of the Court of Lilliput described. The Author hath his Liberty granted him upon certain Conditions.

MY GENTLENESS and good Behaviour had gained so far on the Emperor and his Court, and indeed upon the Army and People in general, that I began to conceive Hopes of getting my Liberty in a short Time. I took all possible Methods to cultivate this favourable Disposition. The Natives came by Degrees to be less apprehensive of any Danger from me. I would sometimes lie down, and let five or six of them dance on my Hand. And at last the Boys and Girls would venture to come and play at Hide and Seek in my Hair. I had now made a good Progress in understanding and speaking their Language. The Emperor had a mind one Day to entertain me with several of the Country Shows; wherein they exceed all Nations I have known, both for Dexterity and Magnificence. I was diverted with none so much as that of the Rope-Dancers,* performed upon a slender white Thread, extended about two Foot, and twelve Inches from the Ground. Upon which, I shall desire Liberty, with the Reader's Patience, to enlarge a little.

This Diversion is only practised by those Persons, who are Candidates for great Employments, and high Favour, at Court. They are trained in this Art from their Youth, and are not always of noble Birth, or liberal Education. When a great Office is vacant, either by Death or Disgrace, (which often happens) five or six of those Candidates petition the Emperor to entertain his Majesty and the Court with a Dance on the Rope; and whoever jumps the highest without falling, succeeds in the Office. Very often the chief Ministers themselves are commanded to shew their Skill, and to convince the Emperor that they have not lost their Faculty. *Flimnap,** the Treasurer, is allowed to cut a Caper on the strait Rope, at least an Inch higher than any other Lord in the whole Empire. I have seen him do the Summerset* several times together, upon a Trencher fixed on the Rope, which is no thicker than a common Packthread in *England*. My Friend *Reldresal*,* principal Secretary for private Affairs, is, in my Opinion, if I am not partial, the second after the Treasurer; the rest of the great Officers are much upon a Par.

These Diversions are often attended with fatal Accidents, whereof great Numbers are on Record. I my self have seen two or three Candidates break a Limb. But the Danger is much greater, when the Ministers themselves are commanded to shew their Dexterity: For, by contending to excel themselves and their Fellows, they strain so far, that there is hardly one of them who hath not received a Fall; and some of them two or three. I was assured, that a Year or two before my Arrival, *Flimnap* would have infallibly broke his Neck, if one of the *King's Cushions*,* that accidentally lay on the Ground, had not weakened the Force of his Fall.

There is likewise another Diversion, which is only shewn before the Emperor and Empress, and first Minister, upon particular Occasions. The Emperor lays on a Table three fine silken Threads* of six Inches long. One is Blue, the other Red, and the third Green. These Threads are proposed as Prizes, for those Persons whom the Emperor hath a mind to distinguish by a peculiar Mark of his Favour. The Ceremony is performed in his Majesty's great Chamber of State; where the Candidates are to undergo a Tryal of Dexterity very different from the former; and such as I have not observed the least Resemblance of in any other Country of the old or the new World. The Emperor holds a Stick in his Hands, both ends parallel to the Horizon, while the Candidates advancing one by one, sometimes leap over the Stick, sometimes creep under it backwards and forwards several times, according as the Stick is advanced or depressed. Sometimes the Emperor holds one End of the Stick, and his first Minister the other; sometimes the Minister has it entirely to himself. Whoever performs his Part with most Agility, and holds out the longest in *leaping* and *creeping*, is rewarded with the Blue-coloured Silk; the Red is given to the next, and the Green to the third, which they all wear girt round about the Middle; and you see few great Persons about this Court, who are not adorned with one of these Girdles.

The Horses of the Army, and those of the Royal Stables, having been daily led before me, were no longer shy, but would come up to my very Feet, without starting. The Riders would leap them over my Hand as I held it on the Ground; and one of the Emperor's Huntsmen, upon a large Courser, took my Foot, Shoe and all; which was indeed a prodigious Leap. I had the good Fortune to divert the Emperor one Day, after a very extraordinary Manner. I desired he would order several Sticks of two Foot high, and the Thickness of an ordinary Cane, to be brought me; whereupon his Majesty commanded the Master of his Woods to give Directions accordingly; and the next Morning six Wood-men arrived with as many Carriages, drawn by eight Horses to each. I took nine of these Sticks,* and fixing them firmly in the ground in a Quadrangle Figure, two Foot and a half square; I took four other Sticks, and tyed them parallel at each Corner, about two Foot from the Ground; then I fastened my Handkerchief to the nine Sticks that stood erect; and extended it on all Sides, till it was as tight as the Top of a Drum; and the four parallel Sticks rising about five inches higher than the Handkerchief, served as Ledges on each Side. When I had finished my Work, I desired the Emperor to let a Troop of his best Horse, Twenty-four in Number,* come and exercise upon this Plain. His Majesty approved of the Proposal, and I took them up one by one in my Hands, ready mounted and armed, with the proper Officers to exercise them. As soon as they got into Order, they divided into two Parties, performed mock Skirmishes, discharged blunt Arrows, drew their Swords, fled and pursued, attacked and retired; and in short discovered* the best military Discipline I ever beheld. The parallel Sticks secured them and their Horses from falling over the Stage; and the Emperor was so much delighted, that he ordered this Entertainment to be repeated several Days; and once was pleased to be lifted up, and give the Word of Command; and, with great Difficulty, persuaded even the Empress her self to let me hold her in her close Chair,* within two Yards of the

Stage, from whence she was able to take a full View of the whole Performance. It was my good Fortune that no ill Accident happened in these Entertainments; only once a fiery Horse that belonged to one of the Captains, pawing with his Hoof struck a Hole in my Handkerchief, and his Foot slipping, he overthrew his Rider and himself; but I immediately relieved them both: For covering the Hole with one Hand, I set down the Troop with the other, in the same Manner as I took them up. The Horse that fell was strained in the left Shoulder, but the Rider got no Hurt; and I repaired my Handkerchief as well as I could: However, I would not trust to the Strength of it any more in such dangerous Enterprizes.

About two or three Days before I was set at Liberty, as I was entertaining the Court with these Kinds of Feats, there arrived an Express to inform his Majesty, that some of his Subjects riding near the Place where I was first taken up, had seen a great black Substance lying on the Ground, very oddly shaped, extending its Edges round as wide as his Majesty's Bedchamber, and rising up in the Middle as high as a Man: That it was no living Creature, as they at first apprehended; for it lay on the Grass without Motion; and some of them had walked round it several Times: That by mounting upon each others Shoulders, they had got to the Top, which was flat and even; and, stamping upon it, they found it was hollow within: That they humbly conceived it might be something belonging to the *Man-Mountain*; and if his Majesty pleased, they would undertake to bring it with only five Horses. I presently* knew what they meant; and was glad at Heart to receive this Intelligence. It seems, upon my first reaching the Shore, after our Shipwreck, I was in such Confusion, that before I came to the Place where I went to sleep, my Hat, which I had fastened with a String to my Head while I was rowing, and had stuck on all the Time I was swimming, fell off after I came to Land; the String, as I conjecture, breaking by some Accident which I never observed, but thought my Hat had been lost at Sea. I intreated his Imperial Majesty to give Orders it might be brought to me as soon as possible, describing to him the Use and the Nature of it: And the next Day the Waggoners arrived with it, but not in a very good Condition;* they bored two Holes in the Brim, within an Inch and a half of the Edge, and fastened two Hooks in the Holes; these Hooks were tied by a long Cord to the Harness, and thus my Hat was dragged along for above half an *English* Mile: But the Ground in that Country being extremely smooth and level, it received less Damage than I expected.

Two Days after this Adventure, the Emperor* having ordered that Part of his Army, which quarters in and about his Metropolis, to be in a Readiness, took a fancy of diverting himself in a very singular Manner. He desired I would stand like a *Colossus*,* with my Legs as far asunder as I conveniently could. He then commanded his General (who was an old experienced Leader, and a great Patron of mine) to draw up the Troops in close Order, and march them under me; the Foot by Twenty-four in a Breast,* and the Horse by Sixteen, with Drums beating, Colours flying, and Pikes advanced. This Body consisted of three Thousand Foot, and a Thousand Horse. His Majesty gave Orders, upon Pain of Death, that every Soldier in his March should observe the strictest Decency, with regard to my Person; which, however, could not prevent some of the younger Officers from turning up their Eyes as they passed under me. And, to confess the Truth, my Breeches were at that Time in so ill a Condition, that they afforded some Opportunities for Laughter and Admiration.

I had sent so many Memorials and Petitions for my Liberty, that his Majesty at length mentioned the Matter first in the Cabinet, and then in a full Council; where it was opposed by none, except *Skyresh Bolgolam*,* who was pleased, without any Provocation, to be my mortal Enemy. But it was carried against him by the whole Board, and confirmed by the Emperor. That Minister was *Galbet*, or Admiral of the Realm; very much in his Master's Confidence, and a Person well versed in Affairs, but of a morose and sour Complection.* However, he was at length persuaded to comply; but prevailed that the Articles and Conditions upon which I should be set free, and to which I must swear, should be drawn up by himself. These Articles were brought to me by *Skyresh Bolgolam* in person, attended by two under Secretaries, and several Persons of Distinction. After they were read, I was demanded to swear to the Performance of them; first in the Manner of my own Country, and afterwards in the Method prescribed by their Laws; which was to hold my right Foot in my left Hand, to place the middle Finger of my right Hand on the Crown of my Head, and my Thumb on the Tip of my right Ear. But, because the Reader may perhaps be curious to have some Idea of the Style and Manner of Expression peculiar to that People, as well as to know the Articles upon which I recovered my Liberty; I have made a Translation of the whole Instrument,* Word for Word, as near as I was able; which I here offer to the Publick.

GOLBASTO MOMAREN EVLAME GURDILO SHEFIN MULLY ULLY GUE, most Mighty Emperor of *Lilliput*, Delight and Terror of the Universe,* whose Dominions extend five Thousand Blustrugs, (about twelve Miles in Circumference) to the Extremities of the Globe: Monarch of all Monarchs: Taller than the Sons of Men; whose Feet press down to the Center,* and whose Head strikes against the Sun: At whose Nod the Princes of the Earth shake their Knees; pleasant as the Spring, comfortable as the Summer, fruitful as Autumn, dreadful as Winter. His most sublime Majesty proposeth to the *Man-Mountain,* lately arrived at our Celestial Dominions, the following Articles, which by a solemn Oath he shall be obliged to perform.

FIRST, The *Man-Mountain* shall not depart from our Dominions, without our Licence under our Great Seal.

SECONDLY, He shall not presume to come into our Metropolis, without our express Order; at which time, the Inhabitants shall have two Hours Warning, to keep within their Doors.

THIRDLY, The said *Man-Mountain* shall confine his Walks to our principal high Roads; and not offer to walk or lie down in a Meadow, or Field of Corn.

FOURTHLY, As he walks the said Roads, he shall take the utmost Care not to trample upon the Bodies of any of our loving Subjects, their Horses, or Carriages; nor take any of our said Subjects into his Hands, without their own Consent.

FIFTHLY, If an Express require extraordinary Dispatch; the *Man-Mountain* shall be obliged to carry in his Pocket the Messenger and Horse, a six Days Journey once in every Moon, and return the said Messenger back (if so required) safe to our Imperial Presence.

SIXTHLY, He shall be our Ally against our Enemies in the Island of *Blefuscu*,* and do his utmost to destroy their Fleet, which is now preparing to invade Us.

SEVENTHLY, That the said *Man-Mountain* shall, at his Times of Leisure, be aiding and assisting our Workmen, in helping to raise certain great Stones, towards covering the Wall of the principal Park, and other our Royal Buildings.

EIGHTHLY, That the said *Man-Mountain* shall, in two Moons Time, deliver in an exact Survey of the Circumference of our Dominions, by a Computation of his own Paces round the Coast.

LASTLY, That upon his solemn Oath to observe all the above Articles, the said *Man-Mountain* shall have a daily Allowance of Meat and Drink, sufficient for the Support of 1728 of our Subjects; with free Access to our Royal Person, and other Marks of our Favour, Given at our Palace at *Belfaborac* the Twelfth Day of the Ninety-first Moon of our Reign.

I swore and subscribed to these Articles with great Chearfulness and Content, although some of them were not so honourable as I could have wished; which proceeded wholly from the Malice of *Skyresh Bolgolam* the High Admiral: Whereupon my Chains were immediately unlocked, and I was at full Liberty: The Emperor himself, in Person, did me the Honour to be by me at the whole Ceremony. I made my

Acknowledgments, by prostrating myself at his Majesty's Feet: But he commanded me to rise; and after many gracious Expressions, which, to avoid the Censure of Vanity, I shall not repeat; he added, that he hoped I should prove a useful Servant, and well deserve all the Favours he had already conferred upon me, or might do for the future.

The Reader may please to observe, that in the last Article for the Recovery of my Liberty, the Emperor stipulates to allow me a Quantity of Meat and Drink sufficient for the Support of 1728 *Lilliputians*. Some time after, asking a Friend at Court how they came to fix on that determinate Number; he told me, that his Majesty's Mathematicians, having taken the Height of my Body by the Help of a Quadrant, and finding it to exceed theirs in the Proportion of Twelve to One, they concluded from the Similarity of their Bodies, that mine must contain at least 1728 of theirs, and consequently would require as much Food* as was necessary to support that Number of *Lilliputians*. By which, the Reader may conceive an Idea of the Ingenuity of that People, as well as the prudent and exact Oeconomy of so great a Prince.

CHAPTER FOUR

Mildendo,* the Metropolis of Lilliput, described, together with the Emperor's Palace. A Conversation between the Author and a principal Secretary, concerning the Affairs of that Empire: The Author's Offers to serve the Emperor in his Wars.

THE FIRST Request I made after I had obtained my Liberty, was, that I might have Licence to see *Mildendo,* the Metropolis; which the Emperor easily granted me, but with a special Charge to do no Hurt, either to the Inhabitants, or their Houses. The People had Notice by Proclamation of my Design to visit the Town. The Wall which encompassed it, is two Foot and a half high, and at least eleven Inches broad, so that a Coach and Horses may be driven very safely round it; and it is flanked with strong Towers at ten Foot Distance. I stept over the great *Western* Gate, and passed very gently, and sideling* through the two principal Streets, only in my short Waistcoat, for fear of damaging the Roofs and Eves of the Houses with the Skirts of my Coat. I walked with the utmost Circumspection, to avoid treading on any Stragglers, who might remain in the Streets, although the Orders were very strict, that all People should keep in their Houses, at their own Peril. The Garret Windows and Tops of Houses were so crowded with Spectators, that I thought in all my Travels I had not seen a more populous Place. The City is an exact Square, each Side of the Wall being five Hundred Foot long. The two great Streets which run cross and divide it into four Quarters, are five Foot wide. The Lanes and Alleys which I could not enter, but only viewed them as I passed, are from Twelve to Eighteen Inches. The Town is capable of holding five Hundred Thousand* Souls. The Houses are from three to five Stories. The Shops and Markets well provided.

The Emperor's Palace is in the Center of the City, where the two great Streets meet. It is inclosed by a Wall of two Foot high, and Twenty Foot distant from the Buildings. I had his

Majesty's Permission to step over this Wall; and the Space being so wide between that and the Palace, I could easily view it on every Side. The outward Court is a Square of Forty Foot, and includes two other Courts: In the inmost are the Royal Apartments, which I was very desirous to see, but found it extremely difficult; for the great Gates, from one Square into another, were but Eighteen Inches high, and seven Inches wide. Now the Buildings of the outer Court were at least five Foot high; and it was impossible for me to stride over them, without infinite Damage to the Pile, although the Walls were strongly built of hewn Stone, and four Inches thick. At the same time, the Emperor had a great Desire that I should see the Magnificence of his Palace: But this I was not able to do till three Days after, which I spent in cutting down with my Knife some of the largest Trees in the Royal Park, about an Hundred Yards distant from the City. Of these Trees I made two Stools, each about three Foot high, and strong enough to bear my Weight. The People having received Notice a second time, I went again through the City to the Palace, with my two Stools in my Hands. When I came to the Side of the outer Court, I stood upon one Stool, and took the other in my Hnad: This I lifted over the Roof, and gently set it down on the Space between the first and second Court, which was eight Foot wide. I then stept over the Buildings very conveniently from one Stool to the other, and drew up the first after me with a hooked Stick. By this Contrivance I got into the inmost Court; and lying down upon my Side, I applied my Face to the Windows of the middle Stories, which were left open on Purpose, and discovered the most splendid Apartments that can be imagined. There I saw the Empress, and the young Princes in their several Lodgings, with their chief Attendants about them. Her Imperial Majesty was pleased to smile very graciously* upon me, and gave me out of the Window her Hand to kiss.

But I shall not anticipate the Reader* with farther Descriptions of this Kind, because I reserve them for a greater Work, which is now almost ready for the Press; containing a general Description of this Empire, from its first Erection, through a long Series of Princes, with a particular Account of their Wars and Politicks, Laws, Learning, and Religion; their Plants and Animals, their peculiar Manners and Customs, with other Matters very curious and useful; my chief Design at present being only to relate such Events and Transactions as happened to the Publick, or to my self, during a Residence of about nine Months in that Empire.

One Morning, about a Fortnight after I had obtained my Liberty; *Reldresal*, Principal Secretary (as they style him) of private Affairs, came to my House, attended only by one Servant. He ordered his Coach to wait at a Distance, and desired I would give him an Hour's Audience; which I readily consented to, on Account of his Quality, and Personal Merits, as well of the many good Offices he had done me during my Sollicitations at Court. I offered to lie down, that he might the more conveniently reach my Ear; but he chose rather to let me hold him in my Hand during our Conversation. He began with Compliments on my Liberty; said, he might pretend to some Merit in it;* but, however, added, that if it had not been for the present Situation of things at Court, perhaps I might not have obtained it so soon. For, *said he,* as flourishing a Condition as we appear to be in to Foreigners, we labour under two mighty Evils; a violent Faction at home, and the Danger of an Invasion by a most potent Enemy from abroad. As to the first, you are to understand, that for above seventy Moons* past, there have been two struggling Parties in this Empire, under the Names of *Tramecksan,* and *Slamecksan,** from the high and low Heels on their Shoes, by which they distinguish themselves.

It is alledged indeed, that the High Heels are most agreeable to our ancient Constitution: But however this be, his Majesty hath determined to make use of only low Heels* in the Administration of the Government, and all Offices in the Gift of the Crown; as you cannot but observe; and particularly, that his Majesty's Imperial Heels are lower at least by a *Drurr* than any of his Court; (*Drurr* is a Measure about the fourteenth Part of an Inch.) The Animosities between these two Parties run so high, that they will neither eat nor drink, nor talk with each other. We compute the *Tramecksan,* or High-Heels, to exceed us in Number; but the Power is wholly on our Side. We apprehend his Imperial Highness, the Heir to the Crown, to have some Tendency towards the High-Heels;* at least we can plainly discover one of his Heels higher than the other; which gives him a Hobble in his Gait. Now, in the midst of these intestine Disquiets, we are threatened with an Invasion from the Island of *Blefuscu*, which is the other great Empire of the Universe, almost as large and powerful as this of his Majesty. For as to what we have heard you affirm, that there are other Kingdoms and States in the World, inhabited by human Creatures as large as your self, our Philosophers are in much Doubt; and would rather conjecture that you dropt from the Moon, or one of the Stars; because it is certain, than an hundred Mortals of your Bulk, would, in a short Time, destroy all the Fruits and Cattle of his Majesty's Dominions. Besides, our Histories of six Thousand Moons* make no Mention of any other Regions, than the two great Empires of *Lilliput* and *Blefuscu*. Which two mighty Powers have, as I was going to tell you, been engaged in a most obstinate War for six and thirty Moons* past. It began upon the following Occasion. It is allowed on all Hands, that the primitive Way of breaking Eggs before we eat them, was upon the larger End: But his present Majesty's Grand-father,* while he was a Boy, going to eat an Egg, and breaking it according to the ancient Practice, happened to cut one of his Fingers. Whereupon the Emperor, his Father, published an Edict, commanding all his Subjects, upon great Penalties, to break the smaller End of their Eggs. The People have so highly resented this Law, that our Histories tell us, there have been six Rebellions raised on that Account; wherein one Emperor* lost his Life, and another* his Crown. These civil Commotions were constantly fomented by the Monarchs of *Blefuscu*;* and when they were quelled, the Exiles always fled for Refuge to that Empire. It is computed, that eleven Thousand Persons have, at several Times, suffered Death, rather than submit to break their Eggs at the smaller End. Many hundred large Volumes have been published upon this Controversy: But the Books of the *Big-Endians* have been long forbidden,* and the whole Party rendred incapable by Law* of holding Employments. During the Course of these Troubles, the Emperors of *Blefuscu* did frequently expostulate by their Ambassadors, accusing us of making a Schism in Religion, by offending against a fundamental doctrine of our great Prophet *Lustrog*, in the fifty-fourth Chapter of the *Brundrecal*, (which is their *Alcoran**). This, however, is thought to be a meer Strain upon the Text: For the Words are these; *That all true Believers shall break their Eggs at the convenient End*: and which is the convenient End, seems, in my humble Opinion, to be left to every Man's Conscience, or at least in the Power of the chief Magistrate* to determine. Now the *Big-Endian* Exiles have found so much Credit in the Emperor of *Blefuscu's* Court; and so much private Assistance and Encouragement from their Party here at home, that a bloody War* hath been carried on between the two Empires for six and thirty Moons with various Success; during which Time we have lost Forty Capital Ships, and a much greater Number of smaller Vessels, together with thirty thousand of our best Seamen and Soldiers; and the Damage received by the Enemy is reckoned to be somewhat greater than ours. However, they have now equipped a numerous Fleet, and are just preparing to make a Descent upon us: And his Imperial Majesty, placing great Confidence in your Valour and Strength, hath commanded me to lay this Account of his Affairs before you.

I desired the Secretary to present my humble Duty to the Emperor, and to let him know, that I thought it would not become me, who was a Foreigner, to interfere with Parties; but I was ready, with the Hazard of my Life, to defend his Person and State against all Invaders.

CHAPTER FIVE

The Author by an extraordinary Stratagem prevents an Invasion. A high Title of Honour is conferred upon him. Ambassadors arrive from the Emperor of Blefuscu and sue for Peace. The Empress's Apartment on fire by an Accident; the Author instrumental in saving the rest of the Palace.

THE EMPIRE of *Blefuscu*, is an Island situated to the North North-East Side of *Lilliput*, from whence it is parted only by a Channel of eight Hundred Yards wide. I had not yet seen it, and upon this Notice of an intended Invasion, I avoided appearing on that Side of the Coast, for fear of being discovered by some of the Enemies Ships, who had received no Intelligence of me; all intercourse between the two Empires having been strictly forbidden during the War, upon Pain of Death; and an Embargo laid by our Emperor upon all Vessels whatsoever. I communicated to his Majesty a Project I had formed of seizing the Enemies whole Fleet; which, as our Scouts assured us, lay at Anchor in the Harbour ready to sail with the first fair Wind. I consulted the most experienced Seamen, upon the Depth of the Channel, which they had often plummed; who told me, that in the Middle at high Water it was seventy *Glumgluffs* deep, which is about six Foot of *European* Measure; and the rest of it fifty *Glumgluffs* at most, I walked to the North-East Coast over against *Blefuscu*; where, lying down behind a Hillock, I took out my small Pocket Perspective Glass, and viewed the Enemy's Fleet at Anchor, consisting of about fifty Men of War, and a great Number of Transports: I then came back to my House, and gave Order (for which I had a Warrant) for a great Quantity of the strongest Cable and Bars of Iron. The Cable was about as thick as Packthread, and the Bars of the Length and Size of a Knitting-Needle. I trebled the Cable to make it stronger; and for same Reason I twisted three of the Iron Bars together, bending the Extremities into a Hook. Having thus fixed fifty

Hooks to as many Cables, I went back to the North-East Coast, and putting off my Coat, Shoes, and Stockings, walked into the Sea in my Leathern Jerken, about half an Hour before high Water. I waded with what Haste I could, and swam in the Middle about thirty Yards until I felt the Ground; I arrived at the Fleet in less than half an Hour. The Enemy was so frighted when they saw me, that they leaped out of their Ships, and swam to Shore; where there could not be fewer than thirty thousand Souls. I then took my Tackling, and fastning a Hook to the Hole at the Prow of each, I tyed all the Cords together at the End. While I was thus employed, the Enemy discharged Several Thousand Arrows, many of which stuck in my Hands and Face; and besides the excessive Smart, gave me much Disturbance in my Work. My greatest Apprehension was for mine Eyes, which I should have infallibly lost, if I had not suddenly thought of an Expedient. I kept, among other little Necessaries, a Pair of Spectacles in a private Pocket, which, as I observed before, had escaped the Emperor's Searchers. These I took out, and fastened as strongly as I could upon my Nose; and thus armed went on boldly with my Work in spight of the Enemy's Arrows; many of which struck against the Glasses of my Spectacles, but without any other Effect, further than a little to discompose them. I had now fastened all the Hooks, and taking the Knot in my Hand, began to pull; but not a Ship would stir, for they were all too fast held by their Anchors; so that the boldest Part of my Enterprize remained. I therefore let go the Cord, and leaving the Hooks fastened to the Ships, I resolutely cut with my Knife the Cables that fastened the Anchors; receiving above two hundred Shots in my Face and Hands: Then I took up the knotted End of the Cables to which my Hooks were tyed; and with great Ease* drew fifty of the Enemy's largest Men of War after me.

The *Blefuscudians*, who had not the least Imagination of what I intended, were at first confounded with Astonishment. They had seen me cut the Cables, and thought my Design was only to let the Ships run a-drift, or fall foul on each other: But when they perceived the whole Fleet moving in Order, and saw me pulling at the End, they set up such a Scream of Grief and Dispair, that it is almost impossible to describe or conceive. When I had got out of Danger, I stopt a while to pick out the Arrows that stuck in my Hands and Face, and rubbed on some of the same Ointment that was given me at my first Arrival, as I have formerly mentioned. I then took off my Spectacles, and waiting about an Hour until the Tyde was a little fallen, I waded through the Middle with my Cargo, and arrived safe at the Royal Port of *Lilliput.*

The Emperor and his whole Court stood on the Shore, expecting* the Issue of this great Adventure. They saw the Ships move forward in a large Half-Moon,* but could not discern me, who was up to my Breast in Water. When I advanced to the Middle of the Channel, they were yet more in Pain because I was under Water to my Neck. The Emperor concluded me to be drowned, and that the Enemy's Fleet was approaching in a hostile Manner: But he was soon Eased of his Fears; for the Channel growing shallower every Step I made, I came in a short Time within Hearing; and holding up the End of the Cable by which the Fleet was fastened, I cryed in a loud Voice, *Long live the most puissant Emperor of Lilliput!* This great Prince received me at my Landing with all possible Encomiums, and created me a *Nardac*∗ upon the Spot, which is the highest Title of Honour among them.

His Majesty desired I would take some other Opportunity of bringing all the rest of his Enemy's Ships into his Ports. And so unmeasurable is the Ambition of Princes, that he seemed to think of nothing less than reducing the whole Empire* of *Blefuscu* into a Province, and governing it by a Viceroy; of destroying the *Big-Endian* Exiles, and compelling that People to break the smaller End of their Eggs; by which he would remain sole Monarch of the whole World. But I endeavoured to divert him from this Design, by many Arguments drawn from the Topicks* of Policy as well as Justice: And I plainly protested, that I would never be an Instrument of bringing a free and brave People into Slavery: And when the Matter was debated in Council, the wisest Part of the Ministry were of my Opinion.

This open bold Declaration of mine was so opposite to the Schemes and Politicks of his Imperial Majesty, that he could never forgive me: He mentioned it in a very artful Manner at

Council, where, I was told, that some of the wisest appeared, at least by their Silence, to be of my Opinion; but others, who were my secret Enemies, could not forbear some Expressions, which by a Side-wind* reflected on me. And from this Time began an Intrigue between his Majesty, and a Junta of Ministers maliciously bent against me, which broke out in less than two Months, and had like to have ended in my utter Destruction. Of so little Weight are the greatest Services to Princes, when put into the Balance with a Refusal to gratify their Passions.

About three Weeks after this Exploit, there arrived a solemn Embassy from *Blefuscu*, with humble Offers of a Peace; which was soon concluded upon Conditions very advantageous to our Emperor; wherewith I shall not trouble the Reader. There were six Ambassadors, with a Train of about five Hundred Persons; and their Entry was very magnificent, suitable to the Grandeur of their Master, and the Importance of their Business. When their Treaty was finished, wherein I did them several good Offices by the Credit I now had, or at least appeared to have at Court; their Excellencies, who were privately told how much I had been their Friend, made me a Visit in Form.* They began with many Compliments upon my Valour and Generosity; invited me to that Kingdom in the Emperor their Master's Name; and desired me to shew them some Proofs of my prodigious Strength, of which they had heard so many Wonders; wherein I readily obliged them, but shall not interrupt the Reader with the Particulars.

When I had for some time entertained their Excellencies to their infinite Satisfaction and Surprize, I desired they would do me the Honour to present my most humble Respects to the Emperor their Master, the Renown of whose Virtues had so justly filled the whole World with Admiration, and whose Royal Person I resolved to attend before I returned to my own Country. Accordingly, the next time I had the Honour to see our Emperor, I desired his general Licence to wait on the *Blefuscudian* Monarch, which he was pleased to grant me, as I could plainly perceive, in a very cold Manner; but could not guess the Reason, till I had a Whisper from a certain Person, that *Flimnap* and *Bolgolam* had represented my Intercourse with those Ambassadors, as a Mark of Disaffection,* from which I am sure my Heart was wholly free. And this was the first time I began to conceive some imperfect Idea of Courts and Ministers.

It is to be observed, that these Ambassadors spoke to me by an Interpreter; the Languages of both Empires differing as much from each other as any two in *Europe*, and each Nation priding itself upon the Antiquity, Beauty, and Energy of their own Tongues, with an avowed Contempt for that of their Neighbour: Yet our Emperor standing upon the Advantage he had got by the Seizure of their Fleet, obliged them to deliver their Credentials, and make their Speech in the *Lilliputian* Tongue. And it must be confessed, that from the great Intercourse of Trade and Commerce between both Realms; from the continual Reception of Exiles, which is mutual among them; and from the Custom in each Empire to send their young Nobility and richer Gentry to the other, in order to polish themselves, by seeing the World, and understanding Men and Manners; there are few Persons of Distinction, or Merchants, or Seamen, who dwell in the Maritime Parts, but what can hold Conversation in both Tongues; as I found some Weeks after, when I went to pay my Respects to the Emperor of *Blefuscu*, which* in the Midst of great Misfortunes, through the Malice of my Enemies, proved a very happy Adventure* to me, as I shall relate in its proper Place.

The Reader may remember, that when I signed those Articles upon which I recovered my Liberty, there were some which I disliked upon Account of their being too servile, neither could any thing but an extreme Necessity have forced me to submit. But being now a *Nardac*, of the highest Rank in that Empire, such Offices were looked upon as below my Dignity; and the Emperor (to do him Justice) never once mentioned them to me. However, it was not long before I had an Opportunity of doing his Majesty, at least, as I then thought, a most signal Service. I was alarmed at Midnight with the Cries of many Hundred People at my Door; by which being suddenly awaked, I was in some Kind of Terror. I heard the Word *Burglum* repeated incessantly; several of the Emperor's Court making their Way through the Croud, intreated me to come immediately to the Palace, where her Imperial Majesty's Apartment was on fire, by the Carelessness of a Maid of Honour, who fell asleep while she was reading a Romance.* I got up in an Instant; and Orders being given to clear the Way before me; and it being likewise a Moonshine Night, I made a shift to get to the Palace without trampling on any of the People. I found they had already applied Ladders to the Walls of the Apartment, and were well provided with Buckets, but the Water was at some Distance. These Buckets were about the Size of a large Thimble, and the poor People supplied me with them as fast as they could; but the Flame was so violent, that they did little Good. I might easily have stifled it with my Coat, which I unfortunately left behind me for haste, and came away only in my Leathern Jerkin. The Case seemed wholly desperate and deplorable; and this magnificent Palace would have infallibly been burnt down to the Ground, if, by a Presence of Mind, unusual to me, I had not suddenly thought of an Expedient. I had the Evening before drank plentifully of a most delicious Wine, called *Glimigrim*, (the *Blefuscudians* call it *Flunec*,* but ours is esteemed the better Sort) which is very diuretick. By the luckiest Chance in the World, I had not discharged myself of any Part of it. The Heat I had contracted by coming very near the Flames, and by my labouring to quench them, made the Wine begin to operate by Urine; which I voided in such a Quantity, and applied so well to the proper Places, that in three Minutes the Fire was wholly extinguished;* and the rest of that Noble Pile, which had cost so many Ages in erecting, preserved from Destruction.

It was now Day-light, and I returned to my House, without waiting to congratulate with* the Emperor; because, although I had done a very eminent Piece of Service, yet I could not tell how his Majesty might resent the Manner by which I had performed it: For, by the fundamental Laws of the Realm, it is Capital* in any Person, of what Quality soever, to make water within the Precincts of the Palace. But I was a little comforted by a Message from his Majesty, that he would give Orders to the Grand Justiciary for passing my Pardon in Form; which, however, I could not obtain. And I was privately assured, that the Empress conceiving the greatest Abhorrence of what I had done, removed to the most distant Side of the Court, firmly resolved that those Buildings should never be repaired for her Use; and, in the Presence of her chief Confidents, could not forbear vowing Revenge.

CHAPTER SIX

Of the Inhabitants* of Lilliput; *their Learning, Laws, and Customs. The Manner of Educating their Children. The Author's Way of living in that Country. His Vindication of a great Lady.*

ALTHOUGH I intend to leave the Description of this Empire to a particular Treatise, yet in the mean time I am content to gratify the curious Reader with some general Ideas. As the common Size of the Natives is somewhat under six Inches, so there is an exact Proportion in all other Animals, as well as Plants and Trees: For Instance, the tallest Horses and Oxen are between four and five Inches* in Height, the Sheep an Inch and a half,* more or less; their Geese about the Bigness of a Sparrow; and so the several Gradations downwards, till you come to the smallest, which, to my Sight, were almost invisible; but Nature hath adapted the Eyes of the *Lilliputians* to all Objects proper for their View: They see with great Exactness, but at no great Distance. And to show the Sharpness of their Sight towards Objects that are near, I have been much pleased with observing a Cook pulling* a Lark, which was not so large as a common Fly; and a young Girl threading an invisible Needle with invisible Silk. Their tallest Trees are about seven Foot high; I mean some of those in the great Royal Park, the Tops whereof I could but just reach with my Fist clinched.* The other Vegetables are in the same Proportion: But this I leave to the Reader's Imagination.

I shall say but little at present of their Learning, which for many Ages hath flourished in all its Branches among them: But their Manner of Writing* is very peculiar; being neither from the Left to the Right, like the *Europeans*; nor from the Right to the Left, like the *Arabians*; nor from up to down, like the *Chinese*; nor from down to up, like the *Cascagians*; but aslant from one Corner of the Paper to the other, like Ladies in *England.*

They bury their Dead with their Heads directly downwards;* because they hold an Opinion, that in eleven Thousand Moons they are all to rise again; in which Period, the Earth (which they conceive to be flat) will turn upside down, and by this Means they shall, at their Resurrection, be found ready standing on their Feet. The Learned among them confess the Absurdity of this Doctrine; but the Practice still continues, in Compliance to the Vulgar.

There are some Laws and Customs in this Empire very peculiar; and if they were not so directly contrary to those of my own dear Country, I should be tempted to say a little in their Justification. It is only to be wished, that they were as well executed. The first I shall mention, relateth to Informers. All Crimes against the State, are punished here with the utmost Severity; but if the Person accused make his Innocence plainly to appear upon his Tryal, the Accuser is immediately put to an ignominious Death; and out of his Goods or Lands, the innocent Person is quadruply recompensed for the Loss of his Time, for the Danger he underwent, for the Hardship of his Imprisonment, and for all the Charges he hath been at* in making his Defence. Or, if that Fund be deficient, it is largely* supplyed by the Crown. The Emperor doth also confer on him some publick Mark of his Favour; and Proclamation is made of his Innocence through the whole City.

They look upon Fraud as a greater Crime than Theft,* and therefore seldom fail to punish it with Death: For they alledge, that Care and Vigilance, with a very common understanding, may preserve a Man's Goods from Thieves; but Honesty hath no Fence against superior Cunning: And since it is necessary that there should be a perpetual Intercourse of buying and selling, and dealing upon Credit; where Fraud is permitted or connived at, or hath no Law to punish it, the honest Dealer is always undone, and the Knave gets the Advantage. I remember when I was once interceeding with the King for a Criminal who had wronged his Master of a great Sum of Money, which he had received by Order, and ran away with; and happening to tell his Majesty, by way of Extenuation, that it was only a Breach of Trust; The Emperor thought it monstrous in me to offer, as a Defence, the greatest

Aggravation of the Crime: And truly, I had little to say in Return, farther than the common Answer, that different Nations had different Customs;* for, I confess, I was heartily ashamed.

Although we usually call Reward and Punishment, the two Hinges* upon which all Government turns; yet I could never observe this Maxim to be put in Practice by any Nation, except that of *Lilliput.** Whoever can there bring sufficient Proof that he hath strictly observed the Laws of his Country for Seventy-three Moons, hath a Claim to certain Privileges, according to his Quality and Condition of Life, with a proportionable Sum of Money out of a Fund appropriated for that Use: He likewise acquires the Title of *Snilpall*, or *Legal*, which is added to his Name, but doth not descend to his Posterity. And these People thought it a prodigious Defect of Policy among us, when I told them that our Laws were enforced only by Penalties, without any Mention of Reward. It is upon this account that the Image of Justice, in their Courts of Judicature, is formed with six Eyes, two before, as many behind, and on each Side one, to signify Circumspection; with a Bag of Gold open in her right Hand, and a Sword sheathed in her left, to shew she is more disposed to reward than to punish.

In chusing Persons* for all Employments, they have more Regard to good Morals than to great abilities: For, since Government is necessary to Mankind, they believe that the common Size of human Understandings, is fitted to some Station or other; and that Providence never intended to make the Management of publick Affairs a Mystery, to be comprehended only by a few Persons of sublime Genius, of which there seldom are three born in an Age: But, they suppose Truth, Justice, Temperance, and the like, to be in every Man's Power; the Practice of which Virtues, assisted by Experience and a good Intention, would qualify any Man for the Service of his Country, except where a Course of Study is required. But they thought the Want of Moral Virtues was so far from being supplied by superior Endowments of the Mind, that Employments could never be put into such dangerous Hands as those of Persons so qualified; and at least, that the Mistakes committed by Ignorance in a virtuous Disposition, would never be of such fatal Consequence to the Publick Weal, as the Practices* of a Man, whose Inclinations led him to be corrupt, and had* great Abilities to manage, to multiply, and defend his Corruptions.

In like Manner, the Disbelief of a Divine Providence renders a Man uncapable of holding any publick Station:* For, since Kings avow themselves to be the Deputies of Providence, the *Lilliputians* think nothing can be more absurd than for a Prince to employ such Men as disown the Authority under which he acteth.

In relating these and the following Laws, I would only be understood to mean the original Institutions, and not the most scandalous Corruptions into which these People are fallen by the degenerate Nature of Man. For as to that infamous Practice of acquiring great Employments by dancing on the Ropes, or Badges of Favour and Distinction by leaping over Sticks, and creeping under them; the Reader is to observe, that they were first introduced by the Grand-father* of the Emperor now reigning; and grew to the present Height, by the gradual Increase of Party and Faction.

Ingratitude is among them a capital Crime,* as we read it to have been in some other Countries: For they reason thus; that whoever makes ill Returns to his Benefactor, must needs be a common Enemy to the rest of Mankind, from whom he hath received no Obligation; and therefore such a Man is not fit to live.

Their Notions relating to the Duties of Parents and Children differ extremely from ours. For, since the Conjunction of Male and Female is founded upon the great Law of Nature, in order to propagate and continue the Species; the *Lilliputians* will needs have it, that Men and Women are joined together like other Animals, by the Motives of Concupiscence; and that their Tenderness towards their Young, proceedeth from the like natural Principle: For which Reason they will never allow, that a Child is under any Obligation to his Father for begetting him, or to his Mother for bringing him into the World,* which, considering the Miseries of human Life, was neither a Benefit in itself, nor intended so by his Parents, whose Thoughts in their Love-encounters were otherwise employed. Upon these, and the like Reasonings, their Opinion is, that Parents are the last of all others to be trusted with the Education of their own Children.* And therefore they have in every Town publick Nurseries, where all Parents, except Cottagers and Labourers, are obliged to send their Infants of both Sexes to be reared and educated when they come to the Age of twenty Moons; at which Time they are supposed to have some Rudiments of Docility. These Schools are of several kinds, suited to different Qualities, and to both Sexes. They have certain Professors* well skilled in preparing Children for such a Condition of Life as befits the Rank of their Parents, and their own Capacities as well as Inclinations. I shall first say something of the Male Nurseries, and then of the Female.

The Nurseries for Males of Noble or Eminent Birth, are provided with grave and learned Professors, and their several Deputies. The Clothes and Food of the Children are plain and simple. They are bred up in the Principles of Honour, Justice, Courage, Modesty, Clemency, Religion, and Love of their Country: They are always employed* in some Business, except in the Times of eating and sleeping, which are very short, and two Hours for Diversions, consisting of bodily Exercises. They are dressed by Men until four Years of Age, and then are obliged to dress themselves, although their Quality be ever so great; and the Women Attendants, who are aged proportionately to ours at fifty, perform only the most menial Offices. They are never suffered to converse with Servants, but go together in small or greater Numbers to take their Diversions, and always in the Presence of a Professor, or one of his Deputies; whereby they avoid those early bad Impressions of Folly and Vice to which our Children are subject. Their Parents are suffered to see them only twice a Year; the Visit is not to last above an Hour; they are allowed to kiss the Child at Meeting and Parting; but a Professor, who always standeth by on those Occasions, will not suffer them to whisper, or use any fondling Expressions, or bring any presents of Toys, Sweet-meats, and the like.*

The Pension* from each Family for the Education and

Entertainment of a Child, upon Failure of due Payment, is levied by the Emperor's Officers.

The Nurseries for Children of ordinary Gentlemen, Merchants, Traders, and Handicrafts, are managed proportionably after the same Manner; only those designed for Trades, are put out Apprentices at seven Years old; whereas those of Persons of Quality continue in their Exercises until Fifteen, which answers to One and Twenty with us: But the Confinement is gradually lessened for the last three Years.

In the Female Nurseries, the young Girls of Quality are educated much like the Males, only they are dressed by orderly Servants of their own Sex, but always in the Presence of a Professor or Deputy, until they come to dress themselves, which is at five Years old. And if it be found that these Nurses ever presume to entertain the Girls with frightful or foolish Stories,* or the common Follies practised by Chamber-Maids among us; they are publickly whipped thrice about the City, imprisoned for a Year, and banished for Life to the most desolate Part of the Country. Thus the young Ladies there are as much ashamed of being Cowards and Fools, as the Men; and despise all personal Ornaments* beyond Decency and Cleanliness; neither did I perceive any Difference* in their Education, made by their Difference of Sex, only that the Exercises of the Females were not altogether so robust; and that some Rules were given them relating to domestick Life, and a smaller Compass of Learning was enjoyned them: For, their Maxim is, that among People of Quality, a Wife should be always a reasonable and agreeable Companion, because she cannot always be young.* When the Girls are twelve years old,* which among them is the marriageable Age, their Parents or Guardians take them home, with great Expressions of Gratitude to the Professors, and seldom without Tears of the young Lady and her Companions.

In the Nurseries of Females of the meaner Sort, the Children are instructed in all Kinds of Works proper for their Sex, and their several Degrees: Those intended for Apprentices are dismissed at seven Years old, the rest are kept to eleven.

The meaner Families who have Children at these Nurseries, are obliged, besides their annual Pension, which is as low as possible, to return to the Steward of the Nursery a small Monthly Share of their Gettings, to be a Portion for the Child; and therefore all Parents are limited in their Expences by the Law. For the *Lilliputians* think nothing can be more unjust, than that People, in Subservience to their own Appetites, should bring Children into the World, and leave the Burthen of supporting them on the Publick. As to Persons of Quality, they give Security to appropriate a certain Sum for each Child, suitable to their Condition; and these Funds are always managed with good Husbandry, and the most exact Justice.

The Cottagers and Labourers keep their Children at home, their Business being only to till and cultivate the Earth; and therefore their Education is of little Consequence to the Publick; but the Old and Diseased among them are supported by Hospitals: For begging is a Trade unknown in this Empire.

And here it may perhaps divert the curious Reader, to give some Account of my Domestick,* and my Manner of living in this Country, during a Residence of nine Months and thirteen Days. Having a Head mechanically turned,* and being likewise forced by Necessity, I had made for myself a Table and Chair convenient enough, out of the largest Trees in the Royal Park. Two hundred Sempstresses were employed to make me Shirts, and Linnen for my Bed and Table, all of the strongest and coarsest kind they could get; which, however, they were forced to quilt together in several Folds; for the thickest was some Degrees finer than Lawn. Their Linnen is usually three Inches wide, and three Foot make a Piece. The Sempstresses took my Measure as I lay on the Ground, one standing at my Neck, and another at my Mid-Leg, with a strong Cord extended, that each held by the End, while the third measured the Length of the Cord with a Rule of an Inch long. Then they measured my right Thumb, and desired no more; for by a mathematical Computation, that twice round the Thumb is once round the Wrist, and so on to the Neck and the Waist; and by the Help of my old Shirt, which I displayed* on the Ground before them for a Pattern, they fitted me exactly. Three hundred Taylors were employed in the same Manner to make me Clothes; but they had another Contrivance for taking my Measure. I kneeled down, and they raised a Ladder from the Ground to my Neck; upon this Ladder one of them mounted, and let fall a Plum-Line from my Collar to the Floor, which just answered the Length of my Coat; but my Waist and Arms I measured myself. When my Cloaths were finished, which was done in my House, (for the largest of theirs would not have been able to hold them) they looked like the Patch-work made by the Ladies in *England*, only that mine were all of a Colour.

I had three hundred Cooks to dress my Victuals, in little convenient Huts built about my House, where they and their Families lived, and prepared me two Dishes a-piece. I took up twenty Waiters in my Hand, and placed them on the Table; an hundred more attended below on the Ground, some with Dishes of Meat, and some with Barrels of Wine, and other Liquors, slung on their Shoulders; all which the Waiters above drew up as I wanted, in a very ingenious Manner, by certain Cords, as we draw the Bucket up a Well in *Europe*. A Dish of their Meat was a good Mouthful, and a Barrel of their Liquor a reasonable Draught. Their Mutton yields to ours,* but their Beef is excellent. I have had a Sirloin so large, that I have been forced to make three Bits* of it; but this is rare. My Servants were astonished to see me eat it Bones and all, as in our Country we do the Leg of a Lark. Their Geese and Turkeys I usually eat at a Mouthful, and I must confess they far exceed ours. Of their smaller Fowl I could take up twenty or thirty at the End of my Knife.

One Day his Imperial Majesty being informed of my Way of living, desired that himself, and his Royal Consort; with the young Princes of the Blood of both Sexes, might have the Happiness (as he was pleased to call it) of dining with me. They came accordingly, and I placed them upon Chairs of State on my Table, just over against me, with their Guards about them. *Flimnap* the Lord High Treasurer attended there likewise, with his white Staff;* and I observed he often looked on me with a sour Countenance, which I would not seem to regard, but eat more than usual, in Honour to my dear Country, as well as to fill the Court with Admiration. I have some private Reasons to believe, that this Visit from his Majesty gave *Flimnap* an Opportunity of doing me ill Offices to his Master. That Minister had always been my secret Enemy, although he outwardly caressed* me more than was usual to the Moroseness of his Nature. He represented to the Emperor the low Condition of his Treasury; that he was forced to take up Money at great Discount;* that Exchequer Bills would not circulate under* nine *per Cent.* below Par; that I had cost his Majesty above a Million and a half of *Sprugs*, (their greatest Gold Coin, about the Bigness of a Spangle;) and upon the whole, that it would be adviseable in the Emperor to take the first fair Occasion of dismissing me.

I am here obliged to vindicate the Reputation of an excellent Lady,* who was an innocent Sufferer on my Account. The Treasurer took a Fancy to be jealous of his Wife, from the Malice of some evil Tongues, who informed him that her Grace had taken a violent Affection for my Person; and the Court-Scandal ran for some Time that she once came privately to my Lodging. This I solemnly declare to be a most infamous Falshood, without any Grounds, farther than that her Grace was pleased to treat me with all innocent Marks of Freedom and Friendship. I own she came often to my House, but always publickly, nor ever without three more in the Coach, who were usually her Sister, and young Daughter, and some particular Acquaintance; but this was common to many other Ladies of the Court. And I still appeal to my Servants round, whether they at any Time saw a Coach at my Door without knowing what Persons were in it. On those Occasions, when a Servant had given me Notice, my Custom was to go immediately to the Door; and after paying my Respects, to take up the Coach and two Horses very carefully in my Hands, (for if there were six Horses, the Postillion always unharnessed four) and place them on a Table, where I had fixed a moveable Rim quite round, of five Inches high, to prevent Accidents. And I have often had four Coaches and Horses at once on my Table full of Company, while I sat in my Chair leaning my Face towards them; and when I was engaged with one Sett, the Coachmen would gently drive the others round my Table. I have passed many an Afternoon very agreeably in these Conversations: But I defy the Treasurer, or his two Informers. (I will name them, and let them make the best of it) *Clustril* and *Drunlo*,* to prove that any Person ever came to me *incognito*,* except the Secretary *Reldresal*, who was sent by express Command of his Imperial Majesty, as I have before related. I should not have dwelt so long upon this Particular, if it had not been a Point wherein the Reputation of a great Lady is so nearly concerned, to say nothing of my own; although I had the Honour to be a *Nardac*, which the Treasurer himself is not; for all the World knows he is only a *Clumglum*, a Title inferior by one Degree,* as that of a Marquess is to a Duke in *England*; yet I allow he preceded me in right of his Post. These false Informations, which I afterwards came to the Knowledge of, by an Accident not proper to mention, made the Treasurer shew his Lady for some Time an ill Countenance, and me a worse: For although he were at last undeceived and reconciled to her, yet I lost all Credit with him; and found my Interest decline very fast with the Emperor himself, who was indeed too much governed by that Favourite.

CHAPTER SEVEN

The Author being informed of a Design to accuse him of High Treason, makes his Escape to Blefuscu. His Reception there.

BEFORE I proceed to give an Account of my leaving this Kingdom, it may be proper to inform the Reader of a private Intrigue which had been for two Months forming against me.

I had been hitherto all my Life a Stranger to Courts, for which I was unqualified by the Meanness of my Condition. I had indeed heard and read enough of the Dispositions of great Princes and Ministers; but never expected to have found such terrible Effects of them in so remote a Country,* governed, as I thought, by very different Maxims from those in *Europe*.

When I was just preparing to pay my Attendance on the Emperor of *Blefuscu*; a considerable Person* at Court (to whom I had been very serviceable at a time when he lay under the highest Displeasure of his Imperial Majesty) came to my House very privately at Night in a close Chair, and without sending his Name, desired Admittance: The Chair-men were dismissed; I put the Chair, with his Lordship in it, into my Coat-Pocket; and giving orders to a trusty Servant to say I was indisposed and gone to sleep, I fastened the Door of my House, placed the Chair on the Table, according to my usual Custom, and sat down by it. After the common Salutations were over, observing his Lordship's Countenance full of Concern; and enquiring* into the Reason, he desired I would hear him with Patience, in a Matter that highly concerned my Honour and my Life. His Speech was to the following Effect, for I took Notes of it as soon as he left me.

You are to know, said he, that several Committees of Council have been lately called in the most private Manner on your

Account: And it is but two Days since his Majesty came to a full Resolution.

You are very sensible that *Skyris Bolgolam* (*Galbet,* or High Admiral) hath been your mortal Enemy almost ever since your Arrival. His original Reasons I know not; but his Hatred is much encreased since your great Success against *Blefuscu,* by which his Glory, as Admiral, is obscured. This Lord, in Conjunction with *Flimnap* the High Treasurer, whose Enmity against you is notorious on Account of his Lady; *Limtoc* the General, *Lalcon* the Chamberlain, and *Balmuff** the grand Justiciary, have prepared Articles of Impeachment against you, for Treason, and other capital Crimes.

This Preface made me so impatient, being conscious of my own Merits and Innocence, that I was going to interrupt; when he intreated me to be silent; and thus proceeded.

Out of Gratitude of the Favours you have done me, I procured Information of the whole Proceedings, and a Copy of the Articles, wherein I venture my Head for your Service.

*Articles of Impeachment** *against* Quinbus Flestrin,
(*the* Man-Mountain.)

ARTICLE I.

Whereas, by a Statute made in the Reign of his Imperial Majesty *Calin Deffar Plune,* it is enacted, That whoever shall make water within the Precincts of the Royal Palace, shall be liable to the Pains and Penalties of High Treason: Notwithstanding, the said *Quinbus Flestrin,* in open Breach of the said Law, under Colour* of extinguishing the Fire kindled in the Apartment of his Majesty's most dear Imperial Consort, did maliciously, traitorously, and devilishly, by discharge of his Urine, put out the said Fire kindled in the said Apartment, lying and being within the Precincts of the said Royal Palace; against the Statute in the Case provided, &c. against the Duty, &c.

ARTICLE II.

That the said *Quinbus Flestrin* having brought the Imperial Fleet of *Blefuscu* into the Royal Port, and being afterwards commanded by his Imperial Majesty to seize all the other Ships of the said Empire of *Blefuscu*, and reduce that Empire to a Province, to be governed by a Vice-Roy from hence; and to destroy and put to death not only all the *Big-Endian Exiles*, but likewise all the People of that Empire, who would not immediately forsake the *Big-Endian* Heresy: He the said *Flestrin*, like a false Traitor against his most Auspicious, Serene, Imperial Majesty, did petition to be excused from the said Service, upon Pretence of Unwillingness to force the Consciences, or destroy the Liberties and Lives of an innocent People.

ARTICLE III.

That, whereas certain Embassadors arrived from the Court of *Blefuscu* to sue for Peace in his Majesty's Court: He the said *Flestrin* did, like a false Traitor, aid, abet, comfort, and divert the said Embassadors; although he knew them to be Servants to a Prince who was lately an open Enemy to his Imperial Majesty, and in open War against his said Majesty.

ARTICLE IV.

That the said *Quinbus Flestrin*, contrary to the Duty of a faithful Subject, is now preparing to make a Voyage to the Court and Empire of *Blefuscu*, for which he hath received only verbal Licence from his Imperial Majesty; and under Colour of the said Licence, doth falsely and traitorously intend to take the said Voyage, and thereby to aid, comfort, and abet the Emperor of *Blefuscu*, so late an Enemy, and in open War with his Imperial Majesty aforesaid.

There are some other Articles, but these are the most important, of which I have read you an Abstract.

In the several Debates upon this Impeachment, it must be confessed that his Majesty gave many Marks of his great *Lenity*; often urging the Services you had done him, and endeavouring to extenuate your Crimes. The Treasurer and Admiral insisted that you should be put to the most painful and ignominious Death, by setting Fire on your House at Night; and the General was to attend with Twenty Thousand Men armed with poisoned Arrows, to shoot you on the Face and Hands. Some of your Servants were to have private Orders to strew a poisonous Juice on your Shirts* and Sheets, which would soon make you tear your own Flesh, and die in the utmost Torture. The General came into the same Opinion; so that for a long time there was a Majority against you. But his Majesty, resolving, if possible, to spare your Life, at last brought off* the Chamberlain.

Upon this Incident, *Reldresal*, principal Secretary for private Affairs, who always approved himself your true Friend, was commanded by the Emperor to deliver his Opinion, which he accordingly did; and therein justified the good Thoughts you have of him. He allowed your Crimes to be great; but that still there was room for Mercy, the most commendable Virtue in a Prince, and for which his Majesty was so justly celebrated. He said, the Friendship between you and him was so well known to the World, that perhaps the most honourable Board might think him partial: However, in Obedience to the Command he had received, he would freely offer his Sentiments. That if his Majesty, in Consideration of your Services, and pursuant to his own merciful Disposition, would please to spare your Life, and only give order to put out both your Eyes;* he humbly conceived, that by this Expedient, Justice might in some measure be satisfied, and all the World would applaud the *Lenity* of the Emperor, as well as the fair and generous Proceedings of those who have the Honour to be his Counsellors. That the Loss of your Eyes would be no Impediment to your bodily Strength,* by which you might still be useful to his Majesty. That Blindness is an Addition to Courage, by concealing Dangers from us; that the Fear you had for your Eyes, was the greatest Difficulty in bringing over the Enemy's Fleet; and it would be sufficient for you to see by the Eyes of the Ministers, since the greatest Princes do no more.*

This Proposal was received with the utmost Disapprobation by the whole Board. *Bolgolam*, the Admiral, could not preserve his Temper; but rising up in Fury, said, he wondered how the Secretary durst presume to give his Opinion for preserving the Life of a Traytor: That the Services you had performed, were, by all true Reasons of State,* the great Aggravation of your Crimes; that you, who were able to extinguish the Fire, by discharge of Urine in her Majesty's Apartment (which he mentioned with Horror) might, at another time, raise an Inundation by the same Means, to drown the whole Palace; and the same Strength which enabled you to bring over the Enemy's Fleet, might serve, upon the first Discontent, to carry it back: That he had good Reasons to think you were a *Big-Endian* in your Heart; and as Treason begins in the Heart before it appears in Overt-Acts; so he accused you as a Traytor on that Account, and therefore insisted you should be put to death.

The Treasurer was of the same Opinion; he shewed to what Streights his Majesty's Revenue was reduced by the Charge of maintaining you, which would soon grow insupportable: That the Secretary's Expedient of putting out your Eyes, was so far from being a Remedy against this Evil, that it would probably increase it; as it is manifest from the common Practice of blinding some Kind of Fowl, after which they fed the faster, and grew sooner fat: That his sacred Majesty, and the Council, who are your Judges, were in their own Consciences fully convinced of your Guilt; which was a sufficient Argument to condemn you to death, without the *formal Proofs* required by the strict Letter of the Law.*

But his Imperial Majesty fully determined against capital Punishment, was graciously pleased to say, that since the Council thought the Loss of your Eyes too easy a Censure,* some other may be inflicted hereafter. And your Friend the Secretary humbly desiring to be heard again, in Answer to what the Treasurer had objected concerning the great Charge his Majesty was at in maintaining you; said, that his Excellency, who had the sole Disposal of the Emperor's Revenue, might easily provide against this Evil, by gradually lessening your Establishment; by which, for want of sufficient Food, you would grow weak and faint, and lose your Appetite, and consequently decay and consume in a few Months; neither would the Stench of your Carcass be then so dangerous, when it should become more than half diminished; and immediately upon your Death, five or six Thousand of his

Majesty's Subjects might, in two or three Days, cut your Flesh from your Bones, take it away by Cart-loads, and bury it in distant Parts to prevent Infection; leaving the Skeleton as a Monument of Admiration to Posterity.

Thus by the great Friendship of the Secretary, the whole Affair was compromised. It was strictly enjoined, that the Project of starving you by Degrees should be kept a Secret; but the Sentence of putting out your Eyes was entered on the Books; none dissenting except *Bolgolam* the Admiral, who being a Creature of the Empress, was perpetually instigated by her Majesty to insist upon your Death; she having born perpetual Malice against you, on Account of that infamous and illegal Method you took to extinguish the Fire in her Apartment.

In three Days your Friend the Secretary will be directed to come to your House, and read before you the Articles of Impeachment; and then to signify the great *Lenity* and Favour of his Majesty and Council; whereby you are only condemned to the Loss of your Eyes, which his Majesty doth not question you will gratefully and humbly submit to; and Twenty of his Majesty's Surgeons will attend, in order to see the Operation well performed, by discharging very sharp pointed Arrows into the Balls of your Eyes, as you lie on the Ground.

I leave to your Prudence what Measures you will take; and to avoid Suspicion, I must immediately return in as private a Manner as I came.

His Lordship did so, and I remained alone, under many Doubts and Perplexities of Mind.

It was a Custom introduced by this Prince and his Ministry, (very different, as I have been assured, from the Practices of former Times) that after the Court had decreed any cruel Execution, either to gratify the Monarch's Resentment, or the Malice of a Favourite; the Emperor always made a Speech to his whole Council, expressing his *great Lenity and Tenderness, as Qualities known and confessed by all the World.* This Speech was immediately published through the Kingdom; nor did any thing terrify the People so much as those Encomiums on his Majesty's Mercy;* because it was observed, that the more these Praises were enlarged and insisted on, the more *inhuman* was the Punishment, and the *Sufferer more innocent.* Yet, as to myself, I must confess, having never been designed for a Courtier, either by my Birth or Education, I was so ill a Judge of Things, that I could not discover the *Lenity* and Favour of this Sentence; but conceived it (perhaps erroneously) rather to be rigorous than gentle. I sometimes thought of standing my Tryal; for although I could not deny the Facts alledged in the several Articles, yet I hoped they would admit of some Extenuations. But having in my Life perused many State-Tryals, which I ever observed to terminate as the Judges thought fit to direct; I durst not rely on so dangerous a Decision, in so critical a Juncture, and against such powerful Enemies.* Once I was strongly bent upon Resistance: For while I had Liberty, the whole Strength of that Empire could hardly subdue me, and I might easily with Stones pelt the Metropolis to Pieces: But I soon rejected that Project with Horror, by remembering the Oath I had made to the Emperor, the Favours I received from him, and the high Title of *Nardac* he conferred upon me. Neither had I so soon learned the Gratitude of Courtiers, to persuade myself that his Majesty's *present Severities acquitted me of all past Obligations.*

At last I fixed upon a Resolution, for which it is probable I may incur some Censure, and not unjustly; for I confess I owe the preserving mine Eyes, and consequently my Liberty, to my own great Rashness and Want of Experience: Because if I had then known the Nature of Princes and Ministers, which I have since observed in many other Courts, and their Methods of treating Criminals less obnoxious than myself; I should with great Alacrity and Readiness have submitted to so *easy* a Punishment. But hurried on by the Precipitancy of Youth;* and having his Imperial Majesty's Licence to pay my Attendance upon* the Emperor of *Blefuscu;* I took this Opportunity, before the three Days were elapsed, to send a Letter to my Friend the Secretary, signifying my Resolution of setting out that Morning for *Blefuscu,* pursuant to the Leave I had got; and without waiting for an Answer, I went to that Side of the Island where our Fleet lay. I seized a large Man of War, tied a Cable to the Prow, and lifting up the Anchors, I stript myself, put my Cloaths (together with my Coverlet, which I carried under my Arm) into the Vessel; and drawing it after me, between wading and swimming, arrived at the Royal Port of *Blefuscu*, where the People had long expected me: They lent me two Guides to direct me to the Capital City, which is of the same Name; I held them in my Hands until I came within two Hundred Yards of the Gate; and desired them to signify my Arrival to one of the Secretaries, and let him know, I there waited his Majesty's Commands. I had an Answer in about an Hour, that his Majesty, attended by the Royal Family, and great Officers of the Court, was coming out to receive me. I advanced a Hundred Yards; the Emperor, and his Train, alighted from their Horses, the Empress and Ladies from their Coaches; and I did not perceive they were in any Fright or Concern. I lay on the Ground to kiss his Majesty's and the Empress's Hand. I told his Majesty, that I was come according to my Promise, and with the Licence of the Emperor my Master, to have the Honour of seeing so mighty a Monarch, and to offer him any Service in my Power, consistent with my Duty to my own Prince; not mentioning a Word of my Disgrace, because I had hitherto no regular Information of it, and might suppose myself* wholly ignorant of any such Design; neither could I reasonably conceive that the Emperor would discover* the Secret while I was out of his Power: Wherein, however, it soon appeared I was deceived.

I shall not trouble the Reader with the particular Account of my Reception at this Court, which was suitable to the Generosity of so great a Prince; nor of the Difficulties I was in for want of a House and Bed, being forced to lie on the Ground, wrapt up in my Coverlet.

CHAPTER EIGHT

*The Author, by a lucky Accident, finds Means to leave Blefuscu;
and, after some Difficulties, returns safe to his Native Country.*

THREE DAYS after my Arrival, walking out of Curiosity to
the North-East Coast of the Island; I observed, about half a
League off, in the Sea, somewhat that looked like a Boat
overturned: I pulled off my Shoes and Stockings, and wading
two or three Hundred Yards, I found the Object to approach
nearer by Force of the Tide; and then plainly saw it to be a
real Boat, which I supposed might, by some Tempest, have
been driven from a Ship. Whereupon I returned immediately
towards the City, and desired his Imperial Majesty to lend me
Twenty of the tallest Vessels he had left after the Loss of his
Fleet, and three Thousand Seamen under the Command of
his Vice-Admiral. This Fleet sailed round, while I went back
the shortest Way to the Coast where I first discovered the
Boat; I found the Tide had driven it still nearer; the Seamen
were all provided with Cordage, which I had beforehand
twisted to a sufficient Strength. When the Ships came up, I
stript myself, and waded till I came within an Hundred Yards
of the Boat; after which I was forced to swim till I got up to it.
The Seamen threw me the End of the Cord, which I fastened
to a Hole in the forepart of the Boat, and the other End to a
Man of War: But I found all my Labour to little Purpose; for
being out of my Depth, I was not able to work. In this Necessity, I was forced to swim behind, and push the Boat forwards
as often as I could, with one of my Hands; and the Tide
favouring me, I advanced so far, that I could just hold up my
Chin and feel the Ground. I rested two or three Minutes, and
then gave the Boat another Shove, and so on till the Sea was
no higher than my Arm-pits. And now the most laborious Part
being over, I took out my other Cables which were stowed in
one of the Ships, and fastening them first to the Boat, and
then to nine of the Vessels which attended me; the Wind

being favourable, the Seamen towed, and I shoved till we arrived within forty Yards of the Shore; and waiting till the Tide was out, I got dry to the Boat, and by the Assistance of two Thousand Men, with Ropes and Engines, I made a shift to turn it on its Bottom, and found it was but little damaged.

I shall not trouble the Reader with the Difficulties I was under by the Help of certain Paddles, which cost me ten Days making, to get my Boat to the Royal Port of *Blefuscu;* where a mighty Concourse of People appeared upon my Arrival, full of Wonder at the Sight of so prodigious a Vessel. I told the Emperor, that my good Fortune had thrown this Boat in my Way, to carry me to some Place from whence I might return into my native Country; and begged his Majesty's Orders for getting Materials to fit it up; together with his Licence to depart; which, after some kind Expostulations, he was pleased to grant.

I did very much wonder, in all this Time, not to have heard of any Express relating to me from our Emperor to the Court of *Blefuscu.* But I was afterwards given privately to understand, that his Imperial Majesty, never imagining I had the least Notice of his Designs, believed I was only gone to *Blefuscu* in Performance of my Promise, according to the Licence he had given me, which was well known at our Court; and would return in a few Days when that Ceremony was ended. But he was at last in pain at my long absence; and, after consulting with the Treasurer, and the rest of that Cabal; a Person of Quality* was dispatched with the Copy of the Articles against me. This Envoy had Instructions to represent to the Monarch of *Blefuscu,* the great *Lenity* of his Master, who was content to punish me no further than with the Loss of mine Eyes: That I had fled from Justice, and if I did not return in two Hours, I should be deprived of my Title of *Nardac,* and declared a Traitor. The Envoy further added; that in order to maintain the Peace and Amity between both Empires, his Master expected, that his Brother of *Blefuscu* would give Orders to have me sent back to *Lilliput,* bound Hand and Foot, to be punished as a Traitor.

The Emperor of *Blefuscu* having taken three Days to consult, returned an Answer consisting of many Civilities and

Excuses. He said, that as for sending me bound, his Brother knew it was impossible; that although I had deprived him of his Fleet, yet he owed great Obligations to me for many good Offices I had done him in making the Peace. That however, both their Majesties would soon be made easy; for I had found a prodigious Vessel on the Shore, able to carry me on the Sea, which he had given order to fit up with my own Assistance and Direction; and he hoped in a few Weeks both Empires would be freed from so insupportable an Incumbrance.

With this Answer the Envoy returned to *Lilliput*, and the Monarch of *Blefuscu* related to me all that had past; offering me at the same time (but under the strictest Confidence) his gracious Protection, if I would continue in his Service; wherein although I believed him sincere, yet I resolved never more to put any Confidence in Princes or Ministers, where I could possibly avoid it; and therefore, with all due Acknowledgements for his favourable Intentions, I humbly begged to be excused. I told him, that since Fortune, whether good or evil, had thrown a Vessel in my Way; I was resolved to venture myself in the Ocean, rather than be an Occasion of Difference between two such mighty Monarchs. Neither did I find the Emperor at all displeased; and I discovered by a certain Accident, that he was very glad* of my Resolution, and so were most of his Ministers.

These Considerations moved me to hasten my Departure somewhat sooner than I intended; to which the Court, impatient to have me gone, very readily contributed. Five hundred Workmen were employed to make two Sails to my Boat, according to my Directions, by quilting thirteen fold of their strongest Linnen together. I was at the Pains* of making Ropes and Cables, by twisting ten, twenty or thirty of the thickest and strongest of theirs. A great Stone that I happened to find, after a long Search by the Sea-shore, served me for an Anchor. I had the Tallow of three hundred Cows for greasing my Boat, and other Uses. I was at incredible Pains in cutting down some of the largest Timber Trees for Oars and Masts, wherein I was, however, much assisted by his Majesty's Ship-Carpenters, who helped me in smoothing them, after I had done the rough Work.

In about a Month, when all was prepared. I sent to receive his Majesty's Commands, and to take my leave. The Emperor and Royal Family came out of the Palace: I lay down on my Face to kiss his Hand, which he very graciously gave me; so did the Empress, and young Princes of the Blood. His Majesty presented me with fifty Purses of two hundred *Sprugs* a-piece, together with his Picture at full length, which I put immediately into one of my Gloves, to keep it from being hurt. The Ceremonies at my Departure were too many to trouble the Reader with at this time.

I stored the Boat with the Carcasses of an hundred Oxen, and three hundred Sheep, with Bread and Drink proportionable, and as much Meat ready dressed as four hundred Cooks could provide. I took with me six Cows and two Bulls alive, with as many Yews and Rams, intending to carry them into my own Country, and propagate the Breed.* And to feed them on board, I had a good Bundle of Hay, and a Bag of Corn. I would gladly have taken a Dozen of the Natives; but this was a thing the Emperor would by no Means permit; and besides a diligent Search into my Pockets, his Majesty engaged my Honour not to carry away any of his Subjects, although with their own Consent and Desire.

Having thus prepared all things as well as I was able; I set sail on the Twenty-fourth Day of *September* 1701, at six in the Morning; and when I had gone about four Leagues to the Northward, the Wind being at South-East; at six in the Evening, I descryed a small Island about half a League to the North West. I advanced forward, and cast Anchor on the Leeside of the Island, which seemed to be uninhabited. I then took some Refreshment, and went to my Rest. I slept well, and as I conjecture at least six Hours; for I found the Day broke in two Hours after I awaked. It was a clear Night; I eat my Breakfast before the Sun was up; and heaving Anchor, the Wind being favourable, I steered the same Course that I had done the Day before, wherein I was directed by my Pocket-Compass. My Intention was to reach, if possible, one of those Islands, which I had reason to believe lay to the North-East of *Van Diemen's* Land. I discovered nothing all that Day; but upon the next, about three in the Afternoon, when I had by my Computation made Twenty-four Leagues from *Blefuscu*, I descryed a Sail steering to the South-East; my Course was due East. I hailed her, but could get no Answer; yet I found I gained upon her, for the Wind slackened. I made all the Sail I could, and in half an Hour she spyed me, then hung out her Antient,* and discharged a Gun. It is not easy to express the Joy I was in upon the unexpected Hope of once more seeing my beloved Country, and the dear Pledges I had left in it. The Ship slackned her Sails, and I came up with her between five and six in the Evening, *September* 26; but my Heart leapt within me to see her *English* Colours. I put my Cows and Sheep into my Coat-Pockets, and got on board with all my little Cargo of Provisions. The Vessel was an *English* Merchantman, returning from *Japan* by the *North* and *South Seas;** the Captain, Mr *John Biddel* of *Deptford,* a very civil Man, and an excellent Sailor. We were now in the Latitude of 30 Degrees South; there were about fifty Men in the Ship; and here I met an old Comrade of mine, one *Peter Williams,* who gave me a good Character to the Captain. This Gentleman treated me with Kindness, and desired I would let him know what Place I came from last, and whither I was bound; which I did in few Words; but he thought I was raving, and that the Dangers I underwent had disturbed my Head; whereupon I took my black Cattle and Sheep out of my Pocket, which, after great Astonishment, clearly convinced him of my Veracity.* I then shewed him the Gold given me by the Emperor of *Blefuscu,* together with his Majesty's Picture at full Length, and some other Rarities of that Country. I gave him two Purses of two Hundred *Sprugs* each, and promised, when we arrived in *England,* to make him a Present of a Cow and a Sheep big with Young.

I shall not trouble the Reader with a particular Account of this Voyage, which was very prosperous for the most Part. We arrived in the *Downs** on the 13th of *April* 1702. I had only one Misfortune, that the Rats on board carried away one of my Sheep; I found her Bones in a Hole, picked clean from the Flesh. The rest of my Cattle I got safe on Shore, and set them a grazing in a Bowling-Green at *Greenwich,* where the Fineness of the Grass made them feed very heartily, although I had always feared the contrary: Neither could I possibly have preserved them in so long a Voyage, if the Captain had not allowed me some of his best Bisket, which rubbed to Powder, and mingled with Water, was their constant Food. The short Time I continued in *England*, I made a considerable Profit* by shewing my Cattle to many Persons of Quality, and others: And before I began my second Voyage, I sold them for six Hundred Pounds. Since my last Return, I find the Breed is considerably increased, especially the Sheep; which I hope will prove much to the Advantage of the Woollen Manufacture, by the Fineness of the Fleeces.*

I stayed but two Months with my Wife and Family; for my insatiable Desire of seeing foreign Countries* would suffer me to continue no longer. I left fifteen Hundred Pounds with my Wife, and fixed her in a good House at *Redriff*. My remaining Stock I carried with me, Part in Money, and Part in Goods, in Hopes to improve my Fortunes. My eldest Uncle, *John*, had left me an Estate in Land, near *Epping*, of about Thirty Pounds a Year; and I had a long Lease of the *Black-Bull** in *Fetter-Lane*, which yielded me as much more: So that I was not in any Danger of leaving my Family upon the Parish. My Son *Johnny*, named so after his Uncle, was at the Grammar School, and a towardly* Child. My Daughter *Betty* (who is now well married, and has Children) was then at her Needle-Work. I took Leave of my Wife, and Boy and Girl, with Tears on both Sides; and went on board the *Adventure*,* a Merchant-Ship of three Hundred Tons, bound for *Surat*, Captain *John Nicholas* of *Liverpool*, Commander. But my Account of this Voyage must be referred to the second part of my Travels.

The End of the First Part.

PART TWO

*A Voyage to Brobdingnag**

BROADINGNAG

Flanflasnic

Lorbrulgrud

Discovered A.D 1703

Plate 2ⁿᵈ Part 2ᵈ Page. 93ᵈ

NORTH AMERICA

Streights of Annian

C. Blanco

St Sebastian

NEW ALBION

C. Mendocino

Mount St Martin

Pᵗ.Sᵗ. Francis Drake

P. Monterey.

CHAPTER ONE

A great Storm described. The long Boat sent to fetch Water, the Author goes with it to discover the Country. He is left on Shoar, is seized by one of the Natives, and carried* to a Farmer's House. His Reception there, with several Accidents that happened there. A Description of the Inhabitants.

HAVING BEEN condemned by Nature and Fortune to an active and restless Life; in two Months after my Return, I again left my native Country, and took Shipping in the *Downs* on the 20th Day of *June* 1702, in the *Adventure*, Capt. *John Nicholas*, a *Cornish* Man, Commander, bound for *Surat*. We had a very prosperous Gale* till we arrived at the *Cape* of *Good-hope*, where we landed for fresh Water; but discovering a Leak we unshipped our Goods, and wintered there; for the Captain falling sick of an Ague, we could not leave the *Cape* till the End of *March*. We then set sail, and had a good Voyage till we passed the *Streights* of *Madagascar*; but having got Northward of that Island, and to about five Degrees South Latitude, the Winds, which in those Seas are observed to blow a constant equal Gale between the North and West, from the Beginning of *December* to the Beginning of *May*, on the 19th of *April* began to blow with much greater Violence, and more Westerly than usual; continuing so for twenty Days together, during which time we were driven a little to the East of the *Molucca* Islands, and about three Degrees Northward of the Line, as our Captain found by an Observation he took the 2d of *May*, at which time the Wind ceased, and it was a perfect Calm, whereat I was not a little rejoyced. But he being a Man well experienced in the Navigation of those Seas, bid us all prepare against a Storm, which accordingly happened the Day following: For a Southern Wind, called the Southern *Monsoon*, began to set in.

Finding it was like to overblow,* we took in our Sprit-sail,* and stood by to hand* the Fore-sail; but making* foul

Weather, we looked the Guns were all fast,* and handed the Missen.* The Ship lay very broad off,* so we thought it better spooning* before the Sea, than trying* or hulling.* We reeft the Foresail and set him, we hawled aft the Fore-sheet;* the Helm was hard a Weather.* The Ship wore* bravely. We belay'd the Foredown-hall;* but the Sail was split, and we hawl'd down the Yard, and got the Sail into the Ship, and unbound all the things clear of it. It was a very fierce Storm; the Sea broke strange and dangerous. We hawl'd off upon the Lanniard of the Wipstaff,* and helped the Man at Helm. We would not get down our Top-Mast, but let all stand, because she scudded before the Sea very well, and we knew that the Top-Mast being aloft, the Ship was the wholesomer,* and made better way through the Sea, seeing we had Sea room. When the Storm was over, we set Fore-sail and Main-sail, and brought the Ship to.* Then we set the Missen, Maintop-Sail and the Foretop-Sail. Our Course was East-North-east, the Wind was at South-west. We got the Star-board Tacks aboard,* we cast off our Weather-braces and Lifts;* we set in the Lee-braces,* and hawl'd forward by the Weather-bowlings,* and hawl'd them tight, and belayed them, and hawl'd over the Missen Tack to Windward, and kept her full and by as near as she would lye.*

During this Storm, which was followed by a strong Wind West South-west, we were carried by my Computation about five hundred Leagues to the East, so that the oldest Sailor on Board could not tell in what part of the World we were. Our Provisions held out well, our Ship was staunch, and our Crew all in good Health; but we lay in the utmost Distress for Water. We thought it best to hold on the same Course rather than turn more Northerly, which might have brought us to the North-west Parts of the great *Tartary*,* and into the frozen Sea.

On the 16*th* Day of *June* 1703, a Boy on the Top-mast discovered Land. On the 17*th* we came in full View of a great Island or Continent, (for we knew not whether*) on the South-side whereof was a small Neck of Land jutting out into the Sea, and a Creek too shallow to hold a Ship of above one hundred Tuns. We cast Anchor within a League of this Creek, and our Captain sent a dozen of his Men well armed in the Long Boat, with Vessels for Water if any could be found. I desired his leave to go with them, that I might see the Country, and make what Discoveries I could. When we came to Land we saw no River or Spring, nor any Sign of Inhabitants. Our Men therefore wandered on the Shore to find out some fresh Water near the Sea, and I walked alone about a Mile on the other side, where I observed the Country all barren and rocky. I now began to be weary, and seeing nothing to entertain my Curiosity, I returned gently down towards the Creek; and the Sea being full in my View, I saw our Men already got into the Boat, and rowing for Life to the Ship. I was going to hollow* after them, although it had been to little purpose, when I observed a huge Creature walking after them in the Sea,* as fast as he could: He waded not much deeper than his Knees,* and took prodigious strides: But our Men had the start of him half a League, and the Sea thereabouts being full of sharp pointed Rocks, the Monster was not able to overtake the Boat. This I was afterwards told, for I durst not stay to see the Issue of that Adventure; but ran as fast as I could the Way I first went; and then climbed up a steep Hill, which gave me some Prospect of the Country. I found it fully cultivated; but that which first surprized me was the Length of the Grass, which in those Grounds that seemed to be kept for Hay, was above twenty Foot high.

I fell into a high Road, for so I took it to be, although it served to the Inhabitants only as a foot Path through a Field of Barley. Here I walked on for sometime, but could see little on either Side, it being now near Harvest, and the Corn rising at least forty Foot. I was an Hour walking to the end of this Field; which was fenced in with a Hedge of at least one hundred and twenty Foot high, and the Trees so lofty that I could make no Computation of their Altitude. There was a Stile to pass from this Field into the next: It had four Steps, and a Stone to cross over when you came to the uppermost. It was impossible for me to climb this Stile, because every Step was six Foot high, and the upper Stone above twenty. I was endeavouring to find some Gap in the Hedge; when I discovered one of the Inhabitants in the next Field advancing

towards the Stile, of the same Size with him whom I saw in the
Sea pursuing our Boat. He appeared as Tall as an ordinary
Spire-steeple; and took about ten Yards at every Stride,* as
near as I could guess. I was struck with the utmost Fear and
Astonishment, and ran to hide my self in the Corn, from
whence I saw him at the Top of the Stile, looking back into
the next Field on the right Hand; and heard him call in a
Voice many Degrees louder than a speaking Trumpet; but the
Noise was so High in the Air, that at first I certainly thought it
was Thunder. Whereupon seven Monsters like himself came
towards him with Reaping-Hooks in their Hands, each Hook
about the largeness of six Scythes. These People were not
so well clad as the first, whose Servants or Labourers they
seemed to be. For, upon some Words he spoke, they went to
reap the Corn in the Field where I lay. I kept from them at as
great a Distance as I could, but was forced to move with
extream Difficulty; for the Stalks of the Corn were sometimes
not above a Foot distant, so that I could hardly squeeze my
Body betwixt them. However, I made a shift to go forward till
I came to a part of the Field where the Corn had been laid by
the Rain and Wind: Here it was impossible for me to advance
a step; for the Stalks were so interwoven that I could not creep
through, and the Beards of the fallen Ears so strong and
pointed, that they pierced through my Cloaths into my Flesh.
At the same time I heard the Reapers not above an hundred
Yards behind me. Being quite dispirited with Toil, and wholly
overcome by Grief and Despair, I lay down between two
Ridges, and heartily wished I might there end my Days. I
bemoaned my desolate Widow, and Fatherless Children: I
lamented my own Folly and Wilfulness in attempting a second
Voyage against the Advice of all my Friends and Relations. In
this terrible Agitation of Mind I could not forbear thinking of
Lilliput, whose Inhabitants looked upon me as the greatest
Prodigy that ever appeared in the World; where I was able to
draw an Imperial Fleet in my Hand, and perform those other
Actions which will be recorded for ever in the Chronicles of
that Empire, while Posterity shall hardly believe them,
although attested by Millions. I reflected what a Mortification
it must prove to me to appear as inconsiderable in this

Nation, as one single *Lilliputian* would be among us. But, this I conceived was to be the least of my Misfortunes: For, as human Creatures are observed to be more Savage and cruel in Proportion to their Bulk;* what could I expect but to be a Morsel in the Mouth of the first among these enormous Barbarians who should happen to seize me? Undoubtedly Philosophers* are in the Right when they tell us, that nothing is great or little otherwise than by Comparison: It might have pleased Fortune to let the *Lilliputians* find some Nation, where the People were as diminutive with respect to them, as they were to me. And who knows but that even this prodigious Race of Mortals might be equally overmatched in some distant Part of the World, whereof we have yet no Discovery?

Scared and confounded as I was, I could not forbear going on with these Reflections; when one of the Reapers approaching within ten Yards of the Ridge where I lay, made me apprehend that with the next Step I should be squashed to Death under his Foot, or cut in two with his Reaping Hook. And therefore when he was again about to move, I screamed as loud as Fear could make me. Whereupon the huge Creature trod short, and looking round about under him for some time, at last espied me as I lay on the Ground. He considered a while with the Caution of one who endeavours to lay hold on a small dangerous Animal in such a Manner that it shall not be able either to scratch or to bite him; as I my self have sometimes done with a *Weasel* in *England*. At length he ventured to take me up behind by the middle between his Forefinger and Thumb, and brought me within three Yards of his Eyes, that he might behold my Shape more perfectly. I guessed his Meaning; and my good Fortune gave me so much Presence of Mind, that I resolved not to struggle in the least as he held me in the Air above sixty Foot from the Ground; although he grievously pinched my Sides, for fear I should slip through his Fingers. All I ventured was to raise mine Eyes towards the Sun, and place my Hands together in a supplicating Posture, and to speak some Words in an humble melancholy Tone, suitable to the Condition I then was in. For, I apprehended every Moment that he would dash me against the Ground, as we usually do any little hateful Animal which we have a Mind to destroy. But my good Star would have it, that he appeared pleased with my Voice and Gestures, and began to look upon me as a Curiosity; much wondering to hear me pronounce articulate Words, although he could not understand them. In the mean time I was not able to forbear Groaning and shedding Tears, and turning my Head towards my Sides; letting him know, as well as I could, how cruelly I was hurt by the Pressure of his Thumb and Finger. He seemed to apprehend my Meaning; for, lifting up the Lappet* of his Coat, he put me gently into it, and immediately ran along with me to his Master, who was a substantial Farmer, and the same Person I had first seen in the Field.

The Farmer having (as I supposed by their Talk) received such an Account of me as his Servant could give him, took a piece of a small Straw, about the Size of a walking Staff, and therewith lifted up the Lappets of my Coat; which it seems he thought to be some kind of Covering that Nature had given me. He blew my Hairs aside to take a better View of my Face. He called his Hinds about him, and asked them (as I afterwards learned) whether they had ever seen in the Fields any little Creature that resembled me. He then placed me softly on the Ground upon all four; but I got immediately up, and walked slowly backwards and forwards, to let those People see I had no Intent to run away. They all sate down in a Circle about me, the better to observe my Motions. I pulled off my Hat, and made a low Bow towards the Farmer: I fell on my Knees, and lifted up my Hands and Eyes, and spoke several Words as loud as I could: I took a Purse of Gold out of my Pocket, and humbly presented it to him. He received it on the Palm of his Hand, then applied it close to his Eye, to see what it was, and afterwards turned it several times with the Point of a Pin, (which he took out of his Sleeve,) but could make nothing of it. Whereupon I made a Sign that he should place his Hand on the Ground: I then took the Purse, and opening it, poured all the Gold into his Palm. There were six *Spanish*-Pieces of four Pistoles* each, besides twenty or thirty smaller Coins. I saw him wet the Tip of his little Finger upon his Tongue, and take up one of my largest Pieces, and then another; but he seemed to be wholly ignorant what they were.

He made a Sign to put them again into my Purse, and the Purse again into my Pocket; which after offering to him several times, I thought it best to do.

The Farmer by this time was convinced I must be a rational Creature. He spoke often to me, but the Sound of his Voice pierced my Ears like that of a Water-Mill; yet his Words were articulate enough.* I answered as loud as I could in several Languages; and he often laid his Ear within two Yards of me, but all in vain, for we were wholly unintelligible to each other. He then sent his Servants to their Work, and taking his Handkerchief out of his Pocket, he doubled and spread it on his Hand, which he placed flat on the Ground with the Palm upwards, making me a Sign to step into it, as I could easily do, for it was not above a Foot in thickness. I thought it my part to obey; and for fear of falling, laid my self at full Length upon the Handkerchief, with the Remainder of which he lapped me up to the Head for further Security; and in this Manner carried me home to his House. There he called his Wife, and shewed me to her; but she screamed and ran back as Women in *England* do at the Sight of a Toad or a Spider. However, when she had a while seen my Behaviour, and how well I observed the Signs her Husband made, she was soon reconciled, and by Degrees grew extreamly tender of me.

It was about twelve at Noon, and the Servant brought in Dinner. It was only one substantial Dish of Meat (fit for the plain Condition of an Husband-Man) in a Dish of about four and twenty Foot Diameter. The Company were the Farmer and his Wife, three Children, and an old Grandmother: When they were sat down, the Farmer placed me at some Distance from him on the Table, which was thirty Foot high from the Floor. I was in a terrible Fright, and kept as far as I could from the Edge, for fear of falling. The Wife minced a bit of Meat, then crumbled some Bread on a Trencher, and placed it before me. I made her a low Bow, took out my Knife and Fork, and fell to eat; which gave them exceeding Delight. The Mistress sent her Maid for a small Dram-cup, which held about two Gallons,* and filled it with Drink: I took up the Vessel with much difficulty in both Hands, and in a most respectful Manner drank to her Ladyship's Health, expressing the Words as loud as I could in *English*; which made the Company laugh so heartily, that I was almost deafened with the Noise. This Liquor tasted like a small Cyder, and was not unpleasant. Then the Master made me a Sign to come to his Trencher side; but as I walked on the Table, being in great surprize* all the time, as the indulgent Reader will easily conceive and excuse, I happened to stumble against a Crust, and fell flat on my Face, but received no hurt. I got up immediately, and observing the good People to be in much Concern, I took my Hat (which I held under my Arm out of good Manners) and waving it over my Head, made three Huzza's, to shew I had got no Mischief by the Fall. But advancing forwards toward my Master (as I shall henceforth call him) his youngest Son who sate next to him, an arch* Boy of about ten Years old, took me up by the Legs, and held me so high in the Air, that I trembled every Limb; but his Father snatched me from him; and at the same time gave him such a Box on the left Ear, as would have felled an *European* Troop of Horse to the Earth; ordering him to be taken from the Table. But, being afraid the Boy might owe me a Spight; and well remembering how mischievous all Children among us naturally are to Sparrows, Rabbits, young Kittens, and Puppy-Dogs; I fell on my Knees, and pointing to the Boy, made my Master understand, as well as I could, that I desired his Son might be pardoned. The Father complied, and the Lad took his Seat again; whereupon I went to him and kissed his Hand, which my Master took, and made him stroak me gently with it.

In the Midst of Dinner my Mistress's favourite Cat leapt into her Lap. I heard a Noise behind me like that of a Dozen Stocking-Weavers* at work; and turning my Head, I found it proceeded from the Purring of this Animal, who seemed to be three Times larger than an Ox, as I computed by the View of her Head, and one of her Paws, while her Mistress was feeding and stroaking her. The Fierceness of this Creature's Countenance altogether discomposed me; although I stood at the further End of the Table, above fifty Foot off; and although my Mistress held her fast for fear she might give a Spring, and seize me in her Talons. But it happened there was no Danger; for the Cat took not the least Notice of me when my Master placed me within three Yards of her. And as I have been always told, and found true by Experience in my Travels, that flying, or discovering Fear before a fierce Animal, is a certain Way to make it pursue or attack you; so I resolved in this dangerous Juncture to shew no Manner of Concern. I walked with Intrepidity five or six Times before the very Head of the Cat, and came within half a Yard of her; whereupon she drew her self back, as if she were more afraid of me: I had less Apprehension concerning the Dogs, whereof three or four came into the Room, as it is usual in Farmers Houses; one of which was a Mastiff equal in Bulk to four Elephants,* and a Grey-hound somewhat taller than the Mastiff, but not so large.

When Dinner was almost done, the Nurse came in with a Child of a Year old in her Arms; who immediately spyed me, and began a Squall that you might have heard from *London-Bridge* to *Chelsea*; after the usual Oratory of Infants, to get me for a Play-thing. The Mother out of pure Indulgence took me up, and put me towards the Child, who presently seized me by the Middle, and got my Head in his Mouth, where I roared so loud that the Urchin was frighted, and let me drop; and I should infallibly have broke my Neck, if the Mother had not held her Apron under me. The Nurse to quiet her Babe made use of a Rattle, which was a Kind of hollow Vessel filled with great Stones, and fastned by a Cable to the Child's Waist: But all in vain so that she was forced to apply the last Remedy by giving it suck. I must confess no Object ever disgusted me so much as the Sight of her monstrous Breast, which I cannot tell what to compare with, so as to give the curious Reader an Idea of its Bulk, Shape and Colour. It stood prominent six Foot, and could not be less than sixteen in Circumference. The Nipple was about half the Bigness of my Head, and the Hue both of that and the Dug so varified with Spots, Pimples and Freckles, that nothing could appear more nauseous: For I had a near Sight of her, she sitting down the more conveniently to give Suck, and I standing on the Table. This made me reflect upon the fair Skins of our *English* Ladies, who appear so beautiful to us, only because they are of our own Size, and their Defects not to be seen but through a magnifying Glass,* where we find by Experiment that the smoothest and whitest Skins look rough and coarse, and ill coloured.

I remember when I was at *Lilliput*, the Complexions of those diminutive People appeared to me the fairest in the World: And talking upon this Subject with a Person of Learning there, who was an intimate Friend of mine; he said, that my Face appeared much fairer and smoother when he looked on me from the Ground, than it did upon a nearer View when I took him up in my Hand, and brought him close; which he confessed was at first a very shocking Sight. He said, he could discover great Holes in my Skin; that the Stumps of my Beard were ten Times stronger than the Bristles of a Boar; and my Complexion made up of several Colours altogether disagreeable: Although I must beg Leave to say for my self, that I am as fair as most of my Sex and Country, and very little Sunburnt by all my Travels. On the other Side, discoursing of the Ladies in that Emperor's Court, he used to tell me, one had Freckles, another too wide a Mouth, a third too large a Nose; nothing of which I was able to distinguish. I confess this Reflection was obvious enough; which, however, I could not forbear, lest the Reader might think those vast Creatures were actually deformed: For I must do them Justice to say they are a comely Race of People; and particularly the Features of my Master's Countenance, although he were but a Farmer, when I beheld him from the Height of sixty Foot, appeared very well proportioned.

When Dinner was done, my Master went out to his Labourers; and as I could discover by his Voice and Gesture, gave his Wife a strict Charge to take Care of me. I was very much tired and disposed to sleep, which my Mistress perceiving, she put me on her own Bed, and covered me with a clean white Handkerchief, but larger and coarser than the Main Sail of a Man of War.

I slept about two Hours, and dreamed I was at home with my Wife and Children, which aggravated my Sorrows when I awaked and found my self alone in a vast Room, between two and three Hundred Foot wide, and above two Hundred high; lying in a Bed twenty Yards wide. My Mistress was gone about her household Affairs, and had locked me in. The Bed was eight Yards from the Floor. Some natural Necessities required me to get down: I durst not presume to call, and if I had, it would have been in vain with such a Voice as mine at so great a Distance from the Room where I lay, to the Kitchen where the Family kept. While I was under these Circumstances, two Rats crept up the Curtains, and ran Smelling backwards and forwards on the Bed: One of them came up almost to my Face; whereupon I rose in a Fright, and drew out my Hanger* to defend my self. These horrible Animals had the Boldness to attack me on both Sides, and one of them held his Forefeet at my Collar; but I had the good fortune to rip up his Belly before he could do me any Mischief. He fell down at my Feet; and the other seeing the Fate of his Comrade, made his Escape, but not without one good Wound on the Back, which I gave him as he fled, and made the Blood run trickling from him. After this Exploit I walked gently to and fro on the Bed, to recover my Breath and Loss of Spirits. These Creatures were of the Size of a large Mastiff, but infinitely more nimble and fierce; so that if I had taken off my Belt before I went to sleep, I must have infallibly been torn to Pieces and devoured. I measured the Tail of the dead Rat, and found it to be two Yards long, wanting an Inch; but it went against my Stomach to drag the Carcass off the Bed, where it lay still bleeding; I observed it had yet some Life, but with a strong Slash cross the Neck, I thoroughly dispatched it.

Soon after, my Mistress came into the Room, who seeing me all bloody, ran and took me up in her Hand. I pointed to the dead *Rat*, smiling and making other Signs to shew I was not hurt; whereat she was extremely rejoyced, calling the Maid to take up the dead *Rat* with a Pair of Tongs, and throw it out of the Window. Then she set me on a Table, where I shewed her my Hanger all bloody, and wiping it on the Lappet of my Coat, returned it to the Scabbard. I was pressed to do more than one Thing, which another could not do for me; and therefore endeavoured to make my Mistress understand that I desired to be set down on the Floor; which after she had done, my Bashfulness would not suffer me to express my self farther than by pointing to the Door, and bowing several Times. The good Woman with much Difficulty at last perceived what I would be at; and taking me up again in her Hand, walked into the Garden where she set me down. I went on one Side about two Hundred Yards; and beckoning to her not to look or to follow me, I hid my self between two Leaves of Sorrel,* and there discharged the Necessities of Nature.

I hope, the gentle Reader will excuse me for dwelling on these and the like Particulars; which however insignificant they may appear to grovelling vulgar Minds, yet will certainly help a Philosopher to enlarge his Thoughts and Imagination, and apply them to the Benefit of publick as well as private Life; which was my sole Design in presenting this and other Accounts of my Travels to the World;* wherein I have been chiefly studious of Truth, without affecting any Ornaments of Learning, or of Style.* But the whole Scene of this Voyage made so strong an Impression on my Mind, and is so deeply fixed in my Memory, that in committing it to Paper, I did not omit one material Circumstance: However, upon a strict Review, I blotted out several Passages of less Moment which were in my first Copy, for fear of being censured as tedious and trifling, whereof Travellers are often, perhaps not without Justice, accused.

CHAPTER TWO

A Description of the Farmer's Daughter. The Author carried to a Market-Town, and then to the Metropolis. The Particulars of his Journey.

MY MISTRESS had a daughter of nine Years old, a Child of towardly Parts* for her Age, very dexterous at her Needle, and skilful in dressing her Baby.* Her Mother and she contrived to fit up the Baby's Cradle for me against Night: The Cradle was put into a small Drawer of a Cabinet, and the Drawer placed upon a hanging Shelf for fear of the *Rats.* This was my Bed all the Time I stayed with those People, although made more convenient by Degrees, as I began to learn their Language, and make my Wants known. This young Girl was so handy, that after I had once or twice pulled off my Cloaths before her, she was able to dress and undress me, although I never gave her that Trouble when she would let me do either my self.* She made me seven Shirts, and some other Linnen of as fine Cloth as could be got, which indeed was coarser than Sackcloth; and these she constantly washed for me with her own Hands. She was likewise my School-Mistress to teach me the Language: When I pointed to any thing, she told me the Name of it in her own Tongue, so that in a few Days I was able to call for whatever I had a mind to. She was very good natured, and not above forty Foot high, being little for her Age. She gave me the Name of *Grildrig,** which the Family took up, and afterwards the whole Kingdom. The Word imports what the *Latins* call *Nanunculus,** the *Italians Homunceletino,** and the *English Mannikin.* To her I chiefly owe my Preservation in that Country: We never parted while I was there; I called her my *Glumdalclitch,** or little Nurse: And I should be guilty of great Ingratitude if I omitted this honourable Mention of her Care and Affection towards me, which I heartily wish it lay in my Power to requite as she deserves, instead of being the innocent but unhappy Instrument of her Disgrace, as I have too much Reason to fear.

It now began to be known and talked of in the Neighbourhood, that my Master had found a strange Animal in the Field, about the Bigness of a *Splacknuck*, but exactly shaped in every Part like a human Creature; which it likewise imitated in all its actions; seemed to speak in a little Language* of its own, had already learned several Words of theirs, went erect upon two Legs, was tame and gentle, would come when it was called, do whatever it was bid, had the finest Limbs in the World, and a Complexion fairer than a Nobleman's Daughter of three Years old. Another Farmer who lived hard by, and was a particular Friend of my Master, came on a Visit on Purpose to enquire into the Truth of this Story. I was immediately produced, and placed upon a Table; where I walked as I was commanded, drew my Hanger, put it up again, made my Reverence* to my Master's Guest, asked him in his own Language how he did, and told him he was welcome; just as my little Nurse had instructed me. This man, who was old and dim-sighted, put on his Spectacles to behold me better, at which I could not forbear laughing very heartily; for his Eyes appeared like the Full-Moon shining into a Chamber at two Windows. Our People, who discovered the Cause of my Mirth, bore me Company in Laughing; at which the old Fellow was Fool enough to be angry and out of Countenance. He had the Character of a great Miser; and to my Misfortune he well deserved it by the cursed Advice he gave my Master, to shew me as a Sight upon a Market-Day in the next Town, which was half an Hour's Riding, about two and twenty Miles from our House. I guessed there was some Mischief contriving, when I observed my Master and his Friend whispering long together, sometimes pointing at me; and my Fears made me fancy that I overheard and understood some of their Words. But, the next Morning *Glumdalclitch* my little Nurse told me the whole Matter, which she had cunningly picked out from her Mother. The poor Girl laid me on her Bosom, and fell a weeping with Shame and Grief. She apprehended some Mischief would happen to me from rude vulgar Folks, who might Squeeze me to Death, or break one of my Limbs by taking me in their Hands. She had also observed how modest I was in my Nature, how nicely I regarded my Honour; and what an Indignity I should conceive it to be exposed for Money as a publick Spectacle* to the meanest of the People. She said, her *Papa* and *Mamma* had promised that *Grildrig* should be hers; but now she found they meant to serve her as they did last Year, when they pretended to give her a Lamb; and yet, as soon as it was fat, sold it to a Butcher. For my own Part, I may truly affirm that I was less concerned than my Nurse. I had a strong Hope which never left me, that I should one Day recover my Liberty; and as to the Ignominy of being carried about for a Monster,* I considered my self to be a perfect Stranger in the Country; and that such a Misfortune could never be charged upon me as a Reproach if ever I should return to *England*; since the King of *Great Britain* himself, in my Condition, must have undergone the same Distress.*

My Master, pursuant to the Advice of his Friend, carried me in a Box* the next Market-Day to the neighbouring Town; and took along with him his little Daughter my Nurse upon a Pillion behind him. The Box was close* on every Side, with a little Door for me to go in and out, and a few Gimlet-holes to let in Air. The Girl had been so careful to* put the Quilt of her Baby's Bed into it, for me to lye down on. However, I was terribly shaken and discomposed in this Journey, although it were but of half an Hour. For the Horse went about forty Foot at every Step; and trotted so high, that the Agitation was equal to the rising and falling of a Ship in a great Storm, but much more frequent: Our Journey was somewhat further than from *London* to St *Albans*.* My Master alighted at an Inn which he used to frequent; and after consulting a while with the Innkeeper, and making some necessary Preparations, he hired the *Grultrud*, or Cryer, to give Notice through the Town, of a strange Creature to be seen at the Sign of the Green *Eagle*, not so big as a *Splacknuck*, (an Animal in that Country very finely shaped, about six Foot long) and in every Part of the Body resembling an human Creature; could speak several Words, and perform an Hundred diverting Tricks.

I was placed upon a Table in the largest Room of the Inn, which might be near three Hundred Foot square. My little

Nurse stood on a low Stool close to the Table, to take care of me, and direct what I should do. My Master, to avoid a Croud, would suffer only Thirty People at a Time to see me. I walked about on the Table as the Girl commanded; she asked me Questions as far as she knew my Understanding of the Language reached, and I answered them as loud as I could. I turned about* several Times to the Company, paid my humble Respects, said they were welcome; and used some other Speeches I had been taught. I took up a Thimble filled with Liquor, which *Glumdalclitch* had given me for a Cup, and drank their Health. I drew out my Hanger, and flourished with it after the Manner of Fencers in *England.* My Nurse gave me Part of a Straw, which I exercised as a Pike, having learned the Art in my Youth. I was that Day shewn to twelve Sets of Company; and as often forced to go over again with the same Fopperies,* till I was half dead with Weariness and Vexation. For, those who had seen me, made such wonderful Reports, that the People were ready to break down the Doors to come in. My Master for his own Interest would not suffer any one to touch me, except my Nurse; and, to prevent Danger, Benches were set round the Table at such a Distance, as put me out of every Body's Reach. However, an unlucky* School-Boy aimed a Hazel Nut directly at my Head, which very narrowly missed me; otherwise, it came with so much Violence, that it would have infallibly knocked out my Brains; for it was almost as large as a small Pumpion:* But I had the Satisfaction to see the young Rogue well beaten, and turned out of the Room.

My Master gave publick Notice, that he would shew me again the next Market-Day: And in the mean time, he prepared a more convenient Vehicle for me,* which he had Reason enough to do; for I was so tired with my first Journey, and with entertaining Company eight Hours together, that I could hardly stand upon my Legs, or speak a Word. It was at least three Days before I recovered my Strength; and that I might have no rest at home, all the neighbouring Gentlemen from an Hundred Miles round, hearing of my Fame, came to see me at My Master's own House. There could not be fewer than thirty Persons with their Wives and Children; (for the Country is very populous;) and my Master demanded the Rate of a full Room whenever he shewed me at Home, although it were only to a single Family. So that for some time I had but little Ease every Day of the Week, (except *Wednesday*, which is their Sabbath*) although I were not carried to the Town.

My Master finding how profitable I was like to be, resolved to carry me to the most considerable Cities of the Kingdom. Having therefore provided himself with all things necessary for a long Journey, and settled his Affairs at Home; he took Leave of his Wife; and upon the 17*th* of *August* 1703, about two Months after my Arrival, we set out for the Metropolis, situated near the Middle of that Empire, and about three Thousand Miles distance from our House: My Master made his Daughter *Glumdalclitch* ride behind him. She carried me on her Lap in a Box tied about her Waist. The Girl had lined it on all Sides with the softest Cloth she could get, well quilted underneath; furnished it with her Baby's Bed, provided me with Linnen and other Necessaries; and made every thing as convenient as she could. We had no other Company but a Boy of the House,* who rode after us with the Luggage.

My Master's Design was to shew me in all the Towns by the Way, and to step out of the Road for Fifty or an Hundred Miles, to any Village or Person of Quality's House where he might expect Custom. We made easy Journies of not above seven or eight Score Miles a Day: For *Glumdalclitch*, on Purpose to spare me, complained she was tired with the trotting of the Horse. She often took me out of my Box at my own Desire, to give me Air, and shew me the Country; but always held me fast by Leading-strings. We passed over five or six Rivers many Degrees broader and deeper than the *Nile* or the *Ganges*; and there was hardly a Rivulet so small as the *Thames* at *London-Bridge*. We were ten Weeks in our Journey; and I was shewn in Eighteen large Towns, besides many Villages and private Families.

On the 26th Day of *October*, we arrived at the Metropolis, called in their Language *Lorbrulgrud*,* or *Pride of the Universe.* My Master took a Lodging in the principal Street of the City, not far from the Royal Palace; and put out Bills in the usual Form, containing an exact Description of my Person and Parts. He hired a large Room between three and four

Hundred Foot wide. He provided a Table sixty Foot in Diameter, upon which I was to act my Part; and pallisadoed it round three Foot from the Edge, and as many high, to prevent my falling over. I was shewn ten Times a Day to the Wonder and Satisfaction of all People. I could now speak the Language tolerably well; and perfectly understood every Word that was spoken to me. Besides, I had learned their Alphabet, and could make a shift to explain* a Sentence here and there; for *Glumdalclitch* had been my Instructer while we were at home, and at leisure Hours during our Journey. She carried a little Book in her Pocket, not much larger than a *Sanson's Atlas;** it was a common Treatise for the use of young Girls, giving a short Account of their Religion; out of this she taught me my Letters, and interpreted the Words.

CHAPTER THREE

The Author sent for to Court. The Queen buys him of his Master the Farmer, and presents him to the King. He disputes with his Majesty's great Scholars. An Apartment at Court provided for the Author. He is in high Favour with the Queen. He stands up for the Honour of his own Country. His Quarrels with the Queen's Dwarf.

THE FREQUENT Labours I underwent every Day, made in a few Weeks a very considerable Change in my Health: The more my Master got by me, the more unsatiable he grew. I had quite lost my Stomach,* and was almost reduced to a Skeleton. The Farmer observed it; and concluding I soon must die, resolved to make as good a Hand of* me as he could. While he was thus reasoning and resolving with himself; a *Slardral,** or Gentleman Usher, came from Court, commanding my Master to bring me immediately thither for the Diversion of the Queen and her Ladies. Some of the latter had already been to see me; and reported strange Things of my Beauty, Behaviour, and good Sense. Her Majesty and those who attended her, were beyond Measure delighted with my Demeanor. I fell on my Knees, and begged the Honour of kissing her Imperial Foot; but this Gracious Princess held out her little Finger towards me (after I was set on a Table) which I embraced in both my Arms, and put the Tip of it, with the utmost Respect, to my Lip. She made me some general Questions about my Country and my Travels, which I answered as distinctly and in as few Words as I could. She asked, whether I would be content to live at Court. I bowed down to the Board of the Table, and humbly answered, that I was my Master's Slave; but if I were at my own Disposal, I should be proud to devote my Life to her Majesty's Service. She then asked my Master whether he were willing to sell me at a good Price. He, who apprehended I could not live a Month, was ready enough to part with me; and demanded a Thousand Pieces of Gold; which were ordered him on the Spot, each

Piece being about the Bigness of eight Hundred Moydores: But, allowing for the Proportion of all Things between that Country and *Europe*, and the high Price of Gold among them; was hardly so great a Sum as a Thousand Guineas would be in *England*. I then said to the Queen; since I was now her Majesty's most humble Creature and Vassal, I must beg the Favour, that *Glumdalclitch*, who had always tended me with so much Care and Kindness, and understood to do it so well, might be admitted into her Service, and continue to be my Nurse and Instructor. Her Majesty agreed to my Petition; and easily got the Farmer's Consent, who was glad enough to have his Daughter preferred at Court: And the poor Girl herself was not able to hide her Joy. My late Master withdrew, bidding me farewell, and saying he had left me in a good Service; to which I replyed not a Word, only making him a slight Bow.

The Queen observed my Coldness; and when the Farmer was gone out of the Apartment, asked me the Reason. I made bold to tell her Majesty, that I owed no other Obligation to my late Master, than his not dashing out the Brains of a poor harmless Creature found by Chance in his Field; which Obligation was amply recompenced by the Gain he had made in shewing me through half the Kingdom, and the Price he had now sold me for. That the Life I had since led, was laborious enough to kill an Animal of ten Times my Strength. That my Health was much impaired by the continual Drudgery of entertaining the Rabble every Hour of the Day; and that if my Master had not thought my Life in Danger, her Majesty perhaps would not have got so cheap a Bargain. But as I was out of all fear of being ill treated under the Protection of so great and good an Empress, the Ornament of Nature, the Darling of the World, the Delight of her Subjects, the Phoenix of the Creation; so, I hoped my late Master's Apprehensions would appear to be groundless; for I already found my Spirits to revive by the Influence of her most August Presence.

This was the Sum of my Speech, delivered with great Improprieties and Hesitation; the latter Part was altogether framed in the Style peculiar to that People,* whereof I learned some Phrases from *Glumdalclitch*, while she was carrying me to Court.

The Queen giving great Allowance for my Defectiveness in speaking, was however surprised at so much Wit and good Sense in so diminutive an Animal. She took me in her own Hand, and carried me to the King, who was then retired to his Cabinet. His Majesty,* a Prince of much Gravity, and austere Countenance, not well observing my Shape at first View, asked the Queen after a cold Manner, how long it was since she grew fond of a *Splacknuck*; for such it seems he took me to be, as I lay upon my Breast in her Majesty's right Hand. But this Princess,* who hath an infinite deal of Wit and Humour, set me gently on my Feet upon the Scrutore;* and commanded me to give His Majesty an Account of my self, which I did in a very few Words; and *Glumdalclitch*, who attended at the Cabinet Door, and could not endure I should be out of her Sight, being admitted; confirmed all that had passed from my Arrival at her Father's House.

The King, although he be as learned a Person as any in his Dominions and had been educated in the Study of Philosophy, and particularly Mathematicks; yet when he observed my Shape exactly, and saw me walk erect, before I began to speak, conceived I might be a piece of Clock-work,* (which is in that Country arrived to a very great Perfection) contrived by some ingenious Artist.* But, when he heard my Voice, and found what I delivered to be regular and rational, he could not conceal his Astonishment. He was by no means satisfied with the Relation I gave him of the Manner I came into his Kingdom; but thought it a Story concerted between *Glumdalclitch* and her Father, who had taught me a Sett of Words to make me sell at a higher Price. Upon this Imagination he put several other Questions to me, and still received rational Answers, no otherwise defective than by a Foreign Accent, and an imperfect Knowledge in the Language; with some rustick Phrases which I had learned at the Farmer's House, and did not suit the polite Style of a Court.

His Majesty sent for three great Scholars who were then in their weekly waiting* (according to the Custom in that Country.) These Gentlemen, after they had a while examined my Shape with much Nicety, were of different Opinions concerning me. They all agreed that I could not be produced according to the regular Laws of Nature;* because I was not framed with a Capacity of preserving my Life, either by Swiftness, or climbing of Trees, or digging Holes in the Earth. They observed by my Teeth, which they viewed with great Exactness, that I was a carnivorous Animal; yet most Quadrupeds being an Overmatch for me; and Field-Mice, with some others, too nimble, they could not imagine how I should be able to support my self, unless I fed upon Snails and other Insects;* which they offered by many learned Arguments to evince* that I could not possibly do. One of them seemed to think that I might be an Embrio, or abortive Birth. But this Opinion was rejected by the other two, who observed my Limbs to be perfect and finished; and that I had lived several Years, as it was manifested from my Beard; the Stumps whereof they plainly discovered through a Magnifying-Glass. They would not allow me to be a Dwarf, because my Littleness was beyond all Degrees of Comparison; for the Queen's favourite Dwarf, the smallest ever known in that Kingdom, was near thirty Foot high. After much Debate, they concluded unanimously that I was only *Relplum Scalcath*, which is interpreted literally *Lusus Naturæ*; a Determination exactly agreeable to the Modern Philosophy of *Europe*: whose Professors,* disdaining the old Evasion of *occult Causes*, whereby the Followers of *Aristotle* endeavour in vain to disguise their Ignorance; have invented this wonderful Solution of all Difficulties, to the unspeakable Advancement of human Knowledge.

After this decisive Conclusion, I entreated to be heard a Word or two. I applied my self to the King, and assured His Majesty, that I came from a Country which abounded with several Millions of both Sexes, and of my own Stature; where the Animals, Trees, and Houses were all in Proportion; and where by Consequence I might be as able to defend my self, and to find Sustenance, as any of his Majesty's Subjects could do here; which I took for a full Answer to those Gentlemens Arguments. To this they only replied with a Smile of Contempt;* saying, that the Farmer had instructed me very well in my Lesson. The King, who had a much better Understanding, dismissing his learned Men, sent for the Farmer, who by good

Fortune was not yet gone out of Town: Having therefore first examined him privately, and then confronted him with me and the young Girl; his Majesty began to think that what we told him might possibly be true. He desired the Queen to order, that a particular Care should be taken of me; and was of Opinion, that *Glumdalclitch* should still continue in her Office of tending me, because he observed we had a great Affection for each other. A convenient Apartment was provided for her at Court; she had a sort of Governess appointed to take care of her Education, a Maid to dress her, and two other Servants for menial Offices; but, the Care of me was wholly appropriated to her self. The Queen commanded her own Cabinet-maker to contrive a Box that might serve me for a Bed-chamber, after the Model that *Glumdalclitch* and I should agree upon. This Man was a most ingenious Artist; and according to my Directions, in three Weeks finished for me a wooden Chamber of sixteen Foot square, and twelve High; with Sash Windows, a Door, and two Closets, like a *London* Bed-chamber. The Board that made the Cieling was to be lifted up and down by two Hinges, to put in a Bed ready furnished by her Majesty's Upholsterer; which *Glumdalclitch* took out every Day to air, made it with her own Hands, and letting it down at Night, locked up the Roof over me. A Nice* Workman, who was famous for little Curiosities, undertook to make me two Chairs, with Backs and Frames, of a Substance not unlike Ivory; and two Tables, with a Cabinet to put my Things in. The Room was quilted on all Sides, as well as the Floor and the Cieling, to prevent any Accident from the Carelessness of those who carried me; and to break the Force of a Jolt when I went in a Coach. I desired a Lock for my Door to prevent Rats and Mice from coming in: The Smith after several Attempts made the smallest that was ever seen among them; for I have known a larger at the Gate of a Gentleman's House in *England.* I made a shift to keep the Key in a Pocket of my own, fearing *Glumdalclitch* might lose it. The Queen likewise ordered the thinnest Silks that could be gotten, to make me Cloaths; not much thicker than an *English* Blanket, very cumbersome till I was accustomed to them. They were after the Fashion of the Kingdom, partly resembling the

Persian, and partly the *Chinese*; and are a very grave decent Habit.

The Queen became so fond of my Company, that she could not dine without me. I had a Table placed upon the same at which her Majesty eat, just at her left Elbow; and a Chair to sit on. *Glumdalclitch* stood upon a Stool on the Floor, near my Table, to assist and take Care of me. I had an entire set of Silver Dishes and Plates, and other Necessaries, which in Proportion to those of the Queen, were not much bigger than what I have seen in a *London* Toy-shop, for the Furniture of a Baby-house:* These my little Nurse kept in her Pocket, in a Silver Box, and gave me at Meals as I wanted them; always cleaning them her self. No Person dined with the Queen but the two Princesses Royal; the elder sixteen Years old, and the younger at that time thirteen and a Month. Her Majesty used to put a Bit of Meat upon one of my Dishes, out of which I carved for my self; and her Diversion was to see me eat in Miniature. For the Queen (who had indeed but a weak Stomach) took up at one Mouthful, as much as a dozen *English* Farmers could eat at a Meal, which to me was for some time a very nauseous Sight. She would craunch* the Wing of a Lark, Bones and all, between her Teeth, although it were nine Times as large as that of a full grown Turkey; and put a Bit of Bread in her Mouth, as big as two twelve-penny Loaves. She drank out of a golden Cup, above a Hogshead at a Draught.* Her Knives were twice as long as a Scythe set strait upon the Handle. The Spoons, Forks, and other Instruments were all in the same Proportion. I remember when *Glumdalclitch* carried me out of Curiosity to see some of the Tables at Court, where ten or a dozen of these enormous Knives and Forks were lifted up together; I thought I had never till then beheld so terrible a Sight.

It is the Custom, that very *Wednesday*, (which as I have before observed, was their Sabbath) the King and Queen, with the Royal Issue of both Sexes, dine together in the Apartments of his Majesty; to whom I was now become a Favourite; and at these Times my little Chair and Table were placed at his left Hand before one of the Salt-sellers. This Prince took a Pleasure in conversing with me; enquiring into the Manners, Religion, Laws, Government, and Learning of *Europe*, wherein I gave him the best Account I was able. His Apprehension was so clear, and his Judgment so exact, that he made very wise Reflexions and Observations upon all I said. But, I confess, that after I had been a little too copious in talking of my own beloved Country; of our Trade, and Wars by Sea and Land, of our Schisms in Religion, and Parties in the State; the Prejudices of his Education prevailed so far, that he could not forbear taking me up in his right Hand, and stroaking me gently with the other; after an hearty Fit of laughing, asked me whether I were a *Whig* or a *Tory*.* Then turning to his first Minister, who waited behind him with a white Staff,* near as tall as the Main-mast of the Royal *Sovereign*;* he observed, how contemptible a Thing was human Grandeur, which could be mimicked by such diminutive Insects as I; And yet, said he, I dare engage,* those Creatures have their Titles and Distinctions of Honour; they contrive little Nests and Burrows, that they call Houses and Cities;* they make a Figure in Dress and Equipage; they love, they fight, they dispute, they cheat, they betray. And thus he continued on, while my Colour came and went several Times, with Indignation to hear our noble Country, the Mistress of Arts and Arms, the Scourge of *France*, the Arbitress of *Europe*, the Seat of Virtue, Piety, Honour and Truth, the Pride and Envy of the World, so contemptuously treated.

But, as I was not in a Condition to resent Injuries, so, upon mature Thoughts, I began to doubt whether I were injured or no. For, after having been accustomed several Months to the Sight and Converse of this People, and observed every Object upon which I cast mine Eyes, to be of proportionable Magnitude; the Horror I had first conceived from their Bulk and Aspect was so far worn off, that if I had then beheld a Company of *English* Lords and Ladies in their Finery and Birth-day Cloaths,* acting their several Parts in the most courtly Manner of Strutting, and Bowing and Prating; to say the Truth, I should have been strongly tempted to laugh as much at them as this King and his Grandees did at me. Neither indeed could I forbear smiling at my self, when the Queen used to place me upon her Hand towards a Looking-Glass, by which both our

Persons appeared before me in full View together; and there could nothing be more ridiculous than the Comparison: So that I really began to imagine my self dwindled many Degrees below my usual Size.

Nothing angred and mortified me so much as the Queen's Dwarf,* who being of the lowest Stature that was ever in that Country, (for I verily think he was not full Thirty Foot high) became so insolent at seeing a Creature so much beneath him, that he would always affect to swagger and look big as he passed by me in the Queen's Antichamber, while I was standing on some Table talking with the Lords or Ladies of the Court; and he seldom failed of a smart Word or two upon my Littleness; against which I could only revenge my self by calling him *Brother*, challenging him to wrestle; and such Repartees as are usual in the Mouths of *Court Pages*. One Day at Dinner, this malicious little Cubb was so nettled with something I had said to him, that raising himself upon the Frame of her Majesty's Chair, he took me up by the Middle, as I was sitting down, not thinking any Harm, and let me drop into a large Silver Bowl of Cream;* and then ran away as fast as he could. I fell over Head and Ears, and if I had not been a good Swimmer, it might have gone very hard with me; for *Glumdalclitch* in that Instant happened to be at the other End of the Room; and the Queen was in such a Fright, that she wanted Presence of Mind to assist me. But my little Nurse ran to my Relief; and took me out, after I had swallowed above a Quart of Cream. I was put to Bed; however I received no other Damage than the Loss of a Suit of Cloaths, which was utterly spoiled. The Dwarf was soundly whipped, and as a further Punishment, forced to drink up the Bowl of Cream, into which he had thrown me; neither was he ever restored to Favour: For, soon after the Queen bestowed him to a Lady of high Quality; so that I saw him no more, to my very great Satisfaction; for I could not tell to what Extremity such a malicious Urchin might have carried his Resentment.

He had before served me a scurvy Trick, which set the Queen a laughing, although at the same time she were heartily vexed, and would have immediately cashiered him, if I had not been so generous as to intercede. Her Majesty had taken a Marrow-bone upon her Plate; and after knocking out the Marrow, placed the Bone again in the Dish erect as it stood before; the Dwarf watching his Opportunity, while *Glumdalclitch* was gone to the Sideboard, mounted the Stool that she stood on to take care of me at Meals; took me up in both Hands, and squeezing my Legs together, wedged them into the Marrow-bone above my Waist; where I stuck for some time, and made a very ridiculous Figure. I believe it was near a Minute before any one knew what was become of me; for I thought it below me to cry out. But, as Princes seldom get their Meat hot, my Legs were not scalded, only my Stockings and Breeches in a sad Condition. The Dwarf at my Entreaty had no other Punishment than a sound whipping.

I was frequently raillied* by the Queen upon Account of my Fearfulness; and she used to ask me whether the People of my Country were as great Cowards as my self. The Occasion was this. The Kingdom is much pestered with Flies in Summer; and these odious Insects, each of them as big as a *Dunstable* Lark,* hardly gave me any Rest while I sat at Dinner, with their continual Humming and Buzzing about mine Ears. They would sometimes alight upon my Victuals, and leave their Loathsome Excrement or Spawn behind, which to me was very visible, although not to the Natives of that Country, whose large Opticks were not so acute as mine in viewing smaller Objects. Sometimes they would fix upon my Nose or Forehead, where they stung me to the Quick, smelling very offensively; and I could easily trace that viscous Matter, which our Naturalists tell us enables those Creatures to walk with their Feet upwards upon a Cieling. I had much ado to defend my self against these detestable Animals, and could not forbear starting when they came on my Face. It was the common Practice of the Dwarf to catch a Number of these Insects in his Hand, as School-boys do among us, and let them out suddenly under my Nose, on Purpose to frighten me, and divert the Queen. My Remedy was to cut them in Pieces with my Knife as they flew in the Air; wherein my Dexterity was much admired.

I remember one Morning when *Glumdalclitch* had set me in my Box upon a Window, as she usually did in fair Days to give me Air, (for I durst not venture to let the Box be hung on a Nail out of the Window, as we do with Cages in *England*) after I had lifted up one of my Sashes,* and sat down at my Table to eat a Piece of Sweet-Cake for my Breakfast; above twenty Wasps, allured by the Smell, came flying into the Room, humming louder than the Drones of as many Bagpipes. Some of them seized my Cake, and carried it piecemeal away; others flew about my Head and Face, confounding me with the Noise, and putting me in the utmost Terror of their Stings. However I had the Courage to rise and draw my Hanger, and attack them in the Air. I dispatched four of them, but the rest got away, and I presently shut my Window. These Insects were as large as Partridges; I took out their Stings, found them an Inch and a half long, and as sharp as Needles. I carefully preserved them all, and having since shewn them with some other Curiosities in several Parts of *Europe*; upon my Return to *England* I gave three of them to *Gresham College*,* and kept the fourth for my self.

CHAPTER FOUR

The Country described. A Proposal for correcting modern Maps. The King's Palace, and some Account of the Metropolis. The Author's Way of travelling. The chief Temple described.

I NOW intend to give the Reader a short Description of this Country, as far as I travelled in it, which was not above two thousand Miles round *Lorbrulgrud* the Metropolis. For, the Queen, whom I always attended, never went further when she accompanied the King in his Progresses; and there staid till his Majesty returned from viewing his Frontiers. The whole Extent* of this Prince's Dominions reacheth about six thousand Miles in Length, and from three to five in Breadth. From whence I cannot but conclude, that our Geographers of *Europe* are in a great Error, by supposing nothing but Sea between *Japan* and *California:* For it was ever my Opinion, that there must be a Balance of Earth to counterpoise the great Continent of *Tartary;* and therefore they ought to correct their Maps and Charts, by joining this vast Tract of Land to the North-west Parts of *America;* wherein I shall be ready to lend them my Assistance.

The Kingdom is a Peninsula,* terminated to the North-east by a Ridge of Mountains thirty Miles high which are altogether impassable by Reason of the Volcanoes upon the Tops. Neither do the most Learned know what sort of Mortals inhabit beyond those Mountains, or whether they be inhabited at all. On the three other Sides it is bounded by the Ocean. There is not one Sea-port in the whole Kingdom; and those Parts of the Coasts into which the Rivers issue, are so full of pointed Rocks, and the Sea generally so rough, that there is no venturing with the smallest of their Boats; so that these People are wholly excluded from any Commerce with the rest of the World. But the large Rivers are full of Vessels, and abound with excellent Fish; for they seldom get any from the Sea, because the Sea-fish are of the same Size with those in

Europe, and consequently not worth catching; whereby it is manifest, that Nature in the Production of Plants and Animals of so extraordinary a Bulk, is wholly confined to this Continent; of which I leave the Reasons to be determined by Philosophers. However, now and then they take a Whale that happens to be dashed against the Rocks, which the common People fêed on heartily. These Whales I have known so large that a Man could hardly carry one upon his Shoulders; and sometimes for Curiosity they are brought in Hampers to *Lorbrulgrud*: I saw one of them in a Dish at the King's Table, which passed for a Rarity; but I did not observe he was fond of it; for I think indeed the Bigness disgusted him, although I have seen one somewhat larger in *Greenland*.

The Country is well inhabited, for it contains fifty-one Cities,* near an hundred walled Towns, and a great Number of Villages. To satisfy my curious Reader, it may be sufficient to describe *Lorbrulgrud*.* This City stands upon almost two equal Parts on each Side the River that passes through. It contains above eighty thousand Houses. It is in Length three *Glonglungs** (which make about fifty four English Miles) and two and a half in Breadth, as I measured it myself in the Royal Map made by the King's Order, which was laid on the Ground on purpose for me, and extended an hundred Feet; I paced the Diameter and Circumference several times Barefoot, and computing by the Scale, measured it pretty exactly.

The King's Palace is no regular Edifice, but an Heap of Buildings about seven Miles round: The chief Rooms are generally two hundred and forty Foot high, and broad and long in Proportion. A Coach was allowed to *Glumdalclitch* and me, wherein her Governess frequently took her out to see the Town, or go among the Shops; and I was always of the Party, carried in my Box; although the Girl at my own Desire would often take me out, and hold me in her Hand, that I might more conveniently view the Houses and the People as we passed along the Streets. I reckoned our Coach to be about a Square of* *Westminster-Hall*, but not altogether so High; however, I cannot be very exact. One Day the Governess ordered our Coachman to stop at several Shops; where the Beggars* watching their Opportunity, crouded to the Sides of the

Coach, and gave me the most horrible Spectacles that ever an *European* Eye beheld. There was a Woman with a Cancer in her Breast, swelled to a monstrous Size, full of Holes, in two or three of which I could have easily crept, and covered my whole Body. There was a Fellow with a Wen in his Neck, larger than five Woolpacks,* and another with a couple of wooden Legs, each about twenty Foot high. But, the most hateful Sight of all was the Lice crawling on their Cloaths: I could see distinctly the Limbs of these Vermin with my naked Eye, much better than those of an *European* Louse through a Microscope;* and their Snouts with which they rooted like Swine. They were the first I had ever beheld; and I should have been curious enough to dissect one of them, if I had proper Instruments (which I unluckily left behind me in the Ship) although indeed the Sight was so nauseous, that it perfectly turned my Stomach.

Beside the large Box in which I was usually carried, the Queen ordered a smaller one to be made for me, of about twelve Foot Square, and ten high, for the Convenience of Travelling; because the other was somewhat too large for *Glumdalclitch's* Lap, and cumbersom in the Coach; it was made by the same Artist, whom I directed in the whole Contrivance. This travelling Closet was an exact Square with a Window in the Middle of three of the Squares,* and each Window was latticed with Iron Wire on the outside, to prevent Accidents in long Journeys. On the fourth Side, which had no Window, two strong Staples were fixed, through which the Person that carried me, when I had a Mind to be on Horseback, put in a Leathern Belt, and buckled it about his Waist. This was always the Office of some grave trusty Servant in whom I could confide, whether I attended the King and Queen in their Progresses, or were disposed to see the Gardens, or pay a Visit to some great Lady or Minister of State in the Court, when *Glumdalclitch* happened to be out of Order:* For I soon began to be known and esteemed among the greatest Officers,* I suppose more upon Account of their Majesty's Favour, than any Merit of my own. In Journeys, when I was weary of the Coach, a Servant on Horseback would buckle my Box, and place it on a Cushion before him; and there I had a full Prospect of the Country on three Sides from my three Windows. I had in this Closet a Field-Bed* and a Hammock hung from the Ceiling, two Chairs and a Table, neatly screwed to the Floor, to prevent being tossed about by the Agitation of the Horse or the Coach. And having been long used to Sea-Voyages, those Motions, although sometimes very violent, did not much discompose me.

Whenever I had a Mind to see the Town, it was always in my Travelling-Closet; which *Glumdalclitch* held in her Lap in a kind of open Sedan, after the Fashion of the Country, born by four Men, and attended by two others in the Queen's Livery. The People who had often heard of me, were very curious to croud about the Sedan; and the Girl was complaisant enough to make the Bearers stop, and to take me in her Hand that I might be more conveniently seen.

I was very desirous to see the chief Temple, and particularly the Tower belonging to it, which is reckoned the highest in the Kingdom. Accordingly one Day my Nurse carried me thither, but I may truly say I came back disappointed; for, the Height is not above three thousand Foot, reckoning from the Ground to the highest Pinnacle top; which allowing for the Difference between the Size of those People, and us in *Europe*, is no great matter for Admiration, nor at all equal in Proportion, (if I rightly remember) to *Salisbury* Steeple.* But, not to detract from a Nation to which during my Life I shall acknowledge myself extremely obliged; it must be allowed, that whatever this famous Tower wants in Height, is amply made up in Beauty and Strength. For the Walls are near an hundred Foot thick, built of hewn Stone, whereof each is about forty Foot square, and adorned on all Sides with Statues of Gods and Emperors cut in Marble larger than the Life, placed in their several Niches. I measured a little Finger* which had fallen down from one of these Statues, and lay unperceived among some Rubbish; and found it exactly four Foot and an Inch in Length. *Glumdalclitch* wrapped it up in a Handkerchief, and carried it home in her Pocket to keep among other Trinkets, of which the Girl was very fond, as Children at her Age usually are.

The King's Kitchen is indeed a noble Building, vaulted at

Top, and about six hundred Foot high. The great Oven is not so wide by ten Paces as the Cupola at St *Paul's*:* For I measured the latter on purpose after my Return. But if I should describe the Kitchen-grate, the prodigious Pots and Kettles, the Joints of Meat turning on the Spits, with many other Particulars; perhaps I should be hardly believed;* at least a severe Critick would be apt to think I enlarged* a little, as Travellers are often suspected to do.* To avoid which Censure, I fear I have run too much into the other Extream; and that if this Treatise should happen to be translated into the Language of *Brobdingnag*, (which is the general Name of that Kingdom) and transmitted thither; the King and his People would have Reason to complain; that I had done them an injury by a false and diminutive* Representation.

His Majesty seldom keeps above six hundred Horses in his Stables: They are generally from fifty-four to sixty Foot high.* But, when he goes abroad on solemn Days, he is attended for State by a Militia Guard of five hundred Horse, which indeed I thought was the most splendid Sight that could be ever beheld, till I saw part of his Army in Battalia:* whereof I shall find another Occasion to speak.

CHAPTER FIVE

Several Adventures that happened to the Author. The Execution of a Criminal. The Author shews his Skill in Navigation.

I SHOULD have lived happy enough in that Country, if my Littleness had not exposed me to several ridiculous and troublesome Accidents; some of which I shall venture to relate. *Glumdalclitch* often carried me into the Gardens of the Court in my smaller Box, and would sometimes take me out of it and hold me in her Hand, or set me down to walk. I remember, before the Dwarf left the Queen, he followed us one Day into those Gardens; and my Nurse having set me down, he and I being close together, near some Dwarf Apple-trees, I must need shew my Wit by a silly Allusion* between him and the Trees, which happens to hold in their Language as it doth in ours. Whereupon, the malicious Rogue watching his Opportunity, when I was walking under one of them, shook it directly over my Head, by which a dozen Apples, each of them near as large as a Bristol *Barrel*,* came tumbling about my Ears; one of them hit me on the Back as I chanced to stoop, and knocked me down flat on my Face, but I received no other Hurt; and the Dwarf was pardoned at my Desire, because I had given the Provocation.

Another Day, *Glumdalclitch* left me on a smooth Grass-plot to divert my self while she walked at some Distance with her Governess. In the mean time, there suddenly fell such a violent Shower of Hail, that I was immediately by the Force of it struck to the Ground: And when I was down, the Hail-stones gave me such cruel Bangs all over the Body, as if I had been pelted with Tennis-Balls; however I made a Shift to creep on all four, and shelter my self by lying flat on my Face on the Lee-side of a Border of Lemmon Thyme;* but so bruised from Head to Foot, that I could not go abroad in ten Days. Neither is this at all to be wondered at; because Nature in that Country observing the same Proportion through all her

Operations, a Hail-stone is near Eighteen Hundred Times* as large as one in *Europe*; which I can assert upon Experience, having been so curious to weigh and measure them.

But, a more dangerous Accident happened to me in the same Garden, when my little Nurse, believing she had put me in a secure Place, which I often entreated her to do, that I might enjoy my own Thoughts; and having left my Box at home to avoid the Trouble of carrying it, went to another Part of the Garden with her Governess and some Ladies of her Acquaintance. While she was absent and out of hearing, a small white Spaniel belonging to one of the chief Gardiners, having got by Accident into the Garden, happened to range near the Place where I lay. The Dog following the Scent, came directly up, and taking me in his Mouth, ran strait to his Master, wagging his Tail, and set me gently on the Ground. By good Fortune he had been so well taught, that I was carried between his Teeth without the least Hurt, or even tearing my Cloaths. But, the poor Gardiner, who knew me well, and had a great Kindness* for me, was in a terrible Fright. He gently took me up in both his Hands, and asked me how I did; but I was so amazed* and out of Breath, that I could not speak a Word. In a few Minutes I came to my self, and he carried me safe to my little Nurse, who by this time had returned to the Place where she left me, and was in cruel Agonies when I did not appear, nor answer when she called; she severely reprimanded the Gardiner on Account of his Dog. But, the Thing was hushed up, and never known at Court; for the Girl was afraid of the Queen's Anger; and truly as to my self, I thought it would not be for* my Reputation that such a Story should go about.

This Accident absolutely determined *Glumdalclitch* never to trust me abroad for the future out of her Sight. I had been long afraid of this Resolution; and therefore concealed from her some little unlucky Adventures that happened in those Times when I was left by my self. Once a Kite hovering over the Garden, made a Stoop at* me, and if I had not resolutely drawn my Hanger, and run under a thick Espalier, he would have certainly carried me away in his Talons. Another time, walking to the Top of a fresh Mole-hill, I fell to my Neck in the

Hole through which that Animal had cast up the Earth; and coined some Lye not worth remembring, to excuse my self for spoiling my Cloaths. I likewise broke my right Shin* against the Shell of a Snail, which I happened to stumble over, as I was walking alone, and thinking on poor *England*.

I cannot tell whether I was more pleased or mortified to observe in those solitary Walks, that the smaller Birds* did not appear to be at all afraid of me;* but would hop about within a Yard Distance, looking for Worms, and other Food, with as much Indifference and Security* as if no Creature at all were near them. I remember, a Thrush had the Confidence to snatch out of my Hand with his Bill, a Piece of Cake that *Glumdalclitch* had just given me for my Breakfast. When I attempted to catch any of these Birds, they would boldly turn against me, endeavouring to pick* my Fingers, which I durst not venture within their Reach; and then they would hop back unconcerned to hunt for Worms or Snails, as they did before. But, one Day I took a thick Cudgel, and threw it with all my Strength so luckily at a Linnet, that I knocked him down, and seizing him by the Neck with both my Hands, ran with him in Triumph to my Nurse. However, the Bird who had only been stunned, recovering himself, gave me so many Boxes with his Wings on both Sides of my Head and Body, although I held him at Arms Length, and was out of the Reach of his Claws, that I was twenty Times thinking to let him go. But I was soon relieved by one of our Servants, who wrung off the Bird's Neck; and I had him next Day for Dinner by the Queen's Command. This Linnet, as near as I can remember, seemed to be somewhat larger than an *English* Swan.

The Maids of Honour* often invited *Glumdalclitch* to their Apartments, and desired she would bring me along with her, on Purpose to have the Pleasure of seeing and touching me. They would often strip me naked from Top to Toe, and lay me at full Length in their Bosoms; wherewith I was much disgusted; because, to say the Truth, a very offensive Smell came from their Skins; which I do not mention or intend to the Disadvantage of those excellent Ladies, for whom I have all Manner of Respect: But, I conceive, that my Sense was more acute in Proportion to my Littleness; and that those illustrious Persons were no more disagreeable to their Lovers, or to each other, than People of the same Quality are with us in *England*. And, after all, I found their natural Smell was much more supportable than when they used Perfumes, under which I immediately swooned away. I cannot forget, that an intimate Friend of mine in *Lilliput* took the Freedom in a warm Day, when I had used a good deal of Exercise, to complain of a strong Smell about me; although I am as little faulty that way as most of my Sex: But I suppose, his Faculty of Smelling was as nice with regard to me, as mine was to that of this People. Upon this point, I cannot forbear doing Justice to the Queen my Mistress, and *Glumdalclitch* my Nurse; whose Persons were as sweet as those of any Lady in *England*.

That which gave me most Uneasiness among these Maids of Honour, when my Nurse carried me to visit them, was to see them use me without any Manner of Ceremony, like a Creature who had no Sort of Consequence. For, they would strip themselves to the Skin, and put on their Smocks in my Presence, while I was placed on their Toylet* directly before their naked Bodies; which, I am sure, to me was very far from being a tempting Sight, or from giving me any other Motions* than those of Horror and Disgust. Their Skins appeared so coarse and uneven, so variously coloured when I saw them near, with a Mole here and there as broad as a Trencher, and Hairs hanging from it thicker than Pack-threads; to say nothing further concerning the rest of their Persons. Neither did they at all scruple while I was by, to discharge what they had drunk, to the Quantity of at least two Hogsheads, in a Vessel that held above three Tuns.* The handsomest among these Maids of Honour, a pleasant* frolicksome Girl of sixteen, would sometimes set me astride upon one of her Nipples; with many other Tricks, wherein the Reader will excuse me for not being over particular. But, I was so much displeased, that I entreated *Glumdalclitch* to contrive some excuse for not seeing that young Lady any more.

One Day, a young Gentleman who was Nephew to my Nurse's Governess, came and pressed them both to see an Execution. It was of a Man who had murdered one of that Gentleman's intimate Acquaintance. *Glumdalclitch* was prevailed on to be of the Company, very much against her Inclination, for she was naturally tender hearted: And, as for myself, although I abhorred such Kind of Spectacles; yet my Curiosity tempted me to see something that I thought must be extraordinary. The Malefactor was fixed in a Chair upon a Scaffold erected for the Purpose; and his Head cut off at one Blow with a Sword of about forty Foot long. The Veins and Arteries spouted up such a prodigious Quantity of Blood, and so high in the Air, that the great *Jet d'Eau at Versailles** was not equal for the Time it lasted; and the Head when it fell on the Scaffold Floor, gave such a Bounce, as made me start, although I were at least an *English* Mile distant.

The Queen, who often used to hear me talk of my Sea-Voyages, and took all Occasions to divert me when I was melancholy, asked me whether I understood how to handle a Sail or an Oar; and whether a little Exercise of Rowing might not be convenient for my Health. I answered, that I understood both very well. For although my proper Employment had been to be Surgeon or Doctor to the Ship; yet often upon a Pinch,* I was forced to work like a common Mariner. But, I could not see how this could be done in their Country, where the smallest Wherry was equal to a first Rate Man of War among us; and such a Boat as I could manage, would never live in any of their Rivers: Her Majesty said, if I would contrive a Boat, her own Joyner should make it, and she would provide a Place for me to sail in. The Fellow was an ingenious Workman, and by my Instructions in ten Days finished a Pleasure-Boat with all its Tackling, able conveniently to hold eight *Europeans.* When it was finished, the Queen was so delighted, that she ran with it in her Lap to the King, who ordered it to be put in a Cistern full of Water, with me in it, by way of Tryal; where I could not manage my two Sculls or little Oars for want of Room. But, the Queen had before contrived another Project. She ordered the Joyner to make a wooden Trough of three Hundred Foot long, fifty broad, and eight deep; which being well pitched to prevent leaking, was placed on the Floor along the Wall, in an outer Room of the Palace. It had a Cock near the Bottom, to let out the Water when it began to grow stale; and two Servants could easily fill it in half an Hour. Here

I often used to row for my Diversion, as well as that of the Queen and her Ladies, who thought themselves agreeably entertained with my Skill and Agility. Sometimes I would put up my Sail, and then my Business was only to steer, while the Ladies gave me a Gale with their Fans; and when they were weary, some of the Pages would blow my Sail forward with their Breath, while I shewed my Art by steering Starboard or Larboard as I pleased. When I had done, *Glumdalclitch* always carried my Boat into her Closet, and hung it on a Nail to dry.

In this Exercise I once met an Accident which had like to have cost me my Life. For, one of the Pages having put my Boat into the Trough; the Governess who attended *Glumdalclitch*, very officiously lifted me up to place me in the Boat; but I happened to slip through her Fingers, and should have infallibly fallen down forty Foot upon the Floor, if by the luckiest Chance in the World, I had not been stop'd by a Corking-pin* that stuck in the good Gentlewoman's Stomacher; the Head of the Pin passed between my Shirt and the Waistband of my Breeches; and thus I was held by the Middle in the Air, till *Glumdalclitch* ran to my Relief.

Another time, one of the Servants, whose Office it was to fill my Trough every third Day with fresh Water; was so careless to let a huge Frog (not perceiving it) slip out of his Pail. The Frog lay concealed till I was put into my Boat, but then seeing a resting Place, climbed up, and made it lean so much on one Side, that I was forced to balance it with all my Weight on the other, to prevent overturning. When the Frog was got in, it hopped at once half the Length of the Boat, and then over my Head, backwards and forwards, dawbing my Face and Cloaths with its odious Slime. The Largeness of its Features made it appear the most deformed Animal that can be conceived. However, I desired *Glumdalclitch* to let me deal with it alone. I banged it a good while with one of my Sculls, and at last forced it to leap out of the Boat.

But, the greatest Danger I ever underwent in that Kingdom, was from a Monkey, who belonged to one of the Clerks of the Kitchen. *Glumdalclitch* had locked me up in her Closet, while she went somewhere upon Business, or a Visit. The Weather being very warm, the Closet Window was left open, as well as the Windows and the Door of my bigger Box, in which I usually lived, because of its Largeness and Conveniency. As I sat quietly meditating at my Table, I heard something bounce in at the Closet Window, and skip about from one Side to the other; whereat, although I were much alarmed, yet I ventured to look out, but not stirring from my Seat; and then I saw this frolicksome Animal, frisking and leaping up and down, till at last he came to my Box, which he seemed to view with great Pleasure and Curiosity, peeping in at the Door and every Window. I retreated to the farther Corner of my Room, or Box; but the Monkey looking in at every Side, put me into such a Fright, that I wanted Presence of Mind to conceal my self under the Bed, as I might easily have done. After some time spent in peeping, grinning, and chattering, he at last espyed me; and reaching one of his Paws in at the Door as a Cat does when she plays with a Mouse, although I often shifted Place to avoid him; he at length seized the Lappet of my Coat (which being made of that Country Silk,* was very thick and strong) and dragged me out. He took me up in his right Fore-foot, and held me as a Nurse doth a Child she is going to suckle; just as I have seen the same Sort of Creature do with a Kitten in *Europe*: And when I offered to struggle, he squeezed me so hard, that I thought it more prudent to submit. I have good Reason to believe that he took me for a young one of his own Species, by his often stroking my Face very gently with his other Paw. In these Diversions he was interrupted by a Noise at the Closet Door, as if some Body were opening it; whereupon he suddenly leaped up to the Window at which he had come in, and thence upon the Leads and Gutters, walking upon three Legs, and holding me in the fourth, till he clambered up to a Roof* that was next to ours. I heard *Glumdalclitch* give a Shriek at the Moment he was carrying me out. The poor Girl was almost distracted: That Quarter of the Palace was all in an Uproar; the Servants ran for Ladders; the Monkey was seen by Hundreds in the Court, sitting upon the Ridge of a Building, holding me like a Baby in one of his Fore-Paws, and feeding me with the other, by cramming into my Mouth some Victuals he had squeezed out of the Bag on one side of his Chaps, and patting me when I would not eat; whereat many of the Rabble below could not forbear laughing; neither do I think they justly ought to be blamed; for without Question, the Sight was ridiculous enough to every Body but my self. Some of the People threw up Stones, hoping to drive the Monkey down; but this was strictly forbidden, or else very probably my Brains had been dashed out.

The Ladders were now applied, and mounted by several Men; which the Monkey observing, and finding himself almost encompassed; not being able to make Speed enough with his three Legs, let me drop on a Ridge-Tyle, and made his Escape. Here I sat for some time five Hundred Yards from the Ground, expecting every Moment to be blown down by the Wind, or to fall by my own Giddiness, and come tumbling over and over from the Ridge to the Eves. But an honest Lad, one of my Nurse's Footmen, climbed up, and putting me into his Breeches Pocket, brought me down safe.

I was almost choaked with the filthy Stuff the Monkey had crammed down my Throat; but, my dear little Nurse picked it out of my Mouth with a small Needle; and then I fell a vomiting, which gave me great Relief. Yet I was so weak and bruised in the Sides with the Squeezes given me by this odious Animal, that I was forced to keep my Bed a Fortnight. The King, Queen, and all the Court, sent every Day to enquire after my Health; and her Majesty made me several Visits during my Sickness. The Monkey was killed, and an Order made that no such Animal should be kept about the Palace.

When I attended the King after my Recovery, to return him Thanks for his Favours, he was pleased to railly me a good deal upon this Adventure. He asked me what my Thoughts and Speculations were while I lay in the Monkey's Paw; how I liked the Victuals he gave me, his Manner of Feeding; and whether the fresh Air on the Roof had sharpened my Stomach. He desired to know what I would have done upon such an Occasion in my own Country. I told his Majesty, that in *Europe* we had no Monkies, except such as were brought for Curiosities from other Places, and so small, that I could deal with a Dozen of them together, if they presumed to attack me. And as for that monstrous Animal with whom I was so lately engaged, (it was indeed as large as an Elephant) if my Fears had suffered me to think so far as to make Use of my Hanger (looking fiercely, and clapping my Hand upon the Hilt as I spoke) when he poked his Paw into my Chamber, perhaps I should have given him such a Wound, as would have made him glad to withdraw it with more Haste than he put it in. This I delivered in a firm Tone, like a Person who was jealous lest his Courage should be called in Question. However, my Speech produced nothing else besides a loud Laughter; which all the Respect due to his Majesty from those about him, could not make them contain. This made me reflect, how vain an Attempt it is for a Man to endeavour doing himself Honour among those who are out of all Degree of Equality or Comparison with him. And yet I have seen the Moral of my own Behaviour very frequent in *England* since my Return; where a little contemptible Varlet, without the least Title to Birth, Person, Wit, or common Sense, shall presume to look with Importance, and put himself upon a Foot* with the greatest Persons of the Kingdom.

I was every Day furnishing the Court with some ridiculous Story; and *Glumdalclitch*, although she loved me to Excess, yet was arch enough to inform the Queen, whenever I committed any Folly that she thought would be diverting to her Majesty. The Girl who had been out of Order, was carried by her Governess to take the Air about an Hour's Distance, or thirty Miles from Town. They alighted out of the Coach near a small Footpath in a Field; and *Glumdalclitch* setting down my travelling Box, I went out of it to walk. There was a Cow-dung* in the Path, and I must needs try my Activity by attempting to leap over it. I took a Run, but unfortunately jumped short, and found my self just in the Middle up to my Knees. I waded through with some Difficulty, and one of the Footmen wiped me as clean as he could with his Handkerchief; for I was filthily bemired, and my Nurse confin . . me to my Box until we returned home; where the Queen was soon informed of what had passed, and the Footmen spread it about the Court; so that all the Mirth, for some Days, was at my Expence.

CHAPTER SIX

Several Contrivances of the Author to please the King and Queen. He shews his Skill in Musick. The King enquires into the State of Europe, which the Author relates to him. The King's Observations thereon.

I USED to attend the King's Levee* once or twice a Week, and had often seen him under the Barber's Hand, which indeed was at first very terrible to behold. For, the Razor was almost twice as long as an ordinary Scythe. His Majesty, according to the Custom of the Country, was only shaved twice a Week. I once prevailed on the Barber to give me some of the Suds or Lather, out of which I picked Forty or Fifty of the strongest Stumps of Hair. I then took a Piece of fine Wood, and cut it like the Back of a Comb, making several Holes in it at equal Distance, with as small a Needle as I could get from *Grumdalclitch*. I fixed in the Stumps so artificially,* scraping and sloping them with my Knife towards the Points, that I made a very tolerable Comb; which was a seasonable Supply,* my own being so much broken in the Teeth, that it was almost useless; Neither did I know any Artist in that Country so nice and exact, as would undertake to make me another.

And this puts me in mind of an Amusement wherein I spent many of my leisure Hours. I desired the Queen's Woman to save for me the Combings of her Majesty's Hair, whereof in time I got a good Quantity; and consulting with my Friend the Cabinet-maker, who had received general Orders to do little Jobbs for me; I directed him to make two Chair-frames, no larger than those I had in my Box, and then to bore little Holes with a fine Awl round those Parts where I designed the Backs and Seats; through these Holes I wove the strongest Hairs I could pick out, just after the Manner of Cane-chairs in *England*. When they were finished, I made a Present of them to her Majesty, who kept them in her Cabinet, and used to shew them for Curiosities; as indeed they were the Wonder of every one who beheld them. The Queen would have had me sit upon one of these Chairs, but I absolutely refused to obey her; protesting I would rather dye a Thousand Deaths than place a dishonourable Part of my Body on those precious Hairs that once adorned her Majesty's Head. Of these Hairs (as I had always a Mechanical Genius*) I likewise made a neat little Purse about five Foot long, with her Majesty's Name decyphered* in Gold Letters; which I gave to *Glumdalclitch*, by the Queen's Consent. To say the Truth, it was more for Shew than Use, being not of Strength to bear the Weight of some of the larger Coins; and therefore she kept nothing in it, but some little Toys that Girls are fond of.

The King, who delighted in Musick, had frequent Consorts* at Court, to which I was sometimes carried, and set in my Box on a Table to hear them: But, the Noise was so great, that I could hardly distinguish the Tunes. I am confident, that all the Drums and Trumpets of a Royal Army, beating and sounding together just at your Ears, could not equal it. My Practice was to have my Box removed from the Places where the Performers sat, as far as I could; then to shut the Doors and Windows of it, and draw the Window-Curtains; after which I found their Musick not disagreeable.*

I had learned in my Youth to play a little upon the Spinet; *Glumdalclitch* kept one in her Chamber, and a Master attended twice a Week to teach her: I call it a Spinet, because it somewhat resembled that Instrument, and was play'd upon in the same Manner. A fancy came into my Head, that I would entertain the King and Queen with an *English* Tune upon this Instrument. But this appeared extremely difficult: For, the Spinet was near sixty Foot long, each Key being almost a Foot wide; so that, with my Arms extended, I could not reach to above five Keys; and to press them down required a good smart stroak with my Fist, which would be too great a Labour, and to no purpose. The Method I contrived was this. I prepared two round Sticks about the Bigness of common Cudgels; they were thicker at one end than the other; and I covered the thicker End with a Piece of a Mouse's Skin, that by rapping on them, I might neither Damage the Tops of the Keys, nor interrupt the Sound. Before the Spinet, a Bench was placed about four Foot below the Keys, and I was put upon the Bench. I ran sideling upon it that way and this, as fast as I could, banging the proper Keys with my two Sticks; and made a shift to play a Jigg to the great Satisfaction of both their Majesties: But, it was the most violent Exercise I ever underwent, and yet I could not strike above sixteen Keys, nor, consequently, play the Bass and Treble together, as other Artists do; which was a great Disadvantage to my Performance.

The King, who as I before observed, was a Prince of excellent Understanding, would frequently order that I should be brought in my Box, and set upon the Table in his Closet. He would then command me to bring one of my Chairs out of the Box, and sit down within three Yards Distance upon the Top of the Cabinet; which brought me almost to a Level with his Face. In this Manner I had several Conversations with him. I one Day took the Freedom to tell his Majesty, that the Contempt he discovered towards *Europe*, and the rest of the World, did not seem answerable to those excellent Qualities of Mind, that he was Master of. That, Reason did not extend itself with the Bulk of the Body: On the contrary, we observed in our Country, that the tallest Persons were usually least provided with it. That among other Animals, Bees and Ants had the Reputation of more Industry, Art, and Sagacity than many of the larger Kinds. And that, as inconsiderable as he took me to be, I hoped I might live to do his Majesty some signal Service. The King heard me with Attention; and began to conceive a much better Opinion of me than he had ever before. He desired I would give him as exact an Account of the Government of *England* as I possibly could; because, as fond as Princes commonly are of their own Customs (for so he conjectured of other Monarchs by my former Discourses) he should be glad to hear of any thing that might deserve Imitation.

Imagine with thy self, courteous Reader, how often I then wished for the Tongue of *Demosthenes* or *Cicero*, that might have enabled me to celebrate the Praise of my own dear native Country in a Style equal to its Merits and Felicity.

I began my Discourse by informing his Majesty, that our

Dominions consisted of two Islands, which composed three mighty Kingdoms* under one Sovereign, besides our Plantations* in *America.* I dwelt long upon the Fertility of our Soil, and the Temperature* of our Climate. I then spoke at large upon the Constitution of an *English* Parliament, partly made up of an illustrious Body called the House of Peers, Persons of the noblest Blood, and of the most ancient and ample Patrimonies. I described that extraordinary Care always taken of their Education* in Arts and Arms, to qualify them for being Counsellors born* to the King and Kingdom; to have a Share in the Legislature, to be Members of the highest Court of Judicature from whence there could be no Appeal;* and to be Champions always ready for the Defence of their Prince and Country by their Valour, Conduct* and Fidelity. That these were the Ornament and Bulwark of the Kingdom; worthy Followers of their most renowned Ancestors, whose Honour had been the Reward of their Virtue; from which their Posterity were never once known to degenerate.* To these were joined several holy Persons, as part of that Assembly, under the Title of Bishops; whose peculiar Business it is, to take care of Religion, and of those who instruct the People therein. These were searched and sought out through the whole Nation, by the Prince and wisest Counsellors, among such of the Priesthood, as were most deservedly distinguished by the Sanctity of their Lives, and the Depth of their Erudition; who were indeed the spiritual Fathers of the Clergy and the People.*

That, the other Part of the Parliament consisted as an Assembly called the House of Commons; who were all principal Gentlemen, *freely* picked and culled out by the People themselves, for their great Abilities, and Love of their Country, to represent the Wisdom of the whole Nation. And, these two Bodies make up the most august Assembly in *Europe*; to whom, in conjunction with the Prince, the whole Legislature is committed.

I then descended to the Courts of Justice, over which the Judges, those venerable Sages and Interpreters of the Law, presided, for determining the disputed Rights and Properties of Men, as well as for the Punishment of Vice, and Protection of Innocence. I mentioned the prudent Management of our Treasury; the Valour and Atchievements of our Forces by Sea and Land. I computed the Number of our People, by reckoning how many Millions there might be of each Religious Sect, or Political Party amongst us. I did not omit even our Sports and Pastimes, or any other Particular which I thought might redound to the Honour of my Country. And, I finished all with a brief historical Account of Affairs and Events in *England* for about an hundred Years past.

This Conversation was not ended under five Audiences, each of several Hours; and the King heard the whole with great Attention; frequently taking Notes of what I spoke, as well as Memorandums of what Questions he intended to ask me.

When I had put an End to these long Discourses, his Majesty in a sixth Audience consulting his Notes, proposed many Doubts, Queries, and Objections, upon every Article. He asked, what Methods were used to cultivate the Minds and Bodies of our young Nobility; and in what kind of Business they commonly spent the first and teachable Part of their Lives. What Course was taken to supply that Assembly, when any noble Family became extinct. What Qualifications were necessary in those who are to be created new Lords: Whether the Humour of the Prince, a Sum of Money to a Court-Lady, or a Prime Minister; or a Design of strengthening a Party opposite to the publick Interest, ever happened to be Motives in those Advancements. What Share of Knowledge these Lords had in the Laws of their Country, and how they came by it, so as to enable them to decide the Properties of their Fellow-Subjects in the last Resort. Whether they were always so free from Avarice, Partialities, or Want, that a Bribe, or some other sinister View,* could have no Place among them. Whether those holy Lords I spoke of, were constantly promoted to that Rank upon Account of their Knowledge in religious Matters, and the Sanctity of their Lives, had never been Compliers with the Times, while they were common Priests; or slavish prostitute Chaplains to some Nobleman,* whose Opinions they continued servilely to follow after they were admitted into that Assembly.

He then desired to know, what Arts were practised in elect-
ing those whom I called Commoners.* Whether, a Stranger
with a strong Purse might not influence the vulgar Voters to
chuse him before their own Landlord, or the most considerable Gentleman in the Neighbourhood. How it came to pass,*
that People were so violently bent upon getting into this
Assembly, which I allowed to be a great Trouble and Expence,
often to the Ruin of their Families, without any Salary or
Pension: Because this appeared such an exalted Strain of
Virtue and publick Spirit, that his Majesty seemed to doubt it
might possibly not be always sincere: And he desired to know,
whether such zealous Gentlemen could have any Views of
refunding themselves for the Charges and Trouble they were
at, by sacrificing the publick Good to the Designs of a weak
and vicious Prince, in Conjunction with a corrupted Ministry.
He multiplied his Questions, and sifted* me thoroughly upon
every Part of this Head;* proposing numberless Enquiries
and Objections, which I think it not prudent or convenient to
repeat.

Upon what I said in relation to our Courts of Justice, his
Majesty desired to be satisfied in several Points: And, this I was
the better able to do, having been formerly almost ruined by
a long Suit in Chancery, which was decreed for me* with
Costs. He asked, what Time was usually spent in determining
between Right and Wrong; and what Degree of Expence.
Whether Advocates and Orators had Liberty to plead in
Causes manifestly known to be unjust, vexatious, or
oppressive. Whether Party in Religion or Politicks were observed to be of any Weight in the Scale of Justice. Whether
those pleading Orators were Persons educated in the general
Knowledge of Equity; or only in provincial, national, and
other local Customs. Whether they or their Judges had any
Part in penning those Laws, which they assumed the Liberty
of interpreting and glossing upon at their Pleasure. Whether
they had ever at different Times pleaded for and against
the same Cause, and cited Precedents to prove contrary
Opinions. Whether they were a rich or a poor Corporation.
Whether they received any pecuniary Reward for pleading or
delivering their Opinions. And particularly whether they were
ever admitted as Members in the lower Senate.

He fell next upon the Management of our Treasury; and said, he thought my Memory had failed me, because I computed our Taxes at about five or six Millions a Year; and when I came to mention the Issues,* he found they sometimes amounted to more than double; for, the Notes he had taken were very particular in this Point; because he hoped, as he told me, that the Knowledge of our Conduct might be useful to him; and he could not be deceived in his Calculations. But, if what I told him were true, he was still at a Loss how a Kingdom could run out of its Estate like a private Person.* He asked me, who were our Creditors? and, where we found Money to pay them? He wondered to hear me talk of such chargeable* and extensive Wars; that, certainly we must be a quarrelsome People, or live among very bad Neighbours; and that our Generals must needs be richer than our Kings.* He asked, what Business we had out of our own Islands, unless upon the Score of Trade or Treaty, or to defend the Coasts with our Fleet. Above all, he was amazed to hear me talk of a mercenary standing Army* in the Midst of Peace, and among a free People. He said, if we were governed by our own Consent in the Persons of our Representatives, he could not imagine of whom we were afraid, or against whom we were to fight; and would hear my Opinion, whether a private Man's House might not better be defended by himself, his Children, and Family; than by half a Dozen Rascals picked up at a Venture in the Streets, for small Wages, who might get an Hundred Times more by cutting their Throats.

He laughed at my odd Kind of Arithmetick* (as he was pleased to call it) in reckoning the Numbers of our People by a Computation drawn from the several Sects among us in Religion and Politicks. He said, he knew no Reason,* why those who entertain Opinions prejudicial to the Publick, should be obliged to change, or should not be obliged to conceal them. And, as it was Tyranny in any Government to require the first, so it was Weakness not to enforce the second: For, a Man may be allowed to keep Poisons in his Closet, but not to vend them about as Cordials.

He observed, that among the Diversions of our Nobility and Gentry, I had mentioned Gaming.* He desired to know at what Age this Entertainment was usually taken up, and when it was laid down. How much of their Time it employed; whether it ever went so high as to affect their Fortunes. Whether mean vicious People, by their Dexterity in that Art, might not arrive at great Riches, and sometimes keep our very Nobles in Dependance, as well as habituate them to vile Companions; wholly take them from the Improvement of their Minds, and force them by the Losses they received, to learn and practice that infamous Dexterity upon others.

He was perfectly astonished with the historical Account I gave him of our Affairs during the last Century; protesting it was only an Heap of Conspiracies, Rebellions, Murders, Massacres, Revolutions, Banishments; the very worst Effects that Avarice, Faction, Hypocrisy, Perfidiousness, Cruelty, Rage, Madness, Hatred, Envy, Lust, Malice, and Ambition could produce.

His Majesty in another Audience, was at the Pains to recapitulate the Sum of all I had spoken; compared the Questions he made, with the Answers I had given; then taking me into his Hands, and stroaking me gently, delivered himself in these Words, which I shall never forget, nor the Manner he spoke them in. My little Friend *Grildrig*, you have made a most admirable Panegyrick upon your Country. You have clearly proved that Ignorance, Idleness, and Vice are the proper Ingredients for qualifying a Legislator. That Laws are best explained, interpreted, and applied by those whose Interest and Abilities lie in perverting, confounding, and eluding them. I observe among you some Lines of an Institution,* which in its Original might have been tolerable; but these half erased, and the rest wholly blurred and blotted by Corruptions. It doth not appear from all you have said, how any one Perfection is required towards the Procurement of any one Station among you; much less that Men are ennobled on Account of their Virtue, that Priests are advanced for their Piety or Learning, Soldiers for their Conduct or Valour, Judges for their Integrity, Senators for the Love of their Country, or Counsellors for their Wisdom. As for yourself (continued the King) who have spent the greatest Part of your Life in travelling; I am well disposed to hope you may hitherto have escaped many Vices of your Country. But, by what I have gathered from your own Relation, and the Answers I have with much Pains wringed and extorted from you; I cannot but conclude the Bulk of your Natives, to be the most pernicious Race of little odious Vermin that Nature ever suffered to crawl upon the Surface of the Earth.

CHAPTER SEVEN

The Author's Love of his Country. He makes a Proposal of much Advantage to the King; which is rejected. The King's great Ignorance in Politicks. The Learning of that Country very imperfect and confined. Their Laws, and military Affairs, and Parties in the State.

NOTHING BUT an extreme Love of Truth could have hindered me from concealing this Part of my Story. It was in vain to discover my Resentments, which were always turned into Ridicule: And I was forced to rest with Patience, while my noble and most beloved Country was so injuriously treated. I am heartily sorry as any of my Readers can possibly be, that such an Occasion was given: But this Prince happened to be so curious and inquisitive upon every Particular, that it could not consist* either with Gratitude or good Manners to refuse giving him what Satisfaction I was able. Yet thus much I may be allowed to say in my own Vindication; that I artfully eluded many of his Questions; and gave to every Point a more favourable turn by many Degrees than the strictness of Truth would allow. For, I have always born that laudable Partiality to my own Country, which *Dionysius Halicarnassensis** with so much Justice recommends to an Historian. I would hide the Frailties and Deformities of my Political Mother, and place her Virtues and Beauties in the most advantageous Light. This was my sincere Endeavour in those many Discourses I had with that Monarch, although it unfortunately failed of Success.

But, great Allowances should be given to a King who lives wholly secluded from the rest of the World, and must therefore be altogether unacquainted with the Manners and Customs that most prevail in other Nations: The want of which Knowledge will ever produce many *Prejudices*, and a certain *Narrowness of Thinking*; from which we and the politer Countries of *Europe* are wholly exempted. And it would be hard indeed, if so remote a Prince's Notions of Virtue and Vice were to be offered as a Standard for all Mankind.

To confirm what I have now said, and further to shew the miserable Effects of a *confined Education*; I shall here insert a Passage which will hardly obtain Belief. In hopes to ingratiate my self farther into his Majesty's Favour, I told him of an Invention discovered between three and four hundred Years ago,* to make a certain Powder; into an heap of which the smallest Spark of Fire falling, would kindle the whole in a Moment, although it were as big as a Mountain; and make it all fly up in the Air together, with a Noise and Agitation greater than Thunder. That, a proper Quantity of this Powder rammed into an hollow Tube of Brass or Iron, according to its Bigness, would drive a Ball of Iron or Lead with such Violence and Speed, as nothing was able to sustain its Force. That, the largest Balls thus discharged, would not only Destroy whole Ranks of an Army at once; but batter the strongest Walls to the Ground; sink down Ships with a thousand Men in each, to the Bottom of the Sea; and when linked together by a Chain,* would cut through Masts and Rigging; divide Hundreds of Bodies in the Middle, and lay all Waste before them. That we often put this Powder into large hollow Balls of Iron, and discharged them by an Engine into some City we were besieging; which would rip up the Pavement, tear the Houses to Pieces, burst and throw Splinters on every Side, dashing out the Brains of all who came near. That I knew the Ingredients very well, which were Cheap, and common; I understood the Manner of compounding them, and could direct his Workmen how to make those Tubes of a Size proportionable to all other Things in his Majesty's Kingdom; and the largest need not be above two hundred Foot long; twenty or thirty of which Tubes, charged with the proper Quantity of Powder and Balls, would batter down the Walls of the strongest Town in his Dominions in a few Hours; or destroy the whole Metropolis, if ever it should pretend to dispute his absolute Commands. This I humbly offered to his Majesty, as a small Tribute of Acknowledgment in return of so many Marks that I had received of his Royal Favour and Protection.

The King was struck with Horror at the Description I had given of those terrible Engines, and the Proposal I had made. He was amazed how so impotent and groveling an Insect as I (these were his Expressions) could entertain such inhuman Ideas, and in so familiar a Manner as to appear wholly unmoved at all the Scenes of Blood and Desolation, which I had painted as the common Effect of those destructive Machines; whereof he said, some evil Genius, Enemy to Mankind, must have been the first Contriver. As for himself, he protested, that although few Things delighted him so much as new Discoveries in Art or in Nature; yet he would rather lose Half his Kingdom than be privy to such a Secret; which he commanded me, as I valued my Life, never to mention any more.

A strange Effect of *narrow Principles* and *short Views!* that a Prince possessed of every Quality which procures Veneration, Love and Esteem, of strong Parts, great Wisdom and profound Learning; endued with admirable Talents for Government, and almost adored by his Subjects; should from a *nice unnecessary Scruple,* whereof in *Europe* we can have no Conception, let slip an Opportunity put into his Hands, that would have made him absolute Master of the Lives, the Liberties, and the Fortunes of his People. Neither do I say this with the least Intention to detract from the many Virtues of that excellent King; whose Character I am sensible will on this Account be very much lessened in the Opinion of an *English* Reader: But, I take this Defect among them to have risen from their Ignorance; by not having hitherto reduced *Politicks* into a *Science,** as the more acute Wits of *Europe* have done. For, I remember very well, in a Discourse one Day with the King; when I happened to say, there were several thousand Books among us written upon the *Art of Government*; it gave him (directly contrary to my Intention) a very mean Opinion of our Understandings. He professed both to abominate and despise all *Mystery, Refinement,* and *Intrigue,* either in a Prince or a Minister. He could not tell what I meant by *Secrets of State,* where an Enemy or some rival Nation were not in the Case. He confined the Knowledge of governing within very *narrow Bounds*; to common Sense and Reason, to Justice and Lenity, to the Speedy Determination of Civil and criminal Causes; with some other obvious Topicks* which are not worth considering. And, he gave it for his Opinion;* that whoever could make two Ears of Corn, or two Blades of Grass to grow upon a Spot of Ground where only one grew before; would deserve better of Mankind, and do more essential Service to his Country, than the whole Race of Politicians put together.

The Learning of this People is very defective; consisting only in Morality, History, Poetry and Mathematicks; wherein they must be allowed to excel. But, the last of these is wholly applied to what may be useful in Life;* to the Improvement of Agriculture and all mechanical Arts; so that among us it would be little esteemed. And as to Ideas,* Entities,* Abstractions and Transcendentals,* I could never drive the least Conception into their Heads.*

No Law* of that Country must exceed in Words the Number of Letters in their Alphabet; which consists only of two and twenty. But indeed, few of them extend even to that Length. They are expressed in the most plain and simple Terms, wherein those People are not Mercurial* enough to discover above one Interpretation. And, to write a Comment upon any Law, is a capital Crime. As to the Decision of civil Causes, or Proceedings against Criminals, their Precedents are so few, that they have little Reason to boast of any extraordinary Skill in either.

They have had the Art of Printing,* as well as the *Chinese*, Time out of Mind. But their Libraries are not very large; for that of the King's, which is reckoned the largest, doth not amount to above a thousand Volumes; placed in a Gallery of twelve hundred Foot long; from whence I had Liberty to borrow what Books I pleased. The Queen's Joyner had contrived in one of *Glumdalclitch*'s Rooms a Kind of wooden Machine five and twenty Foot high, formed like a standing Ladder; the Steps were each fifty Foot long: It was indeed a moveable Pair of Stairs, the lowest End placed at ten Foot Distance from the Wall of the Chamber. The Book I had a Mind to read was put up leaning against the Wall. I first mounted to the upper Step of the Ladder, and turning my Face towards the Book, began at the Top of the Page, and so walking to the Right and Left about eight or ten Paces according to the Length of the Lines, till I had gotten a little below the Level of mine Eyes; and then descending gradually till I came to the Bottom: After which I mounted again, and began the other Page in the same Manner, and so turned over the Leaf, which I could easily do with both my Hands, for it was as thick and stiff as a Paste-board, and in the largest Folio's not above eighteen or twenty Foot long.

Their Stile* is clear, masculine, and smooth, but not Florid; for they avoid nothing more than multiplying unnecessary Words, or using various Expressions. I have perused many of their Books, especially those in History and Morality. Among the latter I was much diverted with a little old Treatise, which always lay in *Glumdalclitch*'s Bedchamber, and belonged to her Governess, a grave elderly Gentlewoman, who dealt in Writings of Morality and Devotion. The Book treats of the Weakness of Human kind; and is in little Esteem except among Women and the Vulgar. However, I was curious to see what an Author of that Country could say upon such a Subject. This Writer went through all the usual Topicks of *European* Moralists; shewing how diminutive, contemptible, and helpless an Animal was Man in his own Nature; how unable to defend himself from the Inclemencies of the Air, or the Fury of wild Beasts: How much he was excelled by one Creature in Strength, by another in Speed, by a third in Foresight, by a fourth in Industry. He added, that Nature was degenerated* in these latter declining Ages of the World, and could now produce only small abortive Births in Comparison of those in ancient Times. He said, it was very reasonable to think, not only that the Species of Men were originally much larger, but also that there must have been Giants in former Ages; which, as it is asserted by History and Tradition, so it hath been confirmed by huge Bones and Sculls casually dug up in several Parts of the Kingdom, far exceeding the common dwindled Race of Man in our Days. He argued, that the very Laws of Nature absolutely required we should have been made in the Beginning, of a Size more large and robust, not so liable to Destruction from every little Accident of a Tile falling* from an House, or a Stone cast from the Hand of a Boy, or of being drowned in a little Brook. From this Way of Reasoning the Author drew several moral Applications useful in the Conduct of Life, but needless here to repeat. For my own Part, I could not avoid reflecting, how universally this Talent was spread of drawing Lectures in Morality, or indeed rather Matter of Discontent and repining, from the Quarrels we raise with Nature. And, I believe upon a strict Enquiry, those Quarrels might be shewn as ill-grounded among us, as they are among that People.

As to their military Affairs; they boast that the King's Army consists of an hundred and seventy six thousand Foot, and thirty two thousand Horse: If that may be called an Army which is made up of Tradesmen* in the several Cities, and Farmers in the Country, whose Commanders are only the Nobility and Gentry, without Pay or Reward. They are indeed perfect enough in their Exercises; and under very good Discipline, wherein I saw no great merit: For, how should it be otherwise, where every Farmer is under the Command of his own Landlord, and every Citizen under that of the principal Men in his own City, chosen after the Manner of *Venice** by *Ballot*?

I have often seen the Militia of *Lorbrulgrud* drawn out to Exercise in a great Field near the City, of twenty Miles Square. They were in all not above twenty five thousand Foot, and six thousand Horse; but it was impossible for me to compute their Number, considering the Space of Ground they took up. A *Cavalier* mounted on a large Steed might be about Ninety Foot high. I have seen this whole Body of Horse upon the Word of Command draw their Swords at once, and brandish them in the Air. Imagination can Figure nothing so Grand, so surprising and so astonishing. It looked as if ten thousand Flashes of Lightning were darting at the same time from every Quarter of the Sky.

I was curious to know how this Prince, to whose Dominions there is no Access from any other Country, came to think of Armies, or to teach his People the Practice of military Discipline. But I was soon informed, both by Conversation, and Reading their Histories. For, in the Course of many Ages they have been troubled with the same Disease,* to which the whole Race of Mankind is Subject: the Nobility often contending for Power, the People for Liberty, and the King for absolute Dominion. All which, however happily tempered by the

Laws of that Kingdom, have been sometimes violated by each of the three Parties; and have more than once occasioned Civil Wars, the last whereof was happily put an End to by this Prince's Grandfather in a general Composition;* and the Militia then settled* with common Consent hath been ever since kept in the strictest Duty.

CHAPTER EIGHT

The King and Queen make a Progress to the Frontiers. The Author attends them. The Manner in which he leaves the Country very particularly related. He returns to England.

I HAD always a strong Impulse* that I should some time recover my Liberty, although it were impossible to conjecture by what Means, or to form any Project with the least Hope of succeeding. The Ship in which I sailed was the first ever known to be driven within Sight of that Coast; and the King had given strict Orders, that if at any Time another appeared, it should be taken ashore, and with all its Crew and Passengers brought in a Tumbril to *Lorbrulgrud.* He was strongly bent to get me a Woman of my own Size,* by whom I might propagate the Breed: But I think I should rather have died than undergone the Disgrace of leaving a Posterity to be kept in Cages like tame Canary Birds,* and perhaps in time sold about the Kingdom to Persons of Quality for Curiosities. I was indeed treated with much Kindness; I was the Favourite of a great King and Queen, and the Delight of the whole Court; but it was upon such a Foot as ill became the Dignity of human Kind. I could never forget those domestick Pledges I had left behind me. I wanted to be among People with whom I could converse upon even* Terms; and walk about the Streets and Fields without Fear of being trod to Death like a Frog or young Puppy. But, my Deliverance came sooner than I expected, and in a Manner not very common: The whole Story and Circumstances of which I shall faithfully relate.

I had now been two Years in this Country; and, about the Beginning of the third, *Glumdalclitch* and I attended the King and Queen in Progress to the South Coast of the Kingdom. I was carried as usual in my Travelling-Box, which, as I have already described, was a very convenient Closet of twelve Foot wide. I had ordered a Hammock to be fixed by silken Ropes from the four Corners at the Top; to break the Jolts, when a

Servant carried me before him on Horseback, as I sometimes desired; and would often sleep in my Hammock while we were upon the Road. On the Roof of my Closet, set not directly over the Middle of the Hammock, I ordered the Joyner to cut out a Hole of a Foot square to give me Air in hot Weather as I slept; which Hole I shut at pleasure with a Board that drew backwards and forwards through a Groove.

When we came to our Journey's End, the King thought proper to pass a few Days at a Palace he hath near *Flanflasnic*, a City within eighteen *English* Miles of the Sea-side. *Glumdalclitch* and I were much fatigued: I had gotten a small Cold; but the poor Girl was so ill as to be confined to her Chamber. I longed to see the Ocean, which must be the only scene of my Escape, if ever it should happen. I pretended to be worse than I really was; and desired leave to take the fresh Air of the Sea, with a Page whom I was very fond of, and who had sometimes been trusted with me. I shall never forget with what Unwillingness *Glumdalclitch* consented; nor the strict Charge she gave the Page to be careful of me; bursting at the same time into a Flood of Tears, as if she had some Foreboding of what was to happen. The Boy took me out in my Box about Half an Hour's Walk from the Palace, towards the Rocks on the Sea-shore. I ordered him to set me down; and lifting up one of my Sashes, cast many a wistful melancholy Look towards the Sea.* I found myself not very well; and told the Page that I had a Mind to take a Nap in my Hammock, which I hoped would do me good. I got in, and the Boy shut the Window close down, to keep out the Cold. I soon fell asleep: And all I can conjecture is, that while I slept, the Page thinking no Danger could happen, went among the Rocks to look for Birds Eggs; having before observed him from my Window searching about, and picking up one or two in the Clefts. Be that as it will, I found my self suddenly awaked with a violent Pull upon the Ring which was fastned at the Top of my Box, for the Conveniency of Carriage. I felt the Box raised very high in the Air, and then born forward with prodigious Speed. The first Jolt had like to have shaken me out of my Hammock; but afterwards the Motion was easy enough. I called out several times as loud as I could raise my Voice, but all to no purpose. I looked towards my Windows, and could see nothing but the Clouds and Sky. I heard a Noise just over my Head like the clapping of Wings; and then began to perceive the woful Condition I was in; that some Eagle* had got the Ring of my Box in his Beak, with an Intent to let it fall on a Rock, like a Tortoise* in a Shell, and then pick out my Body and devour it. For the Sagacity and Smell of this Bird enable him to discover his Quarry at a great Distance, although better concealed than I could be within a two Inch Board.

In a little time I observed the Noise and flutter of Wings to encrease very fast; and my Box was tossed up and down like a Sign-post* in a windy Day. I heard several Bangs or Buffets, as I thought, given to the Eagle (for such I am certain it must have been that held the Ring of my Box in his Beak) and then all on a sudden felt my self falling perpendicularly down for above a Minute; but with such incredible Swiftness that I almost lost my Breath. My Fall was stopped by a terrible Squash,* that sounded louder to mine Ears than the Cataract of *Niagara*; after which I was quite in the Dark for another Minute, and then my Box began to rise so high that I could see Light from the Tops of my Windows. I now perceived that I was fallen into the Sea.* My Box, by the Weight of my Body, the Goods that were in, and the broad Plates of Iron fixed for Strength at the four Corners of the Top and Bottom, floated about five Foot deep in Water. I did then, and do now suppose, that the Eagle which flew away with my Box was pursued by two or three others, and forced to let me drop while he was defending himself against the Rest, who hoped to share in the Prey. The Plates of Iron fastned at the Bottom of the Box, (for those were the strongest) preserved the Balance while it fell; and hindred it from being broken on the Surface of the Water. Every Joint of it was well grooved, and the Door did not move on Hinges, but up and down like a Sash; which kept my Closet so tight that very little Water came in. I got with much Difficulty out of my Hammock, having first ventured to draw back the Slip board on the Roof already mentioned, contrived on purpose to let in Air; for want of which I found my self almost stifled.

How often did I then wish my self with my dear *Glumdalclitch*, from whom one single Hour had so far divided me! And I may say with Truth, that in the midst of my own Misfortune, I could not forbear lamenting my poor Nurse, the Grief she would suffer for my Loss, the Displeasure of the Queen, and the Ruin of her Fortune. Perhaps many Travellers have not been under greater Difficulties and Distress than I was at this Juncture; expecting every Moment to see my Box dashed in Pieces, or at least overset by the first violent Blast, or a rising Wave. A Breach in one single Pane of Glass would have been immediate Death: Nor could any thing have preserved the Windows but the strong Lattice Wires placed on the outside against Accidents in Travelling. I saw the Water ooze in at several Crannies, although the Leaks were not considerable; and I endeavoured to stop them as well as I could. I was not able to lift up the Roof of my Closet, which otherwise I certainly should have done, and sat on the Top of it, where I might at least preserve myself from being shut up, as I may call it, in the Hold. Or, if I escaped these Dangers for a Day or two, what could I expect but a miserable Death of Cold and Hunger! I was four Hours under these Circumstances, expecting and indeed wishing every Moment to be my last.

I have already told the Reader, that there were two strong Staples fixed upon the Side of my Box which had no Window, and into which the Servant, who used to carry me on Horseback, would put a Leathern Belt, and buckle it about his Waist. Being in this disconsolate State, I heard, or at least thought I heard some kind of grating Noise on that Side of my Box where the Staples were fixed; and soon after I began to fancy that the Box was pulled, or towed along in the Sea; for I now and then felt a sort of tugging, which made the Waves rise near the Tops of my Windows, leaving me almost in the Dark. This gave me some faint Hopes of Relief, although I were not able to imagine how it could be brought about. I ventured to unscrew one of my Chairs, which were always fastned to the Floor; and having made a hard shift to screw it down again directly under the Slipping-board that I had lately opened; I mounted on the Chair, and putting my Mouth as near as I could to the Hole, I called for Help in a loud Voice, and in all the Languages I understood. I then fastned my Handkerchief to a Stick I usually carried, and thrusting it up the Hole, waved it several times in the Air; that if any Boat or Ship were near, the Seamen might conjecture some unhappy Mortal to be shut up in the Box.

I found no Effect from all I could do, but plainly perceived my Closet to be moved along; and in the Space of an Hour, or better,* that Side of the Box where the Staples were, and had no Window, struck against something that was hard. I apprehended it to be a Rock, and found my self tossed more than ever. I plainly heard a Noise upon the Cover of my Closet, like that of a Cable, and the grating of it as it passed through the Ring. I then found my self hoisted up by Degrees at least three Foot higher than I was before. Whereupon, I again thrust up my Stick and Handkerchief, calling for Help till I was almost hoarse. In return to which, I heard a great Shout repeated three times, giving me such Transports of Joy as are not to be conceived but by those who feel them. I now heard a trampling over my Head; and somebody calling through the Hole with a loud Voice in the *English* Tongue: *If there be any Body below, let them speak.* I answered, I was an *Englishman*, drawn by ill Fortune into the greatest Calamity that ever any Creature underwent; and begged, by all that was moving,* to be delivered out of the Dungeon I was in. The Voice replied, I was safe, for my Box was fastned to their Ship; and the Carpenter should immediately come, and saw an Hole in the Cover, large enough to pull me out. I answered, that was needless, and would take up too much Time; for there was no more to be done, but let one of the Crew put his Finger into the Ring, and take the Box out of the Sea into the Ship, and so into the Captain's Cabbin. Some of them upon hearing me talk so wildly, thought I was mad; others laughed; for indeed it never came into my Head, that I was now got among People of my own Stature and Strength. The Carpenter came, and in a few Minutes sawed a Passage about four Foot square; then let down a small Ladder, upon which I mounted, and from thence was taken into the Ship in a very weak Condition.

The Sailors were all in Amazement, and asked me a thousand Questions, which I had no Inclination to answer. I was equally confounded at the Sight of so many Pigmies; for such

I took them to be, after having so long accustomed mine Eyes to the monstrous Objects I had left. But the Captain, Mr *Thomas Wilcocks*, an honest worthy *Shropshire* Man, observing I was ready to faint, took me into his Cabbin, gave me a Cordial to comfort me, and made me *turn in* upon his own Bed; advising me to take a little Rest, of which I had great need. Before I went to sleep I gave him to understand, that I had some valuable Furniture in my Box too good to be lost; a fine Hammock, an handsome Field-Bed, two Chairs, a Table and a Cabinet: That my Closet was hung on all Sides, or rather quilted with Silk and Cotton: That if he would let one of the Crew bring my Closet into his Cabbin,* I would open it before him, and shew him my Goods. The Captain hearing me utter these Absurdities, concluded I was raving: However, (I suppose to pacify me) he promised to give Order as I desired; and going upon Deck, sent some of his Men down into my Closet, from whence (as I afterwards found) they drew up all my Goods, and stripped off the Quilting; but the Chairs, Cabinet and Bed-sted being screwed to the Floor, were much damaged by the Ignorance of the Seamen, who tore them up by Force. Then they knocked off some of the Boards for the Use of the Ship; and when they had got all they had a Mind for, let the Hulk drop into the Sea, which by Reason of many Breaches made in the Bottom and Sides, sunk *to rights.** And indeed I was glad not to have been a Spectator of the Havock they made; because I am confident it would have sensibly touched me by bringing former Passages* into my Mind, which I had rather forget.

I slept some Hours, but perpetually disturbed with Dreams of the Place I had left, and the Dangers I had escaped. However, upon waking I found my self much recovered. It was now about eight a Clock at Night, and the Captain ordered Supper immediately, thinking I had already fasted too long. He entertained me with great Kindness, observing me not to look wildly, or talk inconsistently; and when we were left alone, desired I would give him a Relation of my Travels, and by what Accident I came to be set adrift in that monstrous wooden Chest. He said, that about twelve a Clock at Noon, as he was looking through his Glass, he spied it at a Distance, and thought it was a Sail, which he had a Mind to make;* being not much out of his Course, in hopes of buying some Biscuit, his own beginning to fall short. That, upon coming nearer, and finding his Error, he sent out his Long-boat to discover what I was; that his Men came back in a Fright, swearing they had seen a swimming House. That he laughed at their Folly, and went himself in the Boat, ordering his Men to take a strong Cable along with them. That the Weather being calm, he rowed round me several times, observed my Windows, and the Wire Lattices that defended them. That he discovered two Staples upon one Side, which was all of Boards, without any Passage for Light. He then commanded his Men to row up to that Side; and fastning a Cable to one of the Staples, ordered his Men to tow my Chest (as he called it) towards the Ship. When it was there, he gave Directions to fasten another Cable to the Ring fixed in the Cover, and to raise up my Chest with Pullies, which all the Sailors were not able to do above two or three Foot. He said, they saw my Stick and Handkerchief thrust out of the Hole, and concluded, that some unhappy Man must be shut up in the Cavity. I asked whether he or the Crew had seen any prodigious Birds in the Air about the Time he first discovered me: To which he answered, that discoursing* this Matter with the Sailors while I was asleep, one of them said he had *observed* three Eagles flying towards the North: but remarked nothing of of their being larger than the usual Size; which I suppose must be imputed to the great Height they were at: And he could not guess the Reason of my Question. I then asked the Captain how far he reckoned we might be from Land; he said, by the best Computation he could make, we were at least an hundred Leagues. I assured him, that he must be mistaken by almost half; for I had not left the Country from whence I came, above two Hours before I dropt into the Sea. Whereupon he began again to think that my Brain was disturbed, of which he gave me a Hint, and advised me to go to Bed in a Cabin he had provided. I assured him I was well refreshed with his good Entertainment and Company, and as much in my Senses as ever I was in my life. He then grew serious, and desired to ask me freely whether I were not troubled in Mind by the Consciousness of some enormous Crime, for which I was punished at the Command of some Prince, by exposing me in that Chest; as great Criminals in other Countries have been forced to Sea in a leaky Vessel without Provisions: For, although he should be sorry to have taken so ill a Man into his Ship, yet he would engage his Word to set me safe on Shore in the first Port where we arrived. He added, that his Suspicions were much increased by some very absurd Speeches I had delivered at first to the Sailors, and afterwards to himself, in relation to my Closet or Chest, as well as by my odd Looks and Behaviour while I was at Supper.

I begged his Patience to hear me tell my Story; which I faithfully did from the last Time I left *England*, to the Moment he first discovered me. And, as Truth always forceth its Way into rational Minds; so, this honest worthy Gentleman, who had some Tincture of Learning, and very good Sense, was immediately convinced of my Candor and Veracity. But, further to confirm all I had said, I entreated him to give Order that my Cabinet should be brought, of which I kept the Key in my Pocket, (for he had already informed me of how the Seamen disposed of my Closet) I opened it in his Presence, and shewed him the small Collection of Rarities I made in the Country from which I had been so strangely delivered. There was the Comb I had contrived out of the Stumps of the King's Beard; and another of the same Materials, but fixed into a paring of her Majesty's Thumb-nail, which served for the Back. There was a Collection of Needles and Pins from a Foot to half a Yard long. Four Wasp-Stings, like Joyners Tacks: Some Combings of the Queen's Hair: a Gold Ring which one Day she made me a Present of in a most obliging Manner, taking it from her little Finger, and throwing it over my Head like a Collar. I desired the Captain would please to accept this Ring in Return of his Civilities; which he absolutely refused. I shewed him a Corn that I had cut off with my own Hand from a Maid of Honour's Toe; it was about the Bigness of a *Kentish* Pippin, and grown so hard, that when I returned to *England*, I got it hollowed into a Cup and set in Silver. Lastly, I desired him to see the Breeches I had then on, which were made of a Mouse's Skin.

I could force nothing on him but a Footman's Tooth, which I observed him to examine with great Curiosity, and found he had a Fancy for it. He received it with abundance of Thanks, more than such a Trifle could deserve. It was drawn by an unskilful Surgeon in a Mistake from one of *Glumdalclitch*'s Men, who was afficted with the Tooth-ach; but it was as sound as any in his Head. I got it cleaned, and put it into my Cabinet. It was about a Foot long, and four Inches in Diameter.

The Captain was well satisfied with this plain Relation I had given him; and said, he hoped when we returned to *England*, I would oblige the World by putting it in Paper, and making it publick. My Answer was, that I thought we were already over-stocked with Books of Travels: That nothing could now pass which was not extraordinary; wherein I doubted, some Authors less consulted Truth than their own Vanity or Interest, or the Diversion of ignorant Readers. That my Story would contain little besides common Events, without those ornamental Descriptions of strange Plants, Trees, Birds, and other Animals; or the barbarous Customs and Idolatry of savage People, with which most Writers abound. However, I thanked him for his good Opinion, and promised to take the Matter into my Thoughts.

He said, he wondered at one Thing very much; which was, to hear me speak so loud; asking me whether the King or Queen of that Country were thick of Hearing. I told him it was what I had been used to for above two Years past; and that I admired as much at the Voices of him and his Men, who seemed to me only to whisper, and yet I could hear them well enough. But, when I spoke in that Country, it was like a Man talking in the Street to another looking out from the Top of a Steeple, unless when I was placed on a Table, or held in any Person's Hand. I told him, I had likewise observed another Thing; that when I first got into the Ship, and the Sailors stood all about me, I thought they were the most little contemptible Creatures I had ever beheld. For, indeed, while I was in that Prince's Country, I could never endure to look in a Glass after mine Eyes had been accustomed to such prodigious Objects; because the Comparison gave me so despicable a Conceit of my self. The Captain said, that while we were at Supper, he observed me to look at every thing with a Sort of Wonder; and that I often seemed hardly able to contain my Laughter; which he knew not well how to take, but imputed it to some Disorder in my Brain. I answered, it was very true; and I wondered how I could forbear, when I saw his Dishes of the Size of a Silver Three-pence, a Leg of Pork hardly a Mouthful, a Cup not so big as a Nutshell: And so I went on, describing the rest of his Household-stuff and Provisions after the same Manner. For although the Queen had ordered a little Equipage of all Things necessary for me while I was in her Service; yet my Ideas were wholly taken up with what I saw on every Side of me; and I winked at my own Littleness, as People do at their own Faults. The Captain understood my Raillery very well, and merrily replied with the old *English* Proverb, that he doubted, mine Eyes were bigger than my Belly; for he did not observe my Stomach so good, although I had fasted all Day: And continuing in his Mirth, protested he would have gladly given an Hundred Pounds to have seen my Closet in the Eagle's Bill, and afterwards in its Fall from so great an Height into the Sea; which would certainly have been a most astonishing Object, worthy to have the Description of it transmitted to future Ages: And the Comparison of *Phaeton** was so obvious, that he could not forbear applying it, although I did not much admire the Conceit.

The Captain having been at *Tonquin,** was in his Return to *England* driven North Eastward* to the Latitude of 44 Degrees, and of Longitude 143. But meeting a Trade Wind two Days after I came on board him, we sailed Southward a long Time, and coasting *New-Holland,* kept our Course West-south-west, and then South-south-west till we doubled the *Cape of Good-hope.* Our Voyage was very prosperous, but I shall not trouble the Reader with a Journal of it. The Captain celled in at one or two Ports, and sent in his Long-boat for Provisions and fresh Water; but I never went out of the Ship till we came into the *Downs,* which was on the 3d Day of *June* 1706, about nine Months after my Escape. I offered to leave my Goods in Security for Payment of my Freight; but the Captain protested he would not receive one Farthing. We took kind Leave of each other; and I made him promise he would come to see me at my House in *Redriff.* I hired a Horse and Guide for five Shillings, which I borrowed of the Captain.

As I was on the Road; observing the Littleness of the Houses, the Trees, the Cattle and the People, I began to think my self in *Lilliput.* I was afraid of trampling on every Traveller I met; and often called aloud to have them stand out of the Way; so that I had like to have gotten one or two broken Heads for my Impertinence.

When I came to my own House, for which I was forced to enquire, one of the Servants opening the Door, I bent down to go in (like a Goose under a Gate) for fear of striking my Head. My Wife ran out to embrace me, but I stooped lower than her Knees, thinking she could otherwise never be able to reach my Mouth. My Daughter kneeled to ask my Blessing, but I could not see her till she arose; having been so long used to stand with my Head and Eyes erect to above Sixty Foot; and then I went to take her up with one Hand, by the Waist. I looked down upon the Servants, and one of two Friends who were in the House, as if they had been Pigmies, and I a Giant. I told my wife, she had been too thrifty; for I found she had starved herself and her Daughter to nothing. In short, I behaved my self so unaccountably, that they were all of the Captain's Opinion when he first saw me; and concluded I had lost my Wits. This I mention as an Instance of the great Power of Habit and Prejudice.

In a little Time I and my Family and Friends came to a right Understanding: But my Wife protested I should never go to Sea any more; although my evil Destiny so ordered, that she had not Power to hinder me; as the Reader may know hereafter. In the mean Time, I here conclude the second Part of my unfortunate Voyages.

The End of the Second Part.

he would not receive one Farthing. We took kind Leave of each other, and I made him promise he would come to see me at my House in Redriff, I hired a Horse and Guide for five Shillings, which I borrowed of the Captain.

As I was on the Road, observing the Littleness of the Houses, the Trees, the Cattle and the People, I began to think my self in Lilliput. I was afraid of trampling on every Traveller I met, and often called aloud to have them stand out of the way; so that I had like to have gotten one or two broken Heads for my Impertinence.

When I came to my own House, for which I was forced to enquire, one of the Servants opening the Door, I bent down to go in (like a Goose under a Gate) for fear of striking my Head. My Wife ran out to embrace me, but I stooped lower than her Knees, thinking she could otherwise never be able to reach my Mouth. My Daughter kneeled to ask my Blessing, but I could not see her till she arose, having been so long used to stand with my Head and Eyes erect to above Sixty Foot; and then I went to take her up with one Hand by the Waist. I looked down upon the Servants and one or two Friends who were in the House, as if they had been Pigmies, and I a Giant. I told my Wife, she had been too thrifty, for I found she had starved herself and her Daughter to nothing. In short, I behaved my self so unaccountably, that they were all of the Captain's opinion when he first saw me, and concluded I had lost my Wits. This I mention as an Instance of the great Power of Habit and Prejudice.

In a little Time I and my Family and Friends came to a right Understanding; but my Wife protested I should never go to Sea any more; although my evil Destiny so ordered, that she had not Power to hinder me, as the Reader may know hereafter. In the mean Time I here conclude the second Part of my unfortunate Voyages.

The End of the Second Part.

PART THREE

A Voyage to Laputa, Balnibarbi, Luggnagg, Glubbdubdrib, and Japan*

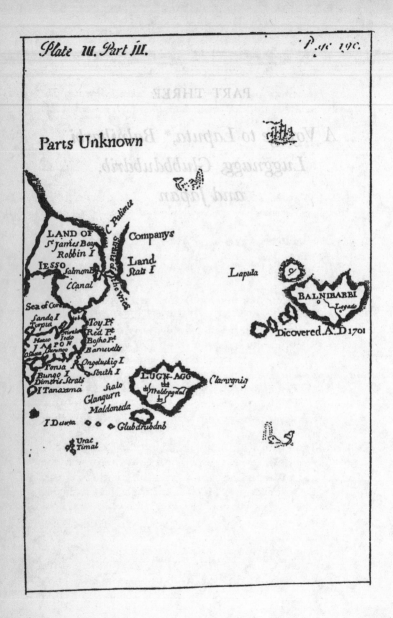

Plate III. Part III.

Page 196.

Parts Unknown

LAND OF
St James Bay
Robbin I
IESSO
Salmon I
I Canal

Sea of Corea

C Patince
Straits the Vries

Companys
Land
Stats I

Laputa

BALNIBARBI
Lagado
Dicovered A.D 1701

Sanda I
Turpu
Meaco
Yedo
Inaba
Ousaca Chrungo
Tonsa
Bungo I
Dimeti Straits
I Tanaxuma

Toy P.t
Red P.t
Bosho P.t
Barnevelts
Ongoluskig I
South I
Sialo
Glangurn
Maldoneda
I Deserta
Glubdubdub

LUGN-AGG
Waldegrad
Clorurgnig

Urat
Timal

CHAPTER ONE

The Author sets out on his Third Voyage. Is taken by Pyrates. The Malice of a Dutchman. *His Arrival at an Island. He is received into* Laputa.

I HAD not been at home above ten Days, when Captain *William Robinson,* a *Cornish* Man, Commander of the *Hopewell,** a stout Ship of three Hundred Tuns, came to my House. I had formerly been Surgeon of another Ship where he was Master, and a fourth Part Owner, in a Voyage to the *Levant.* He had always treated me more like a Brother than an inferior Officer; and hearing of my Arrival made me a Visit, as I apprehended only out of Friendship, for nothing passed more than what is usual after long Absence. But repeating his Visits often, expressing his Joy to find me in good Health, asking whether I were now settled for Life, adding that he intended a Voyage to the *East-Indies,* in two Months, at last he plainly invited me, although with some Apologies, to be Surgeon of the Ship. That* I should have another Surgeon under me, besides our two Mates; that my Sallary should be double to the usual Pay; and that having experienced my Knowledge is Sea-Affairs to be at least equal to his, he would enter into any Engagement to follow my Advice, as much as if I had Share in the Command.

He said so many other obliging things, and I knew him to be so honest a Man, that I could not reject his Proposal; the Thirst I had of seeing the World,* notwithstanding my past Misfortunes, continuing as violent as ever. The only Difficulty that remained, was to persuade my Wife, whose Consent however I at last obtained, by the Prospect of Advantage she proposed* to her Children.

We set out the 5th Day of *August,* 1706, and arrived at Fort St *George,** the 11th of *April* 1707. We stayed there three Weeks to refresh our Crew, many of whom were sick. From thence we went to *Tonquin,* where the Captain resolved to continue some time; because many of the Goods he intended to buy were not ready, nor could he expect to be dispatched* in several Months. Therefore in hopes to defray some of the Charges he must be at, he bought a Sloop, loaded it with several Sorts of Goods, wherewith the *Tonquinese* usually trade to the neighbouring Islands; and putting Fourteen Men on Board, whereof three were of the Country, he appointed me Master of the Sloop, and gave me Power to traffick, while he transacted his Affairs at *Tonquin*.

We had not sailed above three Days, when a great Storm arising, we were driven five Days to the North-North-East, and then to the East; after which we had fair Weather, but still with a pretty strong Gale from the West. Upon the tenth Day we were chased by two Pyrates,* who soon overtook us; for my Sloop was so deep loaden, that she sailed very slow; neither were we in a Condition to defend our selves.

We were boarded about the same Time by both the Pyrates, who entered furiously at the Head of their Men; but finding us all prostrate upon our Faces, (for so I gave Order,) they pinioned us with strong Ropes, and setting a Guard upon us, went to search the Sloop.

I observed among them a *Dutchman*, who seemed to be of some Authority, although he were not Commander of either Ship. He knew us by our Countenances to be *Englishmen*, and jabbering to us in his own Language, swore we should be tyed Back to Back, and thrown into the Sea. I spoke *Dutch* tolerably well; I told him who we were, and begged him in Consideration of our being Christians and Protestants, of neighbouring Countries, in strict Alliance,* that he would move the Captains to take some Pity on us. This inflamed his Rage; he repeated his Threatnings, and turning to his Companions, spoke with great Vehemence, in the *Japanese* Language, as I suppose; often using the Word *Christianos*.

The largest of the two Pyrate Ships was commanded by a *Japanese* Captain, who spoke a little *Dutch*, but very imperfectly. He came up to me, and after several Questions, which I answered in great Humility, he said we should not die. I made the Captain a very low Bow, and then turning to the *Dutchman*, said, I was sorry to find more Mercy in a Heathen, than in a Brother Christian. But I had soon Reason to repent those foolish Words; for that malicious Reprobate, having often endeavoured in vain to persuade both the Captains that I might be thrown into the Sea, (which they would not yield to after the Promise made me, that I should not die) however prevailed so far as to have a Punishment inflicted on me, worse in all human Appearance than Death it self. My Men were sent by an equal Division into both the Pyrate-Ships, and my Sloop new manned. As to my self, it was determined that I should be set a-drift, in a small Canoe, with Paddles and a Sail, and four Days Provisions; which last the *Japanese* Captain was so kind to double out of his own Stores, and would permit no Man to search me. I got down into the Canoe, while the *Dutchman* standing upon the Deck, loaded me with all the Curses and injurious Terms his Language could afford.

About an Hour before we saw the Pyrates, I had taken an Observation, and found we were in the Latitude of 46 N. and of Longitude 183.* When I was at some Distance from the Pyrates, I discovered by my Pocket-Glass several Islands to the South-East. I set up my Sail, the Wind being fair, with a Design to reach the nearest of those Islands, which I made a Shift to do in about three Hours. It was all rocky; however I got many Birds Eggs; and striking Fire, I kindled some Heath* and dry Sea Weed, by which I roasted my Eggs. I eat no other Supper, being resolved to spare my Provisions as much as I could. I passed the Night under the Shelter of a Rock, strowing some Heath under me, and slept pretty well.

The next Day I sailed to another Island, and thence to a third and fourth, sometimes using my Sail, and sometimes my Paddles. But not to trouble the Reader with a particular Account of my Distresses; let it suffice, that on the 5th Day, I arrived at the last Island in my Sight, which lay South-South-East to the former.

This Island was at a greater Distance than I expected, and I did not reach it in less than five Hours. I encompassed it almost round before I could find a convenient Place to land in, which was a small Creek, about three Times the Wideness of my Canoe. I found the Island to be all rocky, only a little intermingled with Tufts of Grass, and sweet smelling Herbs. I took out my small Provisions, and after having refreshed myself, I secured the Remainder in a Cave, whereof there were great Numbers. I gathered Plenty of Eggs upon the Rocks, and got a Quantity of dry Seaweed, and parched Grass, which I designed to kindle the next Day, and roast my Eggs as well as I could. (For I had about me my Flint, Steel, Match, and Burning-glass.) I lay all Night in the Cave where I had lodged my Provisions. My Bed was the same dry Grass and Sea-weed which I intended for Fewel. I slept very little; for the Disquiets of my Mind prevailed over my Wearyness, and kept me awake. I considered how impossible it was to preserve my Life, in so desolate a Place; and how miserable my End must be. Yet I found my self so listless and desponding, that I had not the Heart to rise; and before I could get Spirits enough to creep out of my Cave, the Day was far advanced. I walked a while among the Rocks, the Sky was perfectly clear, and the Sun so hot, that I was forced to turn my Face from it: When all on a Sudden it became obscured, as I thought, in a Manner very different from what happens by the Interposition of a Cloud. I turned back, and perceived a vast Opake Body* between me and the Sun, moving forwards towards the Island: It seemed to be about two Miles high, and hid the Sun six or seven Minutes, but I did not observe the Air to be much colder, or the Sky more darkned, than if I had stood under the Shade of a Mountain. As it approached nearer over the Place where I was, it appeared to be a firm Substance, the Bottom flat, smooth, and shining very bright* from the Reflexion of the Sea below. I stood upon a Height about two Hundred Yards from the Shoar, and saw this vast Body descending almost to a Parallel with me, at less than an *English* Mile Distance. I took out my Pocket-Perspective, and could plainly discover Numbers of People moving up and down the Sides of it, which appeared to be sloping, but what those People were doing, I was not able to distinguish.

The natural Love of Life gave me some inward Motions of Joy; and I was ready to entertain a Hope, that this Adventure* might some Way or other help to deliver me from the desolate Place and Condition I was in. But, at the same Time, the Reader can hardly conceive my Astonishment, to behold an

Island in the Air, inhabited by Men, who were able (as it should seem) to raise, or sink, or put it into a progressive Motion, as they pleased.* But not being, at that Time, in a Disposition to philosophise upon this Phænomenon, I rather chose to observe what Course the Island would take; because it seemed for a while to stand still. Yet soon after it advanced nearer; and I could see the Sides of it, encompassed with several Gradations of Galleries and Stairs, at certain Intervals, to descend from one to the other. In the lowest Gallery, I beheld some People fishing with long Angling Rods, and others looking on. I waved my Cap, (for my Hat was long since worn out,) and my Handkerchief towards the Island; and upon its nearer Approach, I called and shouted with the utmost Strength of my Voice; and then looking circumspectly, I beheld a Crowd gathered to that Side which was most in my View. I found by their pointing towards me and to each other, that they plainly discovered me, although they made no Return to my Shouting: But I could see four or five Men running in great Haste up the Stairs to the Top of the Island, who then disappeared. I happened rightly to conjecture, that these were sent for Orders to some Person in Authority upon this Occasion.

The Number of People increased; and in less than Half an Hour, the Island was moved and raised in such a Manner, that the lowest Gallery appeared in a Parallel of less than an Hundred Yards Distance from the Height where I stood. I then put my self into the most supplicating Postures, and spoke in the humblest Accent, but received no Answer. Those who stood nearest over against me, seemed to be Persons of Distinction, as I supposed by their Habit. They conferred earnestly with each other, looking often upon me. At length one of them called out in a clear, polite,* smooth Dialect, not unlike in Sound to the *Italian*; and therefore I returned an Answer in that Language, hoping at least that the Cadence might be more agreeable to his Ears. Although neither of us understood the other, yet my Meaning was easily known, for the People saw the Distress I was in.

They made Signs for me to come down from the Rock, and go towards the Shoar, which I accordingly did; and the flying

Island being raised to a convenient Height, the Verge directly over me, a Chain was let down from the lowest Gallery, with a Seat fastned to the Bottom, to which I fixed my self, and was drawn up by Pullies.

CHAPTER TWO

The Humours* and Dispositions of the Laputians *described. An Account of their Learning. Of the King and his Court. The Author's Reception there. The Inhabitants subject to Fears and Disquietudes. An Account of the Women.*

AT MY alighting I was surrounded by a Crowd of People, but those who stood nearest seemed to be of better Quality. They beheld me with all the Marks and Circumstances of Wonder; neither indeed was I much in their Debt;* having never till then seen a Race of Mortals so singular* in their Shapes, Habits, and Countenances. Their Heads were all reclined either to the Right, or the Left; one of their Eyes turned inward, and the other directly up to the Zenith.* Their outward Garments were adorned with the Figures of Suns, Moons, and Stars, interwoven with those of Fiddles, Flutes, Harps, Trumpets, Guittars, Harpsicords, and many more Instruments of Musick, unknown to us in *Europe.* I observed here and there many in the Habit of Servants, with a blown Bladder fastned like a Flail to the End of a short Stick, which they carried in their Hands. In each Bladder was a small Quantity of dried Pease, or little Pebbles, (as I was afterwards informed). With these Bladders they now and then flapped the Mouths and Ears of those who stood near them, of which Practice I could not then conceive the Meaning. It seems, the Minds of these People are so taken up with intense Speculations, that they neither can speak, nor attend to the Discourses of others, without being rouzed by some external Taction* upon the Organs of Speech and Hearing; for which Reason, those Persons who are able to afford it, always keep a *Flapper,* (the Original is *Climenole**) in their Family, as one of their Domesticks; nor ever walk abroad or make Visits without him. And the Business of this Officer is, when two or more Persons are in Company, gently to strike with his Bladder the Mouth of him who is to speak, and the Right Ear of him or them to whom the Speaker addresseth himself. This *Flapper* is likewise employed diligently to attend his Master in his Walks, and upon Occasion to give him a soft Flap on his Eyes; because he is always so wrapped up* in Cogitation, that he is in manifest Danger of falling down every Precipice, and bouncing his Head against every Post; and in the Streets, of jostling others, or being jostled himself into the Kennel.*

It was necessary to give the Reader this Information, without which he would be at the same Loss with me, to understand the Proceedings of these People, as they conducted me up the Stairs, to the Top of the Island, and from thence to the Royal Palace. While we were ascending, they forgot several Times what they were about, and left me to my self, till their Memories were again rouzed by their *Flappers*; for they appeared altogether unmoved by the Sight of my foreign Habit and Countenance, and by the Shouts of the Vulgar, whose Thoughts and Minds were more disengaged.

At last we entered the Palace, and proceeded into the Chamber of Presence; where I saw the King seated on his Throne, attended on each Side by Persons of prime Quality. Before the Throne, was a large Table filled with Globes and Spheres, and Mathematical Instruments* of all Kinds. His Majesty took not the least Notice of us, although our Entrance were not without sufficient Noise, by the Concourse of all Persons belonging to the Court. But, he was then deep in a Problem, and we attended* at least an Hour, before he could solve it. There stood by him on each Side, a young Page, with Flaps in their Hands; and when they saw he was at Leisure, one of them gently struck his Mouth, and the other his Right Ear; at which he started like one awaked on the sudden, and looking towards me, and the Company I was in, recollected the Occasion of our coming, whereof he had been informed before. He spoke some Words; whereupon immediately a young Man with a Flap came up to my Side, and flapt me gently on the Right Ear; but I made Signs as well as I could, that I had no Occasion for such an Instrument; which as I afterwards found, gave his Majesty and the whole Court a very mean Opinion of my Understanding. The King, as far as I could conjecture, asked me several Questions, and I addressed my self to him in all the Languages I had. When it was found, that I could neither understand nor be understood, I was conducted by his Order to an Apartment in his Palace, (this Prince being distinguished above all his Predecessors for his Hospitality to Strangers,*) where two Servants were appointed to attend me. My Dinner was brought, and four Persons of Quality, whom I remembered to have seen very near the King's Person, did me the Honour to dine with me. We had two Courses, of three Dishes each. In the first Course, there was a Shoulder of Mutton, cut into an Æquilateral Triangle; a Piece of Beef into a Rhomboides; and a Pudding into a Cycloid. The second Course was two Ducks, trussed up into the Form of Fiddles; Sausages and Puddings resembling Flutes and Haut-boys, and a Breast of Veal in the Shape of a Harp. The Servants cut our Bread into Cones, Cylinders, Parallelograms, and several other Mathematical Figures.

While we were at Dinner, I made bold to ask the Names of several Things in their Language; and those noble Persons, by the Assistance of their *Flappers*, delighted to give me Answers, hoping to raise my Admiration of their great Abilities, if I could be brought to converse with them. I was soon able to call for Bread, and Drink, or whatever else I wanted.

After Dinner my Company withdrew, and a Person was sent to me by the King's Order, attended by a *Flapper*. He brought with him Pen, Ink, and Paper, and three or four Books; giving me to understand by Signs, that he was sent to teach me the Language. We sat together four Hours, in which Time I wrote down a great Number of Words in Columns, with the Translations over against them. I likewise made a Shift to learn several short Sentences. For my Tutor would order one of my Servants to fetch something, to turn about, to make a Bow, to sit, or stand, or walk, and the like. Then I took down the Sentence in Writing. He shewed me also in one of his Books, the Figures of the Sun, Moon, and Stars, the Zodiack, the Tropics, and Polar Circles, together with the Denominations of many Figures of Planes and Solids. He gave me the Names and Descriptions of all the Musical Instruments, and the general Terms of Art* in playing on each of them. After he had left me, I placed all my Words with their Interpretations in alphabetical Order. And thus in a few Days, by the Help of a very faithful Memory, I got some Insight into their Language.

The Word, which I interpret the *Flying* or *Floating Island*,* is in the Original *Laputa*; whereof I could never learn the true Etymology.* *Lap* in the old obsolete Language signifieth *High*, and *Untuh* a *Governor*; from which they say by Corruption was derived *Laputa* from *Lapuntuh*. But I do not approve of this Derivation, which seems to be a little strained. I ventured to offer to the Learned among them a Conjecture of my own, that *Laputa* was *quasi Lap outed*; *Lap* signifying properly the dancing of the Sun Beams in the Sea; and *outed* a Wing, which however I shall not obtrude, but submit to the judicious Reader.

Those to whom the King had entrusted me, observing how ill I was clad, ordered a Taylor to come next Morning, and take my Measure for a Suit of Cloths. This Operator did his Office after a different Manner from those of his Trade in *Europe*. He first took my Altitude by a Quadrant, and then with Rule and Compasses, described the Dimensions and Out-Lines of my whole Body; all which he entered upon Paper, and in six Days brought my Cloths very ill made, and quite out of Shape, by happening to mistake a Figure* in the Calculation. But my Comfort was, that I observed such Accidents very frequent, and little regarded.

During my Confinement for want of Cloaths, and by an Indisposition that held me some Days longer, I much enlarged my Dictionary; and when I went next to Court, was able to understand many Things the King spoke, and to return him some Kind of Answers. His Majesty had given Orders, that the Island should move North-East and by East,* to the vertical Point over *Lagado*,* the Metropolis of the whole Kingdom, below upon the firm Earth. It was about Ninety Leagues distant, and our Voyage lasted four Days and an Half. I was not in the least sensible of the progressive Motion made in the Air by the Island. On the second Morning, about Eleven o'Clock, the King himself in Person, attended by his Nobility, Courtiers, and Officers, having prepared all their Musical Instruments,* played on them for three Hours without Intermission; so that I was quite stunned with the Noise; neither could I possibly guess the Meaning, till my Tutor informed me. He said, that the People of their Island had their Ears adapted to hear the Musick of the Spheres,* which always played at certain Periods; and the Court was now prepared to bear their Part in whatever Instrument they most excelled.

In our Journey towards *Lagado* the Capital City, his Majesty ordered that the Island should stop over certain Towns and Villages, from whence he might receive the Petitions of his Subjects. And to this Purpose, several Packthreads were let down* with small Weights at the Bottom. On these Packthreads the People strung their Petitions, which mounted up directly like the Scraps of Paper fastned by School-boys at the End of the String that holds their Kite. Sometimes we received Wine and Victuals from below, which were drawn up by Pullies.

The Knowledge I had in Mathematicks gave me great Assistance in acquiring their Phraseology, which depended much upon that Science and Musick; and in the latter I was not unskilled. Their Ideas are perpetually conversant in Lines and Figures. If they would, for Example, praise the Beauty of a Woman, or any other Animal, they describe it by Rhombs, Circles, Parallelograms, Ellipses, and other Geometrical Terms; or else by Words of Art drawn from Musick, needless here to repeat. I observed in the King's Kitchen all Sorts of Mathematical and Musical Instruments, after the Figures of which they cut up the Joynts that were served to his Majesty's Table.

Their Houses are very ill built, the Walls bevil,* without one right Angle in any Apartment; and this Defect ariseth from the Contempt they bear for practical Geometry; which they despise as vulgar and mechanick, those Instructions they give being too refined for the Intellectuals* of their Workmen; which occasions perpetual Mistakes. And although they are dextrous enough upon a Piece of Paper in the Management of the Rule, the Pencil, and the Divider, yet in the common Actions and Behaviour of Life, I have not seen a more clumsy, awkward, and unhandy People, nor so slow and perplexed in their Conceptions upon all other Subjects, except those of

Mathematicks and Musick. They are very bad Reasoners, and vehemently given to Opposition, unless when they happen to be of the right Opinion,* which is seldom their Case. Imagination, Fancy, and Invention, they are wholly Strangers to, nor have any Words in their Language by which those Ideas can be expressed; the whole Compass of their Thoughts and Mind, being shut up within the two forementioned Sciences.

Most of them, and especially those who deal in the Astronomical Part, have great Faith in judicial Astrology,* although they are ashamed to own it publickly. But, what I chiefly admired, and thought altogether unaccountable, was the strong Disposition I observed in them towards News and Politicks;* perpetually enquiring into publick Affairs, giving their Judgments in Matters of State; and passionately disputing every Inch of a Party Opinion. I have indeed observed the same Disposition among most of the Mathematicians* I have known in *Europe*; although I could never discover the least Analogy between the two Sciences; unless those People suppose, that because the smallest Circle hath as many Degrees as the largest, therefore the Regulation and Management of the World require no more Abilities than the handling and turning of a Globe. But, I rather take this Quality to spring from a very common Infirmity of human Nature, inclining us to be more curious and conceited* in Matters where we have least Concern, and for which we are least adapted either by Study or Nature.

These People are under continual Disquietudes, never enjoying a Minute's Peace of Mind; and their Disturbances proceed from Causes which very little affect the rest of Mortals. Their Apprehensions arise from several Changes they dread in the Celestial Bodies. For Instance; that the Earth by the continual Approaches of the Sun towards it, must in Course of Time be absorbed or swallowed up.* That the Face of the Sun will by Degrees be encrusted with its own Effluvia,* and give no more Light to the World. That, the Earth very narrowly escaped a Brush from the Tail of the last Comet,* which would have infallibly reduced it to Ashes; and that the next, which they have calculated for One and Thirty Years hence, will probably destroy us.* For, if in its Perihelion it should approach within a certain Degree of the Sun, (as by their Calculations they have Reason to dread) it will conceive a Degree of Heat ten Thousand Times more intense than that of red hot glowing Iron; and in its Absence from the Sun, carry a blazing Tail Ten Hundred Thousand and Fourteen Miles long; through which if the Earth should pass at the Distance of one Hundred Thousand Miles from the *Nucleus*, or main Body of the Comet, it must in its Passage be set on Fire, and reduced to Ashes. That the Sun daily spending its Rays without any Nutriment to supply them, will at last be wholly consumed and annihilated;* which must be attended with the Destruction of this Earth, and of all the Planets that receive their Light from it.*

They are so perpetually alarmed with the Apprehensions of these and the like impending Dangers, that they can neither sleep quietly in their Beds, nor have any Relish for the common Pleasures or Amusements of Life. When they meet an Acquaintance in the Morning, the first Question is about the Sun's Health; how he looked at his Setting and Rising, and what Hopes they have to avoid the Stroak of the approaching Comet. This conversation they are apt to run into with the same Temper that Boys discover, in delighting to hear terrible Stories of Sprites and Hobgoblins, which they greedily listen to, and dare not go to Bed for fear.

The Women of the Island have Abundance of Vivacity; they contemn their Husbands, and are exceedingly fond of Strangers, whereof there is always a considerable Number from the Continent below, attending at Court, either upon Affairs of the several Towns and Corporations, or their own particular Occasions; but are much despised, because they want the same Endowments.* Among these the Ladies chuse their Gallants: But the Vexation is, that they act with too much Ease and Security; for the Husband is always so rapt in Speculation, that the Mistress and Lover may proceed to the greatest Familiarities before his Face, if he be but provided with Paper and Implements,* and without his *Flapper* at his Side.

The Wives and Daughters lament their Confinement to the Island, although I think it the most delicious Spot of Ground in the World; and although they live here in the greatest Plenty and Magnificence, and are allowed to do whatever they please: They long to see the World, and take the Diversions of the Metropolis, which they are not allowed to do without a particular Licence from the King; and this is not easy to obtain, because the People of Quality have found by frequent Experience, how hard it is to persuade their Women to return from below. I was told, that a great Court Lady, who had several Children, is married to the prime Minister,* the richest Subject in the Kingdom, a very graceful Person, extremely fond of her, and lives in the finest Palace of the Island; went down to *Lagado,* on the Pretence of Health, there hid herself for several Months, till the King sent a Warrant to search for her; and she was found in an obscure Eating-House all in Rags, having pawned her Cloths to maintain an old deformed Footman, who beat her every Day, and in whose Company she was taken much against her Will. And although her Husband received her with all possible Kindness, and without the least Reproach; she soon after contrived to steal down again with all her Jewels, to the same Gallant, and hath not been heard of since.

This may perhaps pass with the Reader rather for an *European* or *English* Story, than for one of a Country so remote. But he may please to consider, that the Caprices of Womankind are not limited by any Climate or Nation; and that they are much more uniform than can be easily imagined.

In about a Month's Time I had made a tolerable Proficiency* in their Language, and was able to answer most of the King's Questions, when I had the Honour to attend him. His Majesty discovered not the least Curiosity to enquire into the Laws, Government, History, Religion, or Manners of the Countries where I had been; but confined his Questions to the State of Mathematicks, and received the Account I gave him, with great Contempt and Indifference, though often rouzed by his *Flapper* on each Side.

CHAPTER THREE

A Phænomenon solved* by modern Philosophy and Astronomy. The Laputians great Improvements in the latter. The King's Method of suppressing Insurrections.

I DESIRED Leave of this Prince to see the Curiosities of the Island; which he was graciously pleased to grant, and ordered my Tutor to attend me. I chiefly wanted to know to what Cause in Art or in Nature, it owed its several Motions; whereof I will now give a philosophical Account to the Reader.

The flying or floating Island is exactly circular; its Diameter* 7837 Yards, or about four Miles and an Half, and consequently contains ten Thousand Acres. It is three Hundred Yards thick. The Bottom, or under Surface, which appears to those who view it from below, is one even regular Plate of Adamant,* shooting up to the Height of about two Hundred Yards. Above it lye the several Minerals in their usual Order;* and over all is a Coat of rich Mould ten or twelve Foot deep. The Declivity of the upper Surface, from the Circumference to the Center, is the natural Cause why all the Dews and Rains which fall upon the Island, are conveyed in small Rivulets towards the Middle, where they are emptied into four large Basons, each of about Half a Mile in Circuit, and two Hundred Yards distant from the Center. From these Basons the Water is continually exhaled by the Sun in the Day-time, which effectually prevents their overflowing. Besides, as it is in the Power of the Monarch to raise the Island above the Region of Clouds and Vapours, he can prevent the falling of Dews and Rains whenever he pleases. For the highest Clouds cannot rise above two Miles, as Naturalists agree,* at least they were never known to do so in that Country.

At the Center of the Island there is a Chasm about fifty Yards in Diameter, from whence the Astronomers descend into a large Dome, which is therefore called *Flandona Gagnole*, or the *Astronomers Cave*;* situated at the Depth of an Hundred

Yards beneath the upper Surface of the Adamant. In this Cave are Twenty Lamps continually burning, which from the Reflection of the Adamant cast a strong Light into every Part. The Place is stored with great Variety of Sextants, Quadrants, Telescopes, Astrolabes, and other Astronomical Instruments. But the greatest Curiosity, upon which the Fate of the Island depends, is a Loadstone* of a prodigious Size, in Shape resembling a Weaver's Shuttle.* It is in Length six Yards, and in the thickest Part at least three Yards over.* This Magnet is sustained by a very strong Axle of Adamant, passing through its Middle, upon which it plays, and is poized so exactly that the weakest Hand can turn it. It is hooped round with an hollow Cylinder of Adamant, four Foot deep, as many thick, and twelve Yards in Diameter, placed horizontally, and supported by Eight Adamantine Feet, each Six Yards high. In the Middle of the Concave Side there is a Groove Twelve Inches deep, in which the Extremities of the Axle are lodged, and turned round* as there is Occasion.

This Stone cannot be moved from its Place by any Force, because the Hoop and its Feet are one continued Piece with that Body of Adamant which constitutes the Bottom of the Island.

By Means of this Load-stone, the Island is made to rise and fall, and move from one Place to another. For, with respect to that Part of the Earth over which the Monarch presides, the Stone is endued at one of its Sides* with an attractive Power, and at the other with a repulsive. Upon placing the Magnet erect with its attracting End towards the Earth, the Island descends; but when the repelling Extremity points downwards, the Island mounts directly upwards. When the Position of the Stone is oblique, the Motion of the Island is so too. For in this Magnet the Forces always act in Lines parallel to its Direction.*

By this oblique Motion the Island is conveyed to different Parts of the Monarch's Dominions. To explain the Manner of its Progress, let *A B* represent a Line drawn cross the Dominions of *Balnibarbi*; let the Line *c d* represent the Loadstone, of which let *d* be the repelling End, and *c* the attracting End, the Island being over *C*; let the stone be placed in the Position *c d* with its repelling End downwards; then the Island will be driven upwards obliquely towards *D*. When it is arrived at *D*, let the Stone be turned upon its Axle till its attracting End points towards *E*, and then the Island will be carried obliquely towards *E*; where if the Stone be again turned upon its Axle till it stands in the Position *E F*, with its repelling Point downwards, the Island will rise obliquely towards *F*, where by directing the attracting End towards *G*, the Island may be carried to *G*, and from *G* to *H*, by turning the Stone, so as to make its repelling Extremity point directly downwards. And thus by changing the Situation of the Stone as often as there is Occasion, the Island is made to rise and fall by Turns in an oblique Direction; and by those alternate Risings and Fallings (the Obliquity being not considerable), is conveyed from one Part of the Dominions to the other.

But it must be observed, that this Island cannot move beyond the Extent of the Dominions below; nor can it rise above the Height of four Miles. For which the Astronomers (who have written large Systems concerning the Stone) assign the following Reason: That the Magnetick Virtue does not extend beyond the Distance of four Miles, and that the Mineral which acts upon the Stone in the Bowels of the Earth, and in the Sea about six Leagues distant from the Shoar, is not diffused through the whole Globe, but terminated with the Limits of the King's Dominions: And it was easy from the great Advantage of such a superior Situation, for a Prince to bring under his Obedience whatever Country lay within the Attraction of that Magnet.

When the Stone* is put parallel to the Plane of the Horizon, the Island standeth still; for in that Case, the Extremities of it being at equal Distance from the Earth, act with equal Force, the one in drawing downwards, the other in pushing upwards; and consequently no Motion can ensue.

This Loadstone is under the Care of certain Astronomers, who from Time to Time give it such Positions as the Monarch directs. They spend the greatest Part of their Lives in observing the celestial Bodies, which they do by the Assistance of Glasses, far excelling ours in Goodness. For, although their largest Telescopes do not exceed three Feet, they magnify

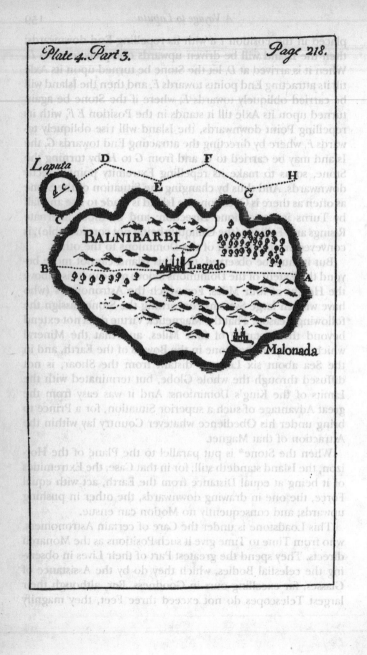

Plate 4. Part 3.   *Page* 218.

Laputa

D   F

E   H

C   G

BALNIBARBI

B   A

Lagado

Malonada

much more than those of a Hundred with us, and shew the Stars with greater Clearness.* This Advantage hath enabled them to extend their Discoveries much farther than our Astronomers in *Europe*. They have made a Catalogue of ten Thousand fixed Stars,* whereas the largest of ours do not contain above one third Part of that Number. They have likewise discovered two lesser Stars, or *Satellites*,* which revolve about *Mars*; whereof the innermost is distant from the Center of the primary Planet exactly three of his Diameters, and the outermost five; the former revolves in the Space of ten Hours, and the latter in Twenty-one and an Half; so that the Squares of their periodical Times, are very near in the same Proportion with the Cubes of their Distance from the Center of *Mars*; which evidently shews them to be governed by the same Law of Gravitation, that influences the other heavenly Bodies.

They have observed Ninety-three different Comets,* and settled their Periods with great Exactness. If this be true, (and they affirm it with great Confidence) it is much to be wished that their Observations were made publick; whereby the Theory of Comets, which at present is very lame and defective, might be brought to the same Perfection with other Parts of Astronomy.

The King would be the most absolute Prince in the Universe, if he could but prevail on a Ministry to join with him; but these having their Estates below on the Continent, and considering that the Office of a Favourite hath a very uncertain Tenure, would never consent to the enslaving their Country.

If any Town should engage in Rebellion or Mutiny, fall into violent Factions, or refuse to pay the usual Tribute; the King hath two Methods of reducing them to Obedience. The first and the mildest Course is by keeping the Island hovering over such a Town, and the Lands about it; whereby he can deprive them of the Benefit of the Sun* and the Rain, and consequently afflict the Inhabitants with Dearth and Diseases. And if the Crime deserve it, they are at the same time pelted from above with great Stones, against which they have no Defence, but by creeping into Cellars or Caves, while the Roofs of their

Houses are beaten to Pieces. But if they still continue obstinate, or offer to raise Insurrections; he proceeds to the last Remedy, by letting the Island drop directly upon their Heads, which makes a universal Destruction both of Houses and Men. However, this is an Extremity to which the Prince is seldom driven, neither indeed is he willing, to put it in Execution; nor dare his Ministers advise him to an Action, which as it would render them odious to the People, so it would be a great Damage to their own Estates that lie all below; for the Island is the King's Demesne.

But there is still indeed a more weighty Reason, why the Kings of this Country have been always averse from executing so terrible an Action, unless upon the utmost Necessity. For if the Town intended to be destroyed should have in it any tall Rocks, as it generally falls in the larger Cities; a Situation probably chosen at first with a View to prevent such a Catastrophe: Or if it abound in high Spires or Pillars of Stone, a sudden Fall might endanger the Bottom or under Surface of the Island, which although it consists as I have said, of one entire Adamant two hundred Yards thick, might happen to crack by too great a Choque, or burst by approaching too near the Fires from the Houses below; as the Backs both of Iron and Stone will often do in our Chimneys. Of all this the People are well apprized, and understand how far to carry their Obstinacy, where their Liberty or Property is concerned. And the King, when he is highest provoked, and most determined to press a City to Rubbish, orders the Island to descend with great Gentleness, out of a Pretence of Tenderness to his People, but indeed for fear of breaking the Adamantine Bottom;* in which Case it is the Opinion of all their Philosophers, that the Load-stone could no longer hold it up, and the whole Mass would fall to the Ground.

[About three Years* before my Arrival among them, while the King was in his Progress over his Dominions, there happened an extraordinary Accident which had like to have put a Period to the Fate of that Monarchy, at least as it is now instituted. Lindalino* the second City in the Kingdom was the first his Majesty visited in his Progress. Three Days after his Departure, the Inhabitants who had often complained of great Oppressions, shut the Town Gates, seized on the Governor, and with incredible Speed and Labour erected four large Towers,* one at every Corner of the City (which is an exact Square) equal in Heigth to a strong pointed Rock* that stands directly in the Center of the City. Upon the Top of each Tower, as well as upon the Rock, they fixed a great Loadstone, and in case their Design should fail, they had provided a vast Quantity of the most combustible Fewel,* hoping to burst therewith the adamantine Bottom of the Island, if the Loadstone Project should miscarry.

It was eight Months* before the King had perfect Notice that the Lindalinians were in Rebellion. He then commanded that the Island should be wafted over the City. The People were unanimous, and had laid in Store of Provisions, and a great River runs through the middle of the Town. The King hovered over them several Days to deprive them of the Sun and the Rain. He ordered many Packthreads to be let down, yet not a Person offered to send up a Petition, but instead thereof, very bold Demands, the Redress of all their Greivances, great Immunitys,* the Choice of their own Governor,* and other the like Exorbitances. Upon which his Majesty commanded all the Inhabitants of the Island to cast great Stones from the lower Gallery into the Town; but the Citizens had provided against this Mischief by conveying their Persons and Effects into the four Towers, and other strong Buildings, and Vaults under Ground.

The King being now determined to reduce this proud People, ordered that the Island should descend gently within fourty Yards of the Top of the Towers and Rock. This was accordingly done; but the Officers employed in that Work found the Descent much speedier than usual, and by turning the Loadstone could not without great Difficulty keep it in a firm position, but found the Island inclining to fall. They sent the King immediate Intelligence of this astonishing Event and begged his Majesty's Permission to raise the Island higher; the King consented, a general Council was called, and the Officers of the Loadstone ordered to attend. One of the oldest and expertest among them obtained leave to try an Experiment. He took a strong Line of an hundred Yards, and the

Island being raised over the Town above the attracting Power they had felt, He fastened a Piece of Adamant to the End of his Line which had in it a Mixture of Iron mineral, of the same Nature with that whereof the Bottom or lower Surface of the Island is composed, and from the lower Gallery let it down slowly towards the Top of the Towers. The Adamant was not descended four Yards, before the Officer felt it drawn so strongly downwards, that he could hardly pull it back. He then threw down several small Pieces of Adamant, and observed that they were all violently attracted by the Top of the Tower. The same Experiment was made on the other three Towers, and on the Rock with the same Effect.

This Incident broke entirely the King's Measures and (to dwell no longer on other Circumstances) he was forced to give the Town their own Conditions.

I was assured by a great Minister, that if the Island had descended so near the Town, as not to be able to raise it self, the Citizens were determined to fix it for ever, to kill the King and all his Servants, and entirely change the Government.]

By a fundamental Law* of this Realm, neither the King nor either of his two elder Sons, are permitted to leave the Island; nor the Queen till she is past Child-bearing.

CHAPTER FOUR

The Author leaves Laputa, *is conveyed to* Balnibarbi, *arrives at the Metropolis. A Description of the Metropolis and the Country adjoining. The Author hospitably received by a great Lord. His Conversation with that Lord.*

ALTHOUGH I cannot say that I was ill treated in this Island, yet I must confess I thought my self too much neglected, not without some Degree of Contempt. For neither Prince nor People appeared to be curious in any Part of Knowledge, except Mathematicks and Musick, wherein I was far their inferior, and upon that Account very little regarded.

On the other Side, after having seen all the Curiosities of the Island, I was very desirous to leave it, being heartily weary of those People.* They were indeed excellent in two Sciences for which I have great Esteem, and wherein I am not unversed; but at the same time so abstracted and involved in Speculation, that I never met with such disagreeable Companions. I conversed only with Women, Tradesmen, *Flappers*, and Court-Pages, during two Months of my Abode there; by which at last I rendered my self extremely contemptible; yet these were the only People from whom I could ever receive a reasonable Answer.

I had obtained by hard Study a good Degree of Knowledge in their Language; I was weary of being confined to an Island where I received so little Countenance;* and resolved to leave it with the first Opportunity.

There was a great Lord at Court, nearly related to the King, and for that Reason alone used with respect. He was universally reckoned the most ignorant and stupid Person among them. He had performed many eminent Services for the Crown, had great natural and acquired Parts, adorned with Integrity and Honour; but so ill an Ear for Musick, that his Detractors reported he had been often known to beat Time in the wrong Place; neither could his Tutors without extreme

Difficulty teach him to demonstrate the most easy Proposition in the Mathematicks. He was pleased to shew me many Marks of Favour, often did me the Honour of a Visit, desired to be informed in the Affairs of *Europe*, the Laws and Customs, the Manners and Learning of the several Countries where I had travelled. He listened to me with great Attention, and made very wise Observations on all I spoke. He had two *Flappers* attending him for State, but never made use of them except at Court, and in Visits of Ceremony; and would always command them to withdraw when we were alone together.

I intreated this illustrious Person to intercede in my Behalf with his Majesty for Leave to depart; which he accordingly did, as he was pleased to tell me, with Regret: For, indeed he had made me several Offers very advantageous, which however I refused with Expressions of the highest Acknowledgment.

On the 16th Day of *February*, I took Leave of his Majesty and the Court. The King made me a Present to the Value of about two Hundred Pounds *English*; and my Protector his Kinsman as much more, together with a Letter of Recommendation to a Friend of his in *Lagado*, the Metropolis: The Island being then hovering over a Mountain about two Miles from it, I was let down from the lowest Gallery, in the same Manner as I had been taken up.

The Continent, as far as it is subject to the Monarch of the *Flying Island*, passeth under the general Name of *Balnibarbi*; and the Metropolis, as I said before, is called *Lagado*. I felt some little Satisfaction in finding my self on firm Ground. I walked to the City without any Concern, being clad like one of the Natives, and sufficiently instructed to converse with them. I soon found out the Person's House to whom I was recommended; presented my Letter from his Friend the Grandee in the Island, and was received with much Kindness. This great Lord, whose Name was *Munodi*,* ordered me an Apartment in his own House, where I continued during my Stay, and was entertained in a most hospitable Manner.

The next Morning after my Arrival he took me in his Chariot to see the Town, which is about half the Bigness of *London*; but the Houses very strangely built, and most of them out of Repair. The People in the Streets walked fast, looked wild, their Eyes fixed, and were generally in Rags. We passed through one of the Town Gates, and went about three Miles into the Country, where I saw many Labourers working with several Sorts of Tools in the Ground, but he was not able to conjecture what they were about; neither did I observe any Expectation either of Corn or Grass, although the Soil appeared to be excellent. I could not forbear admiring at these odd Appearances both in Town and Country; and I made bold to desire my Conductor, that he would be pleased to explain to me what could be meant by so many busy Heads, Hands and Faces, both in the Streets and the Fields, because I did not discover any good Effects they produced; but on the contrary, I never knew a Soil so unhappily cultivated, Houses so ill contrived and so ruinous, or a People whose Countenances and Habit expressed so much Misery and Want.*

This Lord *Munodi* was a Person of the first Rank, and had been some Years Governor of *Lagado*; but by a Cabal of Ministers was discharged for Insufficiency.* However the King treated him with Tenderness, as a well-meaning Man, but of a low contemptible Understanding.

When I gave that free Censure of the Country and its Inhabitants, he made no further Answer than by telling me, that I had not been long enough among them to form a Judgment; and that the different Nations of the World had different Customs; with other common Topicks to the same Purpose. But when we returned to his Palace, he asked me how I liked the Building, what Absurdities I observed, and what Quarrel I had with the Dress and Looks of his Domesticks. This he might safely do; because every Thing about him was magnificent, regular and polite.* I answered, that his Excellency's Prudence, Quality, and Fortune, had exempted him from those Defects which Folly and Beggary had produced in others. He said, if I would go with him to his Country House about Twenty Miles distant, where his Estate lay, there would be more Leisure for this Kind of Conversation. I told his Excellency, that I was entirely at his Disposal; and accordingly we set out next Morning.

During our Journey, he made me observe the several

Methods used by Farmers in managing their Lands; which to me were wholly unaccountable: For except in some very few Places, I could not discover one Ear of Corn, or Blade of Grass. But, in three Hours travelling, the Scene was wholly altered; we came into a most beautiful Country; Farmers Houses at small Distances, neatly built, the Fields enclosed, containing Vineyards, Corngrounds and Meadows. Neither do I remember to have seen a more delightful Prospect. His Excellency observed my Countenance to clear up; he told me with a Sigh, that there his Estate began, and would continue the same till we should come to his House. That his Countrymen ridiculed and despised him for managing his Affairs no better, and for setting so ill an Example to the Kingdom; which however was followed by very few, such as were old and wilful, and weak like himself.

We came at length to the House, which was indeed a noble Structure, built according to the best Rules of ancient Architecture. The Fountains, Gardens, Walks, Avenues, and Groves were all disposed with exact Judgment and Taste. I gave due Praises to every Thing I saw, whereof his Excellency took not the least Notice till after Supper; when, there being no third Companion, he told me with a very melancholy Air, that he doubted he must throw down his Houses in Town and Country, to rebuild them after the present Mode; destroy all his Plantations, and cast others into such a Form as modern Usage required; and give the same Directions to all his Tenants, unless he would submit to incur the Censure of Pride, Singularity, Affectation, Ignorance, Caprice; and perhaps encrease his Majesty's Displeasure.

That the Admiration I appeared to be under, would cease or diminish when he had informed me of some Particulars, which probably I never heard of at Court, the People there being too much taken up in their own Speculations, to have Regard to what passed here below.

The Sum of his Discourse was to this Effect. That about Forty Years ago,* certain Persons went up to *Laputa*, either upon Business or Diversion; and after five Months Continuance, came back with a very little Smattering in Mathematicks, but full of Volatile Spirits acquired in that Airy* Region. That these Persons upon their Return, began to dislike the Management of every Thing below; and fell into Schemes of putting all Arts, Sciences, Languages, and Mechanicks upon a new Foot. To this End they procured a Royal Patent for erecting an Academy of PROJECTORS* in *Lagado*: And the Humour prevailed so strongly among the People, that there is not a Town of any Consequence in the Kingdom without such an Academy. In these Colleges, the Professors contrive new Rules and Methods of Agriculture and Building, and new Instruments and Tools for all Trades and Manufactures, whereby, as they undertake, one Man shall do the Work of Ten; a Palace may be built in a Week, of Materials so durable as to last for ever without repairing. All the Fruits of the Earth shall come to Maturity at whatever Season we think fit to chuse,* and increase an Hundred Fold more than they do at present; with unnumerable other happy Proposals. The only Inconvenience is, that none of these Projects are yet brought to Perfection; and in the mean time, the whole Country lies miserably waste, the Houses in Ruins, and the People without Food or Cloaths. By all which, instead of being discouraged, they are Fifty Times more violently bent upon prosecuting their Schemes, driven equally on by Hope and Despair: That, as for himself, being not of an enterprizing Spirit, he was content to go on in the old Forms; to live in the Houses his Ancestors had built, and act as they did in every Part of Life without Innovation. That, some few other Persons of Quality and Gentry had done the same; but were looked on with an Eye of Contempt and ill Will, as Enemies to Art, ignorant, and ill Commonwealthsmen,* preferring their own Ease and Sloth before the general Improvement of their Country.

His Lordship added, that he would not by any further Particulars prevent* the Pleasure I should certainly take in viewing the grand Academy, whither he was resolved I should go. He only desired me to observe a ruined Building* upon the Side of a Mountain about three Miles distant, of which he gave me this Account. That he had a very convenient Mill within Half a Mile of his House, turned by a Current from a large River, and sufficient for his own Family as well as a great Number of his Tenants. That, about seven Years ago, a Club of those Projectors came to him with Proposals to destroy this Mill, and build another on the Side of that Mountain, on the long Ridge whereof a long Canal must be cut for a Repository of Water, to be conveyed up by Pipes and Engines to supply the Mill: Because the Wind and Air upon a Height agitated the Water, and thereby made it fitter for Motion: And because the Water descending down a Declivity would turn the Mill with half the Current of a River whose Course is more upon a Level. He said, that being then not very well with* the Court, and pressed by many of his Friends, he complied with the Proposal; and after employing an Hundred Men for two Years, the Work miscarried, the Projectors went off, laying the Blame intirely upon him; railing at him ever since, and putting others upon* the same Experiment, with equal Assurance of Success, as well as equal Disappointment.

In a few Days we came back to Town; and his Excellency, considering the bad Character he had in the Academy, would not go with me himself, but recommended me to a Friend of his to bear me Company thither. My Lord was pleased to represent me as a great Admirer of Projects, and a Person of much Curiosity and easy Belief; which indeed was not without Truth; for I had my self been a Sort of Projector in my younger Days.

CHAPTER FIVE

The Author permitted to see the grand Academy of Lagado. The Academy largely* described. The Arts wherein the Professors employ themselves.

THIS ACADEMY is not an entire single Building, but a Continuation of several Houses* on both Sides of a Street; which growing waste,* was purchased and applyed to that Use.

I was received very kindly by the Warden, and went for many Days to the Academy. Every Room hath in it one or more Projectors; and I believe I could not be* in fewer than five Hundred Rooms.*

The first Man I saw was of a meagre Aspect, with sooty Hands and Face, his Hair and Beard long, ragged and singed in several Places. His Clothes, Shirt, and Skin were all of the same Colour. He had been Eight Years upon a Project for extracting Sun-Beams out of Cucumbers,* which were to be put into Vials hermetically sealed, and let out to warm the Air in raw inclement Summers. He told me, he did not doubt in Eight Years more, that he should be able to supply the Governors Gardens with Sun-shine at a reasonable Rate; but he complained that his Stock was low, and intreated me to give him something as an Encouragement to Ingenuity, especially since this had been a very dear Season for Cucumbers. I made him a small Present, for my Lord had furnished me with Money on purpose, because he knew their Practice of begging* from all who go to see them.

I went into another Chamber, but was ready to hasten back, being almost overcome with a horrible Stink.* My Conductor pressed me forward, conjuring me in a Whisper to give no Offence, which would be highly resented; and therefore I durst not so much as stop my Nose. The Projector of this Cell was the most ancient Student of the Academy. His Face and Beard were of a pale Yellow; his Hands and Clothes dawbed over with Filth. When I was presented to him, he gave me a very close Embrace, (a Compliment I could well have excused.) His Employment from his first coming into the Academy, was an Operation to reduce human Excrement to its original Food, by separating the several Parts, removing the Tincture which it receives from the Gall, making the Odour exhale, and scumming off the Saliva. He had a weekly Allowance from the Society, of a Vessel filled with human Ordure, about the Bigness of a *Bristol* Barrel.

I saw another at work to calcine Ice into Gunpowder; who likewise shewed me a Treatise he had written concerning the Malleability of Fire,* which he intended to publish.

There was a most ingenious Architect who had contrived a new Method for building Houses, by beginning at the Roof, and working downwards to the Foundation; which he justified to me by the like Practice of those two prudent Insects the Bee and the Spider.

There was a Man born blind,* who had several Apprentices in his own Condition: Their Employment was to mix Colours for Painters, which their Master taught them to distinguish by feeling and smelling. It was indeed my Misfortune to find them at that Time not very perfect in their Lessons; and the Professor himself happened to be generally mistaken: This Artist is much encouraged and esteemed by the whole Fraternity.

In another Apartment I was highly pleased with a Projector, who had found a Device of plowing the Ground with Hogs,* to save the Charges of Plows, Cattle, and Labour. The Method is this: In an Acre of Ground you bury at six Inches Distance, and eight deep, a Quantity of Acorns, Dates, Chesnuts, and other Maste* or Vegetables whereof these Animals are fondest; then you drive six Hundred or more of them into the Field, where in a few Days they will root up the whole Ground in search of their Food, and make it fit for sowing, at the same time manuring it with their Dung. It is true, upon Experiment they found the Charge and Trouble very great, and they had little or no Crop. However, it is not doubted that this Invention may be capable of great Improvement.

I went into another Room, where the Walls and Ceiling

were all hung round with Cobwebs, except a narrow Passage for the Artist* to go in and out. At my Entrance he called aloud to me not to disturb his Webs. He lamented the fatal Mistake the World had been so long in of using Silk-Worms, while we had such plenty of domestick Insects, who infinitely excelled the former, because they understood how to weave as well as spin. And he proposed farther, that by employing Spiders, the Charge of dying Silks would be wholly saved; whereof I was fully convinced when he shewed me a vast Number of Flies most beautifully coloured, wherewith he fed his Spiders; assuring us, that the Webs would take a Tincture from them; and as he had them of all Hues, he hoped to fit every Body's Fancy, as soon as he could find proper Food for the Flies, of certain Gums, Oyls, and other glutinous Matter, to give a Strength and Consistence to the Threads.

There was an Astronomer who had undertaken to place a Sun-Dial upon the great Weather-Cock* on the Town-House,* by adjusting the annual and diurnal Motions of the Earth and Sun, so as to answer and coincide with all accidental Turnings of the Wind.

I was complaining of a small Fit of the Cholick; upon which my Conductor led me into a Room, where a great Physician resided, who was famous for curing that Disease by contrary Operations from the same Instrument. He had a large Pair of Bellows,* with a long slender Muzzle of Ivory. This he conveyed eight Inches up the Anus, and drawing in the Wind, he affirmed he could make the Guts as lank as a dried Bladder. But when the Disease was more stubborn and violent, he let in the Muzzle while the Bellows was full of Wind, which he discharged into the Body of the Patient; then withdrew the Instrument to replenish it, clapping his Thumb strongly against the Orifice of the Fundament; and this being repeated three or four Times, the adventitious Wind would rush out, bringing the noxious along with it (like Water put into a Pump) and the Patient recovers. I saw him try both Experiments upon a Dog, but could not discern any Effect from the former. After the latter, the Animal was ready to burst, and made so violent a Discharge, as was very offensive to me and my Companions. The Dog died on the Spot, and

Plate 5 Part 3.   Page 232.

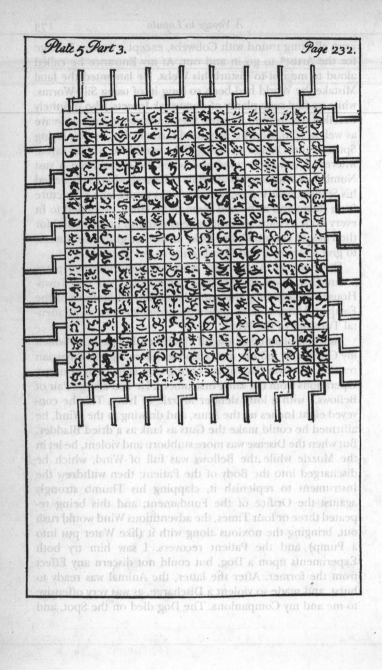

we left the Doctor endeavouring to recover him by the same Operation.

I visited many other Apartments, but shall not trouble my Reader with all the Curiosities I observed, being studious of Brevity.

I had hitherto seen only one Side of the Academy, the other being appropriated to the Advancers of speculative Learning; of whom I shall say something when I have mentioned one illustrious Person more, who is called among them *the universal Artist.** He told us, he had been Thirty Years employing his Thoughts for the Improvement of human Life. He had two large Rooms full of wonderful Curiosities, and Fifty Men at work. Some were condensing Air into a dry tangible Substance, by extracting the Nitre, and letting the aqueous or fluid Particles percolate: Others softening Marble for Pillows and Pin-cushions; others petrifying the Hoofs of a living Horse to preserve them from foundring. The Artist himself was at that Time busy upon two great designs: The first, to sow Land with Chaff,* wherein he affirmed the true seminal Virtue* to be contained, as he demonstrated by several Experiments which I was not skilful enough to comprehend. The other was, by a certain Composition of Gums, Minerals, and Vegetables outwardly applied, to prevent the Growth of Wool upon two young Lambs; and he hoped in a reasonable Time to propagate the Breed of naked Sheep all over the Kingdom.*

We crossed a Walk to the other Part of the Academy, where, as I have already said, the Projectors in speculative Learning resided.

The first Professor I saw was in a very large Room, with Forty Pupils about him. After Salutation, observing me to look earnestly upon a Frame,* which took up the greatest Part of both the Length and Breadth of the Room; he said, perhaps I might wonder to see him employed in a Project for improving speculative Knowledge by practical and mechanical Operations. But the World would soon be sensible of its Usefulness; and the flattered himself, that a more noble exalted Thought never sprang in any other Man's Head. Every one knew how laborious the usual Method is of attaining to

Arts and Sciences; whereas by his Contrivance, the most ignorant Person* at a reasonable Charge, and with a little bodily Labour, may write Books in Philosophy, Poetry, Politicks, Law, Mathematicks and Theology, without the least Assistance from Genius or Study. He then led me to the Frame, about the Sides whereof all his Pupils stood in Ranks. It was Twenty Foot square, placed in the Middle of the Room. The Superficies was composed of several Bits of Wood, about the Bigness of a Dye, but some larger than others. They were all linked together by slender Wires. These Bits of Wood were covered on every Square with Paper pasted on them; and on these Papers were written all the Words of their language in their Order. The Professor then desired me to observe, for he was going to set his Engine at work. The Pupils at his Command took each of them hold of an Iron Handle, whereof there were Forty fixed round the Edges of the Frame; and giving them a sudden Turn, the whole Disposition of the Words was entirely changed. He then commanded Six and Thirty of the Lads to read the several Lines softly as they appeared upon the Frame; and where they found three or four Words together that might make Part of a Sentence, they dictated to the four remaining Boys who were Scribes. This Work was repeated three or four Times, and at every Turn the Engine was so contrived, that the Words shifted into new Places, as the square Bits of Wood moved upside down.

Six Hours a-Day the young Students were employed in this Labour; and the Professor shewed me several Volumes in large Folio already collected, of broken Sentences, which he intended to piece together; and out of those rich Materials to give the World a compleat Body of all Arts and Sciences,* which however might be still improved, and much expedited, if the Publick would raise a Fund for making and employing five Hundred such Frames in *Lagado*, and oblige the Managers to contribute in common their several Collections.

He assured me, that this Invention had employed all his Thoughts from his Youth; that he had emptyed the whole Vocabulary into his Frame, and made the strictest Computation of the general Proportion there is in Books between the Numbers of Particles, Nouns, and Verbs, and other Parts of Speech.

I made my humblest Acknowledgments to this illustrious Person for his great Communicativeness; and promised if ever I had the good Fortune to return to my native Country, that I would do him Justice, as the sole Inventer of this wonderful Machine; the Form and Contrivance of which I desired Leave to delineate upon Paper as in the Figure here annexed. I told him, although it were the Custom of our Learned in *Europe* to steal Inventions from each other,* who had thereby at least this Advantage, that it became a Controversy which was the right Owner; yet I would take such Caution, that he should have the Honour entire without a Rival.

We next went to the School of Languages,* where three Professors sat in Consultation upon improving that of their own Country.

The first Project was to shorten Discourse* by cutting Polysyllables into one, and leaving out Verbs and Participles; because in Reality all things imaginable are but Nouns.*

The other, was a Scheme for entirely abolishing all Words whatsoever: And this was urged as a great Advantage in Point of Health as well as Brevity. For, it is plain, that every Word we speak is in some Degree a Diminution of our Lungs* by Corrosion; and consequently contributes to the shortning of our Lives. An Expedient was therefore offered, that since Words are only Names for *Things*,* it would be more convenient for all Men to carry about them, such *Things* as were necessary to express the particular Business they are to discourse on. And this Invention would certainly have taken Place, to the great Ease as well as Health of the Subject,* if the Women in Conjunction with the Vulgar and Illiterate had not threatned to raise a Rebellion, unless they might be allowed the Liberty to speak with their Tongues, after the Manner of their Forefathers: Such constant irreconcileable Enemies to Science are the common People. However, many of the most Learned and Wise adhere to the new Scheme of expressing themselves by *Things*; which hath only this Inconvenience* attending it; that if a Man's Business be very great, and of various Kinds, he must be obliged in Proportion to carry a greater Bundle of *Things* upon his Back, unless he can afford one or two strong Servants to attend him. I have often beheld two of those Sages almost sinking under the Weight of their Packs, like Pedlars among us; who when they met in the Streets would lay down their Loads, open their Sacks, and hold Conversation for an Hour together; then put up their Implements, help each other to resume their Burthens, and take their Leave.

But, for short Conversations, a Man may carry Implements in his Pockets and under his Arms, enough to supply him, and in his House he cannot be at a Loss; therefore the Room where Company meet who practice this Art, is full of all *Things* ready at Hand, requisite to furnish Matter for this Kind of artificial Converse.

Another great Advantage proposed by this Invention, was, that it would serve as an universal Language* to be understood in all civilized Nations, whose Goods and Utensils are generally of the same Kind, or nearly resembling, so that their Uses might easily be comprehended. And thus, Embassadors would be qualified to treat with foreign Princes or Ministers of State, to whose Tongues they were utter Strangers.

I was at* the Mathematical School, where the Master taught his Pupils after a Method scarce imaginable to us in *Europe.* The Proposition and Demonstration were fairly written on a thin Wafer, with Ink composed of a Cephalick Tincture.* This the Student was to swallow upon a fasting Stomach, and for three Days following eat nothing but Bread and Water. As the Wafer digested, the Tincture mounted to his Brain, bearing the Proposition along with it. But the Success hath not hitherto been answerable, partly by some Error in the *Quantum** or Composition, and partly by the Perverseness of Lads; to whom this Bolus is so nauseous, that they generally steal aside, and discharge it upwards before it can operate; neither have they been yet persuaded to use so long an Abstinence as the Prescription requires.

CHAPTER SIX

A further Account of the Academy. The Author proposeth some Improvements, which are honourably received.

IN THE School of political Projectors I was but ill entertained; the Professors appearing in my Judgment wholly out of their Senses;* which is a Scene that never fails to make me melancholy. These unhappy People were proposing Schemes for persuading Monarchs to chuse Favourites upon the Score of their Wisdom, Capacity and Virtue; of teaching Ministers to consult the publick Good; of rewarding Merit, great Abilities and eminent Services; of instructing Princes to know their true Interest, by placing it on the same Foundation with that of their People: Of chusing for Employments Persons qualified to exercise them; with many other wild impossible Chimæras, that never entered before into the Heart of Man to conceive; and confirmed in me the old Observation, that there is nothing so extravagant and irrational which some Philosophers have not maintained for Truth.

But, however I shall so far do Justice to this Part of the Academy, as to acknowledge that all of them were not so visionary. There was a most ingenious Doctor who seemed to be perfectly versed in the whole Nature and System of Government. This illustrious Person had very usefully employed his Studies in finding out effectual Remedies for all Diseases and Corruptions, to which the several Kinds of publick Administration are subject by the Vices or Infirmities of those who govern, as well as by the Licentiousness of those who are to obey. For Instance: Whereas all Writers and Reasoners have agreed, that there is a strict universal Resemblance between the natural and the political Body,* can there be any thing more evident, than that the Health of both must be preserved, and the Diseases cured by the same Prescriptions? It is allowed, that Senates and great Councils are often troubled with redundant, ebullient, and other peccant

Humours;* with many Diseases of the Head, and more of the
Heart; with strong Convulsions, with grievous Contractions of
the Nerves and Sinews in both Hands, but especially the
Right:* With Spleen, Flatus,* Vertigoes and Deliriums; with
scrophulous Tumours full of fœtid purulent Matter; with
sower frothy Ructations;* with Canine Appetites* and Crudeness of Digestion;* besides many others needless to mention.
This Doctor therefore proposed, that upon the meeting of a
Senate, certain Physicians should attend at the three first Days
of their sitting, and at the Close of each Day's Debate, feel the
Pulses of every Senator; after which having maturely considered, and consulted upon the Nature of the several Maladies,
and the Methods of Cure; they should on the fourth Day
return to the Senate-House, attended by their Apothecaries
stored with proper Medicines; and before the Members sat,
administer to each of them Lenitives, Aperitives, Abstersives,
Corrosives, Restringents, Palliatives, Laxatives, Cephalalgicks,
Ictericks, Apophlegmaticks, Acousticks, as their several Cases
required,* and according as these Medicines should operate,
repeat, alter, or omit them at the next Meeting.

This Project could not be of any great Expence to the
Publick; and might in my poor Opinion, be of much Use for
the Dispatch of Business in those Countries where Senates
have any Share in the legislative Power; beget Unanimity,
shorten Debates, open a few Mouths which are now closed,
and close many more which are now open; curb the Petulancy
of the Young, and correct the Positiveness of the Old; rouze
the Stupid, and damp the Pert.

Again; Because it is a general Complaint that the Favourites
of Princes are troubled with short and weak Memories; the
same Doctor proposed, that whoever attended a first Minister, after having told his Business with the utmost Brevity, and
in the plainest Words; should at his Departure give the said
Minister a Tweak by the Nose, or a Kick in the Belly, or tread
on his Corns, or lug him thrice by both Ears, or run a Pin into
his Breech, or pinch his Arm black and blue; to prevent
Forgetfulness: And at every Levee Day repeat the same Operation, till the Business were done or absolutely refused.

He likewise directed, that every Senator in the Great

Council of a Nation, after he had delivered his Opinion, and argued in the Defence of it, should be obliged to give his Vote directly contrary; because if that were done, the Result would infallibly terminate in the Good of the Publick.

When Parties in a State are violent,* he offered a wonderful Contrivance to reconcile them. The Method is this. You take an Hundred Leaders of each Party; you dispose them into Couples of such whose Heads are nearest of a Size; then let two nice Operators saw off the *Occiput* of each Couple at the same Time, in such a Manner that the Brain may be equally divided. Let the *Occiputs* thus cut off be interchanged, applying each to the Head of his opposite Party-man. It seems indeed to be a Work that requireth some Exactness; but the Professor assured us, that if it were dextrously performed, the Cure would be infallible. For he argued thus; that the two half Brains being left to debate the Matter between themselves within the Space of one Scull, would soon come to a good Understanding, and produce that Moderation as well as Regularity of Thinking, so much to be wished for in the Heads of those, who imagine they came into the World only to watch and govern its Motion: And as to the Difference of Brains in Quantity or Quality, among those who are Directors in Faction; the Doctor assured us from his own Knowledge, that it was a perfect Trifle.

I heard a very warm Debate between two Professors, about the most commodious and effectual Ways and Means of raising Money without grieving the Subject. The first affirmed, the justest Method would be to lay a certain Tax upon Vices and Folly; and the Sum fixed upon every Man, to be rated after the fairest Manner by a Jury of his Neighbours. The second was of an Opinion directly contrary; to tax those Qualities of Body and Mind for which Men chiefly value themselves; the Rate to be more or less according to the Degrees of excelling; the Decision whereof should be left entirely to their own Breast. The highest Tax was upon Men, who are the greatest Favourites of the other Sex; and the Assessments according to the Number and Natures of the Favours they have received; for which they are allowed to be their own Vouchers. Wit, Valour, and Politeness were likewise proposed to be largely taxed, and collected in the same Manner, by every Person giving his own Word for the Quantum of what he possessed. But, as to Honour, Justice, Wisdom and Learning, they should not be taxed at all; because, they are Qualifications of so singular a Kind, that no Man will either allow them in his Neighbour, or value them in himself.

The Women were proposed to be taxed according to their Beauty and Skill in Dressing; wherein they had the same Privilege with the Men, to be determined by their own Judgment. But Constancy, Chastity, good Sense, and good Nature were not rated, because they would not bear the charge of Collecting.

To keep Senators in the Interest of the Crown, it was proposed that the Members should raffle for Employments; every Man first taking an Oath and giving Security that he would vote for the Court, whether he won or no; after which the Losers had in their Turn the Liberty of raffling upon the next Vacancy. Thus, Hope and Expectation would be kept alive; none would complain of broken Promises, but impute their Disappointments wholly to Fortune, whose Shoulders are broader and stronger than those of a Ministry.

Another Professor shewed me a large Paper of Instructions for discovering Plots and Conspiracies against the Government. He advised great Statesmen to examine into the Dyet of all suspected Persons; their Times of eating; upon which Side they lay in Bed; with which Hand they wiped their Posteriors; to take a strict View of their Excrements,* and from the Colour, the Odour, the Taste, the Consistence, the Crudeness, or Maturity of Digestion, form a Judgment of their Thoughts and Designs: Because Men are never so serious, thoughtful, and intent, as when they are at Stool; which he found by frequent Experiment: For in such Conjunctions,* when he used merely as a Trial* to consider which was the best Way of murdering the King, his Ordure would have a Tincture of Green; but quite different when he thought only of raising an Insurrection, or burning the Metropolis.

The whole Discourse was written with great Acuteness, containing many Observations both curious and useful for Politicians, but as I conceived not altogether compleat. This I ventured to tell the Author, and offered if he pleased to supply him with some Additions. He received my Proposition with more Compliance than is usual among Writers, especially those of the Projecting Species; professing he would be glad to recieve farther Information.

I told him, that in the Kingdom of *Tribnia*,* by the Natives called *Langden*,* where I had long sojourned, the Bulk of the People consisted wholly of Discoverers, Witnesses, Informers, Accusers, Prosecutors, Evidences,* Swearers; together with their several subservient and subaltern Instruments;* all under the Colours, the Conduct, and pay of Ministers and their Deputies. The Plots in that Kingdom* are usually the Workmanship of those Persons who desire to raise their own Characters of profound Politicians; to restore new Vigour to a crazy Administration; to stifle or divert general Discontents; to fill their Coffers with Forfeitures;* and raise or sink the Opinion of publick Credit,* as either shall best answer their private Advantage. It is first agreed and settled among them, what suspected Persons shall be accused of a Plot: Then effectual Care is taken to secure all their Letters and other Papers, and put the Owners in Chains. These Papers are delivered to a Set of Artists very dextrous in finding out the mysterious Meanings of Words, Syllables and Letters. For Instance, they can decypher a Close-stool to signify a Privy-Council; a Flock of Geese, a Senate; a lame Dog, an Invader;* the Plague,* a standing Army; a Buzard,* a Minister; the Gout, a High Priest;* a Gibbet, a Secretary of State; a Chamber pot, a Committee of Grandees; a Sieve,* a Court Lady; a Broom, a Revolution; a Mouse-trap, an Employment;* a bottomless Pit, the Treasury; a Sink, a C——t;* a Cap and Bells, a Favourite; a broken Reed, a Court of Justice; an empty Tun, a General; a running Sore, the Administration.

When this Method fails, they have two others more effectual; which the Learned among them call Acrosticks, and Anagrams. *First*, they can decypher all initial Letters into political Meanings: Thus, *N*, shall signify a Plot; *B*, a Regiment of Horse: *L*, a Fleet at Sea. Or *Secondly*, by transposing the Letters of the Alphabet, in any suspected Paper, they can lay open the deepest Designs of a discontented Party. So for Example, if I should say in a Letter to a Friend, *Our Brother* Tom *has just got the Piles;** a Man of Skill in this Art would discover how the same Letters which compose that Sentence, may be analysed into the following words; *Resist,—— a Plot is brought home—— The Tour.** And this is the Anagrammatick Method.

The Professor made me great Acknowledgments for communicating these Observations, and promised to make honourable mention of me in his Treatise.

I saw nothing in this Country that could invite me to a longer Continuance; and began to think of returning home to *England*.

CHAPTER SEVEN

The Author leaves Lagado, *arrives at* Maldonada.* *No Ship ready. He takes a Short Voyage to* Glubbdubdrib.* *His reception by the Governor.*

THE CONTINENT of which this Kingdom is a part, extends itself, as I have Reason to believe, Eastward to that unknown Tract of *America*, Westward of *California*, and North to the Pacifick Ocean, which is not above an hundred and fifty Miles from *Lagado*; where there is a good Port and much Commerce with the great Island of *Luggnagg*,* situated to the North-West* about 29 Degrees North Latitude, and 140 Longitude. This Island of *Luggnagg* stands South Eastwards of *Japan*, about an hundred Leagues distant. There is a strict Alliance between the *Japanese* Emperor and the King of *Luggnagg*, which affords frequent Opportunities of sailing from one Island to the other. I determined therefore to direct my Course this Way, in order to my Return to *Europe*. I hired two Mules with a Guide to shew me the Way, and carry my small Baggage. I took leave of my noble Protector, who had shewn me so much Favour, and made me a generous Present at my Departure.

My Journey was without any Accident or Adventure worth relating. When I arrived at the Port of *Maldonada*,* (for so it is called) there was no Ship in the Harbour bound for *Luggnagg*, nor like to be in some Time. The Town is about as large as *Portsmouth*. I soon fell into some Acquaintance, and was very hospitably received. A Gentleman of Distinction said to me, that since the Ships bound for *Luggnagg* could not be ready in less than a Month, it might be no disagreeable Amusement for me to take a Trip to the little Island of *Glubbdubdrib*, about five Leagues to the South-West.* He offered himself and a Friend to accompany me, and that I should be provided with a small convenient Barque for the Voyage.

GLUBBDUBDRIB, as nearly as I can interpret the Word, signifies the Island of *Sorcerers* or *Magicians*. It is about one third as large as the Isle of *Wight*, and extreamly fruitful: It is governed by the Head of a certain Tribe, who are all Magicians. This Tribe marries only among each other; and the eldest in Succession is Prince or Governor. He hath a noble Palace, and a Park of about three thousand Acres, surrounded by a Wall of hewn Stone twenty Foot high. In this Park are several small Inclosures for Cattle, Corn and Gardening.

The Governor and his Family are served and attended by Domesticks of a Kind somewhat unusual. By his Skill in Necromancy, he hath Power of calling whom he pleaseth from the Dead, and commanding their Service for twenty-four Hours, but no longer; nor can he call the same Persons up again in less than three Months, except upon very extraordinary Occasions.

When we arrived at the Island, which was about Eleven in the Morning, one of the Gentlemen who accompanied me, went to the Governor and desired Admittance for a Stranger, who came on purpose to have the Honour of attending on his Highness. This was immediately granted, and we all three entered the Gate of the Palace between two Rows of Guards, armed and dressed after a very antick* Manner, and something in their Countenances that made my Flesh creep with a Horror I cannot express. We passed through several Apartments between Servants of the same Sort, ranked on each Side as before, till we came to the Chamber of Presence, where after three profound Obeysances, and a few general Questions, we were permitted to sit on three Stools near the lowest Step of his Highness's Throne. He understood the Language of *Balnibarbi*, although it were different from that of his Island. He desired me to give him some Account of my Travels; and to let me see that I should be treated without Ceremony, he dismissed all his Attendants with a Turn of his Finger, at which to my great Astonishment they vanished in an Instant, like Visions in a Dream, when we awake on a sudden. I could not recover myself in some Time, till the

Governor assured me that I should receive no Hurt; and observing my two Companions to be under no Concern, who had been often entertained in the same Manner, I began to take Courage; and related to his Highness a short History of my several Adventures, yet not without some Hesitation, and frequently looking behind me to the Place where I had seen those domestick Spectres. I had the Honour to dine with the Governor, where a new Set of Ghosts served up the Meat, and waited at Table. I new observed myself to be less terrified than I had been in the Morning. I stayed till Sun-set, but humbly desired his Highness to excuse me for not accepting his Invitation of lodging in the Palace. My two Friends and I lay at a private House in the Town adjoining, which is the Capital of this little Island; and the next Morning we returned to pay our Duty to the Governor, as he was pleased to command us.

After this Manner we continued in the Island for ten Days, most Part of every Day with the Governor, and at Night in our Lodging. I soon grew so familiarized to the Sight of Spirits, that after the third or fourth Time they gave me no Emotion at all; or if I had any Apprehensions left, my Curiosity prevailed over them. For his Highness the Governor ordered me to call up whatever Persons I would chuse to name,* and in whatever Numbers among all the Dead from the Beginning of the World to the present Time, and command them to answer any Questions I should think fit to ask; with this Condition, that my Questions must be confined within the Compass of the Times they lived in. And one Thing I might depend upon, that they would certainly tell me Truth; for Lying was a Talent of no Use in the lower World.

I made my humble Acknowledgments to his Highness for so great a Favour. We were in a Chamber, from whence there was a fair Prospect into the Park. And because my first Inclination was to be entertained with Scenes of Pomp and Magnificence. I desired to see *Alexander* the Great, at the Head of his Army just after the Battle of Arbela;* which upon a Motion of the Governor's Finger immediately appeared in a large Field under the Window, where we stood. *Alexander* was called up into the Room; It was with great Difficulty that I understood his *Greek,* and had but little of my own. He assured me upon his Honour that he was not poisoned, but dyed of a Fever by excessive Drinking.*

Next I saw *Hannibal* passing the *Alps,* who told me he had not a Drop of Vinegar in his Camp.*

I saw *Cæsar* and *Pompey* at the Head of their Troops just ready to engage.* I saw the former in his last great Triumph.* I desired that the Senate of *Rome* might appear before me in one large Chamber, and a modern Representative, in counterview,* in another. The first seemed to be an Assembly of Heroes and Demy-Gods; the other a Knot of Pedlars, Pick-pockets, Highwaymen and Bullies.

The Governor at my Request gave the Sign for *Cæsar* and *Brutus* to advance towards us. I was struck with a profound Veneration at the Sight of *Brutus;** and could easily discover the most consummate Virtue, the greatest Intrepidity, and Firmness of Mind, the truest Love of his Country, and general Benevolence for Mankind in every Lineament of his Counten-ance. I observed with much Pleasure, that these two Persons were in good Intelligence* with each other; and *Cæsar* freely confessed to me, that the greatest Actions of his own Life were not equal by many Degrees to the Glory of taking it away. I had the Honour to have much Conversation with *Brutus*; and was told that his Ancestor *Junius,** *Socrates,** *Epaminondas,** *Cato* the Younger,* Sir *Thomas More** and himself, were per-petually together: A *Sextumvirate** to which all the Ages of the World cannot add a Seventh.

It would be tedious to trouble the Reader with relating what vast Numbers of illustrious Persons were called up, to gratify that insatiable Desire I had to see the World in every Period of Antiquity placed before me. I chiefly fed mine Eyes with beholding the Destroyers of Tyrants and Usurpers, and the Restorers of Liberty to oppressed and injured Nations. But it is impossible to express the Satisfaction I received in my own Mind, after such a Manner as to make it a suitable Entertain-ment to the Reader.

CHAPTER EIGHT

HAVING A Desire to see those Antients, who were most renowned for Wit and Learning, I set apart one Day on purpose. I proposed that *Homer** and *Aristotle* might appear at the Head of all their Commentators; but these were so numerous, that some Hundreds were forced to attend in the Court and outward Rooms of the Palace. I knew and could distinguish those two Heroes at first Sight, not only from the Croud, but from each other. *Homer* was the taller and comelier Person of the two, walked very erect for one of his Age, and his Eyes were the most quick and piercing* I ever beheld. *Aristotle* stooped much, and made use of a Staff. His Visage was meager, his Hair lank and thin, and his Voice hollow. I soon discovered, that both of them were perfect Strangers to the rest of the Company, and had never seen or heard of them before. And I had a Whisper from a Ghost,* who shall be nameless, that these Commentators always kept in the most distant Quarters from their Principals in the lower World, through a Consciousness of Shame and Guilt, because they had so horribly misrepresented the Meaning of those Authors to Posterity. I introduced *Didymus** and *Eustathius** to *Homer,* and prevailed on him to treat them better than perhaps they deserved; for he soon found they wanted a Genius to enter into the Spirit of a Poet.* But *Aristotle* was out of all Patience with the Account I gave him of *Scotus** and *Ramus,** as I presented them to him; and he asked them whether the rest of the Tribe were as great Dunces as themselves.

I then desired the Governor to call up *Descartes** and *Gassendi,** with whom I prevailed to explain their Systems to *Aristotle.* This great Philosopher freely acknowledged his own Mistakes in Natural Philosophy, because he proceeded in many things upon Conjecture, as all Men must do; and he found, that *Gassendi*,* who had made the Doctrine of *Epicurus* as palatable as he could, and the *Vortices* of *Descartes*, were equally exploded. He predicted the same Fate to *Attraction*,* whereof the present Learned are such zealous Asserters. He said, that new Systems of Nature were but new Fashions, which would vary in every Age; and even those who pretend to demonstrate them from Mathematical Principles,* would flourish but a short Period of Time, and be out of Vogue when that was determined.*

I spent five Days in conversing with many others of the antient Learned. I saw most of the first *Roman* Emperors. I prevailed on the Governor to call up *Eliogabalus*'s* Cooks to dress us a Dinner; but they could not shew us much of their Skill, for want of Materials. A *Helot** of *Agesilaus** made us a Dish of *Spartan* Broth,* but I was not able to get down a second *Spoonful*.

The two Gentlemen who conducted me to the Island were pressed by their private Affairs to return in three Days, which I employed in seeing some of the modern Dead, who had made the greatest Figure for two or three Hundred Years past in our own and other Countries of *Europe*; and having been always a great Admirer of old illustrious Families, I desired the Governor would call up a Dozen or two of Kings with their Ancestors in order, for eight or nine Generations. But my Disappointment was grievous and unexpected. For, instead of a long Train with Royal Diadems, I saw in one Family two Fidlers, three spruce Courtiers, and an *Italian* Prelate. In another, a Barber, an Abbot, and two Cardinals.* I have too great a Veneration for crowned Heads to dwell any longer on so nice a Subject: But as to Counts, Marquesses, Dukes, Earls, and the like, I was not so scrupulous. And I confess it was not without some Pleasure that I found my self able to trace the particular Features, by which certain Families are distinguished up to their Originals. I could plainly discover from whence one Family derives a long Chin; why a second hath abounded with Knaves for two Generations, and Fools for two more; why a third happened to be crack-brained, and a fourth to be Sharpers. Whence it came, what *Polydore Virgil** says of a certain great House, *Nec Vir fortis, nec Fœmina Casta.** How

Cruelty, Falshood, and Cowardice grew to be Characteristicks by which certain Families are distinguished as much as by their Coat of Arms. Who first brought the *Pox** into a noble House, which hath lineally descended in scrophulous Tumours to their Posterity. Neither could I wonder at all this, when I saw such an Interruption of Lineages by Pages, Lacqueys, Valets, Coachmen, Gamesters, Fidlers, Players, Captains, and Pick-pockets.

I was chiefly disgusted with modern History. For having strictly examined all the Persons of greatest Name in the Courts of Princes for an Hundred Years past, I found how the World had been misled by prostitute Writers,* to ascribe the greatest Exploits in War to Cowards, the wisest Counsel to Fools, Sincerity to Flatterers, *Roman* Virtue to Betrayers of their Country, Piety to Atheists, Chastity to Sodomites, Truth to Informers. How many innocent and excellent Persons had been condemned to Death or Banishment, by the practising of great Ministers upon* the Corruption of Judges, and the Malice of Factions. How many Villains had been exalted to the highest Places of Trust, Power, Dignity, and Profit: How great a Share in the Motions and Events of Courts, Councils, and Senates might be challenged by Bawds, Whores, Pimps, Parasites, and Buffoons: How low an Opinion I had of human Wisdom and Integrity, when I was truly informed of the Springs and Motives of great Enterprizes and Revolutions in the World, and of the contemptible Accidents to which they owed their Success.*

Here I discovered the Roguery and Ignorance of those who pretend to write *Anecdotes*, or secret History;* who send so many Kings to their Graves with a Cup of Poison; will repeat the Discourse between a Prince and chief Minister, where no Witness was by; unlock the Thoughts and Cabinets of Embassadors and Secretaries of State; and have the perpetual Misfortune to be mistaken. Here I discovered the true Causes of many great Events that have surprized the World: How a Whore can govern the Back-stairs, the Back-stairs a Council, and the Council a Senate. A General confessed in my Presence, that he got a Victory purely by the Force of Cowardice and ill Conduct:* And an Admiral,* that for want of proper

Intelligence, he beat the Enemy to whom he intended to betray the Fleet. Three Kings* protested to me, that in their whole Reigns they did never once prefer any Person of Merit, unless by Mistake or Treachery of some Minister in whom they confided: Neither would they do it if they were to live again; and they shewed with great Strength of Reason, that the Royal Throne could not be supported without Corruption; because, that positive, confident, restive Temper, which Virtue infused into Man, was a perpetual Clog to publick Business.

I had the Curiosity to enquire in a particular Manner, by what Method great Numbers had procured to themselves high Titles of Honour, and prodigious Estates; and I confined my Enquiry to a very modern Period: However, without grating upon* present Times, because I would be sure to give no Offence even to Foreigners, (for I hope the Reader need not be told that I do not in the least intend my own Country in what I say upon this Occasion) a great Number of Persons concerned were called up, and upon a very slight Examination, discovered such a Scene of Infamy, that I cannot reflect upon it without some Seriousness. Perjury, Oppression, Subornation, Fraud, Pandarism, and the like *Infirmities** were amongst the most excusable Arts they had to mention; and for these I gave, as it was reasonable, due Allowance. But when some confessed, they owed their Greatness and Wealth to Sodomy or Incest; others to the prostituting of their own Wives and Daughters; others to the betraying their Country or their Prince; some to poisoning, more to the perverting of Justice in order to destroy the Innocent: I hope I may be pardoned if these Discoveries inclined me a little to abate of that profound Veneration which I am naturally apt to pay to Persons of high Rank, who ought to be treated with the utmost Respect due to their sublime Dignity, by us their Inferiors.

I had often read of some great Services done to Princes and States, and desired to see the Persons by whom those Services were performed. Upon Enquiry I was told, that their Names were to be found on no Record, except a few of them whom History hath represented as the vilest Rogues and Traitors. As to the rest, I had never once heard of them. They all appeared with dejected Looks, and in the meanest Habit; most of them telling me they died in Poverty and Disgrace, and the rest on a Scaffold or a Gibbet.

Among others there was one Person whose Case appeared a little singular.* He had a Youth about Eighteen Years old standing by his Side. He told me, he had for many Years been Commander of a Ship; and in the Sea Fight at *Actium,** had the good Fortune to break through the Enemy's great Line of Battle, sink three of their Capital Ships, and take a fourth, which was the sole Cause of *Antony*'s Flight,* and of the Victory that ensued: That the Youth standing by him, his only Son, was killed in the Action. He added, that upon the Confidence of some Merit, the War being at an End, he went to *Rome,* and solicited at the Court of *Augustus* to be preferred to a greater Ship, whose Commander had been killed; but without any regard to his Pretensions, it was given to a Boy who had never seen the Sea, the Son of a *Libertina,** who waited on one of the Emperor's Mistresses. Returning back to his own Vessel, he was charged with Neglect of Duty, and the Ship given to a favourite Page of *Publicola** the Vice-Admiral; whereupon he retired to a poor Farm, at a great Distance from *Rome,* and there ended his Life. I was so curious to know the Truth of this Story, that I desired *Agrippa** might be called, who was Admiral in that Fight. He appeared, and confirmed the whole Account, but with much more Advantage to the Captain, whose Modesty had extenuated or concealed a great Part of his Merit.

I was surprized to find Corruption grown so high and so quick in that Empire, by the Force of Luxury so lately introduced; which made me less wonder at many parallel Cases in other Countries where Vices of all Kinds have reigned so much longer, and where the whole Praise as well as Pillage hath been engrossed by the chief Commander,* who perhaps had the least Title to either.

As every Person called up made exactly the same Appearance he had done in the World, it gave me melancholy Reflections to observe how much the Race of human Kind was degenerate among us, within these Hundred Years past. How the Pox under all its Consequences and Denominations had altered every Lineament of an *English* Countenance: shortened the Size of Bodies, unbraced the Nerves, relaxed the Sinews and Muscles, introduced a sallow Complexion, and rendered the Flesh loose and *rancid.**

I descended so low as to desire that some *English* Yeomen of the old Stamp, might be summoned to appear; once so famous for the Simplicity of their Manners, Dyet and Dress; for Justice in their Dealings; for their true Spirit of Liberty; for their Valour and Love of their Country. Neither could I be wholly unmoved after comparing the Living with the Dead, when I considered how all these pure native Virtues were prostituted for a Piece of Money by their Grand-children; who in selling their Votes, and managing* at Elections have acquired every Vice and Corruption than can possibly be learned in a Court.

The Author's Return to Maldonada. *Sails to the Kingdom of* Luggnagg. *The Author confined. He is sent for to Court. The Manner of his Admittance. The King's great Lenity to his Subjects.*

THE DAY of our Departure being come, I took leave of his Highness the Governor of *Glubbdubdribb*, and returned with my two companions to *Maldonada*, where after a Fortnight's waiting, a Ship was ready to sail for *Luggnagg*. The two Gentlemen and some others were so generous and kind as to furnish me with Provisions, and see me on Board. I was a Month in this Voyage. We had one violent Storm, and were under a Necessity of steering Westward to get into the Trade-Wind, which holds for above sixty Leagues. On the 21st of *April*, 1708, we sailed in the River of *Clumegnig*, which is a Sea-port Town, at the South-East Point of *Luggnagg*. We cast Anchor within a League of the Town, and made a Signal for a Pilot. Two of them came on Board in less than half an Hour, by whom we were guided between certain Shoals and Rocks, which are very dangerous in the Passage, to a large Basin, where a Fleet may ride in Safety within a Cable's Length of the Town-Wall.

Some of our Sailors, whether out of Treachery or Inadvertence, had informed the Pilots that I was a Stranger and a great Traveller, whereof these gave Notice to a Custom-House Officer, by whom I was examined very strictly upon my landing. This Officer spoke to me in the Language of *Balnibarbi*, which by the Force of much Commerce is generally understood in that Town, especially by Seamen, and those employed in the Customs. I gave him a short Account of some Particulars, and made my Story as plausible and consistent as I could; but I thought it necessary to disguise my Country, and call my self a *Hollander*; because my Intentions were for *Japan*, and I knew the Dutch were the only *Europeans* permitted to enter into that Kingdom.* I therefore told the Officer, that having been shipwrecked on the Coast of *Balnibarbi*, and cast on a Rock, I was received up into *Laputa*, or the flying Island (of which he had often heard) and was now endeavouring to get to *Japan*, from whence I might find a Convenience* of returning to my own Country. The Officer said, I must be confined till he could receive Orders from Court, for which he would write immediately, and hoped to receive an Answer in a Fortnight. I was carried to a convenient Lodging, with a Centry placed at the Door; however I had the Liberty of a large Garden, and was treated with Humanity enough, being maintained all the Time at the King's Charge. I was visited by several Persons, chiefly out of Curiosity, because it was reported I came from Countries very remote, of which they had never heard.

I hired a young Man who came in the same Ship to be an Interpreter; he was a Native of *Luggnagg*, but had lived some Years at *Maldonada*, and was a perfect Master of both Languages. By his Assistance I was able to hold a Conversation with those that came to visit me; but this consisted only of their Questions and my Answers.

The Dispatch came from Court about the Time we expected. It contained a Warrant for conducting me and my Retinue to *Traldragdubb* or *Trildrogdrib*,* (for it is pronounced both Ways as near as I can remember) by a Party of Ten Horse. All my Retinue was that poor Lad for an Interpreter, whom I persuaded into my Service. At my humble Request we had each of us a Mule to ride on. A Messenger was dispatched half a Day's Journey before us, to give the King Notice of my Approach, and to desire that his Majesty would please to appoint a Day and Hour, when it would be his gracious Pleasure that I might have the Honour to *lick the Dust** *before his Footstool*. This is the Court Style, and I found it to be more than Matter of Form: For upon my Admittance two Days after my Arrival, I was commanded to crawl upon my Belly, and lick the Floor as I advanced; but on account of my being a Stranger, Care was taken to have it so clean that the Dust was not offensive. However, this was a peculiar Grace, not allowed to any but Persons of the highest Rank, when they desire an Admittance: Nay, sometimes the Floor is strewed with Dust on purpose, when the Person to be admitted happens to have powerful Enemies at Court: And I have seen a great Lord with his Mouth so crammed, that when he had crept to the proper Distance from the Throne, he was not able to speak a Word. Neither is there any Remedy, because it is capital for those who receive an Audience to spit or wipe their Mouths in his Majesty's Presence. There is indeed another Custom, which I cannot altogether approve of. When the King hath a Mind to put any of his Nobles to Death in a gentle indulgent Manner; he commands to have the Floor strowed with a certain brown Powder, of a deadly Composition, which being licked up infallibly kills him in twenty-four Hours. But in Justice to this Prince's great Clemency, and the Care he hath of his Subjects Lives, (wherein it were much to be wished that the Monarchs of *Europe* would imitate him) it must be mentioned for his Honour, that strict Orders are given to have the infected Parts of the Floor well washed after every such Execution; which if his Domesticks neglect, they are in Danger of incurring his Royal Displeasure. I my self heard him give Directions, that one of his Pages should be whipt, whose Turn it was to give Notice about washing the Floor after an Execution, but maliciously* had omitted it; by which Neglect a young Lord of great Hopes coming to an Audience, was unfortunately poisoned, although the King at that Time had no Design against his Life. But this good Prince was so gracious, as to forgive the Page his Whipping, upon Promise that he would do so no more, without special Orders.

To return from this Digression; when I had crept within four Yards of the Throne, I raised my self gently upon my Knees, and then striking my Forehead seven Times against the Ground, I pronounced the following Words, as they had been taught me the Night before, *Ickpling Gloffthrobb Squutserumm blhiop Mlashnalt Zwin tnodbalkguffh Slhiophad Gurdlubh Asht.* This is the Compliment established by the Laws of the Land for all Persons admitted to the King's Presence. It may be rendered into *English* thus: *May your cœlestial Majesty out-live the Sun, eleven Moons and an half.* To this the King returned some Answer, which although I could not understand, yet I replied as I had been directed; *Fluft drin Yalerick*

Dwuldum prastrad mirplush, which properly signifies, *My Tongue is in the Mouth of my Friend;** and by this Expression was meant that I desired leave to bring my Interpreter; whereupon the young Man already mentioned was accordingly introduced; by whose Intervention I answered as many Questions as his Majesty could put in above an Hour. I spoke in the *Balnibarbian* Tongue, and my Interpreter delivered my Meaning in that of *Luggnagg.*

The King was much delighted with my Company, and ordered his *Bliffmarklub* or High Chamberlain to appoint a Lodging in the Court for me and my Interpreter, with a daily Allowance for my Table, and a large Purse of Gold for my common Expences.

I stayed three Months in this Country* out of perfect Obedience to his Majesty, who was pleased highly to favour me, and made me very honourable Offers. But I thought it more consistent with Prudence and Justice to pass the Remainder of my Days with my Wife and Family.

CHAPTER TEN

The Luggnuggians *commended. A particular Description of the* Struldbrugs,* *with many Conversations between the Author and some eminent Persons upon that Subject.*

THE LUGGNUGGIANS are a polite and generous People, and although they are not without some Share of that Pride which is peculiar to all *Eastern* Countries, yet they shew themselves courteous to Strangers, especially such who are countenanced by the Court. I had many Acquaintance among Persons of the best Fashion, and being always attended by my Interpreter, the Conversation we had was not disagreeable.

One Day in much good Company, I was asked by a Person of Quality, whether I had seen any of their *Struldbrugs* or *Immortals.* I said I had not; and desired he would explain to me what he meant by such an Appellation, applyed to a mortal Creature. He told me, that sometimes, although very rarely, a Child happened to be born in a Family with a red circular Spot in the Forehead, directly over the left Eye-brow, which was an infallible Mark that it should never dye. The Spot, as he described it, was about the Compass of a Silver Threepence, but in the Course of Time grew larger, and changed its Colour; for at Twelve Years old it became green, so continued till Five and Twenty, then turned to a deep blue; at Five and Forty it grew coal black, and as large as an *English* Shilling; but never admitted any farther Alteration. He said these Births were so rare, that he did not believe there could be above Eleven Hundred *Struldbrugs* of both Sexes in the whole Kingdom, of which he computed about Fifty in the Metropolis, and among the rest a young Girl born about three Years ago. That, these Productions were not peculiar to any Family, but a meer Effect of Chance; and the Children of the *Struldbruggs* themselves, were equally mortal with the rest of the People.

I freely own myself to have been struck with inexpressible

Delight upon hearing this Account: And the Person who gave it me happening to understand the *Balnibarbian* Language, which I spoke very well, I could not forbear breaking out into Expressions perhaps a little too extravagant. I cryed out as in a Rapture; Happy Nation, where every Child hath at least a Chance for being immortal! Happy People who enjoy so many living Examples of antient Virtue, and have Masters ready to instruct them in the Wisdom of all former Ages! But, happiest* beyond all Comparison are those excellent *Struldbruggs*, who being born exempt from that universal Calamity of human Nature, have their Minds free and disingaged, without the Weight and Depression of Spirits caused by the continual Apprehension of Death. I discovered my Admiration that I had not observed any of these illustrious Persons at Court; the black Spot on the Forehead, being so remarkable a Distinction, that I could not have easily over-looked it: And it was impossible that his Majesty, a most judicious Prince, should not provide himself with a good Number of such wise and able Counsellors. Yet perhaps the Virtue of those Reverend Sages was too strict for the corrupt and libertine Manners of a Court. And we often find by Experience, that young Men are too opinionative and volatile to be guided by the sober Dictates of their Seniors. However, since the King was pleased to allow me Access to his Royal Person, I was resolved upon the very first Occasion to deliver my Opinion to him on this Matter freely, and at large by the Help of my Interpreter; and whether he would please to take my Advice or no, yet in one Thing I was determined, that his Majesty having frequently offered me an Establishment in this Country, I would with great Thankfulness accept the Favour, and pass my Life here in the Conversation of those superiour Beings the *Struldbruggs*, if they would please to admit me.

The Gentleman to whom I addressed my Discourse, be-cause (as I have already observed) he spoke the Language of *Balnibarbi*, said to me with a Sort of a Smile, which usually ariseth from Pity to the Ignorant, that he was glad of any Occasion to keep me among them, and desired my Per-mission to explain to the Company what I had spoke. He did so; and they talked together for some time in their own

Language, whereof I understood not a Syllable, neither could I observe by their Countenances what Impression my Discourse had made on them. After a short Silence, the same Person told me, that his Friends and mine (so he thought fit to express himself) were very much pleased with the judicious Remarks I had made on the great Happiness and Advantages of immortal Life; and they were desirous to know in a particular Manner, what Scheme of Living I should have formed to myself, if it had fallen to my Lot to have been born a *Struldbrugg*.

I answered, it was easy to be eloquent on so copious and delightful a Subject, especially to me who have been often apt to amuse myself with Visions of what I should do if I were a King, a General, or a great Lord: And upon this very Case I had frequently run over the whole System how I should employ myself, and pass the Time if I were to live for ever.

That, if it had been my good Fortune to come into the World a *Struldbrugg*, as soon as I could discover my own Happiness by understanding the Difference between Life and Death, I would first resolve by all Arts and Methods whatsoever to procure myself Riches: In the Pursuit of which, by Thrift and Management, I might reasonably expect in about two Hundred Years, to be the wealthiest Man in the Kingdom. In the second Place, I would from my earliest Youth apply myself to the Study of Arts and Sciences, by which I should arrive in time to excel all others in Learning. Lastly, I would carefully record every Action and Event of Consequence that happened in the Publick,* impartially draw the Characters of the several Successions of Princes, and great Ministers of State; with my own Observations on every Point. I would exactly set down the several Changes in Customs, Language, Fashion of Dress, Dyet and Diversions. By all which Acquirements, I should be a living Treasury of Knowledge and Wisdom, and certainly become the Oracle of the Nation.

I would never marry after Threescore,* but live in an hospitable Manner, yet still on the saving Side. I would entertain myself in forming and directing the Minds of hopeful young Men, by convincing them from my own Remembrance, Experience and Observation, fortified by numerous Examples, of the Usefulness of Virtue in publick and private Life. But, my choise and constant Companions should be a Sett of my own immortal Brotherhood, among whom I would elect a Dozen from the most ancient down to my own Contemporaries. Where any of these wanted Fortunes, I would provide them with convenient Lodges round my own Estate, and have some of them always at my Table, only mingling a few of the most valuable among you Mortals, whom Length of Time would harden me to lose with little or no Reluctance, and treat your Posterity after the same Manner; just as a Man diverts himself with the annual Succession of Pinks and Tulips in his Garden, without regretting the Loss of those which withered the preceding Year.

These *Struldbruggs* and I would mutually communicate our Observations and Memorials* through the Course of Time; remark the several Gradations by which Corruption steals into the World, and oppose it in every Step, by giving perpetual Warning and Instruction to Mankind; which, added to the strong Influence of our own Example, would probably prevent that continual Degeneracy of human Nature, so justly complained of in all Ages.

Add to all this, the Pleasure of seeing the various Revolutions of States and Empires; the Changes in the lower and upper World;* antient Cities in Ruins, and obscure Villages become the Seats of Kings. Famous Rivers lessening into shallow Brooks;* the Ocean leaving one Coast dry, and overwhelming another: The Discovery of many Countries yet unknown. Barbarity overrunning the politest Nations, and the most barbarous becoming civilized. I should then see the Discovery of the *Longitude,** the *perpetual Motion,** the *universal Medicine,** and many other great Inventions brought to the utmost Perfection.

What wonderful Discoveries should we make in Astronomy, by outliving and confirming our own Predictions; by observing the Progress and Returns of Comets, with the Changes of Motion in the Sun, Moon and Stars.

I enlarged upon many other Topicks, which the natural Desire of endless Life and sublunary Happiness could easily furnish me with. When I had ended, and the Sum of my

Discourse had been interpreted as before, to the rest of the Company, there was a good Deal of Talk among them in the Language of the Country, not without some Laughter at my Expence. At last the same Gentleman who had been my Interpreter, said, he was desired by the rest to set me right in a few Mistakes, which I had fallen into through the common Imbecility* of human Nature, and upon that Allowance was less answerable for them. That, this Breed of *Struldbruggs* was peculiar to their Country, for there were no such People either in *Balnibarbi* or *Japan*, where he had the Honour to be Embassador from his Majesty, and found the Natives in both those Kingdoms very hard to believe* that the Fact was possible; and it appeared from my Astonishment when he first mentioned the Matter to me, that I received it as a Thing wholly new, and scarcely to be credited. That in the two Kingdoms above-mentioned, where during his Residence he had conversed very much, he observed long Life to be the universal Desire and Wish of Mankind. That, whoever had one Foot in the Grave, was sure to hold back the other as strongly as he could. That the oldest had still Hopes of living one Day longer, and looked on Death as the greatest Evil, from which Nature always prompted him to retreat; only in this Island of *Luggnagg*, the Appetite for living was not so eager, from the continual Example of the *Struldbruggs* before their Eyes.

That the System of Living contrived by me was unreasonable and unjust,* because it supposed a Perpetuity of Youth, Health, and Vigour, which no Man could be so foolish to hope, however extravagant he might be in his Wishes. That, the Question therefore was not whether a Man would chuse to be always in the Prime of Youth, attended with Prosperity and Health; but how he would pass a perpetual Life under all the usual Disadvantages which old Age brings along with it. For although few Men will avow their Desires of being immortal upon such hard Conditions, yet in the two Kingdoms beforementioned of *Balnibarbi* and *Japan*, he observed that every Man desired to put off Death for sometime longer, let it approach ever so late; and he rarely heard of any Man who died willingly, except he were incited by the Extremity of

Grief or Torture. And he appealed to me whether in those Countries I had travelled as well as my own, I had not observed the same general Disposition.

After this Preface, he gave me a particular Account of the *Struldbruggs* among them. He said they commonly acted like Mortals, till about Thirty Years old, after which by Degrees they grew melancholy and dejected, increasing in both till they came to Fourscore. This he learned from their own Confession; for otherwise there not being above two or three of that Species born in an Age, they were too few to form a general Observation by. When they came to Fourscore Years, which is reckoned the Extremity of living in this Country, they had not only all the Follies and Infirmities of other old Men, but many more which arose from the dreadful Prospect of never dying. They were not only opinionative, peevish, covetous, morose, vain, talkative; but uncapable of Friendship, and dead to all natural Affection, which never descended below their Grand-children. Envy and impotent Desires, are their prevailing Passions. But those Objects against which their Envy seems principally directed, are the Vices of the younger Sort, and the Deaths of the old. By reflecting on the former, they find themselves cut off from all Possibility of Pleasure; and whenever they see a Funeral, they lament and repine that others are gone to an Harbour of Rest, to which they themselves never can hope to arrive. They have no Remembrance of any thing but what they learned and observed in their Youth and middle Age, and even that is very imperfect: And for the Truth or Particulars of any Fact, it is safer to depend on common Traditions than upon their best Recollections. The least miserable among them, appear to be those who turn to Dotage, and entirely lose their Memories; these meet with more Pity and Assistance, because they want many bad Qualities which abound in others.

If a *Struldbrugg* happen to marry one of his own Kind, the Marriage is dissolved of Course* by the Courtesy of the Kingdom,* as soon as the younger of the two comes to be Fourscore. For the Law thinks it a reasonable Indulgence, that those who are condemned without any Fault of their own to a perpetual Continuance in the World, should not have their Misery doubled by the Load of a Wife.

As soon as they have compleated the Term of Eighty Years, they are looked on as dead in Law; their Heirs immediately succeed to their Estates, only a small Pittance is reserved for their Support; and the poor ones are maintained at the publick Charge. After that Period they are held incapable of any Employment of Trust or Profit; they cannot purchase Lands, or take Leases, neither are they allowed to be Witnesses in any Cause, either Civil or Criminal, not even for the Decision of Meers* and Bounds.

At Ninety* they lose their Teeth and Hair; they have at that Age no Distinction of Taste, but eat and drink whatever they can get, without Relish or Appetite. The Diseases they were subject to, still continue without encreasing or diminishing. In talking they forget the common Appellation of Things, and the Names of Persons, even of those who are their nearest Friends and Relations. For the same Reason they never can amuse themselves with reading, because their Memory will not serve to carry them from the Beginning of a Sentence to the End; and by this Defect they are deprived of the only Entertainment whereof they might otherwise be capable.

The Language of this Country being always upon the Flux,* the *Struldbruggs* of one Age do not understand those of another; neither are they able after two Hundred Years to hold any Conversation (farther than by a few general Words) with their Neighbours the Mortals; and thus they lye under the Disadvantage of living like Foreigners in their own Country.

This was the Account given me of the *Struldbruggs*, as near as I can remember. I afterwards saw five or six of different Ages, the youngest not above two Hundred Years old, who were brought to me at several Times by some of my Friends; but although they were told that I was a great Traveller, and had seen all the World, they had not the least Curiosity to ask me a Question; only desired I would give them *Slumskudask*, or a Token of Remembrance; which is a modest Way of begging, to avoid the Law that strictly forbids it, because they are provided for by the Publick, although indeed with a very scanty Allowance.

They are despised and hated by all Sorts of People: When one of them is born, it is reckoned ominous,* and their Birth is recorded very particularly; so that you may know their Age by consulting the Registry, which however hath not been kept above a Thousand Years past, or at least hath been destroyed by Time or publick Disturbances. But the usual Way of computing how old they are, is, by asking them what Kings or great Persons they can remember, and then consulting History; for infallibly the last Prince in their Mind did not begin his Reign after they were Fourscore Years old.

They were the most horrifying Sight I ever beheld; and the Women more horrible than the Men. Besides the usual Deformities in extreme old Age, they acquired an additional Ghastliness in Proportion to their Number of Years, which is not to be described; and among half a Dozen I soon distinguished which was the eldest, although there were not above a Century or two between them.

The Reader will easily believe, that from what I had heard and seen, my keen Appetite for Perpetuity of Life was much abated. I grew heartily ashamed of the pleasing Visions I had formed; and thought no Tyrant could invent a Death into which I would not run with Pleasure from such a Life. The King heard of all that had passed between me and my Friends upon this Occasion, and raillied me very pleasantly; wishing I would send a Couple of *Struldbruggs* to my own Country, to arm our People against the Fear of Death; but this it seems is forbidden by the fundamental Laws of the Kingdom; or else I should have been well content with the Trouble and Expence of transporting them.

I could not but agree, that the Laws of this Kingdom relating to the *Struldbruggs*, were founded upon the strongest Reasons, and such as any other Country would be under the Necessity of enacting in the like Circumstances. Otherwise, as Avarice is the necessary Consequent* of old Age, those Immortals would in time become Proprietors of the whole Nation, and engross the Civil Power; which, for want of Abilities to manage, must end in the Ruin of the Publick.

CHAPTER ELEVEN

The Author leaves Luggnagg *and sails to* Japan. *From thence he returns in a* Dutch *Ship to* Amsterdam, *and from* Amsterdam *to* England.

I THOUGHT this Account of the *Struldbruggs* might be some Entertainment to the Reader, because it seems to be a little out of the common Way; at least, I do not remember to have met the like in any Book of Travels* that hath come to my Hands: And if I am deceived, my Excuse must be, that it is necessary for Travellers, who describe the same Country, very often to agree in dwelling on the same Particulars, without deserving the Censure of having borrowed or transcribed from those who wrote before them.

There is indeed a perpetual Commerce between this Kingdom and the great Empire of *Japan*; and it is very probable that the *Japanese* Authors may have given some Account of the *Struldbruggs*; but my Stay in *Japan* was so short, and I was so entirely a Stranger to the Language, that I was not qualified to make any Enquiries. But I hope the *Dutch** upon this Notice will be curious and able enough to supply my Defects.

His Majesty having often pressed me to accept some Employment in his Court, and finding me absolutely determined to return to my Native Country; was pleased to give me his Licence to depart; and honoured me with a Letter of Recommendation under his own Hand to the Emperor of *Japan*. He likewise presented me with four Hundred forty-four large Pieces of Gold (this Nation delighting in even Numbers) and a red Diamond* which I sold in *England* for Eleven Hundred Pounds.

On the 6th Day of *May*, 1709, I took a solemn Leave of his Majesty, and all my Friends. This Prince was so gracious as to order a Guard to conduct me to *Glanguenstald*, which is a Royal Port to the *South-West* Part of the Island. In six Days I found a Vessel ready to carry me to *Japan*; and spent fifteen

Days in the Voyage. We landed at a small Port-Town called *Xamoschi*, situated on the *South-East* Part of *Japan*. The Town lies on the *Western* Part, where there is a narrow Streight, leading *Northward* into a long Arm of the Sea, upon the *North-West* Part of which *Yedo** the Metropolis stands. At landing I shewed the Custom-House Officers my Letter from the King of *Luggnagg* to his Imperial Majesty: They knew the Seal perfectly well; it was as broad as the Palm of my Hand. The Impression was, *A King lifting up a lame Beggar from the Earth.** The Magistrates of the Town hearing of my Letter, received me as a publick Minister; they provided me with Carriages and Servants, and bore my Charges to *Yedo*, where I was admitted to an Audience, and delivered my Letter; which was opened with great Ceremony, and explained to the Emperor by an Interpreter, who gave me Notice of his Majesty's Order, that I should signify my Request; and whatever it were, it should be granted for the sake of his Royal Brother of *Luggnagg*. This Interpreter was a Person employed to transact Affairs with the *Hollanders*: He soon conjectured by my Countenance that I was an *European*, and therefore repeated his Majesty's Commands in *Low-Dutch*,* which he spoke perfectly well. I answered, (as I had before determined) that I was a *Dutch* Merchant, shipwrecked in a very remote Country, from whence I travelled by Sea and Land to *Luggnagg*, and then took Shipping for *Japan*, where I knew my Countrymen often traded, and with some of these I hoped to get an Opportunity of returning into *Europe*: I therefore most humbly entreated his Royal Favour to give Order, that I should be conducted in Safety to *Nangasac*.* To this I added another Petition, that for the sake of my Patron the King of *Luggnagg*, his Majesty would condescend to excuse my performing the Ceremony imposed on my Countrymen, of *trampling upon the Crucifix*,* because I had been thrown into his Kingdom by my Misfortunes, without any Intention of trading. When this latter Petition was interpreted to the Emperor, he seemed a little surprised; and said, he believed I was the first of my Countrymen who ever made any Scruple in this Point; and that he began to doubt whether I were a real *Hollander* or no; but rather suspected I must be a CHRISTIAN.* However, for the Reasons I had offered, but chiefly to gratify the King of *Luggnagg*, by an uncommon Mark of his Favour, he would comply with the *singularity* of my Humour; but the Affair must be managed with Dexterity, and his Officers should be commanded to let me pass as it were by Forgetfulness. For he assured me, that if the Secret should be discovered by my Countrymen, the *Dutch*, they would cut my Throat in the Voyage. I returned my Thanks by the Interpreter for so unusual a Favour; and some Troops being at that Time on their March to *Nangasac*, the Commanding Officer had Orders to convey me safe thither, with particular Instructions about the Business of the *Crucifix*.

On the 9th Day of *June*, 1709, I arrived at *Nangasac*, after a very long and troublesome Journey. I soon fell into Company of some *Dutch* Sailors belonging to the *Amboyna** of *Amsterdam*, a stout Ship of 450 Tuns. I had lived long in *Holland*, pursuing my Studies at *Leyden*, and I spoke *Dutch* well: The Seamen soon knew from whence I came last; they were curious to enquire into my Voyages and Course of Life. I made up a Story as short and probable as I could, but concealed the greatest Part. I knew many Persons in *Holland*; I was able to invent Names for my Parents, whom I pretended to be obscure People in the Province of *Guelderland*. I would have given the Captain (one *Theodorus Vangrult**) what he pleased to ask for my Voyage to *Holland*; but, understanding I was a Surgeon, he was contented to take half the usual Rate, on Condition that I would serve him in the Way of my Calling. Before we took Shipping, I was often asked by some of the Crew, whether I had performed the Ceremony above-mentioned? I evaded the Question by general Answers, that I had satisfied the Emperor and Court in all Particulars. However, a malicious Rogue of a Skipper* went to an Officer, and pointing to me, told him, I had not yet *trampled on the Crucifix*: But the other, who had received Instructions to let me pass, gave the Rascal twenty Strokes on the Shoulders with Bamboo; after which I was no more troubled with such Questions.

Nothing happened worth mentioning in this Voyage. We sailed with a fair Wind to the *Cape of Good Hope*, where we staid only to take in fresh Water. On the 6th of *April* we arrived safe at *Amsterdam*, having lost only three Men by Sickness in the

Voyage, and a fourth who fell from the Foremast into the Sea, not far from the Coast of *Guinca*. From *Amsterdam* I soon after set sail for *England* in a small Vessel belonging to that City.

On the 10th of *April*, 1710, we put in at the Downs. I landed the next Morning, and saw once more my Native Country after an Absence of five Years and six Months compleat. I went strait to *Redriff*, whither I arrived the same Day at two in the Afternoon, and found my Wife and Family in good Health.

The End of the Third Part.

PART FOUR

A Voyage to the Country of
The Houyhnhnms*

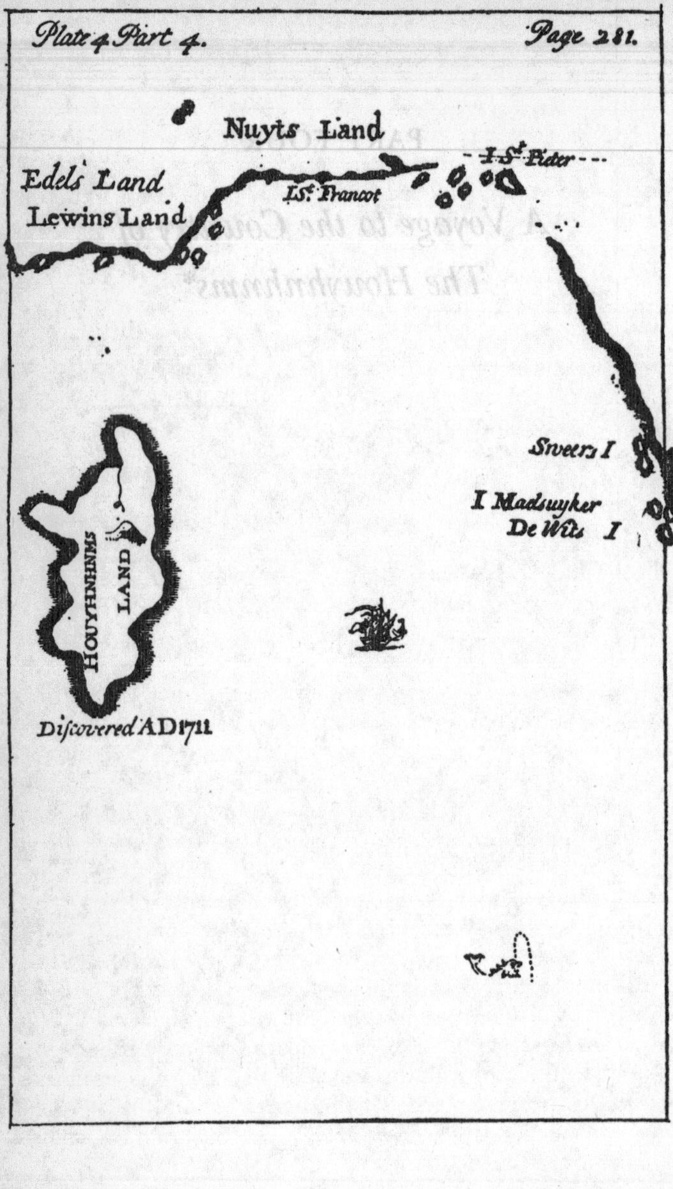

Plate 4 Part 4.   Page 281.

Nuyts Land

Edels Land
Lewins Land

I St: Francot

I St: Pieter

Sweers I

I Madsuyker
De Wits I

HOUYHNHNMS LAND

Discovered AD 1711

CHAPTER ONE

The Author sets out as Captain of a Ship. His Men conspire against him, confine him a long Time to his Cabbin, set him on Shore in an unknown Land. He travels up into the Country. The Yahoos,* *a strange Sort of Animal, described. The Author meets two* Houyhnhnms.

I CONTINUED at home with my Wife and Children about five Months in a very happy Condition, if I could have learned the Lesson of knowing when I was well. I left my poor Wife big with Child, and accepted an advantageous Offer made me to be Captain of the *Adventure,** a stout Merchant-man of 350 Tuns: For I understood Navigation well, and being grown weary of a Surgeon's Employment at Sea, which however I could exercise upon Occasion, I took a skilful young Man of that Calling, one *Robert Purefoy,** into my Ship. We set sail from *Portsmouth* upon the 7th Day of *September*, 1710; on the 14th we met with Captain *Pocock** of *Bristol*, at *Tenariff*, who was going to the Bay of *Campeachy*, to cut Logwood.* On the 16th he was parted from us by a Storm: I heard since my Return, that his Ship foundered and none escaped, but one Cabbin-Boy. He was an honest Man, and a good Sailor, but a little too positive in his own Opinions,* which was the Cause of his Destruction, as it hath been of several others. For if he had followed my Advice, he might at this Time have been safe at home with his Family as well as my self.

I had several Men died in my Ship of Calentures,* so that I was forced to get Recruits out of *Barbadoes*, and the *Leeward Islands*, where I touched by the Direction of the Merchants who employed me; which I had soon too much Cause to repent; for I found afterwards that most of them had been Buccaneers. I had fifty Hands on Board; and my Orders were, that I should trade with the *Indians* in the *South-Sea*, and make what Discoveries I could. These Rogues* whom I had picked up, debauched my other Men, and they all formed a

Conspiracy to seize the Ship and secure me; which they did one Morning, rushing into my Cabbin, and binding me Hand and Foot, threatening to throw me overboard, if I offered to stir. I told them, I was their Prisoner, and would submit. This they made me swear to do, and then unbound me, only fastening one of my Legs with a Chain near my Bed; and placed a Centry at my Door with his Piece* charged, who was commanded to shoot me dead if I attempted my Liberty. They sent me down Victuals and Drink, and took the Government of the Ship to themselves. Their Design was to turn Pirates, and plunder the *Spaniards*, which they could not do, till they got more Men. But first they resolved to sell the Goods in the Ship, and then go to *Madagascar** for Recruits, several among them having died since my Confinement. They sailed many Weeks, and traded with the *Indians*; but I knew not what Course they took, being kept close Prisoner in my Cabbin, and expecting nothing less than to be murdered, as they often threatened me.

Upon the 9th Day of *May*, 1711, one *James Welch* came down to my Cabbin; and said he had Orders from the Captain to set me ashore. I expostulated with him, but in vain; neither would he so much as tell me who their new Captain was. They forced me into the Long-boat, letting me put on my best Suit of Cloaths, which were as good as new, and a small Bundle of Linnen, but no Arms except my Hanger; and they were so civil as not to search my Pockets, into which I conveyed what Money I had, with some other little Necessaries. They rowed about a League; and then set me down on a Strand. I desired them to tell me what Country it was: They all swore, they knew no more than my self, but said, that the Captain (as they called him) was resolved, after they had sold the Lading, to get rid of me in the first Place where they discovered Land. They pushed off immediately, advising me to make haste, for fear of being overtaken by the Tide; and bade me farewell.

In this desolate Condition I advanced forward, and soon got upon firm Ground, where I sat down on a Bank to rest my self, and consider what I had best to do. When I was a little refreshed I went up into the Country, resolving to deliver my self to the first Savages I should meet; and purchase my Life

from them by some Bracelets, Glass Rings, and other Toys,*
which Sailors usually provide themselves with in those Voyages, and whereof I had some about me: The Land was divided by long Rows of Trees, not regularly planted, but
naturally growing; there was great Plenty of Grass, and several
Fields of Oats. I walked very circumspectly for fear of being
surprised, or suddenly shot with an Arrow from behind, or on
either Side. I fell into a beaten Road, where I saw many Tracks
of human Feet, and some of Cows, but most of Horses. At last
I beheld several Animals in a Field,* and one or two of the
same Kind sitting in Trees. Their Shape was very singular, and
deformed, which a little discomposed me, so that I lay down
behind a Thicket to observe them better. Some of them
coming forward near the Place where I lay, gave me an Opportunity of distinctly marking their Form. Their Heads and
Breasts were covered with a thick Hair, some frizzled and
others lank; they had Beards like Goats, and a Long Ridge of
Hair down their Backs, and the fore Parts of their Legs and
Feet; but the rest of their Bodies were bare, so that I might see
their Skins, which were of a brown Buff Colour. They had no
Tails, nor any Hair at all on their Buttocks, except about the
Anus; which, I presume Nature had placed there to defend
them as they sat on the Ground; for this Posture they used, as
well as lying down, and often stood on their hind Feet. They
climbed high Trees, as nimbly as a Squirrel, for they had
strong extended Claws before and behind, terminating in
sharp Points, and hooked.* They would often spring, and
bound, and leap with prodigious Agility. The Females were
not so large as the Males; they had long lank Hair on their
Heads, and only a Sort of Down on the rest of their Bodies,
except about the *Anus*, and *Pudenda*. Their Dugs hung between their fore Feet, and often reached almost to the
Ground as they walked.* The Hair of both Sexes was of several Colours, brown, red, black and yellow. Upon the whole,
I never beheld in all my Travels so disagreeable an Animal, or
one against which I naturally conceived so strong an Antipathy. So that thinking I had seen enough, full of Contempt and
Aversion, I got up and pursued the beaten Road, hoping it
might direct me to the Cabbin* of some *Indian*. I had not

gone far when I met one of these Creatures full in my Way, and coming up directly to me. The ugly Monster, when he saw me, distorted several Ways every Feature of his Visage, and stared as at an Object he had never seen before; then approaching nearer, lifted up his fore Paw, whether out of Curiosity or Mischief, I could not tell: But I drew my Hanger, and gave him a good Blow with the flat Side of it; for I durst not strike him with the Edge, fearing the Inhabitants might be provoked against me, if they should come to know, that I had killed or maimed any of their Cattle. When the Beast felt the Smart, he drew back, and roared so loud, that a Herd of at least forty came flocking about me from the next Field, howling and making odious Faces; but I ran to the Body of a Tree, and leaning my Back against it, kept them off, by waving my Hanger. Several of this cursed Brood getting hold of the Branches behind, leaped up into the Tree, from whence they began to discharge their Excrements on my Head:* However, I escaped pretty well, by sticking close to the Stem of the Tree, but was almost stifled with the Filth, which fell about me on every Side.

In the Midst of this Distress, I observed them all to run away on a sudden as fast as they could; at which I ventured to leave the Tree, and pursue the Road, wondering what it was that could put them into this Fright. But looking on my Left-Hand, I saw a Horse walking softly in the Field; which my Persecutors having sooner discovered, was the Cause of their Flight. The Horse started a little when he came near me, but soon recovering himself, looked full in my Face with manifest Tokens of Wonder: He viewed my Hands and Feet, walking round me several times. I would have pursued my Journey, but he placed himself directly in the Way, yet looking with a very mild Aspect, never offering the least Violence. We stood gazing at each other for some time; at last I took the Boldness, to reach my Hand towards his Neck, with a Design to stroak it; using the common Style and Whistle of Jockies when they are going to handle a strange Horse. But, this Animal seeming to receive my Civilities with Disdain, shook his Head, and bent his Brows, softly raising up his Left Fore-Foot to remove my Hand. Then he neighed three or four times, but in so different a Cadence, that I almost began to think he was speaking to himself in some Language of his own.

While He and I were thus employed, another Horse came up; who applying himself to* the first in a very formal Manner, they gently struck each others Right Hoof before, neighing several times by Turns, and varying the Sound, which seemed to be almost articulate. They went some Paces off, as if it were to confer together, walking Side by Side, backward and forward, like Persons deliberating upon some Affair of Weight; but often turning their Eyes towards me, as it were to watch that I might not escape. I was amazed to see such Actions and Behaviour in Brute Beasts; and concluded with myself, that if the Inhabitants of this Country were endued with a proportionable Degree of Reason, they must needs be the wisest People upon Earth. This Thought gave me so much Comfort, that I resolved to go forward until I could discover some House or Village, or meet with any of the Natives; leaving the two Horses to discourse together as they pleased. But the first, who was a Dapple-Grey, observing me to steal off, neighed after me in so expressive a Tone, that I fancied myself to understand what he meant; whereupon I turned back, and came near him, to expect* his farther Commands; but concealing my Fear as much as I could; for I began to be in some Pain, how this Adventure might terminate: and the Reader will easily believe I did not much like my present Situation.

The two Horses came up close to me, looking with great Earnestness upon my Face and Hands. The grey Steed rubbed my Hat all round with his Right Fore-hoof, and discomposed it so much, that I was forced to adjust it better, by taking it off, and settling it again; whereat both he and his Companion (who was a brown Bay) appeared to be much surprized; the latter felt the Lappet of my Coat, and finding it to hang loose about me, they both looked with new Signs of Wonder. He stroked my Right Hand, seeming to admire the Softness, and Colour; but he squeezed it so hard between his Hoof and his Pastern, that I was forced to roar; after which they both touched me with all possible Tenderness. They were under great Perplexity about my Shoes and Stockings, which they felt very often, neighing to each other, and using various Gestures, not unlike those of a Philosopher,* when he would attempt to solve some new and difficult Phænomenon.

Upon the whole, the Behaviour of these Animals was so orderly and rational, so acute and judicious, that I at last concluded, they must needs be Magicians, who had thus metamorphosed* themselves upon some Design; and seeing a Stranger in the Way, were resolved to divert themselves with him; or perhaps were really amazed at the Sight of a Man so very different in Habit, Feature and Complexion from those who might probably live in so remote a Climate.* Upon the Strength of this Reasoning, I ventured to address them in the following Manner: Gentlemen, if you be Conjurers,* as I have good Cause to believe, you can understand any Language; therefore I make bold to let your Worships know, that I am a poor distressed *Englishman*, driven by his Misfortunes upon your Coast; and I entreat one of you, to let me ride upon his Back, as if he were a real Horse, to some House or Village, where I can be relieved. In return of which Favour, I will make you a Present of this Knife and Bracelet, (taking them out of my Pocket.) The two Creatures stood silent while I spoke, seeming to listen with great Attention; and when I had ended, they neighed frequently towards each other, as if they were engaged in serious Conversation. I plainly observed, that their Language expressed the Passions* very well, and the Words might with little Pains be resolved into an Alphabet more easily than the *Chinese.*

I could frequently distinguish the Word *Yahoo,* which was repeated by each of them several times; and although it were impossible for me to conjecture what it meant, yet while the two Horses were busy in Conversation, I endeavoured to practice this Word upon my Tongue; and as soon as they were silent, I boldly pronounced *Yahoo* in a loud Voice, imitating, at the same time, as near as I could, the Neighing of a Horse; at which they were both visibly surprized,* and the Grey repeated the same Word twice, as if he meant to teach me the right Accent, wherein I spoke after him as well as I could, and found myself perceivably to improve every time, although very far from any Degree of Perfection. Then the Bay tried me with a second Word, much harder to be pronounced; but reducing it to the *English Orthography*, may be spelt thus, *Houyhnhnm*. I did not succeed in this so well as the former, but after two or three farther Trials, I had better Fortune; and they both appeared amazed at my Capacity.

After some farther Discourse, which I then conjectured might relate to me, the two Friends took their Leaves, with the same Compliment of striking each other's Hoof; and the Grey made me Signs that I should walk before him; wherein I thought it prudent to comply, till I could find a better Director. When I offered to slacken my Pace, he would cry *Hhuun, Hhuun*; I guessed his Meaning, and gave him to understand, as well as I could, that I was weary, and not able to walk faster; upon which, he would stand a while to let me rest.

CHAPTER TWO

The Author conducted by a Houyhnhnm *to his House. The House described. The Author's Reception. The Food of the* Houyhnhnms. *The Author in Distress for want of Meat, is at last relieved. His Manner of feeding in that Country.*

HAVING TRAVELLED about three Miles, we came to a long Kind of Building, made of Timber, stuck in the Ground, and wattled a-cross; the Roof was low, and covered with Straw. I now began to be a little comforted; and took out some Toys, which Travellers usually carry for Presents to the Savage *Indians* of *America* and other Parts, in hopes the People of the House would be thereby encouraged to receive me kindly. The Horse made me a Sign to go in first; it was a large Room with a smooth Clay Floor, and a Rack and Manger extending the whole Length on one Side. There were three Nags, and two Mares, not eating, but some of them sitting down upon their Hams, which I very much wondered at; but wondered more to see the rest employed in domestick Business: The last seemed but ordinary Cattle; however this confirmed my first Opinion, that a People who could so far civilize brute Animals, must needs excel in Wisdom all the Nations of the World. The Grey came in just after, and thereby prevented any ill Treatment, which the others might have given me. He neighed to them several times in a Style of Authority, and received Answers.

Beyond this Room there were three others, reaching the Length of the House, to which you passed through three Doors, opposite to each other, in the Manner of a Vista:* We went through the second Room towards the third; here the Grey walked in first, beckoning me to attend: I waited in the second Room, and got ready my Presents, for the Master and Mistress of the House: They were two Knives, three Bracelets of false Pearl, a small Looking Glass and a Bead Necklace. The Horse neighed three or four Times, and I waited to hear some Answers in a human Voice, but I heard no other Returns than in the same Dialect, only one or two a little shriller than his. I began to think that this House must belong to some Person of great Note among them, because there appeared so much ceremony before I could gain Admittance. But, that a Man of Quality should be served all by Horses, was beyond my Comprehension. I feared my Brain was disturbed by my Sufferings and Misfortunes: I roused my self, and looked about me in the Room where I was left alone; this was furnished as the first, only after a more elegant Manner. I rubbed mine Eyes often, but the same Objects still occurred.* I pinched my Arms and Sides, to awake my self, hoping I might be in a Dream. I then absolutely concluded, that all these Appearances could be nothing else but Necromancy and Magick. But I had no Time to pursue these Reflections; for the Grey Horse came to the Door, and made me a Sign to follow him into the third Room; where I saw a very comely Mare, together with a Colt and Fole, sitting on their Haunches, upon Mats of Straw, not unartfully made, and perfectly neat and clean.

The Mare soon after my Entrance, rose from her Mat, and coming up close, after having nicely observed my Hands and Face, gave me a most contemptuous Look; then turning to the Horse, I heard the Word *Yahoo* often repeated betwixt them; the meaning of which Word I could not then comprehend, although it were the first I had learned to pronounce; but I was soon better informed, to my everlasting Mortification: For the Horse beckoning to me with his Head, and repeating the Word *Hhuun, Hhuun,* as he did upon the Road, which I understood was to attend him, led me out into a kind of Court, where was another Building at some Distance from the House. Here we entered, and I saw three of those detestable Creatures, which I first met after my landing, feeding upon Roots, and the Flesh of some Animals, which I afterwards found to be that of Asses and Dogs, and now and then a Cow dead by Accident or Disease.* They were all tied by the Neck with strong Wyths,* fastened to a Beam; they held their Food between the Claws of their fore Feet, and tore it with their Teeth.

The Master Horse ordered a Sorrel Nag, one of his Servants, to untie the largest of these Animals, and take him into the Yard. The Beast and I were brought close together; and our Countenances diligently compared, both by Master and Servant, who thereupon repeated several Times the Word *Yahoo*. My Horror and Astonishment are not to be described, when I observed, in this abominable Animal, a perfect human Figure; the Face of it indeed was flat and broad, the Nose depressed, the Lips large, and the Mouth wide: But these Differences are common to all savage Nations, where the Lineaments of the Countenance are distorted by the Natives suffering their Infants to lie grovelling on the Earth, or by carrying them on their Backs,* nuzzling with their Face against the Mother's Shoulders. The Fore-feet of the *Yahoo* differed from my Hands in nothing else, but the Length of the Nails, the Coarseness and Brownness of the Palms, and the Hairiness on the Backs. There was the same Resemblance between our Feet, with the same Differences, which I knew very well, although the Horses did not, because of my Shoes and Stockings; the same in every Part of our Bodies, except as to Hairiness and Colour, which I have already described.

The great Difficulty that seemed to stick with the two Horses, was, to see the rest of my Body so very different from that of a *Yahoo*, for which I was obliged to my Cloaths, whereof they had no Conception:* The Sorrel Nag offered me a Root, which he held (after their Manner, as we shall describe in its proper Place) between his Hoof and Pastern; I took it in my Hand, and having smelt it, returned it to him again as civilly as I could. He brought out of the *Yahoo*'s Kennel a Piece of Ass's Flesh, but it smelt so offensively that I turned from it with loathing; he then threw it to the *Yahoo*, by whom it was greedily devoured. He afterwards shewed me a Wisp of Hay, and a Fettlock full of Oats; but I shook my Head, to signify, that neither of these were Food for me. And indeed, I now apprehended, that I must absolutely starve, if I did not get to some of my own Species: For as to those filthy *Yahoos*, although there were few greater Lovers of Mankind, at that time, than myself; yet I confess I never saw any sensitive Being so detestable on all Accounts; and the more I came near them, the more hateful they grew, while I stayed in that Country. This the Master Horse observed by my Behaviour, and therefore sent the *Yahoo* back to his Kennel. He then put his Forehoof to his Mouth, at which I was much surprized, although he did it with Ease, and with a Motion that appear'd perfectly natural; and made other Signs to know what I would eat; but I could not return him such an Answer as he was able to apprehend; and if he had understood me I did not see how it was possible to contrive any way for finding myself Nourishment. While we were thus engaged, I observed a Cow passing by; whereupon I pointed to her, and expressed a Desire to let me go and milk her. This had its Effect; for he led me back into the House, and ordered a Mare-servant to open a Room, where a good Store of Milk lay in Earthen and Wooden Vessels, after a very orderly and cleanly Manner. She gave me a large Bowl full, of which I drank very heartily, and found myself well refreshed.

About Noon I saw coming towards the House a Kind of Vehicle, drawn like a Sledge by four *Yahoos*. There was in it an old Steed, who seemed to be of Quality: he alighted with his Hind-feet forward, having by Accident got a Hurt in his Left Fore-foot. He came to dine with our Horse, who received him with great Civility. They dined in the best Room, and had Oats boiled in Milk for the second Course, which the old Horse ate warm, but the rest cold. Their Mangers were placed circular in the Middle of the Room, and divided into several Partitions, round which they sat on their Haunches upon Bosses of Straw. In the Middle was a large Rack with Angles answering to every Partition of the Manger. So that each Horse and Mare eat their own Hay, and their own Mash of Oats and Milk, with much Decency and Regularity. The Behaviour of the young Colt and Fole appeared very modest; and that of the Master and Mistress extremely chearful and complaisant* to their Guest. The Grey ordered me to stand by him; and much Discourse passed between him and his Friend concerning me, as I found by the Stranger's often looking on me, and the frequent Repetition of the Word *Yahoo*.

I happened to wear my Gloves; which the Master Grey observing, seemed perplexed; discovering Signs of Wonder

what I had done to my Fore-feet; he put his Hoof three or four
times to them, as if he would signify, that I should reduce
them to their former Shape, which I presently did, pulling off
both my Gloves, and putting them into my Pocket. This occasioned farther Talk, and I saw the Company was pleased
with my Behaviour, whereof I soon found the good Effects. I
was ordered to speak the few Words I understood; and while
they were at Dinner, the Master taught me the Names for
Oats, Milk, Fire, Water, and some others; which I could readily pronounce after him; having from my Youth a great Facility in learning Languages.

When Dinner was done, the Master Horse took me aside,
and by Signs and Words made me understand the Concern
he was in, that I had nothing to eat. Oats in their Tongue are
called *Hlunnh*. This Woud I pronounced two or three times;
for although I had refused them at first, yet upon second
Thoughts, I considered that I could contrive to make of them
a Kind of Bread, which might be sufficient with Milk to keep
me alive, till I could make my Escape to some other Country,
and to Creatures of my own Species. The Horse immediately
ordered a white Mare-servant of his Family to bring me a good
Quantity of Oats in a Sort of wooden Tray. These I heated
before the Fire as well as I could, and rubbed them till the
Husks came off, which I made a shift to winnow from the
Grain; I ground and beat them between two Stones, then took
Water, and made them into a Paste or Cake, which I toasted
at the Fire, and eat warm with Milk. It was at first a very insipid
Diet, although common enough in many Parts of *Europe*, but
grew tolerable by Time; and having been often reduced to
hard Fare in my Life, this was not the first Experiment I had
made how easily Nature is satisfied.* And I cannot but observe, that I never had one Hour's Sickness, while I staid in
this Island. It is true, I sometimes made a shift to catch a
Rabbet, or Bird, by Springes made of *Yahoos* Hairs; and I often
gathered wholesome Herbs, which I boiled, or eat as Salades
with my Bread; and now and then, for a Rarity, I made a little
Butter, and drank the Whey. I was at first at a great Loss for
Salt; but Custom soon reconciled the* Want of it; and I am
confident that the frequent Use of Salt among us is an Effect

of Luxury, and was first introduced only as a Provocative to Drink;* except where it is necessary for preserving of Flesh in long Voyages, or in Places remote from great Markets. For we observe no Animal to be fond of it but Man:* And as to myself, when I left this Country, it was a great while before I could endure the Taste of it in any thing that I eat.

This is enough to say upon the Subject of my Dyet, where-with other Travellers fill their Books, as if the Readers were personally concerned, whether we fare* well or ill. However, it was necessary to mention this Matter, lest the World should think it impossible that I could find Sustenance for three Years in such a Country, and among such Inhabitants.

When it grew towards Evening, the Master Horse ordered a Place for me to lodge in; it was but Six Yards from the House, and separated from the Stable of the *Yahoos.* Here I got some Straw, and covering myself with my own Cloaths, slept very sound. But I was in a short time better accommodated, as the Reader shall know hereafter, when I come to treat more particularly about my Way of living.

CHAPTER THREE

The Author studious to learn the Language, the Houyhnhnm *his Master assists in teaching him. The Language described. Several* Houyhnhnms *of Quality come out of Curiosity to see the Author. He gives his Master a short Account of his Voyage.*

MY PRINCIPAL Endeavour was to learn the Language, which my Master (for so I shall henceforth call him) and his Children, and every Servant of his House were desirous to teach me. For they looked upon it as a Prodigy, that a brute Animal should discover such Marks of a rational Creature. I pointed to every thing, and enquired the Name of it, which I wrote down in my *Journal Book* when I was alone, and corrected my bad Accent, by desiring those of the Family to pronounce it often. In this Employment, a Sorrel Nag, one of the under Servants, was very ready to assist me.

In speaking, they pronounce through the Nose and Throat, and their Language approaches nearest to the *High Dutch* or *German*, of any I know in *Europe*; but is much more graceful and significant.* The Emperor *Charles* V. made almost the same Observation* when he said, that if he were to speak to his Horse, it should be in *High Dutch*.

The Curiosity and Impatience of my Master were so great, that he spent many Hours of his Leisure to instruct me. He was convinced (as he afterwards told me) that I must be a *Yahoo*, but my Teachableness, Civility and Cleanliness astonished him; which were Qualities altogether so opposite to those Animals. He was most perplexed about my Cloaths, reasoning sometimes with himself, whether they were a Part of my Body; for I never pulled them off till the Family were asleep, and got them on before they waked in the Morning. My Master was eager to learn from whence I came; how I acquired those Appearances of Reason, which I discovered in all my Actions; and to know my Story from my own Mouth, which he hoped he should soon do by the great Proficiency

I made in learning and pronouncing their Words and Sentences. To help my Memory, I formed all I learned into the *English* Alphabet, and writ the Words down with the Translations. This last, after some time, I ventured to do in my Master's Presence. It cost me much Trouble to explain to him what I was doing; for the Inhabitants have not the least Idea of Books or Literature.*

In about ten Weeks time I was able to understand most of his Questions; and in three Months could give him some tolerable Answers. He was extremely curious to know from what Part of the Country I came, and how I was taught to imitate a rational Creature; because the *Yahoos,* (whom he saw I exactly resembled in my Head, Hands and Face, that were only visible,) with some Appearance of Cunning, and the strongest Disposition to Mischief, were observed to be the most unteachable of all Brutes. I answered; that I came over the Sea, from a far Place, with many others of my own Kind, in a great hollow Vessel made of the Bodies of Trees: That, my Companions forced me to land on this Coast, and then left me to shift for myself. It was with some Difficulty, and by the Help of many Signs, that I brought him to understand me. He replied, That I must needs be mistaken, or that I *Said the thing which was not.* (For they have no Word in their Language to express Lying or Falshood.) He knew it was impossible* that there could be a Country beyond the Sea, or that a Parcel of Brutes could move a wooden Vessel whither they pleased upon Water. He was sure no *Houyhnhnm* alive could make such a Vessel, or would trust *Yahoos* to manage it.

The Word *Houyhnhnm,* in their Tongue, signifies a *Horse;* and in its Etymology, *the Perfection of Nature.** I told my Master, that I was at a Loss for Expression, but would improve as fast as I could; and hoped in a short time I would be able to tell him Wonders: He was pleased to direct his own Mare, his Colt and Fole, and the Servants of the Family to take all Opportunities of instructing me; and every Day for two or three Hours, he was at the same Pains himself: Several Horses and Mares of Quality in the Neighbourhood came often to our House, upon the Report spread of a wonderful *Yahoo,* that could speak like a *Houyhnhnm,* and seemed in his Words and

Actions to discover some Glimmerings of Reason. These delighted to converse with me; they put many Questions, and received such Answers, as I was able to return. By all which Advantages, I made so great a Progress, that in five Months from my Arrival, I understood whatever was spoke, and could express myself tolerably well.

The *Houyhnhnms* who came to visit my Master, out of a Design of seeing and talking with me, could hardly believe me to be a right* *Yahoo*, because my Body had a different Covering* from others of my Kind. They were astonished to observe me without the usual Hair or Skin, except on my Head, Face and Hands: But I discovered that Secret to my Master, upon an Accident, which happened about a Fortnight before.

I have already told the Reader, that every Night when the Family were gone to Bed, it was my Custom to strip and cover myself with my Cloaths: It happened one Morning early, that my Master sent for me, by the Sorrel Nag, who was his Valet; when he came, I was fast asleep, my Cloaths fallen off on one Side, and my Shirt above my Waste. I awaked at the Noise he made, and observed him to deliver his Message in some Disorder; after which he went to my Master, and in a great Fright gave him a very confused Account of what he had seen: This I presently discovered; for going as soon as I was dressed, to pay my Attendance upon his Honour, he asked me the Meaning of what his Servant had reported; that I was not the same Thing when I slept as I appeared to be at other times; that his Valet assured him, some Part of me was white, some yellow, at least not so white, and some brown.

I had hitherto concealed the Secret of my Dress, in order to distinguish myself as much as possible, from that cursed Race of *Yahoos*; but now I found it in vain to do so any longer. Besides, I considered that my Cloaths and Shoes would soon wear out, which already were in a declining Condition, and must be supplied by some Contrivance from the Hides of *Yahoos*,* or other Brutes; whereby the whole Secret would be known. I therefore told my Master, that in the Country from whence I came, those of my Kind always covered their Bodies with the Hairs of certain Animals prepared by Art, as well for Decency, as to avoid Inclemencies of Air both hot and cold; of which, as to my own Person I would give him immediate Conviction, if he pleased to command me; only desiring his Excuse, if I did not expose those Parts that Nature taught us to conceal. He said, my Discourse was all very strange, but especially the last Part; for he could not understand why Nature should teach us to conceal what Nature had given.* That neither himself nor Family were ashamed of any Parts of their Bodies; but however I might do as I pleased. Whereupon I first unbuttoned my Coat, and pulled it off. I did the same with my Wastecoat; I drew off my Shoes, Stockings and Breeches. I let my Shirt down to my Waste, and drew up the Bottom, fastening it like a Girdle about my Middle to hide my Nakedness.

My Master observed the whole Performance with great Signs of Curiosity and Admiration. He took up all my Cloaths in his Pastern, one Piece after another, and examined them diligently; he then stroaked my Body very gently, and looked round me several Times; after which he said, it was plain I must be a perfect *Yahoo*; but that I differed very much from the rest of my Species in the Whiteness, and Smoothness of my Skin, my want of Hair in several Parts of my Body, the Shape and Shortness of my Claws behind and before, and my Affectation of walking continually on my two hinder Feet. He desired to see no more; and gave me leave to put on my Cloaths again, for I was shuddering with Cold.

I expressed my Uneasiness at his giving me so often the Appellation of *Yahoo*, an odious Animal, for which I had so utter an Hatred and Contempt. I begged he would forbear applying that Word to me, and take the same Order in his Family, and among his Friends whom he suffered to see me. I requested likewise, that the Secret of my having a false Covering to my Body might be known to none but himself, at least as long as my present Cloathing should last: For as to what the Sorrel Nag his Valet had observed, his Honour might command him to conceal it.

All this my Master very graciously consented to;* and thus the Secret was kept till my Cloaths began to wear out, which I was forced to supply by several Contrivances, that shall hereafter be mentioned. In the mean Time, he desired I would go on with my utmost Diligence to learn their Language, because he was more astonished at my Capacity for Speech and Reason, than at the Figure of my Body, whether it were covered or no; adding, that he waited with some Impatience to hear the Wonders which I promised to tell him.

From thenceforward he doubled the Pains he had been at to instruct me; he brought me into all Company, and made them treat me with Civility, because, as he told them privately, this would put me into good Humour, and make me more diverting.

Every Day when I waited on him, beside the Trouble he was at in teaching, he would ask me several Questions concerning my self, which I answered as well as I could; and by those Means he had already received some general Ideas, although very imperfect. It would be tedious to relate the several Steps, by which I advanced to a more regular Conversation. But the first Account I gave of my self in any Order and Length, was to this Purpose:

That, I came from a very far Country, as I already had attempted to tell him, with about fifty more of my own Species; that we travelled upon the Seas, in a great hollow Vessel made of Wood, and larger than his Honour's House. I described the Ship to him in the best Terms I could; and explained by the help of my Handkerchief displayed, how it was driven forward by the Wind. That, upon a Quarrel among us, I was set on Shoar on this Coast, where I walked forward without knowing whither, till he delivered me from the Persecution of those execrable *Yahoos*. He asked me, Who made the Ship, and how it was possible that the *Houyhnhnms* of my Country would leave it to the Management of Brutes? My Answer was, that I durst proceed no farther in my Relation, unless he would give me his Word and Honour that he would not be offended; and then I would tell him the Wonders I had so often promised. He agreed; and I went on by assuring him, that the Ship was made by Creatures like myself, who in all the Countries I had travelled, as well as in my own, were the only governing, rational Animals; and that upon my Arrival hither, I was as much astonished to see the *Houyhnhnms* act like rational Beings, as he or his Friends could be in finding some

Marks of Reason in a Creature he was pleased to call a *Yahoo*;
to which I owned my Resemblance in every Part, but could
not account for their degenerate and brutal Nature. I said
farther, That if good Fortune ever restored me to my native
Country, to relate my Travels hither, as I resolved to do; every
Body would believe that I *said the Thing which was not*; that I
invented the Story out of my own Head: And with all possible
respect to Himself, his Family, and Friends, and under his
Promise of not being offended, our Countrymen would
hardly think it probable, that a *Houyhnhnm* could be the
presiding Creature of a Nation, and a *Yahoo* the brute.

CHAPTER FOUR

The Houyhnhnms *Notion of Truth and Falshood. The Author's Discourse disapproved by his Master. The Author gives a more particular Account of himself, and the Accidents of his Voyage.*

MY MASTER heard me with great Appearances of Uneasiness in his Countenance; because *Doubting* or *not believing*, are so little known in this Country, that the Inhabitants cannot tell how to behave themselves under such Circumstances. And I remember in frequent Discourses with my Master concerning the Nature of Manhood,* in other Parts of the World; having Occasion to talk of *Lying*, and *false Representation*, it was with much Difficulty that he comprehended what I meant; although he had otherwise a most acute Judgment. For he argued thus; That the Use of Speech was to make us understand one another, and to receive Information of Facts; now if any one *said the Thing which was not*, these Ends were defeated; because I cannot properly be said to understand him; and I am so far from receiving Information, that he leaves me worse than in Ignorance; for I am led to believe a Thing *Black* when it is *White*, and *Short* when it is *Long*. And these were all the Notions he had concerning that Faculty of *Lying*, so perfectly well understood, and so universally practised among human Creatures.

To return from this Digression; when I asserted that the *Yahoos* were the only governing Animals in my Country, which my Master said was altogether past his Conception, he desired to know, whether we had *Houyhnhnms* among us, and what was their Employment: I told him, we had great Numbers; that in Summer they grazed in the Fields, and in Winter were kept in Houses, with Hay and Oats, where *Yahoo*-servants were employed to rub their Skins smooth, comb their Manes, pick their Feet, serve them with Food, and make their Beds. I understand you well, said my Master; it is now very plain from all you have spoken, that whatever Share of Reason the *Yahoos* pretend to, the *Houyhnhnms* are your Masters;* I heartily wish our *Yahoos* would be so tractable. I begged his Honour would please to excuse me from proceeding any farther, because I was very certain that the Account he expected from me would be highly displeasing. But he insisted in commanding me to let him know the best and the worst: I told him he should be obeyed. I owned, that the *Houyhnhnms* among us, whom we called *Horses*, were the most generous and comely Animal we had; that they excelled in Strength and Swiftness; and when they belonged to Persons of Quality, employed in Travelling, Racing, and drawing Chariots, they were treated with much Kindness and Care, till they fell into Diseases, or became foundered in the Feet; but then they were sold, and used to all kind of Drudgery till they died; after which their Skins were stripped and sold for what they were worth, and their Bodies left to be devoured by Dogs and Birds of Prey.* But the common Race of Horses had not so good Fortune, being kept by Farmers and Carriers, and other mean people, who put them to greater Labour, and feed them worse. I described as well as I could, our Way of Riding; the Shape and Use of a Bridle, a Saddle, a Spur, and a Whip; of Harness and Wheels. I added, that we fastened Plates of a certain hard Substance called *Iron* at the Bottom of their Feet, to preserve their Hoofs from being broken by the Stony Ways on which we often travelled.

My Master, after some Expressions of great Indignation, wondered how we dared to venture upon a *Houyhnhnm*'s Back; for he was sure, that the weakest Servant in his House would be able to shake off the strongest *Yahoo*; or by lying down, and rolling upon his Back, squeeze the Brute to Death. I answered, That our Horses were trained up from three or four Years old to the several Uses we intended them for; That if any of them proved intolerably vicious, they were employed for Carriages; that they were severely beaten while they were young for any mischievous Tricks: That the Males, designed for the common Use of Riding or Draught, were generally *castrated* about two Years after their Birth, to take down their Spirits, and make them more tame and gentle: That they were indeed sensible of Rewards and Punishments; but his Honour would please to consider, that they had not the least Tincture of Reason any more than the *Yahoos* in this Country.

It put me to the Pains of many Circumlocutions to give my Master a right Idea of what I spoke; for their Language doth not abound in Variety of Words, because their Wants and Passions are fewer* than among us. But it is impossible to express his noble Resentment at our savage Treatment of the *Houyhnhnm* Race; particularly after I had explained the Manner and Use of *Castrating* Horses among us, to hinder them from propagating their Kind, and to render them more servile. He said, if it were possible there could be any Country where *Yahoos* alone were endued with Reason, they certainly must be the governing Animal, because Reason will in Time always prevail against Brutal Strength. But, considering the Frame of our Bodies, and especially of mine, he thought no Creature of equal Bulk was so ill-contrived, for employing that Reason in the common Offices of Life; whereupon he desired to know whether those among whom I lived, resembled me or the *Yahoos* of his Country. I assured him, that I was as well shaped as most of my Age; but the younger and the Females were much more soft and tender, and the Skins of the latter generally as white as Milk. He said, I differed indeed from other *Yahoos*, being much more cleanly, and not altogether so deformed; but in point of real Advantage, he thought I differed for the worse. That my Nails were of no Use either to my fore or hinder Feet: As to my fore Feet,* he could not properly call them by that Name, for he never observed me to walk upon them; that they were too soft to bear the Ground; that I generally went with them uncovered, neither was the Covering I sometimes wore on them, of the same Shape, or so strong as that on my Feet behind. That I could not walk with any Security; for if either of my hinder Feet slipped, I must inevitably fall. He then began to find fault with other parts of my Body; the Flatness of my Face, the Prominence of my Nose, mine Eyes placed directly in Front, so that I could not look on either Side without turning my Head: That I was not able to feed my self, without lifting one of my fore Feet to my Mouth: And therefore Nature had placed those joints to answer that Necessity. He knew not what could be the use of these several Clefts and Divisions in my Feet behind; that these were too soft to bear the Hardness and Sharpness of Stone without a Covering made from the Skin of some other Brute; that my whole Body wanted a Fence against Heat and Cold, which I was forced to put on and off every Day with Tediousness and Trouble. And lastly, that he observed every Animal in this Country naturally to abhor the *Yahoos*, whom the Weaker avoided, and the Stronger drove from them. So that supposing us to have the Gift of Reason, he could not see how it were possible to cure that natural Antipathy which every Creature discovered against us; nor consequently, how we could tame and render them serviceable. However, he would (as he said) debate the Matter no farther, because he was more desirous to know my own Story, the Country, where I was born, and the several Actions and Events of my life before I came hither.

I assured him, how extreamly desirous I was that he should be satisfied in every Point; but I doubted much, whether it would be possible for me to explain my self on several Subjects whereof his Honour could have no Conception, because I saw nothing in his Country to which I could resemble them.* That however, I would do my best, and strive to express my self by Similitudes, humbly desiring his Assistance when I wanted proper Words; which he was pleased to promise me.

I said, my Birth was of honest Parents, in an Island called *England*, which was remote from this Country, as many Days Journey as the strongest of his Honour's Servants could travel in the Annual Course of the Sun. That I was bred a Surgeon, whose Trade it is to cure Wounds and Hurts in the Body, got by Accident or Violence. That my Country was governed by a Female Man, whom we called a *Queen*. That I left it to get Riches,* whereby I might maintain my self and Family when I should return. That in my last Voyage, I was Commander of the Ship and had about fifty *Yahoos* under me, many of which died at Sea, and I was forced to supply them by others picked out from several Nations. That our Ship was twice in Danger of being sunk; the first Time by a great Storm, and the second, by striking against a Rock. Here my Master interposed, by asking me, How I could persuade Strangers out of different Countries to venture with me, after the Losses I had sustained, and the Hazards I had run. I said, they were Fellows of desperate Fortunes, forced to fly from the Places of their Birth, on Account of their Poverty or their Crimes. Some were undone by Law-suits; others spent all they had in Drinking, Whoring and Gaming; others fled for Treason; many for Murder, Theft, Poysoning, Robbery, Perjury, Forgery, Coining false Money; for committing Rapes or Sodomy; for flying from their Colours,* or deserting to the Enemy; and most of them had broken Prison. None of these durst return to their native Countries for fear of being hanged, or of starving in a Jail; and therefore were under a Necessity of seeking a Livelihood in other Places.

During this Discourse, my Master was pleased often to interrupt me. I had made Use of many Circumlocutions in describing to him the Nature of the several Crimes, for which most of our Crew had been forced to fly their Country. This Labour took up several Days Conversation before he was able to comprehend me. He was wholly at a Loss to know what could be the Use or Necessity of practising those Vices. To clear up which I endeavoured to give him some Ideas of the Desire of Power and Riches; of the terrible Effects of Lust, Intemperance, Malice, and Envy. All this I was forced to define and describe by putting of Cases, and making Suppositions. After which, like one whose Imagination was struck with something never seen or heard of before, he would lift up his Eyes with Amazement and Indignation. Power, Government, War, Law, Punishment, and a Thousand other Things had no Terms, wherein that Language could express them; which made the Difficulty almost insuperable to give my Master any Conception of what I meant: But being of an excellent Understanding, much improved by Contemplation and Converse, he at last arrived at a competent Knowledge of what human Nature in our Parts of the World is capable to perform; and desired I would give him some particular Account of that Land, which we call *Europe*, especially, of my own Country.

CHAPTER FIVE

The Author at his Master's Commands informs him of the State of England. *The Causes of War among the Princes of* Europe. *The Author begins to explain the English Constitution.*

THE READER may please to observe, that the following Extract of many Conversations I had with my Master, contains a Summary of the most material Points, which were discoursed at several times for above two Years; his Honour often desiring fuller Satisfaction as I farther improved in the *Houyhnhnm* Tongue. I laid before him, as well as I could, the whole State of *Europe*; I discoursed of Trade and Manufactures, of Arts and Sciences; and the Answers I gave to all the Questions he made, as they arose upon several Subjects, were a Fund of Conversation not to be exhausted. But I shall here only set down the Substance of what passed between us concerning my own Country, reducing it into Order as well as I can, without any Regard to Time or other Circumstances, while I strictly adhere to Truth. My only Concern is, that I shall hardly be able to do Justice to my Master's Arguments and Expressions, which must needs suffer by my Want of Capacity, as well as by a Translation into our barbarous *English*.*

In obedience therefore to his Honour's Commands, I related to him the *Revolution*＊ under the Prince of *Orange*; the long War* with *France* entered into by the said Prince, and renewed by his Successor the present Queen; wherein the greatest Powers of *Christendom* were engaged, and which still continued: I computed at his Request, that about a Million of *Yahoos* might have been killed in the whole Progress of it; and perhaps a Hundred or more Cities taken, and five times as many Ships burnt or sunk.

He asked me what were the usual Causes or Motives that made one Country go to War with another. I answered, they were innumerable; but I should only mention a few of the chief. Sometimes the Ambition of Princes, who never think they have Land or People enough to govern:* Sometimes the Corruption of Ministers, who engage their Master in a War in order to stifle or divert the Clamour of the Subjects against their evil Administration. Difference in Opinions* hath cost many Millions of Lives: For Instance, whether *Flesh* be *Bread*, or *Bread* be *Flesh*:* Whether the Juice of a certain *Berry* be *Blood* or *Wine*: Whether *Whistling* be a Vice or a Virtue:* Whether it be better to *kiss a Post*,* or throw it into the Fire: What is the best Colour for a *Coat*, whether *Black, White, Red* or *Grey*;* and whether it should be *long* or *short, narrow* or *wide, dirty* or *clean*; with many more. Neither are any Wars so furious and bloody, or of so long Continuance, as those occasioned by Difference in Opinion, especially of it be in things indifferent.*

Sometimes the Quarrel between two Princes is to decide which of them shall dispossess a Third of his Dominions, where neither of them pretend to any Right.* Sometimes one Prince quarrelleth with another, for fear the other should quarrel with him. Sometimes a War is entered upon, because the Enemy is too *strong*, and sometimes because he is too *weak*. Sometimes our Neighbours *want* the *Things* which we *have*, or *have* the Things which we want; and we both fight, till they take ours or give us theirs. It is a very justifiable Cause of War to invade a Country after the People have been wasted by Famine, destroyed by Pestilence, or embroiled by Factions amongst themselves. It is justifiable to enter into a War against our nearest Ally, when one of his Towns lies convenient for us, or a Territory of Land, that would render our Dominions round and compact. If a Prince send Forces into a Nation, where the People are poor and ignorant, he may lawfully put half of them to Death, and make Slaves of the rest, in order to civilize and reduce* them from their barbarous Way of Living. It is a very kingly, honourable, and frequent Practice, when one Prince desires the Assistance of another to secure him against an Invasion, that the Assistant, when he hath driven out the Invader, should seize on the Dominions himself, and kill, imprison or banish the Prince he came to relieve. Allyance by Blood or Marriage, is a sufficient Cause of War between Princes; and the nearer the

Kindred is, the greater is their Disposition to quarrel: *Poor* Nations are *hungry*, and *rich* Nations are *proud*; and Pride and Hunger will ever be at Variance. For these Reasons, the Trade of a *Soldier* is held the most honourable of all others: Because a *Soldier* is a *Yahoo* hired to kill in cold Blood as many of his own Species, who have never offended him, as possibly he can.

There is likewise a Kind of beggarly Princes in *Europe*, not able to make War by themselves, who hire out their Troops to richer Nations for so much a Day to each Man; of which they keep three Fourths to themselves, and it is the best Part of their Maintenance; such are those in many *Northern* Parts of *Europe*.*

What you have told me, (said my Master) upon the Subject of War, doth indeed discover most admirably the Effects of that Reason you pretend to: However, it is happy that the *Shame* is greater than the *Danger*; and that Nature hath left you utterly uncapable of doing much Mischief: For your Mouths lying flat with your Faces, you can hardly bite each other to any Purpose, unless by Consent. Then, as to the Claws upon your Feet before and behind, they are so short and tender, that one of our *Yahoos* would drive a Dozen of yours before him. And therefore in recounting the Numbers of those who have been killed in Battle, I cannot but think that you have *said the Thing which is not*.

I could not forbear shaking my Head and smiling a little at his Ignorance. And, being no Stranger to the Art of War, I gave him a Description of Cannons, Culverins,* Muskets, Carabines,* Pistols, Bullets, Powder, Swords, Bayonets, Sieges, Retreats, Attacks, Undermines,* Countermines,* Bombardments, Sea-fights; Ships sunk with a Thousand Men; twenty Thousand killed on each Side; dying Groans, Limbs flying in the Air: Smoak, Noise, Confusion, trampling to Death under Horses Feet: Flight, Pursuit, Victory; Fields strewed with Carcases left for Food to Dogs, and Wolves, and Birds of Prey; Plundering, Stripping, Ravishing, Burning and Destroying. And, to set forth the Valour of my own dear Countrymen, I assured him, that I had seen them blow up a Hundred Enemies at once in a Siege, and as many in a Ship; and beheld the dead Bodies drop down in Pieces from the Clouds, to the great Diversion of all the Spectators.

I was going on to more Particulars, when my Master commanded me Silence. He said, whoever understood the Nature of *Yahoos* might easily believe it possible for so vile an Animal, to be capable of every Action I had named, if their Strength and Cunning equalled their Malice. But, as my Discourse had increased his Abhorrence of the whole Species, so he found it gave him a Disturbance in his Mind, to which he was wholly a Stranger before. He thought his Ears being used to such abominable Words, might by Degrees admit them with less Detestation. That, although he hated the *Yahoos* of this Country, yet he no more blamed them for their odious Qualities, than he did a *Gnnayh* (a Bird of Prey) for its Cruelty, or a sharp Stone for cutting his Hoof.* But, when a Creature pretending to Reason, could be capable of such Enormities, he dreaded lest the Corruption of that Faculty might be worse than Brutality itself. He seemed therefore confident, that instead of Reason, we were only possessed of some Quality fitted to increase our natural Vices; as the Reflection from a troubled Stream returns the Image of an ill-shapen Body, not only *larger*, but more *distorted*.

He added, That he had heard too much upon the Subject of War, both in this, and some former Discourses. There was another Point which a little perplexed him at present. I had said, that some of our Crew left their Country on Account of being ruined by *Law*: That I had already explained the Meaning of the Word: but he was at a Loss how it should come to pass, that the *Law* which was intended for *every* Man's Preservation, should be any Man's Ruin. Therefore he desired to be farther satisfied what I meant by *Law*, and the Dispensers thereof, according to the present Practice in my own Country: Because he thought, Nature and Reason were sufficient Guides for a reasonable Animal,* as we pretended to be, in shewing us what we ought to do, and what to avoid.

I assured his Honour, that *Law* was a Science wherein I had not much conversed,* further than by employing Advocates, in vain, upon some Injustices that had been done me. However, I would give him all the Satisfaction I was able.

I said there was a Society of Men among us,* bred up from their Youth in the Art of proving by Words multiplied for the Purpose, that *White* is *Black*, and *Black* is *White*, according as they are paid. To this Society all the rest of the People are Slaves.

For Example. If my Neigbour hath a mind to my *Cow*, he hires a Lawyer to prove that he ought to have my *Cow* from me. I must then hire another to defend my Right; it being against all Rules of *Law* that any Man should be allowed to speak for himself.* Now in this Case, I who am the true Owner lie under two great Disadvantages. First, my Lawyer being practiced almost from his Cradle in defending Falshood; is quite out of his Element when he would be an Advocate for Justice, which as an Office unnatural, he always attempts with great Awkwardness, if not with Ill-will. The second Disadvantage is, that my Lawyer must proceed with great Caution: Or else he will be reprimanded by the Judges, and abhorred by his Brethren, as one who would lessen the Practice* of the Law. And therefore I have but two Methods to preserve my *Cow.* The first is, to gain over my Adversary's Lawyer with a double Fee; who will then betray his Client, by insinuating that he hath Justice on his Side. The second way is for my Lawyer to make my Cause appear as unjust as he can; by allowing the *Cow* to belong to my Adversary; and this if it be skilfully done, will certainly bespeak the Favour of the Bench.

Now, your Honour is to know, that these Judges are Persons appointed to decide all Controversies of Property, as well as for the Tryal of Criminals; and picked out from the most dextrous Lawyers who are grown old or lazy: And having been byassed all their Lives against Truth and Equity, are under such a fatal Necessity of favouring Fraud, Perjury and Oppression; that I have known some of them to have refused a large Bribe from the Side where Justice lay, rather than injure the *Faculty*,* by doing any thing unbecoming their Nature or their Office.

It is a Maxim among these Lawyers, that whatever hath been done before, may legally be done again: And therefore they take special Care to record all the Decisions formerly made against common Justice and the general Reason of

Mankind. These, under the Name of *Precedents*, they produce as Authorities to justify the most iniquitous Opinions; and the Judges never fail of decreeing accordingly.

In pleading, they studiously avoid entering into the *Merits* of the Cause; but are loud, violent and tedious in dwelling upon all *Circumstances* which are not to the Purpose. For Instance, in the Case already mentioned: They never desire to know what Claim or Title my Adversary hath to my *Cow*; but whether the said *Cow* were Red or Black; her Horns long or short; whether the Field I graze her in be round or square; whether she were milked at home or abroad; what Diseases she is subject to, and the like. After which they consult *Precedents*, adjourn the Cause, from Time to Time, and in Ten, Twenty, or Thirty Years come to an Issue.

It is likewise to be observed, that this Society hath a peculiar Cant and Jargon of their own, that no other Mortal can understand, and wherein all their Laws are written, which they take special Care to multiply; whereby they have wholly confounded the very Essence of Truth and Falshood, of Right and Wrong; so that it will take Thirty Years to decide whether the Field, left me by my Ancestors for six Generations, belong to me, or to a Stranger three Hundred Miles off.

In the Tryal of Persons accused for Crimes against the State, the Method is much more short and commendable: The Judge, first sends to sound to Disposition of those in Power;* after which he can easily hang or save the Criminal, strictly preserving all the Forms of Law.

Here my Master interposing, said it was a Pity, that Creatures endowed with such prodigious Abilities of Mind as these Lawyers, by the Description I gave of them must certainly be, were not encouraged to be Instructors of others in Wisdom and Knowledge. In Answer to which, I assured his Honour, that in all Points out of their own Trade, they were usually the most ignorant and stupid Generation* among us, the most despicable in common Conversation, avowed Enemies to all Knowledge and Learning; and equally disposed to pervert the general Reason of Mankind, in every other Subject of Discourse, as in that of their own Profession.

CHAPTER SIX

A Continuation of the State of England, under Queen Anne.* The Character of a first Minister in the Courts of Europe.

MY MASTER was yet wholly at a Loss to understand what Motives could incite this Race of Lawyers to perplex, disquiet, and weary themselves by engaging in a Confederacy of Injustice, merely for the Sake of injuring their Fellow-Animals; neither could he comprehend what I meant in saying they did it for *Hire.* Whereupon I was at much Pains to describe to him the Use of *Money,* the Materials it was made of, and the Value of the Metals:* That when a *Yahoo* had got a great Store of this precious Substance, he was able to purchase whatever he had a mind to; the finest Cloathing, the noblest Houses, great Tracts of Land, the most costly Meats and Drinks; and have his Choice of the most beautiful Females. Therefore since *Money* alone, was able to perform all these Feats, our *Yahoos* thought, they could never have enough of it to spend or to save, as they found themselves inclined from their natural Bent either to Profusion or Avarice. That, the rich Man enjoyed the Fruit of the poor Man's Labour, and the latter were a Thousand to One in Proportion to the former. That the Bulk of our People was forced to live miserably, by labouring every Day for small Wages to make a few live plentifully.* I enlarged myself much on these and many other Particulars to the same Purpose: But his Honour was still to seek:* For he went upon a Supposition that all Animals had a Title to their Share in the Productions of the Earth; and especially those who presided over the rest.* Therefore he desired I would let him know, what these costly Meats were, and how any of us happened to want them. Whereupon I enumerated as many Sorts as came into my Head, with the Various Methods of dressing them, which could not be done without sending Vessels by Sea to every Part of the World, as well for Liquors to drink, as for Sauces, and innumerable other

Conveniencies. I assured him, that this whole Globe of Earth must be at least three Times gone round,* before one of our better Female *Yahoos* could get her Breakfast, or a Cup to put it in. He said, That must needs be a miserable Country which cannot furnish Food for its own Inhabitants. But what he chiefly wondered at, was how such vast Tracts of Ground as I described, should be wholly without *Fresh water*, and the People put to the Necessity of sending over the Sea for Drink. I replied, that *England* (the dear Place of my Nativity) was computed to produce three Times the Quantity of Food, more than its Inhabitants are able to consume, as well as Liquors extracted from Grain, or pressed out of the Fruit of certain Trees, which made excellent Drink; and the same Proportion in every other Convenience of Life. But, in order to feed the Luxury and Intemperance of the Males, and the Vanity of the Females, we sent away the greatest Part of our necessary Things to other Countries, from whence in Return we brought the Materials of Diseases, Folly, and Vice, to spend among ourselves. Hence it follows of Necessity, that vast Numbers of our People are compelled to seek their Livelihood by Begging, Robbing, Stealing, Cheating, Pimping, Forswearing, Flattering, Suborning, Forging, Gaming, Lying, Fawning, Hectoring, Voting, Scribling, Stargazing,* Poysoning, Whoring, Canting, Libelling, Free-thinking, and the like Occupations: Every one of which Terms, I was at much Pains to make him understand.

That, *Wine* was not imported among us from foreign Countries, to supply the Want of Water or other Drinks, but because it was a Sort of Liquid which made us merry, by putting us out of our Senses; diverted all melancholy Thoughts, begat wild extravagant Imaginations in the Brain, raised our Hopes, and banished our Fears; suspended every Office of Reason for a Time, and deprived us of the Use of our Limbs, untill we fell into a profound Sleep; although it must be confessed, that we always awaked sick and dispirited; and that the Use of this Liquor filled us with Diseases, which made our Lives uncomfortable and short.*

But beside all this, the Bulk of our People supported themselves by furnishing the Necessities or Conveniencies of Life to the Rich, and to each other. For Instance, when I am at home and dressed as I ought to be, I carry on my Body the Workmanship of an Hundred Tradesmen,* the Building and Furniture of my House employ as many more; and five Times the Number to adorn my Wife.

I was going on to tell him of another Sort of People, who get their Livelihood by attending the Sick; having upon some Occasions informed his Honour that many of my Crew had died of Diseases. But here it was with the utmost Difficulty, that I brought him to apprehend what I meant. He could easily conceive, that a *Houyhnhnm* grew weak and heavy a few Days before his Death; or by some Accident might hurt a Limb. But that Nature, who worketh all things to Perfection, should suffer any Pains to breed in our Bodies, he thought impossible;* and desired to know the Reason of so unaccountable an Evil. I told him, we fed on a Thousand Things which operated contrary to each other; that we eat when we were not hungry, and drank without the Provocation of Thirst: That we sat whole Nights drinking strong Liquors without eating a Bit; which disposed us to Sloth, enflamed our Bodies, and precipitated or prevented Digestion. That, prostitute Female *Yahoos* acquired a certain Malady, which bred Rottenness in the Bones of those, who fell into their Embraces: That this and many other Diseases, were propagated from Father to Son; so that great Numbers come into the World with complicated Maladies upon them: That, it would be endless to give him a Catalogue of all Diseases incident to human Bodies; for they could not be fewer than five or six Hundred, spread over every Limb, and Joynt: In short, every Part, external and intestine, having Diseases appropriated to each. To remedy which, there was a Sort of People bred up among us, in the Profession or Pretence of curing the Sick. And because I had some Skill in the Faculty, I would in Gratitude to his Honour, let him know the whole Mystery* and Method by which they proceed.

Their Fundamental is, that all Diseases arise from *Repletion*; from whence they conclude, that a great *Evacuation* of the Body is necessary, either through the natural Passage, or upwards at the Mouth. Their next Business is, from Herbs,

Minerals, Gums, Oyls, Shells, Salts, Juices, Sea-weed, Excrements, Barks of Trees, Serpents, Toads, Frogs, Spiders, dead Mens Flesh and Bones, Birds, Beasts and Fishes, to form a Composition for Smell and Taste the most abominable, nauseous and detestable, that they can possibly contrive, which the Stomach immediately rejects with Loathing: And this they call a *Vomit.** Or else from the same Store-house, with some other poysonous Additions, they command us to take in at the Orifice *above* or *below*, (just as the Physician then happens to be disposed) a Medicine equally annoying and disgustful to the Bowels; which relaxing the Belly, drives down all before it: And this they call a *Purge*, or a *Clyster.** For Nature (as the Physicians alledge) having intended the superior anterior Orifice only for the *Intromission* of Solids and Liquids, and the inferior Posterior for Ejection; these Artists ingeniously considering that in all Diseases Nature is forced out of her Seat; therefore to replace her in it, the Body must be treated in a Manner directly contrary, by interchanging the Use of each Orifice; forcing Solids and Liquids in at the *Anus*, and making Evacuations at the Mouth.

But, besides real Diseases, we are subject to many that are only imaginary, for which the Physicians have invented imaginary Cures; these have their several Names, and so have the Drugs that are proper for them; and with these our Female *Yahoos* are always infested.

One great Excellency in this Tribe is their Skill at *Prognosticks*, wherein they seldom fail; their Predictions in real Diseases, when they rise to any Degree of Malignity, generally portending *Death*, which is always in their Power, when Recovery is not: And therefore, upon any unexpected Signs of Amendment, after they have pronounced their Sentence, rather than be accused as false Prophets, they know how to approve their Sagacity to the World by a seasonable Dose.*

They are likewise of special Use to Husbands and Wives, who are grown weary of their Mates; to eldest Sons, to great Ministers of State, and often to Princes.

I had formerly upon Occasion discoursed with my Master upon the Nature of *Government* in general, and particularly of our own *excellent Constitution*, deservedly the Wonder and

Envy of the whole World. But having here accidentally mentioned a *Minister of State*, he commanded me some Time after to inform him, what Species of *Yahoo* I particularly meant by that Appellation.

I told him, that a *First* or *Chief Minister** of State, whom I intended to describe, was a Creature wholly exempt from Joy and Grief, Love and Hatred, Pity and Anger; at least makes use of no other Passions but a violent Desire of Wealth, Power, and Titles: That he applies his Words to all Uses, except to the Indication of his Mind;* That he never tells a *Truth*, but with an Intent that you should take it for a *Lye*; nor a *Lye*, but with a Design that you should take it for a *Truth*; That those he speaks worst of behind their Backs, are in the surest way to Preferment; and whenever he begins to praise you to others or to your self, you are from that Day forlorn.* The worst Mark you can receive is a *Promise*, especially when it is confirmed with an Oath; after which every wise Man retires, and gives over all Hopes.

There are three Methods by which a Man may rise to be Chief Minister: The first is, by knowing how with Prudence to dispose of a Wife, a Daughter, or a Sister: The second, by betraying or undermining his Predecessor: And the third is, by a *furious Zeal* in publick Assemblies against the Corruptions of the Court. But a wise Prince would rather chuse to employ those who practise the last of these Methods; because such Zealots prove always the most obsequious and subservient to the Will and Passions of their Master. That, these *Ministers* having all Employments at their Disposal, preserve themselves in Power by bribing the Majority of a Senate or great Council; and at last by an Expedient called an *Act of Indemnity** (whereof I described the Nature to him) they secure themselves from After-reckonings, and retire from the Publick, laden with the Spoils of the Nation.

The Palace of a *Chief Minister*, is a Seminary to breed up others in his own Trade: The Pages, Lacquies, and Porter, by imitating their Master, become *Ministers of State* in their several Districts, and learn to excel in the three principal *Ingredients*, of *Insolence*, *Lying*, and *Bribery*. Accordingly, they have a *Subaltern* Court paid to them by Persons of the best Rank; and sometimes by the Force of Dexterity and Impudence, arrive through several Gradations to be Successors to their Lord.

He is usually governed by a decayed Wench,* or favourite Footman, who are the Tunnels* through which all Graces* are conveyed, and may properly be called, *in the last Resort,** Governors of the Kingdom.

One Day, my Master, having heard me mention the *Nobility* of my Country, was pleased to make me a Compliment which I could not pretend to deserve: That, he was sure, I must have been born of some Noble Family, because I far exceeded in Shape, Colour, and Cleanliness, all the *Yahoos* of his Nation, although I seemed to fail in Strength, and Agility, which must be imputed to my different Way of Living from those other Brutes; and besides, I was not only endowed with the Faculty of Speech, but likewise with some Rudiments of Reason, to a Degree, that with all his Acquaintance I passed for a Prodigy.

He made me observe, that among the *Houyhnhnms*, the *White*, the *Sorrel*, and the *Iron-grey*, were not so exactly shaped as the *Bay*, the *Dapple-grey*, and the *Black*; nor born with equal Talents of Mind, or a Capacity to improve them; and therefore continued always in the Condition of Servants, without ever aspiring to match* out of their own Race, which in that Country would be reckoned monstrous and unnatural.

I made his Honour my most humble Acknowledgments for the good Opinion he was pleased to conceive of me; but assured him at the same Time, that my Birth was of the lower Sort, having been born of plain, honest Parents, who were just able to give me a tolerable Education: That, *Nobility* among us was altogether a different Thing from the Idea he had of it; That, our young *Noblemen* are bred from their Childhood in Idleness and Luxury; that, as soon as Years will permit, they consume their Vigour, and contract odious Diseases among lewd Females; and when their Fortunes are almost ruined, they marry some Woman of mean Birth, disagreeable Person, and unsound Constitution, merely for the sake of Money, whom they hate and despise. That, the Productions of such Marriages are generally scrophulous, rickety or deformed Children; by which Means the Family seldom continues above three Generations, unless the Wife take Care to provide a healthy Father among her Neighbours, or Domesticks, in order to improve and continue the Breed. That, a weak diseased Body, a meager Countenance, and sallow Complexion, are the true Marks of *noble Blood*; and a healthy robust Appearance is so disgraceful in a Man of Quality, that the World concludes his real Father to have been a Groom or a Coachman. The Imperfections of his Mind run parallel with those of his Body; being a Composition of Spleen, Dulness, Ignorance, Caprice, Sensuality and Pride.

Without the Consent of this illustrious Body, no Law can be enacted, repealed, or altered: And these Nobles have likewise the Decision of all our Possessions without Appeal.*

CHAPTER SEVEN

The Author's great Love of his Native Country. His Master's Observations upon the Constitution and Administration of England, as described by the Author, with parallel Cases and Comparisons. His Master's Observations upon human Nature.

THE READER may be disposed to wonder how I could prevail on my self to give so free a Representation of my own Species, among a Race of Mortals who were already too apt to conceive the vilest Opinion of Human Kind, from that entire Congruity betwixt me and their *Yahoos*. But I must freely confess, that the many Virtues of those excellent *Quadrupeds* placed in opposite View to human Corruptions, had so far opened mine Eyes, and enlarged my Understanding, that I began to view the Actions and Passions of Man in a very different Light; and to think the Honour of my own Kind not worth managing;* which, besides, it was impossible for me to do before a Person of so acute a Judgment as my Master, who daily convinced me of a thousand Faults in my self, whereof I had not the least Perception before, and which with us would never be numbered even among human Infirmities. I had likewise learned from his Example an utter Detestation of all Falsehood or Disguise; and *Truth* appeared so amiable to me,* that I determined upon sacrificing every thing to it.

Let me deal so candidly with the Reader, as to confess, that there was yet a much stronger Motive for the Freedom I took in my Representation of Things. I had not been a Year in this Country, before I contracted such a Love and Veneration for the Inhabitants, that I entered on a firm Resolution never to return to human Kind, but to pass the rest of my Life among these admirable *Houyhnhnms* in the Contemplation and Practice of every Virtue; where I could have no Example or Incitement to Vice. But it was decreed by Fortune, my perpetual Enemy, that so great a Felicity should not fall to my Share. However, it is now some Comfort to reflect, that in what I said of my Countrymen, I *extenuated* their Faults as much as I durst before so strict an Examiner; and upon every Article, gave as *favourable* a Turn as the Matter would bear. For, indeed, who is there alive that will not be swayed by his Byass and Partiality to the Place of his Birth?

I have related the Substance of several Conversations I had with my Master, during the greatest Part of the Time I had the Honour to be in his Service; but have indeed for Brevity sake omitted much more than is here set down.

When I had answered all his Questions, and his Curiosity seemed to be fully satisfied; he sent for me one Morning early, and commanding me to sit down at some Distance, (an Honour which he had never before conferred upon me) He said, he had been very seriously considering my whole Story, as far as it related both to my self and my Country: That, he looked upon us as a Sort of Animals to whose Share, by what Accident he could not conjecture, some small Pittance of *Reason* had fallen, whereof we made no other Use than by its Assistance to aggravate our *natural* Corruptions, and to acquire new ones which Nature had not given us. That, we disarmed our selves of the few Abilities she had bestowed; had been very successful in multiplying our original Wants, and seemed to spend our whole Lives in vain Endeavours to supply them by our own Inventions. That, as to my self, it was manifest I had neither the Strength or Agility of a common *Yahoo*; that I walked infirmly on my hinder Feet; had found out a Contrivance to make my Claws of no Use or Defence, and to remove the Hair from my Chin, which was intended as a Shelter from the Sun and the Weather. Lastly, that I could neither run with Speed, nor climb Trees like my *Brethren* (as he called them) the *Yahoos* in this Country.

That, our Institutions of *Government* and *Law* were plainly owing to our gross Defects in *Reason*, and by consequence, in *Virtue*; because *Reason** alone is sufficient to govern a *Rational* Creature; which was therefore a Character we had no Pretence to challenge,* even from the Account I had given of my own People; although he manifestly perceived, that in order to favour them, I had concealed many Particulars, and often *said the Thing which was not.*

He was the more confirmed in this Opinion, because he observed, that as I agreed in every Feature of my Body with other *Yahoos*, except where it was to my real Disadvantage in point of Strength, Speed and Activity, the Shortness of my Claws, and some other Particulars where Nature had no Part; so, from the Representation I had given him of our Lives, our Manners, and our Actions, he found as near a Resemblance in the Disposition of our Minds. He said, the *Yahoos* were known to hate one another more than they did any different Species of Animals; and the Reason usually assigned, was, the Odiousness of their own Shapes, which all could see in the rest, but not in themselves. He had therefore begun to think it not unwise in us to *cover* our Bodies, and by that Invention, conceal many of our Deformities from each other, which would else be hardly supportable. But, he now found he had been mistaken; and that the Dissentions of those Brutes in his Country were owing to the same Cause with ours, as I had described them. For, if (said he) you throw among five *Yahoos* as much Food as would be sufficient for fifty, they will, instead of eating peaceably, fall together by the Ears, each single one impatient to *have all to it self*; and therefore a Servant was usually employed to stand by while they were feeding abroad, and those kept at home were tied at a Distance from each other. That, if a Cow died of Age or Accident, before a *Houyhnhnm* could secure it for his own *Yahoos*, those in the Neighbourhood would come in Herds to seize it, and then would ensue such a Battle as I had described, with terrible Wounds made by their Claws on both Sides, although they seldom were able to kill one another, for want of such convenient Instruments of Death as we had invented. At other Times the like Battles have been fought between the *Yahoos* of several Neighbourhoods without any visible Cause: Those of one District watching all Opportunities to surprise the next before they are prepared. But if they find their Project hath miscarried, they return home, and for want of Enemies, engage in what I call a *Civil War* among themselves.

That, in some Fields of his Country, there are certain *shining Stones* of several Colours, whereof the *Yahoos* are violently fond; and when Part of these *Stones* are fixed in the

Earth, as it sometimes happeneth, they will dig with their Claws for whole Days to get them out, and carry them away, and hide them by Heaps in their Kennels; but still looking round with great Caution, for fear their Comrades should find out their Treasure. My Master said, he could never discover the Reason of this unnatural Appetite,* or how these *Stones* could be of any Use to a *Yahoo*; but now he believed it might proceed from the same Principle of *Avarice*, which I had ascribed to Mankind. That he had once by way of Experiment,* privately removed a Heap of these *Stones* from the Place where one of his *Yahoos* had buried it: Whereupon, the sordid* Animal missing his Treasure, by his loud lamenting brought the whole Herd to the Place, there miserably howled, then fell to biting and tearing the rest; began to pine away, would neither eat nor sleep, nor work, till he ordered a Servant privately to convey the *Stones* into the same Hole, and hide them as before; which when his *Yahoo* had found, he presently recovered his Spirits and good Humour; but took Care to remove them to a better hiding Place; and hath ever since been a very serviceable Brute.

My Master farther assured me, which I also observed my self; That in the Fields where these *shining Stones* abound, the fiercest and most frequent Battles are fought, occasioned by perpetual Inroads of the neighbouring *Yahoos*.

He said, it was common when two *Yahoos* discovered such a *Stone* in a Field, and were contending which of them should be the Proprietor, a third would take the Advantage,* and carry it away from them both; which my Master would needs contend to have some Resemblance with our *Suits at Law*; wherein I thought it for our Credit not to undeceive him; since the Decision he mentioned was much more equitable than many Decrees among us: Because the Plaintiff and Defendant there lost nothing beside the *Stone* they contended for; whereas our *Courts of Equity*,* would never have dismissed the Cause while either of them had any thing left.

My Master continuing his Discourse, said, There was nothing that rendered the *Yahoos* more odious, than their undistinguishing Appetite* to devour every thing that came in their Way, whether Herbs, Roots, Berries, corrupted Flesh of Animals, or all mingled together: And it was peculiar in their Temper, that they were fonder of what they could get by Rapine or Stealth at a greater Distance, than much better Food provided for them at home. If their Prey held out, they would eat till they were ready to burst, after which Nature had pointed out to them a certain *Root* that gave them a general Evacuation.

There was also another Kind of *Root* very *juicy*, but something rare and difficult to be found, which the *Yahoos* sought for with much Eagerness, and would suck it with great Delight: It produced the same Effects that Wine hath upon us. It would make them sometimes hug, and sometimes tear one another; they would howl and grin, and chatter, and reel, and tumble, and then fall asleep in the Mud.

I did indeed observe, that the *Yahoos* were the only Animals in his Country subject to any Diseases; which however, were much fewer than Horses have among us, and contracted not by any ill Treatment they meet with, but by the Nastiness and Greediness of that sordid Brute. Neither has their Language* any more than a general Appellation for those Maladies; which is borrowed from the Name of the Beast, and called *Hnea Yahoo*, or the *Yahoo's-Evil*; and the Cure prescribed is a Mixture of *their own Dung* and *Urine*, forcibly put down the *Yahoo's* Throat. This I have since often known to have been taken with Success: And do here freely recommend it to my Countrymen, for the publick Good, as an admirable Specifick against all Diseases produced by Depletion.

As to Learning, Government, Arts, Manufactures, and the like; my Master confessed he could find little or no Resemblance between the *Yahoos* of that country and those in ours. For, he only meant to observe what Parity there was in our Natures. He had heard indeed some curious *Houyhnhnms* observe, that in most Herds there was a Sort of ruling *Yahoo*, (as among us there is generally some leading or principal Stag in a Park) who was always more *deformed* in Body, and *mischievous in Disposition*, than any of the rest. That, this *Leader* had usually a Favourite as *like himself* as he could get, whose Employment was to *lick his Master's Feet and Posteriors, and drive the Female* Yahoos *to his Kennel*; for which he was now and then rewarded with a Piece of Ass's Flesh. This *Favourite* is hated by the whole Herd; and therefore to protect himself, keeps always *near the Person of his Leader.* He usually continues in Office till a worse can be found; but the very Moment he is discarded, his Successor, at the Head of all the *Yahoos* in that District, Young and Old, Male and Female, come in a Body, and discharge their Excrements upon him from Head to Foot. But how far this might be applicable to our *Courts* and *Favourites,* and *Ministers of State,* my Master said I could best determine.

I durst make no Return to this malicious Insinuation, which debased human Understanding below the Sagacity of a common *Hound,* who hath Judgment enough to distinguish and follow the Cry of the *ablest Dog in the Pack,* without being ever mistaken.

My Master told me, there were some Qualities remarkable in the *Yahoos,* which he had not observed me to mention, or at least very slightly, in the Accounts I had given him of human Kind. He said, those Animals, like other Brutes, had their Females in common;* but in this they differed, that the She-*Yahoo* would admit the Male, while she was pregnant; and that the Hees would quarrel and fight with the Females as fiercely as with each other. Both which Practices were such Degrees of infamous Brutality, that no other sensitive Creature ever arrived at.

Another Thing he wondered at in the *Yahoos,* was their strange Disposition to Nastiness and Dirt; whereas there appears to be a natural Love of Cleanliness in all other Animals. As to the two former Accusations, I was glad to let them pass without any Reply, because I had not a Word to offer upon them in Defence of my Species, which otherwise I certainly had done from my own Inclinations. But I could have easily vindicated human Kind from the Imputation of Singularity upon the last Article, if there had been any *Swine* in that Country, (as unluckily for me there were not) which although it may be a *sweeter Quadruped* than a *Yahoo,* cannot I humbly conceive in Justice pretend to more Cleanliness; and so his Honour himself must have owned, if he had seen their filthy Way of feeding, and their Custom of wallowing and sleeping in the Mud.

My Master likewise mentioned another Quality, which his

Servants had discovered in several *Yahoos*, and to him was wholly unaccountable. He said, a Fancy would sometimes take a *Yahoo*, to retire into a Corner, to lie down and howl, and groan, and spurn away all that came near him, although he were young and fat, and wanted neither Food nor Water; nor did the Servants imagine what could possibly ail him. And the only Remedy they found was to set him to hard Work, after which he would infallibly come to himself. To this I was silent out of Partiality to my own Kind; yet here I could plainly discover the true Seeds of *Spleen*,* which only seizeth on the *Lazy*, the *Luxurious*, and the *Rich*; who, if they were forced to undergo the *same Regimen*, I would undertake for the Cure.

His Honour had farther observed, that a Female *Yahoo** would often stand behind a Bank or a Bush, to gaze on the young Males passing by, and then appear, and hide, using many antick Gestures and Grimaces; at which time it was observed, that she had a most *offensive Smell*; and when any of the Males advanced, would slowly retire, looking often back, and with a counterfeit Shew of Fear, run off into some convenient Place where she knew the Male would follow her.

At other times, if a Female Stranger came among them, three or four of her own Sex would get about her, and stare and chatter, and grin, and smell her all over; and then turn off with Gestures that seemed to express Contempt and Disdain.

Perhaps my Master might refine a little* in these Speculations, which he had drawn from what he observed himself, or had been told him by others: However, I could not reflect without some Amazement, and much Sorrow, that the Rudiments of *Lewdness, Coquetry, Censure*, and *Scandal*, should have Place by Instinct in Womankind.

I expected every Moment, that my Master would accuse the *Yahoos* of those unnatural Appetites in both Sexes, so common among us. But Nature it seems hath not been so expert a Schoolmistress; and these politer Pleasures* are entirely the Productions of Art and Reason, on our Side of the Globe.

CHAPTER EIGHT

The Author relateth several Particulars of the Yahoos. *The great Virtues of the* Houyhnhnms. *The Education and Exercise of their Youth. Their general Assembly.*

As I ought to have understood human Nature much better than I supposed it possible for my Master to do, so it was easy to apply the Character he gave of the *Yahoos* to myself and my Countrymen; and I believed I could yet make farther Discoveries from my own Observation. I therefore often begged his Honour to let me go among the Herds of *Yahoos* in the Neighbourhood; to which he always very graciously consented, being perfectly convinced that the Hatred I bore those Brutes would never suffer me to be corrupted by them; and his Honour ordered one of his Servants, a strong Sorrel Nag, very honest and good-natured, to be my Guard; without whose Protection I durst not undertake such Adventures. For I have already told the Reader how much I was pestered by those odious Animals upon my first Arrival. I afterwards failed very narrowly three or four times of falling into their Clutches, when I happened to stray at any Distance without my Hanger. And I have Reason to believe, they had some Imagination that I was of their own Species, which I often assisted myself, by stripping up my Sleeves, and shewing my naked Arms and Breast in their Sight, when my Protector was with me: At which times they would approach as near as they durst, and imitate my Actions after the Manner of Monkeys, but ever with great Signs of Hatred; as a tame *Jack Daw* with Cap and Stockings, is always persecuted by the wild ones, when he happens to be got among them.

They are prodigiously nimble from their Infancy; however, I once caught a young Male of three Years old, and endeavoured by all Marks of Tenderness to make it quiet; but the little Imp fell a squalling, and scratching, and biting with such Violence, that I was forced to let it go; and it was high time, for a whole Troop of old ones came about us at the Noise; but finding the Cub was safe, (for away it ran) and my Sorrel Nag being by, they durst not venture near us. I observed the young Animal's Flesh to smell very rank, and the Stink was somewhat between a *Weasel* and a *Fox*, but much more disagreeable. I forgot another Circumstance, (and perhaps I might have the Reader's Pardon, if it were wholly omitted) that while I held the odious Vermin in my Hands, it voided its filthy Excrements of a yellow liquid Substance, all over my Cloaths; but by good Fortune there was a small Brook hard by, where I washed myself as clean as I could; although I durst not come into my Master's Presence, until I were sufficiently aired.

By what I could discover, the *Yahoos* appear to be the most unteachable of all Animals, their Capacities never reaching higher than to draw or carry Burthens. Yet I am of Opinion, this Defect ariseth chiefly from a perverse, restive Disposition. For they are cunning, malicious, treacherous and revengeful. They are strong and hardy, but of a cowardly Spirit, and by Consequence insolent, abject, and cruel. It is observed, that the *Red-haired* of both Sexes are more libidinous and mischievous than the rest,* whom yet they much exceed in Strength and Activity.

The *Houyhnhnms* keep the *Yahoos* for present* Use in Huts not far from the House; but the rest are sent abroad to certain Fields, where they dig up Roots, eat several Kinds of Herbs, and search about for Carrion, or sometimes catch *Weasels* and *Luhimuhs** (a Sort of *wild Rat*) which they greedily devour. Nature hath taught them to dig deep Holes with their Nails on the Side of a rising Ground, wherein they lie by themselves; only the Kennels* of the Females are larger, sufficient to hold two or three Cubs.

They swim from their Infancy like Frogs, and are able to continue long under Water, where they often take Fish, which the Females carry home to their Young. And upon this Occasion, I hope the Reader will pardon my relating an odd Adventure.

Being one Day abroad with my Protector the Sorrel Nag, and the Weather exceeding hot, I entreated him to let me bathe in a River that was near. He consented, and I immediately stripped myself stark naked, and went down softly* into the Stream. It happened that a young Female *Yahoo** standing behind a Bank, saw the whole Proceeding; and inflamed by Desire, as the Nag and I conjectured, came running with all Speed, and leaped into the Water within five Yards of the Place where I bathed. I was never in my Life so terribly frighted; the Nag was grazing at some Distance, not suspecting any Harm: She embraced me after a most fulsome Manner; I roared as loud as I could, and the Nag came galloping towards me, whereupon she quitted her Grasp, with the utmost Reluctancy, and leaped upon the opposite Bank, where she stood gazing and howling all the time I was putting on my Cloaths.

This was Matter of Diversion to my Master and his Family, as well as of Mortification to my self. For now I could no longer deny, that I was a real *Yahoo*, in every Limb and Feature, since the Females had a natural Propensity to me as one of their own Species: Neither was the Hair of this Brute of a Red Colour, (which might have been some Excuse for an Appetite a little irregular) but black as a Sloe, and her Countenance did not make an Appearance altogether so hideous as the rest of the Kind; for, I think, she could not be above Eleven Years old.*

Having already lived three Years in this Country, the Reader I suppose will expect, that I should, like other Travellers, give him some Account of the Manners and Customs of its Inhabitants, which it was indeed my principal Study to learn.

As these noble *Houyhnhnms* are endowed by Nature with a general Disposition to all Virtues, and have no Conceptions or Ideas of what is evil in a rational Creature; so their grand Maxim* is, to cultivate *Reason*, and to be wholly governed by it. Neither is *Reason* among them a Point problematical as with us, where Men can argue with Plausibility on both Sides of a Question; but strikes you with immediate Conviction;* as it must needs do where it is not mingled, obscured, or discoloured by Passion and Interest. I remember it was with extreme Difficulty that I could bring my Master to understand the Meaning of the Word *Opinion*, or how a Point could be disputable; because *Reason* taught us to affirm or deny only where we are certain; and beyond our Knowledge we cannot do either.* So that Controversies, Wranglings, Disputes, and Positiveness in false or dubious Propositions, are Evils unknown among the *Houyhnhnms*. In the like Manner when I used to explain to him our several Systems of *Natural Philosophy*, he would laugh that a Creature pretending to *Reason*, should value itself upon the Knowledge of other Peoples Conjectures, and in Things, where that Knowledge, if it were certain, could be of no Use. Wherein he agreed entirely with the Sentiments of *Socrates*,* as *Plato* delivers them; which I mention as the highest Honour I can do that Prince of Philosophers. I have often since reflected what Destruction such a Doctrine would make in the Libraries of *Europe*; and how many Paths to Fame would be then shut up in the Learned World.

Friendship and *Benevolence** are the two principal Virtues among the *Houyhnhnms*; and these not confined to particular Objects, but universal to the whole Race. For, a Stranger from the remotest Part, is equally treated with the nearest Neighbour, and where-ever he goes, looks upon himself as at home.* They preserve *Decency* and *Civility* in the highest Degrees, but are altogether ignorant of *Ceremony.** They have no Fondness* for their Colts or Foles; but the Care they take in educating them proceedeth entirely from the Dictates of *Reason*. And, I observed my Master to shew the same Affection to his Neighbour's Issue that he had for his own.* They will have it that *Nature* teaches them to love the whole *Species*, and it is *Reason* only that maketh a Distinction of Persons, where there is a superior Degree of Virtue.*

When the Matron *Houyhnhnms* have produced one of each Sex, they no longer accompany with their Consorts,* except they lose one of their Issue by some Casualty, which very seldom happens: But in such a Case they meet again; or when the like Accident befalls a Person, whose Wife is past bearing, some other Couple bestows on him one of their own Colts, and then go together a second Time, until the Mother be pregnant. This Caution is necessary to prevent the Country from being over-burthened with Numbers.* But the Race of inferior *Houyhnhnms* bred up to be Servants is not so strictly limited upon this Article; these are allowed to produce three of each Sex, to be Domesticks in the Noble Families.

In their Marriages* they are exactly careful to chuse such Colours as will not make any disagreeable Mixture in the Breed. *Strength* is chiefly valued in the Male, and *Comeliness* in the Female; not upon the Account of *Love*, but to preserve the Race from degenerating: For, where a Female happens to excel in *Strength*, a Consort is chosen with regard to *Comeliness*. Courtship, Love, Presents, Joyntures, Settlements, have no place in their Thoughts; or Terms whereby to express them in their Language. The young Couple meet and are joined, merely because it is the Determination of their Parents and Friends: It is what they see done every Day; and they look upon it as one of the necessary Actions in a reasonable Being.* But the Violation of Marriage, or any other Unchastity, was never heard of:* And the married Pair pass their Lives with the same Friendship, and mutual Benevolence that they bear to all others of the same Species, who come in their Way; without Jealousy, Fondness, Quarrelling, or Discontent.

In educating the Youth of both Sexes, their Method is admirable, and highly deserveth our Imitation. These are not suffered to taste a Grain of *Oats*, except upon certain Days, till Eighteen Years old; nor *Milk*, but very rarely; and in Summer they graze two Hours in the Morning, and as many in the Evening, which* their Parents likewise observe; but the Servants are not allowed above half that Time; and a great Part of their Grass is brought home, which they eat at the most convenient Hours, when they can be best spared from Work.

Temperance, *Industry*, *Exercise* and *Cleanliness*, are the Lessons equally enjoyned to the young ones of both Sexes: And my Master thought it monstrous in us to give the Females a different Kind of Education from the Males,* except in some Articles of Domestick Management; whereby, as he truly observed, one Half of our Natives were good for nothing but bringing Children into the World: And to trust the Care of their Children to such useless Animals, he said was yet a greater Instance of Brutality.

But the *Houyhnhnms* train up their Youth to Strength,

Speed, and Hardiness, by exercising them in running Races up and down steep Hills, or over hard stony Grounds; and when they are all in a Sweat, they are ordered to leap over Head and Ears into a Pond or a River. Four times a Year the Youth of certain Districts meet to shew their Proficiency in Running, and Leaping, and other Feats of Strength or Agility; where the Victor is rewarded with a Song made in his or her Praise. On this Festival the Servants drive a Herd of *Yahoos* into the Field, laden with Hay, and Oats, and Milk for a Repast to the *Houyhnhnms*; after which, these Brutes are immediately driven back again, for fear of being noisome to the Assembly.

Every fourth Year, at the *Vernal Equinox*, there is a Representative Council of the whole Nation,* which meets in a Plain about twenty Miles from our House, and continueth about five or six Days. Here they inquire into the State and Condition of the several Districts; whether they abound or be deficient in Hay or Oats, or Cows or *Yahoos*? And where-ever there is any Want (which is but seldom) it is immediately supplied by unanimous Consent and Contribution. Here likewise the Regulation of Children is settled: As for instance, if a *Houyhnhnm* hath two Males, he changeth one of them with another who hath two Females: And when a Child hath been lost by any Casualty, where the Mother is past Breeding, it is determined what Family shall breed another to supply the Loss.

CHAPTER NINE

A grand Debate at the General Assembly of the Houyhnhnms; *and how it was determined. The Learning of the* Houyhnhnms. *Their Buildings. Their Manner of Burials. The Defectiveness of their Language.*

ONE OF these Grand Assemblies was held in my time, about three Months before my Departure, whither my Master went as the Representative of our District. In this Council was resumed their old Debate, and indeed, the only Debate that ever happened in their Country; whereof my Master after his Return gave me a very particular Account.

The Question to be debated was, Whether the *Yahoos* should be exterminated* from the Face of the Earth. One of the *Members* for the Affirmative offered several Arguments of great Strength and Weight; alledging, That, as the *Yahoos* were the most filthy, noisome, and deformed Animal which Nature ever produced, so they were the most restive and indocible,* mischievous and malicious: They would privately suck the Teats of the *Houyhnhnms* Cows; kill and devour their Cats, trample down their Oats and Grass, if they were not continually watched; and commit a Thousand other Extravagancies. He took Notice of a general Tradition, that *Yahoos* had not been always in their Country: But, that many Ages ago, two of these Brutes appeared together upon a Mountain,* whether produced by the Heat of the Sun upon corrupted Mud and Slime, or from the Ooze and Froth of the Sea,* was never known. That these *Yahoos* engendered, and their Brood in a short time grew so numerous as to overrun and infest the whole Nation. That the *Houyhnhnms* to get rid of this Evil, made a general Hunting, and at last inclosed the whole Herd; and destroying the Older, every *Houyhnhnm* kept two young Ones in a Kennel, and brought them to such a Degree of Tameness, as an Animal so savage by Nature can be capable of acquiring; using them for Draught and Carriage.

That, there seemed to be much Truth in this Tradition, and that those Creatures could not be *Ylnhniamshy** (or *Aborigines* of the Land) because of the violent Hatred the *Houyhnhnms* as well as all other Animals, bore them; which although their evil Disposition sufficiently deserved, could never have arrived at so high a Degree, if they had been *Aborigines*, or else they would have long since been rooted out. That, the Inhabitants taking a Fancy to use the Service of the *Yahoos*, had very imprudently neglected to cultivate the Breed of *Asses*,* which were a comely Animal, easily kept, more tame and orderly, without any offensive Smell, strong enough for Labour, although they yield to the other in Agility of Body; and if their Braying be no agreeable Sound, it is far preferable to the horrible Howlings of the *Yahoos*.

Several others declared their Sentiments to the same purpose; when my Master proposed an Expedient to the Assembly, whereof he had indeed borrowed the Hint from me. He approved of the Tradition, mentioned by the *Honourable Member*, who spoke before; and affirmed, that the two *Yahoos* said to be first seen among them, had been driven thither over the Sea; that coming to Land, and being forsaken by their Companions, they retired to the Mountains, and degenerating by Degrees, became in Process of Time, much more savage then those of their own Species in the Country from whence these two Originals came. The Reason of his Assertion was, that he had now in his Possession, a certain wonderful *Yahoo*, (meaning myself) which most of them had heard of, and many of them had seen. He then related to them, how he first found me; that, my Body was all covered with an artificial Composure* of the Skins and Hairs of other Animals: That, I spoke in a Language of my own, and had thoroughly learned theirs: That, I had related to him the Accidents which brought me thither: That, when he saw me without my covering, I was an exact *Yahoo* in every Part, only of a whiter Colour, less hairy, and with shorter Claws. He added, how I had endeavoured to persuade him, that in my own and other Countries the Yahoos acted as the governing, rational Animal, and held the *Houyhnhnms* in Servitude: That, he observed in me all the Qualities of a *Yahoo*, only a little more civilized by some Tincture of Reason; which however was in a Degree as far inferior to the *Houyhnhnm* Race, as the *Yahoos* of their Country were to me: That, among other things, I mentioned a Custom we had of *castrating Houyhnhnms* when they were young, in order to render them tame; that the Operation was easy and safe; that it was no Shame to learn Wisdom from Brutes, as Industry is taught by the Ant, and Building by the Swallow. (For so I translate the Word *Lyhannh*, although it be a much larger Fowl) That, this Invention might be practiced upon the younger *Yahoos* here, which, besides rendering them tractable and fitter for Use, would in an Age put an End to the whole Species without destroying Life. That, in the mean time the *Houyhnhnms* should be *exhorted** to cultivate the Breed of Asses, which, as they are in all respects more valuable Brutes; so they have this Advantage, to be fit for Service at five Years old, which the others are not till Twelve.

This was all my Master thought fit to tell me at that Time, of what passed in the Grand Council. But he was pleased to conceal* one Particular, which related personally to myself, whereof I soon felt the unhappy Effect, as the Reader will know in its proper Place, and from whence I date all the succeeding Misfortunes of my Life.

The *Houyhnhnms* have no Letters, and consequently, their Knowledge is all traditional.* But there happening few Events of any Moment among a People so well united, naturally disposed to every Virtue, wholly governed by Reason, and cut off from all Commerce with other Nations; the historical Part is easily preserved without burthening their Memories. I have already observed, that they are subject to no Diseases, and therefore can have no Need of Physicians. However, they have excellent Medicines composed of Herbs, to cure accidental Bruises and Cuts in the Pastern or Frog of the Foot by sharp Stones, as well as other Maims and Hurts in the several Parts of the Body.

They calculate the Year by the Revolution of the Sun and the Moon, but use no Subdivisions into Weeks. They are well enough acquainted with the Motions of those two Luminaries, and understand the Nature of *Eclipses*; and this is the utmost Progress of their *Astronomy*.

In *Poetry* they must be allowed to excel all other Mortals;*

wherein the Justness of their Similes, and the Minuteness, as
well as Exactness of their Descriptions, are indeed inimitable.
Their Verses abound very much in both of these; and usually
contain either some exalted Notions of Friendship and
Benevolence, or the Praises of those who were Victors in
Races, and other bodily Exercises.* Their Buildings, although
very rude and simple, are not inconvenient, but well contrived to defend them from all Injuries of Cold and Heat.
They have a Kind of Tree, which at Forty Years old loosens in
the Root, and falls with the first Storm; it grows very strait, and
being pointed like Stakes with a sharp Stone, (for the
Houyhnhnms know not the Use of Iron) they stick them erect
in the Ground about ten Inches asunder, and then weave in
Oat-straw, or sometimes Wattles betwixt them. The Roof is
made after the same Manner, and so are the Doors.

The *Houyhnhnms* use the hollow Part between the Pastern
and the Hoof of their Fore-feet, as we do our Hands, and this
with greater Dexterity, than I could at first imagine. I have
seen a white Mare of our Family thread a Needle (which I lent
her on Purpose) with that Joynt. They milk their Cows, reap
their Oats, and do all the Work which requires Hands, in the
same Manner. They have a Kind of hard Flints, which by
grinding against other Stones, they form into Instruments,
that serve instead of Wedges, Axes, and Hammers. With Tools
made of these Flints they likewise cut their Hay, and reap
their Oats, which there groweth naturally in several Fields:
The *Yahoos* draw home the Sheaves in Carriages, and the
Servants tread them in certain covered Hutts, to get out the
Grain, which is kept in Stores. They make a rude Kind of
earthen and wooden Vessels, and bake the former in the Sun.

If they can avoid Casualties, they die only of old Age, and
are buried in the obscurest Places that can be found, their
Friends and Relations expressing neither Joy nor Grief* at
their Departure; nor does the dying Person discover the least
Regret that he is leaving the World, any more than if he were
upon returning* home from a Visit to one of his Neighbours:
I remember, my Master having once made an Appointment
with a Friend and his Family to come to his House upon some
Affair of Importance; on the Day fixed, the Mistress and her

two Children came very late; she made two Excuses, first for her Husband, who, as she said, happened that very Morning to *Lhnuwnh*. The Word is strongly expressive in their Language, but not easily rendered into *English*; it signifies, *to retire to his first Mother*. Her Excuse for not coming sooner, was, that her Husband dying late in the Morning, she was a good while consulting her Servants about a convenient Place where his Body should be laid; and I observed she behaved herself at our House, as chearfully as the rest: She died about three Months after.

They live generally to Seventy or Seventy-five Years, very seldom to Fourscore: Some Weeks before their Death they feel a gradual Decay, but without Pain. During this time they are much visited by their Friends, because they cannot go abroad with their usual Ease and Satisfaction. However, about ten Days before their Death, which they seldom fail in computing they return the Visits that have been made them by those who are nearest in the Neighbourhood, being carried in a convenient Sledge drawn by *Yahoos*; which Vehicle they use, not only upon this Occasion, but when they grow old, upon long Journeys, or when they are lamed by any Accident. And therefore when the dying *Houyhnhnms* return those Visits, they take a solemn Leave of their Friends, as if they were going to some remote Part of the Country, where they designed to pass the rest of their Lives.

I know not whether it may be worth observing, that the *Houyhnhnms* have no Word in their Language to express any thing that is *evil*, except what they borrow from the Deformities or ill Qualities of the *Yahoos*. Thus they denote the Folly of a Servant, an Omission of a Child, a Stone that cuts their Feet, a Continuance of foul or unseasonable Weather, and the like, by adding to each the Epithet of *Yahoo*. For Instance, *Hhnm Yahoo, Whnaholm Yahoo, Ynlhmnawihlma Yahoo*, and an ill contrived House, *Ynholmhnmrohlnw Yahoo*.*

I could with great Pleasure enlarge farther upon the Manners and Virtues of this excellent People; but intending in a short time to publish a Volume by itself expressly upon that Subject, I refer the Reader thither. And in the mean time, proceed to relate my own sad Catastrophe.

CHAPTER TEN

The Author's Oeconomy and happy Life among the Houyhnhnms. *His great Improvement in Virtue, by conversing with them. Their Conversations. The Author hath Notice given him by his Master that he must depart from the Country. He falls into a Swoon for Grief, but submits. He contrives and finishes a Canoo, by the Help of a Fellow-Servant, and puts to Sea at a Venture.*

I HAD settled my little Oeconomy to my own Heart's Content. My Master had ordered a Room to be made for me after their Manner, about six Yards from the House; the Sides and Floors of which I plaistered with Clay, and covered with Rush-mats of my own contriving: I had beaten Hemp, which there grows wild, and made of it a Sort of Ticking: This I filled with the Feathers of several Birds I had taken with Springes made of *Yahoos* Hairs; and were excellent Food. I had worked two Chairs with my Knife, the Sorrel Nag helping me in the grosser and more laborious Part. When my Cloaths were worn to Rags, I made my self others with the Skins of Rabbets, and of a certain beautiful Animal about the same Size, called *Nnuhnoh*, the Skin of which is covered with a fine Down. Of these I likewise made very tolerable Stockings. I soaled my Shoes with Wood which I cut from a Tree, and fitted to the upper Leather, and when this was worn out, I supplied it with the Skins of *Yahoos*,* dried in the Sun. I often got Honey out of hollow Trees, which I mingled with Water,* or eat it with my Bread. No man could more verify the Truth of these two Maxims, *That, Nature is very easily satisfied;** and, *That, Necessity is the Mother of Invention.* I enjoyed perfect Health of Body, and Tranquility of Mind;* I did not feel the Treachery or Inconstancy of a Friend, nor the Injuries of a secret or open Enemy. I had no Occasion of bribing, flattering or pimping, to procure the Favour of any great Man, or of his Minion. I wanted no Fence against Fraud or Oppression: Here was neither Physician to destroy my Body, nor Lawyer to ruin my Fortune:

No Informer to watch my Words and Actions, or forge Accusations against me for Hire: Here were no Gibers, Censurers, Backbiters, Pickpockets, Highwaymen, House-breakers, Attorneys, Bawds, Buffoons, Gamesters, Politicians, Wits, Spleneticks, tedious Talkers, Controvertists,* Ravishers, Murderers, Robbers, Virtuoso's;* no Leaders or Followers of Party and Faction; no Encouragers to Vice, by Seducement or Examples: No Dungeon, Axes, Gibbets, Whipping-posts, or Pillories; No cheating Shopkeepers or Mechanicks:* No Pride, Vanity or Affectation: No Fops, Bullies, Drunkards, strolling Whores, or Poxes: No ranting, lewd, expensive Wives: No stupid, proud Pedants: No importunate, over-bearing quarrelsome, noisy, roaring, empty, conceited, swearing Companions: No Scoundrels raised from the Dust upon the Merit of their Vices; or Nobility thrown into it on account of their Virtues: No Lords, Fidlers, Judges or Dancing-masters.

I had the Favour of being admitted to several *Houyhnhnms*, who came to visit or dine with my Master; where his Honour graciously suffered me to wait in the Room, and listen to their Discourse. Both he and his Company would often descend* to ask me Questions, and receive my Answers. I had also sometimes the Honour of attending my Master in his Visits to others. I never presumed to speak, except in answer to a Question; and then I did it with inward Regret, because it was a Loss of so much Time for improving my self: But I was infinitely delighted with the Station of an humble Auditor in such Conversations, where nothing passed but what was useful, expressed in the fewest and most significant Words:* Where (as I have already said) the greatest *Decency* was observed, without the least Degree of Ceremony; where no Person spoke without being pleased himself, and pleasing his Companions: Where there was no Interruption, Tediousness, Heat, or Difference of Sentiments. They have a Notion, That when People are met together, a short Silence doth much improve Conversation: This I found to be true; for during those little Intermissions of Talk, new Ideas would arise in their Minds, which very much enlivened the Discourse. Their Subjects* are generally on Friendship and Benevolence; on Order and Oeconomy; sometimes upon the visible

Operations of Nature, or ancient Traditions; upon the Bounds and Limits of Virtue; upon the unerring Rules of Reason; or upon some Determinations, to be taken at the next great Assembly; and often upon the various Excellencies of *Poetry*. I may add, without Vanity, that my Presence often gave them sufficient Matter for Discourse, because it afforded my Master an Occasion of letting his Friends into the History of me and my Country, upon which they were all pleased to discant in a Manner not very advantageous to human Kind; and for that Reason I shall not repeat what they said: Only I may be allowed to observe, That his Honour, to my great Admiration, appeared to understand the Nature of *Yahoos* much better than my self. He went through all our Vices and Follies, and discovered many which I had never mentioned to him; by only supposing what Qualities a *Yahoo* of their Country, with a small Proportion of Reason, might be capable of exerting: And concluded, with too much Probability, how vile as well as miserable such a Creature must be.

I freely confess, that all the little Knowledge I have of any Value, was acquired by the Lectures I received from my Master, and from hearing the Discourses of him and his Friends; to which I should be prouder to listen, than to dictate to the greatest and wisest Assembly in *Europe*. I admired the Strength, Comeliness and Speed of the Inhabitants; and such a Constellation of Virtues in such amiable Persons produced in me the highest Veneration. At first, indeed, I did not feel that natural Awe which the *Yahoos* and all other Animals bear towards them; but it grew upon me by Degrees, much sooner than I imagined, and was mingled with a respectful Love and Gratitude, that they would condescend to distinguish me from the rest of my Species.

When I thought of my Family, my Friends, my Countrymen, or human Race in general, I considered them as they really were, *Yahoos* in Shape and Disposition, perhaps a little more civilized, and qualified with the Gift of Speech; but making no other Use of Reason, than to improve and multiply those Vices, whereof their Brethren in this Country had only the Share that Nature allotted them. When I happened to behold the Reflection of my own Form in a Lake or Fountain, I

turned away my Face in Horror and detestation of my self;*
and could better endure the Sight of a common *Yahoo*, than
of my own Person. By conversing with the *Houyhnhnms*, and
looking upon them with Delight, I fell to imitate their Gait
and Gesture, which is now grown into a Habit; and my Friends
often tell me in a blunt Way, that I *trot like a Horse*; which,
however, I take for a great Compliment: Neither shall I disown, that in speaking I am apt to fall into the Voice and
manner of the *Houyhnhnms*, and hear my self ridiculed on
that Account without the least Mortification.

In the Midst of this Happiness, when I looked upon my self
to be fully settled for Life, my Master sent for me one Morning a little earlier than his usual Hour. I observed by his
Countenance that he was in some Perplexity, and at a Loss
how to begin what he had to speak. After a short Silence, he
told me, he did not know how I would take what he was going
to say: That, in the last general Assembly, when the Affair of
the *Yahoos* was entered upon, the Representatives had taken
Offence at his keeping a *Yahoo* (meaning my self) in his
Family more like a *Houyhnhnm* than a Brute Animal. That, he
was known frequently to converse with me, as if he could
receive some Advantage or Pleasure in my Company: That,
such a Practice was not agreeable to Reason or Nature, nor a
thing ever heard of before among them. The Assembly did
therefore *exhort* him, either to employ me like the rest of my
Species, or command me to swim back to the Place from
whence I came. That, the first of these Expedients was utterly
rejected by all the *Houyhnhnms*, who had ever seen me at his
House or their own: For, they alledged, That because I had
some Rudiments of Reason, added to the natural Pravity of
those Animals, it was to be feared, I might be able to seduce
them into the woody and mountainous Parts of the Country,
and bring them in Troops by Night to destroy the
Houyhnhnms Cattle, as being naturally of the ravenous* Kind,
and averse from Labour.

My Master added, That he was daily pressed by the
Houyhnhnms of the Neighbourhood to have the Assembly's
Exhortation executed, which he could not put off much
longer. He doubted,* it would be impossible for me to swim

to another Country; and therefore wished I would contrive some Sort of Vehicle* resembling those I had described to him, that might carry me on the Sea; in which Work I should have the Assistance of his own Servants, as well as those of his Neighbours. He concluded, that for his own Part he could have been content to keep me in this Service as long as I lived; because he found I had cured myself of some bad Habits and Dispositions, by endeavouring, as far as my inferior Nature was capable, to imitate the *Houyhnhnms*.

I should here observe to the Reader, that a Decree of the general Assembly in this Country, is expressed by the Word *Hnhloayn*, which signifies an *Exhortation*; as near as I can render it: For they have no Conception how a rational Creature can be *compelled*, but only advised, or *exhorted*; because no Person can disobey Reason, without giving up his Claim to be a rational Creature.

I was struck with the utmost Grief and Despair at my Master's Discourse; and being unable to support the Agonies I was under, I fell into a Swoon at his Feet: When I came to myself, he told me, that he concluded I had been dead. (For these People are subject to no such Imbecillities of Nature.) I answered, in a faint Voice, that Death would have been too great an Happiness; that although I could not blame the Assembly's *Exhortation*, or the Urgency* of his Friends; yet in my weak and corrupt Judgment, I thought it might consist with Reason* to have been less rigorous. That, I could not swim a League, and probably the nearest Land to theirs might be distant above an Hundred: That, many Materials, necessary for making a small Vessel to carry me off, were wholly wanting in this Country, which however, I would attempt in Obedience and Gratitude to his Honour, although I concluded the thing to be impossible, and therefore looked on myself as already devoted to Destruction. That, the certain Prospect of an unnatural Death, was the least of my Evils: For, supposing I should escape with Life by some strange Adventure, how could I think with Temper,* of passing my Days among *Yahoos*, and relapsing into my old Corruptions, for want of Examples to lead and keep me within the Paths of Virtue. That, I knew too well upon what solid Reasons all the

Determinations of the wise *Houyhnhnms* were founded, not to be shaken by Arguments of mine, a miserable *Yahoo*; and therefore after presenting him with my humble Thanks for the Offer of his Servants Assistance in making a Vessel, and desiring a reasonable Time for so difficult a Work, I told him, I would endeavour to preserve a wretched Being; and, if ever I returned to *England*, was not without Hopes of being useful to my own Species, by celebrating the Praises of the renowned* *Houyhnhnms*, and proposing their Virtues to the Imitation of Mankind.

My Master in a few Words made me a very gracious Reply, allowed me the Space of two *Months* to finish my Boat; and ordered the Sorrel Nag, my Fellow-Servant, (for so at this Distance I may presume to call him) to follow my Instructions, because I told my Master, that his help would be sufficient, and I knew he had a Tenderness for me.

In his Company my first Business was to go to that Part of the Coast, where my rebellious Crew had ordered me to be set on Shore. I got upon a Height, and looking on every Side into the Sea, fancied I saw a small Island, towards the *North-East*: I took out my Pocket-glass, and could then clearly distinguish it about five Leagues off, as I computed; but it appeared to the Sorrel Nag to be only a blue Cloud: For, as he had no Conception of any Country beside his own, so he could not be as expert in distinguishing remote Objects at Sea, as we who so much converse in that Element.

After I had discovered this Island, I considered no farther; but resolved, it should, if possible, be the first Place of my Banishment, leaving the Consequence to Fortune.

I returned home, and consulting with the Sorrel Nag, we went into a Copse at some Distance, where I with my Knife, and he with a sharp Flint fastened very artificially, after their Manner, to a wooden Handle, cut down several Oak Wattles* about the Thickness of a Walking-staff, and some larger Pieces. But I shall not trouble the Reader with a particular Description of my own Mechanicks: Let it suffice to say, that in six Weeks time, with the Help of the Sorrel Nag, who performed the Parts that required most Labour, I finished a Sort of *Indian* Canoo, but much larger, covering it with the

Skins of *Yahoos*, well stitched together, with hempen Threads of my own making. My Sail was likewise composed of the Skins of the same Animal; but I made use of the youngest I could get,* the older being too tough and thick; and I likewise provided myself with four Paddles. I laid in a Stock of boiled Flesh, of Rabbets and Fowls; and took with me two Vessels, one filled with Milk, and the other with Water.

I tried my Canoo in a large Pond near my Master's House, and then corrected in it what was amiss; stopping all the Chinks with *Yahoos* Tallow, till I found it stanch,* and able to bear me, and my Freight. And when it was as compleat as I could possibly make it, I had it drawn on a Carriage very gently by *Yahoos*, to the Sea-side, under the Conduct of the Sorrel Nag, and another Servant.

When all was ready, and the Day came for my Departure, I took Leave of my Master and Lady, and the whole Family, mine Eyes flowing with Tears, and my Heart quite sunk with Grief. But his Honour, out of Curiosity, and perhaps (if I may speak it without Vanity) partly out of Kindness,* was determined to see me in my Canoo; and got several of his neighbouring Friends to accompany him. I was forced to wait above an Hour for the Tide, and then observing the Wind very fortunately bearing towards the Island, to which I intended to steer my Course, I took a second Leave of my Master: But as I was going to prostrate myself to kiss his Hoof, he did me the Honour to raise it gently to my Mouth.* I am not ignorant how much I have been censured for mentioning this last Particular. Detractors are pleased to think it improbable, that so illustrious a Person should descend to give so great a Mark of Distinction to a Creature so inferior as I. Neither have I forgot, how apt some Travellers are to boast of extraordinary Favours they have received. But, if these Censurers were better acquainted with the noble and courteous Disposition of the *Houyhnhnms*, they would soon change their Opinion.

I paid my Respects to the rest of the *Houyhnhnms* in his Honour's Company; then getting into my Canoo, I pushed off from Shore.

CHAPTER ELEVEN

The Author's dangerous Voyage. He arrives at New-Holland, *hoping to settle there. Is wounded with an Arrow by one of the Natives. Is seized and carried by Force into a* Portugueze *Ship. The great Civilities of the Captain. The Author arrives at* England.

I BEGAN this desperate Voyage on *February* 15, 171$\frac{4}{5}$*, at 9 o'Clock in the Morning. The Wind was very favourable; however, I made use at first only of my Paddles; but considering I should soon be weary, and that the Wind might probably chop about, I ventured to set up my little Sail; and thus, with the Help of the Tide, I went at the Rate of a League and a Half an Hour, as near as I could guess. My Master and his Friends continued on the Shoar, till I was almost out of Sight; and I often heard the Sorrel Nag (who always loved me) crying out, *Hnuy illa nyha maiah Yahoo*, Take Care of thy self, gentle *Yahoo*.

My Design was, if possible, to discover some small Island uninhabited, yet sufficient by my Labour to furnish me with Necessaries of Life, which I would have thought a greater Happiness than to be first Minister in the politest Court of *Europe*; so horrible was the Idea I conceived of returning to live in the Society and under the Government of *Yahoos*. For in such a Solitude as I desired, I could at least enjoy my own Thoughts, and reflect with Delight on the Virtues of those inimitable *Houyhnhnms*, without any Opportunity of degenerating into the Vices and Corruptions of my own Species.

The Reader may remember what I related when my Crew conspired against me, and confined me to my Cabbin. How I continued there several Weeks, without knowing what Course we took; and when I was put ashore in the Long-boat, how the Sailors told me with Oaths, whether true or false, that they knew not in what Part of the World we were. However, I did then believe us to be about ten Degrees *Southward* of the *Cape of Good Hope*, or about 45 Degrees *Southern* Latitude, as I gathered from some general Words I overheard among them, being I supposed to the *South-East* in their intended Voyage to *Madagascar*. And although this were but little better than Conjecture, yet I resolved to steer my Course *Eastward*, hoping to reach the *South-West* Coast of *New-Holland*, and perhaps some such Island as I desired, lying *Westward* of it. The Wind was full *West*, and by six in the Evening I computed I had gone *Eastward* at least eighteen Leagues; when I spied a very small Island about half a League off, which I soon reached. It was nothing but a Rock with one Creek, naturally arched by the Force of Tempests. Here I put in my Canoo, and climbing a Part of the Rock, I could plainly discover Land to the *East*, extending from *South* to *North*. I lay all Night in my Canoo; and repeating my Voyage early in the Morning, I arrived in seven Hours to the *South-East* Point of *New-Holland*.* This confirmed me in the Opinion I have long entertained, that the *Maps* and *Charts* place this Country at least three Degrees more to the *East* than it really is;* which Thought I communicated many Years ago to my worthy Friend Mr *Herman Moll*,* and gave him my Reasons for it, although he hath rather chosen to follow other Authors.*

I saw no Inhabitants in the Place where I landed; and being unarmed, I was afraid of venturing far into the Country. I found some Shell-Fish on the Shore, and eat them raw, not daring to kindle a Fire, for fear of being discovered by the Natives. I continued three Days feeding on Oysters and Limpits, to save my own Provisions; and I fortunately found a Brook of excellent Water, which gave me great Relief.

On the fourth Day, venturing out early a little too far, I saw twenty or thirty Natives upon a Height, not above five hundred Yards from me. They were stark naked, Men, Women and Children round a Fire, as I could discover by the Smoke. One of them spied me, and gave Notice to the rest; five of them advanced towards me, leaving the Women and Children at the Fire. I made what haste I could to the Shore, and getting into my Canoo, shoved off: The Savages observing me retreat, ran after me; and before I could get far enough into the Sea, discharged an Arrow, which wounded me deeply on the Inside of my left Knee (I shall carry the Mark to my

Grave.) I apprehended the Arrow might be poisoned; and paddling out of the Reach of their Darts (being a calm Day) I made a shift to suck the Wound, and dress it as well as I could.

I was at a Loss what to do, for I durst not return to the same Landing-place, but stood to* the *North,* and was forced to paddle; for the Wind, although very gentle, was against me, blowing *North-West.* As I was looking about for a secure Landing-place, I saw a Sail to the *North North-East,* which appearing every Minute more visible, I was in some Doubt, whether I should wait for them or no; but at last my Detestation of the *Yahoo* Race prevailed; and turning my Canoo, I sailed and paddled together to the *South,* and got into the same Creek from whence I set out in the Morning; choosing rather to trust my self among these *Barbarians,* than live with *European Yahoos.* I drew up my Canoo as close as I could to the Shore, and hid my self behind a Stone by the little Brook, which, as I have already said, was excellent Water.

The Ship came within half a League of this Creek, and sent out her Long-Boat with Vessels to take in fresh Water (for the Place it seems was very well known) but I did not observe it until the Boat was almost on Shore; and it was too late to seek another Hiding-Place. The Seamen at their landing observed my Canoo, and rummaging it all over, easily conjectured that the Owner could not be far off. Four of them well armed searched every Cranny and Lurking-hole, till at last they found me flat on my Face behind the Stone. They gazed a while in Admiration at my strange uncouth Dress; my Coat made of Skins, my wooden-soaled Shoes, and my furred Stockings; from whence, however, they concluded I was not a Native of the Place, who all go naked. One of the Seamen in *Portugueze* bid me rise, and asked who I was. I understood that Language very well, and getting upon my Feet, said, I was a poor *Yahoo,* banished from the *Houyhnhnms,* and desired they would please to let me depart. They admired to hear me answer them in their own Tongue, and saw by my Complection I must be an European; but were at a Loss to know what I meant by *Yahoos* and *Houyhnhnms,* and at the same Time fell a laughing at my strange Tone in speaking, which resembled the Neighing of a Horse. I trembled all the while betwixt Fear and Hatred: I again desired Leave to depart, and was gently moving to my Canoo; but they laid hold on me, desiring to know what Country I was of? whence I came? with many other Questions. I told them, I was born in *England*, from whence I came about five Years ago,* and then their Country and ours were at Peace. I therefore hoped they would not treat me as an Enemy, since I meant them no Harm, but was a poor *Yahoo*, seeking some desolate Place where to pass the Remainder of his unfortunate Life.

When they began to talk, I thought I never heard or saw any thing so unnatural; for it appeared to me as monstrous as if a Dog or a Cow should speak in *England*, or a *Yahoo* in *Houyhnhnm-Land*. The honest Portuguese were equally amazed at my strange Dress, and the odd Manner of delivering* my Words, which however they understood very well. They spoke to me with great Humanity, and said they were sure their Captain would carry me *gratis* to *Lisbon*, from whence I might return to my own Country; that two of the Seamen would go back to the Ship, to inform the Captain of what they had seen, and receive his Orders; in the mean Time, unless I would give my solemn Oath not to fly, they would secure me by Force. I thought it best to comply with their Proposal. They were very curious to know my Story, but I gave them very little Satisfaction; and they all conjectured, that my Misfortunes had impaired my Reason. In two Hours the Boat, which went loaden with Vessels of Water, returned with the Captain's Commands to fetch me on Board. I fell on my Knees to preserve my Liberty; but all was in vain, and the Men having tied me with Cords, heaved me into the Boat, from whence I was taken into the Ship, and from thence into the Captain's Cabbin.

His Name was *Pedro de Mendez*; he was a very courteous and generous Person; he entreated me to give some Account of my self, and desired to know what I would eat or drink; said, I should be used as well as himself, and spoke so many obliging Things, that I wondered to find such Civilities from a *Yahoo*. However, I remained silent and sullen; I was ready to faint at the very Smell of him and his Men. At last I desired something to eat out of my own Canoo; but the ordered me a

Chicken and some excellent Wine, and then directed that I should be put to Bed in a very clean Cabbin. I would not undress my self, but lay on the Bed-cloaths; and in half an Hour stole out, when I thought the Crew was at Dinner; and getting to the Side of the Ship, was going to leap into the Sea, and swim for my Life, rather than continue among *Yahoos*. But one of the Seamen prevented me, and having informed the Captain, I was chained to my Cabbin.

After Dinner *Don Pedro* came to me, and desired to know my Reason for so desperate an Attempt; assured me he only meant to do me all the Service he was able; and spoke so very movingly, that at last I descended to treat him like an Animal which had some little Portion of Reason. I gave him a very short Relation of my Voyage; of the Conspiracy against me by my own Men; of the Country where they set me on Shore, and of my five* Years Residence there. All which he looked upon as if it were a Dream or a Vision; whereat I took great Offence: For I had quite forgot the Faculty of Lying, so peculiar to *Yahoos* in all Countries where they preside, and consequently the Disposition of suspecting Truth in others of their own Species. I asked him, Whether it were the Custom of his Country to *say the Thing that was not?* I assured him I almost forgot what he meant by Falshood; and if I had lived a thousand Years in *Houyhnhnmland*, I should never have heard a Lie from the meanest Servant. That I was altogether indifferent whether he believed me or no; but however, in return for his Favours, I would give so much Allowance to the Corruption of his Nature, as to answer any Objection he would please to make; and he might easily discover the Truth.

The Captain, a wise Man, after many Endeavours to catch me tripping in some Part of my Story, at last began to have a better Opinion of my Veracity.* But the added, that since I professed so inviolable an Attachment to Truth, I must give him my Word of Honour to bear him Company in this Voyage without attempting any thing against my Life; or else he would continue me a Prisoner till we arrived at *Lisbon*. I gave him the Promise he required; but at the same time protested that I would suffer the greatest hardships rather than return to live among *Yahoos*.

Our Voyage passed without any considerable Accident.* In

Gratitude to the Captain I sometimes sate with him at his earnest Request, and strove to conceal my Antipathy against human Kind, although it often broke out; which he suffered to pass without Observation. But the greatest Part of the Day, I confined myself to my Cabbin, to avoid seeing any of the Crew. The Captain had often intreated me to strip myself of my savage Dress, and offered to lend me the best Suit of Cloaths he had. This I would not be prevailed on to accept, abhorring to cover myself with any thing that had been on the Back of a *Yahoo*. I only desired he would lend me two clean Shirts, which having been washed since he wore them, I believed would not so much defile me. These I changed every second Day, and washed them myself.

We arrived at *Lisbon, Nov.* 5, 1715. At our landing, the Captain forced me to cover myself with his Cloak, to prevent the Rabble from crouding about me. I was conveyed to his own House; and at my earnest Request, he led me up to the highest Room backwards.* I conjured him to conceal from all Persons what I had told him of the *Houyhnhnms*; because the least Hint of such a Story would not only draw Numbers of People to see me, but probably put me in Danger of being imprisoned, or burnt by the *Inquisition*.* The Captain persuaded me to accept a Suit of Cloaths newly made; but I would not suffer the Taylor to take my Measure; however, Don *Pedro* being almost of my Size,* they fitted me well enough. He accoutred me with other Necessaries all new, which I aired for Twenty-four Hours before I would use them.

The Captain had no Wife, nor above three Servants, none of which were suffered to attend at Meals; and his whole Deportment was so obliging, added to very good *human* Understanding, that I really began to tolerate his Company. He gained so far upon me that I ventured to look out of the back Window. By Degrees I was brought into another Room, from whence I peeped into the Street, but drew my Head back in a Fright. In a Week's Time he seduced me down to the Door. I found my Terror gradually lessened, but my Hatred and Contempt seemed to increase. I was at last bold enough to walk the Street in his Company, but kept my Nose well stopped with Rue, or sometimes with Tobacco.

In ten Days, Don *Pedro*, to whom I had given some Account of my domestick Affairs, put it upon me* as a Point of Honour and Conscience, that I ought to return to my native Country, and live at home with my Wife and Children. He told me, there was an *English* Ship in the Port just ready to sail, and he would furnish me with all things necessary. It would be tedious to repeat his Arguments, and my Contradictions. He said, it was altogether impossible to find such a solitary Island as I had desired to live in; but I might command in my own House, and pass my time in a Manner as recluse as I pleased.

I complied at last, finding I could not do better. I left *Lisbon* the 24th Day of *November*, in an *English* Merchantman, but who was the Master I never inquired. Don *Pedro* accompanied me to the Ship, and lent me Twenty Pounds. He took kind Leave of me, and embraced me at parting; which I bore as well as I could. During this last Voyage I had no Commerce* with the Master, or any of his Men; but pretending I was sick kept close in my Cabbin. On the Fifth of *December*, 1715, we cast Anchor in the *Downs* about Nine in the Morning, and at Three in the Afternoon I got safe to my House at *Redriff*.

My Wife and Family received me with great Surprize and Joy, because they concluded me certainly dead; but I must freely confess, the Sight of them filled me only with Hatred, Disgust and Contempt; and the more, by reflecting on the near Alliance I had to them. For, although since my unfortunate Exile from the *Houyhnhnm* Country, I had compelled myself to tolerate the Sight of *Yahoos*, and to converse with Don *Pedro de Mendez*; yet my Memory and Imaginations were perpetually filled with the Virtues and Ideas of those exalted *Houyhnhnms*. And when I began to consider, that by copulating with one of the *Yahoo*-Species, I had become a Parent of more; it struck me with the utmost Shame, Confusion and Horror.

As soon as I entered the House, my Wife took me in her Arms, and kissed me; at which, having not been used to the Touch of that odious Animal for so many Years, I fell in a Swoon for almost an Hour.* At the Time I am writing, it is five Years since my last Return to *England*: During the first Year I could not endure my Wife or Children in my Presence, the very Smell of them was intolerable; much less could I suffer them to eat in the same Room. To this Hour they dare not presume to touch my Bread, or drink out of the same Cup; neither was I ever able to let one of them take me by the Hand.* The first Money I laid out was to buy two young Stone-Horses,* which I keep in a good Stable, and next to them the Groom is my greatest Favourite; for I feel my Spirits revived by the Smell he contracts in the Stable. My Horses understand me tolerably well; I converse with them at least four Hours every Day. They are Strangers to Bridle or Saddle; they live in great Amity with me, and Friendship to each other.

CHAPTER TWELVE

The Author's Veracity. His Design in publishing this Work. His Censure of those Travellers who swerve from the Truth. The Author clears himself from any sinister End in writing. An Objection answered. The Method of planting Colonies. His Native Country commended. The Right of the Crown to those Countries described by the Author, is justified. The Difficulty of conquering them. The Author takes his last Leave of the Reader; proposeth his Manner of Living for the future; gives good Advice, and concludeth.

THUS, GENTLE Reader,* I have given thee a faithful History* of my Travels for Sixteen Years, and above Seven Months; wherein I have not been so studious of Ornament as of Truth. I could perhaps like others have astonished thee with strange improbable Tales; but I rather chose to relate plain Matter of Fact in the simplest Manner and Style; because my principal Design was to inform, and not to amuse thee.

It is easy for us who travel into remote Countries, which are seldom visited by *Englishmen* or other *Europeans*, to form Descriptions of wonderful Animals both at Sea and Land. Whereas, a Traveller's chief Aim should be to make Men wiser and better, and to improve their Minds by the bad, as well as good Example of what they deliver concerning foreign Places.*

I could heartily wish a Law were enacted, that every Traveller, before he were permitted to publish his Voyages, should be obliged to make Oath before the *Lord High Chancellor*, that all he intended to print was absolutely true to the best of his Knowledge; for then the World would no longer be deceived as it usually is, while some Writers, to make their Works pass the better upon the Publick, impose the grossest Falsities on the unwary Reader. I have perused several Books of Travels with great Delight in my younger Days; but having since gone over most Parts of the Globe, and been able to contradict many fabulous Accounts from my own Observation; it hath given me a great Disgust against this Part of Reading, and some Indignation to see the Credulity of Mankind so impudently abused. Therefore since my Acquaintance were pleased to think my poor Endeavours might not be unacceptable to my Country; I imposed on myself as a Maxim, never to be swerved from, that I would *strictly adhere to Truth*; neither indeed can I be ever under the least Temptation to vary from it, while I retain in my Mind the Lectures and Example of my noble Master, and the other illustrious *Houyhnhnms*, of whom I had so long the Honour to be an humble Hearer.

> ———*Nec si miserum Fortuna Sinonem*
> *Finxit, vanum etiam, mendacemque improba finget.**

I know very well, how little Reputation is to be got by Writings which require neither Genius nor Learning, nor indeed any other Talent, except a good Memory, or an exact *Journal.** I know likewise, that Writers of Travels, like *Dictionary*-Makers, are sunk into Oblivion by the Weight and Bulk of those who come last, and therefore lie uppermost And it is highly probable, that such Travellers who shall hereafter visit the Countries described in this Work of mine, may by detecting my Errors, (if there be any) and adding many new Discoveries of their own, jostle me out of Vogue, and stand in my Place; making the World forget that ever I was an Author. This indeed would be too great a Mortification if I wrote for Fame: But, as my sole Intention was the PUBLICK GOOD,* I cannot be altogether disappointed. For, who can read of the Virtues I have mentioned in the glorious *Houyhnhnms*, without being ashamed of his own Vices, when he considers himself as the reasoning, governing Animal of his Country? I shall say nothing of those remote nations where *Yahoos* preside; amongst which the least corrupted are the *Brobdingnagians*, whose wise Maxims in Morality and Government, it would be our Happiness to observe. But I forbear descanting further, and rather leave the judicious Reader to his own Remarks and Applications.

I am not a little pleased that this Work of mine can possibly meet with no* Censurers: For what Objections can be made against a Writer who relates only plain Facts that happened in such distant Countries, where we have not the least Interest with respect either to Trade or Negotiations? I have carefully avoided every Fault with which common Writers of Travels are often too justly charged. Besides, I meddle not the least with any *Party*, but write without Passion, Prejudice, or Ill-will against any Man or Number of Men whatsover. I write for the noblest End, to inform and instruct Mankind, over whom I may, without Breach of Modesty, pretend to some Superiority, from the Advantages I received by conversing so long among the most accomplished *Houyhnhnms*. I write without any View towards Profit or Praise. I never suffer a Word to pass that may look like Reflection, or possibly give the least Offence even to those who are most ready to take it. So that, I hope, I may with Justice pronounce myself an Author perfectly blameless; against whom the Tribes of Answerers, Considerers, Observers, Reflecters, Detecters, Remarkers, will never be able to find Matter for exercising their Talents.*

I confess, it was whispered to me, that I was bound in Duty as a Subject of *England*, to have given in a Memorial to a Secretary of State, at my first coming over; because, whatever Lands are discovered by a Subject, belong to the Crown. But I doubt, whether our Conquests in the Countries I treat of, would be as easy as those of *Ferdinando Cortez** over the naked *Americans*. The *Lilliputians* I think, are hardly worth the Charge of a Fleet and Army to reduce them; and I question whether it might be prudent or safe to attempt the *Brobdingnagians*: Or, whether an *English* Army would be much at their Ease with the Flying Island over their Heads. The *Houyhnhnms*, indeed, appear not to be so well prepared for War, a Science to which they are perfect Strangers, and especially against missive Weapons.* However, supposing myself to be a Minister of State, I could never give my Advice for invading them. Their Prudence, Unanimity, Unacquaintedness with Fear, and their Love of their Country would amply supply all Defects in the military Art. Imagine twenty Thousand of them breaking into the Midst of an *European* Army, confounding the Ranks, overturning the Carriages, battering the Warriors Faces into Mummy,* by terrible

Yerks* from their hinder Hoofs: For they would well deserve the Character given to *Augustus*; *Recalcitrat undique tutus.** But instead of Proposals for conquering that magnanimous Nation, I rather wish they were in a Capacity or Disposition to send a sufficient Number of their Inhabitants for civilizing *Europe*; by teaching us the first Principles of Honour, Justice, Truth, Temperance, publick Spirit, Fortitude, Chastity, Friendship, Benevolence, and Fidelity. The *Names* of all which Virtues are still retained among us in most Languages, and are to be met with in modern as well as ancient Authors; which I am able to assert from my own small Reading.

But, I had another Reason which made me less forward to enlarge his Majesty's Dominions by my Discoveries: To say the Truth, I had conceived a few Scruples with relation to the distributive* Justice of Princes upon those Occasions. For Instance, A Crew of Pyrates* are driven by a Storm they know not whither; at length a Boy discovers Land from the Top-mast; they go on Shore to rob and plunder; they see an harmless People, are entertained with Kindness, they give the Country a new Name, they take formal Possession of it for the King, they set up a rotten Plank or a Stone for a Memorial, they murder two or three Dozen of the Natives, bring away a Couple more by Force for a Sample, return home, and get their Pardon. Here commences a new Dominion acquired with a Title by *Divine Right*. Ships are sent with the first Opportunity; the Natives driven out or destroyed, their Princes tortured to discover their Gold;* a free Licence given to all Acts of Inhumanity and Lust; the Earth reeking with the Blood of its Inhabitants: And this execrable Crew of Butchers employed in so pious an Expedition, is a *modern Colony* sent to convert* and civilize an idolatrous and barbarous People.

But this Description,* I confess, doth by no means affect the *British* Nation, who may be an Example to the whole World for their Wisdom, Care, and Justice in planting Colonies; their liberal Endowments* for the Advancement of Religion and Learning; their Choice of devout and able Pastors to propagate *Christianity*; their Caution in stocking their Provinces with People of sober Lives and Conversations from this the Mother Kingdom; their strict Regard to the Distribution of Justice, in supplying the Civil Administration through all their Colonies with Officers of the greatest Abilities, utter Strangers to Corruption: And to crown all, by sending the most vigilant and virtuous Governors, who have no other Views than the Happiness of the People over whom they preside, and the Honour of the King their Master.

But, as those Countries which I have described do not appear to have a Desire of being conquered, and enslaved, murdered or driven out by Colonies; nor abound either in Gold, Silver, Sugar or Tobacco; I did humbly conceive they were by no Means proper Objects of our Zeal, our Valour, or our Interest. However, if those whom it more concerns, think fit to be of another Opinion, I am ready to depose, when I shall be lawfully called, That no *European* did ever visit these Countries before me. I mean, if the Inhabitants ought to be believed.*

But, as to the Formality of taking Possession in my Sovereign's Name, it never came once into my Thoughts; and if it had, yet as my Affairs then stood, I should perhaps in point of Prudence and Self-Preservation, have put it off to a better Opportunity.

Having thus answered the *only* Objection that can be raised against me as a Traveller; I here take a final Leave of my Courteous Readers, and return to enjoy my own Speculations in my little Garden at *Redriff*; to apply those excellent Lessons of Virtue which I learned among the *Houyhnhnms*; to instruct the *Yahoos* of my own Family as far as I shall find them docible* Animals; to behold my Figure often in a Glass, and thus if possible habituate my self by Time to tolerate the Sight of a human Creature: To lament the Brutality of *Houyhnhnms* in my own Country, but always treat their Persons with Respect, for the Sake of my noble Master, his Family, his Friends, and the whole *Houyhnhnm* Race, whom these of ours have the Honour to resemble in all their Lineaments, however their Intellectuals* came to degenerate.

I began last Week to permit my Wife to sit at Dinner with me, at the farthest End of a long Table; and to answer (but with the utmost Brevity) the few Questions I asked her. Yet the Smell of a Yahoo continuing very offensive, I always keep my

Nose well stopt with Rue, Lavender, or Tobacco-Leaves. And although it be hard for a Man late in Life to remove old Habits; I am not altogether out of Hopes in some Time to suffer a Neighbour *Yahoo* in my Company, without the Apprehensions I am yet under of his Teeth or his Claws.

My Reconcilement to the *Yahoo*-kind in general might not be so difficult, if they would be content with those Vices and Follies only which Nature hath entitled them to. I am not in the least provoked at the Sight of a Lawyer, a Pick-pocket, a Colonel, a Fool, a Lord, a Gamester, a Politician, a Whoremunger, a Physician, an Evidence,* a Suborner, an Attorney, a Traytor, or the like: This is all according to the due Course of Things: But, when I behold a Lump of Deformity, and Diseases both in Body and Mind, smitten with *Pride*, it immediately breaks all the Measures of my Patience; neither shall I ever be able to comprehend how such an Animal and such a Vice could tally together. The wise and virtuous *Houyhnhnms*, who abound in all Excellencies that can adorn a rational Creature, have no Name for this Vice in their Language, which hath no Terms to express any thing that is evil, except those whereby they describe the detestable Qualities of their *Yahoos*; among which they were not able to distinguish this of Pride, for want of thoroughly understanding Human Nature, as it sheweth it self in other Countries, where that Animal presides. But I, who had more Experience, could plainly observe some Rudiments of it among the wild *Yahoos*.

But the *Houyhnhnms*, who live under the Government of Reason, are no more proud of the good Qualities they possess, than I should be for not wanting a Leg or an Arm, which no Man in his Wits would boast of, although he must be miserable without them. I dwell the longer upon this Subject from the Desire I have to make the Society of an *English Yahoo* by any Means not insupportable; and therefore I here intreat those who have any Tincture of this absurd Vice, that they will not presume to appear in my Sight.*

FINIS.

EXPLANATORY NOTES

xxxii ADVERTISEMENT: added in Faulkner's edn. (1735). For the story of Motte's 1st edn. (1726), see Introduction, pp. xv–xvi.

Mr Sympson's Letter to Captain Gulliver: a mistake for 'Captain Gulliver's Letter to Mr Sympson'.

Interpolations: made by Motte in his 1st edn., apparently to reduce the risk of prosecution.

compliment the Memory: the scathing account of a Chief Minister (p. 247) was obviously aimed at Walpole; but Motte prudently turned the satire back into the past, by inserting a lengthy statement that, although Queen Anne was too good a ruler to employ a Chief Minister, some of her predecessors had employed Chief Ministers quite bad enough to justify Gulliver's description.

a very worthy Gentleman: probably Swift's friend Charles Ford, whose interleaved copy of *GT*, with minor corrections noted in the margins and major corrections written on the blank leaves, is now in the Victoria & Albert Museum.

xxxiii A LETTER FROM CAPT. GULLIVER TO HIS COUSIN SYMPSON: added in Faulkner's edn. (1735) and perhaps written specially for it.

Gulliver: a name doubtless meant to suggest this character's gullibility. His first name, Lemuel ('devoted to God'), should be taken ironically, like his 'Veracity' (see note to p. xxxvii), the meaning of which is stressed by the words beneath his portrait in the 1735 edn.: '*Splendide mendax*' (a magnificent liar).

Sympson: the pseudonym used by Swift when first negotiating with Motte for the publication of *GT*. The name may have been chosen to imply a relationship between Gulliver and Captain William Sympson, the equally fictitious author of *A New Voyage to the East-Indies* (1715), which was plagiarized from an earlier travel-book (R. W. Frantz, *HLQ* i. (1938), 329–34).

Dampier: William Dampier (1652–1715), pirate, explorer, and author of *A New Voyage Round the World* (1697) and *A Voyage to New Holland* (1703–9), in which he wrote: 'Others have taxed me ... with Insufficiency, as if I was not myself the Author of what I write, but published Things digested and drawn up by others . . . I think it so far from being a Diminution to one of my Education and Employment, to have what I write, Revised and Corrected by Friends; that on the contrary, the best and most eminent Authors are not ashamed to own the same Thing, and look upon it as an Advantage' (*Voyages*, ii. 342).

xxxiii *a Paragraph*: see fourth note to p. xxxii.

of our Composition: made like us, i.e. a human being.

my Master Houyhnhnm: the horse that takes charge of Gulliver in Part IV.

say the thing that was not: the only equivalent for *tell a lie* in Houyhnhnm-language (see p. 227).

I do hardly know mine own Work: Swift was exasperated by these alterations, and probably composed the letter of protest which Ford sent to Motte on 3 Jan. 1726–7 (*Corr.*, iii. 194–5).

xxxiv *Yahoos*: the Houyhnhnms' term for human beings.

these: the Houyhnhnms; *those*: the Yahoos.

Retirement hither: see p. 10.

Smithfield: an open space outside the north-west walls of the City of London, where heretics had been burnt in the 16th century.

Cotten: the context would suggest that this means paper, which was normally made of cotton or linen rags; but there may be a sort of pun on the word *bombast*, which originally meant cotton.

xxxv *Libels*: satires, lampoons, e.g. *Two Lilliputian Odes: The First, On the Famous Engine with which Captain Gulliver extinguish'd the Flames in the Royal Palace . . .* (1727). See p. 43.

Keys: e.g. *Lemuel Gulliver's Travels . . . Compendiously methodized . . . A Key . . .* By Signor Corolini [i.e. Edmund Curll] (1726).

Memoirs, and Second Parts: e.g. *Memoirs of the Court of Lilliput. Written by Captain Gulliver. Containing an Account of the Intrigues and some other particular Transactions of that Nation, omitted in the two Volumes of his Travels* (1727).

confound the Times: the time scheme of *GT* is generally consistent, but there are a few discrepancies for which the printer may not be wholly responsible (Case, 61–8).

Manuscript . . . destroyed: if the manuscript delivered to the printers was in Swift's handwriting, Motte may have destroyed it deliberately, as an incriminating document (Case, 7).

stand to them: insist on them.

xxxv *nor now in Use*: it was largely taken from a book first published
in 1669 (see third note to p. 71).

deliver our Conceptions: express our thoughts.

xxxvi *Utopia*: the imaginary island described in Sir Thomas More's
book (1516). The word means 'nowhere'.

Truth immediately . . . . : a Houyhnhnm doctrine (see p. 259).

these miserable Animals: his human critics.

xxxvii *The Publisher to the Reader*: this was the Preface to the 1st edn.
(1726). *Publisher* here means 'editor'.

Redriff: Rotherhithe.

Banbury: a town famous for its Puritanism (cf. note to p. 5).
Several Gulliver tombstones are still legible in the churchyard
of St Mary's, and the parish register records the burial of a
Samuel Gulliver on 17 Aug. 1728. Like Lemuel (see p. 68),
Samuel was an innkeeper, and the name of his inn, the 'Dol-
phin' (on the south side of the Horsefair) had associations with
seafaring. The inventory of his possessions (valued at £19. 5*s*.
6*d*.) is among the records of the Peculiar Court of Banbury, now
in the Bodleian Library; it is dated 3 Sept. 1729, and shows that
Samuel's wife, like Lemuel's daughter (see p. 68), was called
Elizabeth. There is a local tradition that Swift once lodged on
the opposite side of the Horsefair, probably at 'The Three
Tuns', the principal inn at Banbury during the 18th century. He
may have passed through the town in the summer of 1726, on
his way to visit his old friend William Rollinson, whose family
home was at Chadlington, about 15 miles south-west of Banbury
(see *Corr.*, iii. 150–1; E. St John Brooks, *TLS*, 16 Sept., 1944,
p. 456).

Veracity: the word repeats the irony of *true* in Lucian's *True
History*, a deliberately fantastic traveller's tale which was one of
Swift's sources.

twice as large: a parody of Dampier, who claimed to have often
omitted 'Sea Phrases, to gratify the Land Reader', and excluded
enough nautical information from *A New Voyage* to make up
another whole book, *Voyages and Descriptions* (Bonner, 162–3).

Part I. A Voyage to Lilliput

3 *Lilliput*: the first two syllables of this name are generally agreed
to mean 'little'; the last has been variously derived from *put* (silly

fellow), a word familiar in Swift's day (H. Morley, *GT* (1890), 17–18); from Latin *puto* (think), so that Lilliput is 'the country of little minds as well as little bodies' (C. C. Seronsy, *NQ* ccii (1957), 471); and from a pun on the verb *put* (place), so that Lilliput is simply 'littleplace' (S. Baker, who also connects the name with a Latin word for 'manikin', *salaputium; NQ* cci (1956), 477–9). Clark (p. 606) expands to *lilliputti*, and decodes as 'little-pretty' or 'pretty little'.

5 *My Father . . . Cambridge*: the implication may be that Gulliver is the average Englishman of his period: the middle son of a middle-class father, born in the middle of England, and educated at a College noted for its Puritanism, the typically middle-class religion (E. A. Block, *MLN* lxviii (1953), 474–5).

at Fourteen: the age at which Swift was admitted to Trinity College, Dublin, where the average age that year was 16 (Ehrenpreis 5, i. 61).

Leyden: a Dutch university famous for its medical school, and therefore attended by many foreign students.

Swallow: the name of two real ships mentioned in records 1705–21 (Quinlan, 412).

I married . . . Portion: possibly a veiled reference to Defoe, who had started life as a hosier, married an heiress called Mary Tuffley, rapidly spent her dowry of nearly £4,000, and passed 5 months in Newgate Prison (J. R. Moore, *NQ* clxxviii (1940), 79). *Mrs* was then used for both single and married women.

6 *Antelope . . . May 4th, 1699*: on 3 June 1699, off the Cape of Good Hope, Dampier met the *Antelope* of London, bound for the East Indies (*Voyages*, ii. 416; Bonner, 168).

trouble the Reader: one of Dampier's favourite phrases (Bonner, 164). Cf. p. 62, l. 9; p. 68, l. 6.

Van Diemen's Land: a name given on 18th-century maps both to north-western Australia and to Tasmania. If it means the former in the map on p. 4, Lilliput should be about 15° south, not 30° 2′ south, as stated in the text; if the latter, Lilliput must lie well inland in Australia. Case (pp. 50–61) discusses the geography of *GT*, and finds Swift's scheme moderately consistent, though somewhat confused by Motte's map-engraver.

a Cable's length: 600 ft.

made a Shift: managed with difficulty.

7 *when I awaked*: this episode was possibly suggested by the

account in Philostratus (*Eikones*, II. xxii) of an attack on the sleeping Hercules by pygmies (Eddy, 53, 76–7).

7 *not six inches high*: the scale of Lilliput is one inch to a foot of the ordinary world. Mogg mentions (pp. 52–4) some biological difficulties: a Lilliputian would have room for far fewer cortical cells (so far less intelligence) than a chimpanzee; his head would be too small to carry useful eyes; and he would need eight times as many calories per ounce of body-weight as a full-scale man needs—twenty-four meals a day instead of three.

8 *Admiration*: astonishment.

   shrill, but distinct Voice: at seven octaves above a normal human voice, it would be almost inaudible to Gulliver (Mogg, 54).

   Hekinah Degul: Pons, who interprets Lilliputian by reference to European languages, translates (pp. 225–6): 'He qu'il n'a de gueule' (Oh, what a mouth he has!). Clark, who regards most 'foreign' words in *GT* as coded versions of English ones (the codes being based on systematic substitution of letters) decodes (p. 600) as 'What in the Devil!'

   Tolgo Phonac: 'Come, let's kill him!', from the Latin and Greek words for *kill*, *tollo* and *phoneuo* (Pons, 227); 'Let go! Vomit!' or 'Let go vomit!', i.e. 'Discharge a shower of arrows!' (Clark, 600).

   Bombs: shells.

   Buff Jerkin: close-fitting leather jacket.

9 *Langro Dehul san*: Clark (p. 601) decodes as 'Run from the wild man!' or 'Run from the devil man!', but the context requires 'Cut the cables!' or 'Let his head turn!'

10 *Half a Pint*: since the lineal scale of Lilliput is 1 to 12 of ours, the cubic scale is 1 to 1728. On this basis our half-pint works out as 108 Lilliputian gallons. A hogshead is a large cask holding 100–140 gallons (Eddy, 93–4).

   Borach Mivola: Pons (p. 227) translates as 'The drunkard is going to smash (his cups)', from Spanish *borracho* (drunkard) and *volar* (make fly into pieces). Clark decodes: 'Volat ciboria', dog-Latin for 'he lets fly the drinking-cups' (p. 601).

11 *determinate*: determined.

   Peplom Selan: 'Flee from the rain!' (Clark, 602–3).

12 *Express*: special messenger.

   Engines: machines.

13 *four Inches and a half*: although Henry VIII had made it illegal

for horses of less than 15 hands (5 ft.) to be grazed on common lands in certain counties, Eastern horses, which were imported in large numbers towards the end of the 17th century, tended to be around 14 hands (4 ft. 8 in.). Lilliputian horses are proportionately smaller than this foreign norm, and Brobdingnagian ones are sometimes rather bigger (see p. 103).

13 *Half-Pike*: short pike carried by infantry officers.

an ancient Temple: perhaps an allusion to Westminster Hall, where Charles I was condemned to death. In his 'Sermon upon the Martyrdom of K. Charles I', preached 30 Jan. 1725–6, Swift refers eight times to this execution as a 'murder' (*Prose*, ix. 219–31).

15 *Stang*: a quarter of an acre.

16 *my Maligners*: this remark seems to come not from Gulliver, but from Swift, whose writings, especially *A Tale of a Tub*, had been charged with 'filthiness', 'lewdness', and 'immodesty' (C. J. Rawson, *Imagined Worlds*, ed. M. Mack and I. Gregor (1968), 56).

had like to have cost: very nearly cost.

a sort of Vehicles: a number of receptacles.

Princes of the Blood: i.e. of the blood royal, members of the royal family.

He is taller: possibly suggested by a passage in Addison's mock-epic, *Praelium Inter Pygmaeos et Grues Commissum* (The Battle between the Pygmies and the Cranes) of 1699, where the Pygmy chief

> reliquos supereminet omnes
> Mole gigantea, mediamque assurgit in ulnam

(ll. 77–8; he towers over all the rest with his gigantic bulk, and rises to a height of almost 2 ft.).

His Features: perhaps a sarcastic description of George I, intended to suggest by contrast his thick, awkward figure, his bad taste in clothes, and (p. 17) the thick German accent which made his English almost unintelligible (Case, 71).

Austrian Lip: the thick under-lip typical of the Hapsburgs.

Countenance: bearing, deportment.

past his Prime: defined by *OED* as over 28. Since 15 in Lilliput equals 21 in Europe (see p. 50), the Emperor is really at least 40. George I was 66 when *GT* appeared.

16 *reigned about seven*: the period that George I had reigned when Swift started serious work on *GT*.

17 *High and Low Dutch*: German and Dutch.

Lingua Franca: a mixture of Italian, French, Greek, and Spanish used in the eastern Mediterranean.

Malice of the Rabble: the following episode may allegorize the arrest by Bolingbroke, and subsequent release without punishment (1712) of some Whig pamphleteers who had written 'bold and abusive' attacks on the Government (Ehrenpreis 3, 882).

18 *Six Hundred Beds*: i.e. mattresses. If arranged in four layers of 150, 10 across and 15 down, they would form a bed about 4 ft. by $7\frac{1}{2}$ ft. (E. E. Calkins, *AM*, July 1952, p. 78); but the depth would be only one–third that of a normal mattress (Eddy, 94–5).

four double: four deep.

19 *six Beeves*: such details of catering may have been suggested by Rabelais, whose Gargantua eats a supper of 'sixteen oxen, three heifers, thirty-two calves, sixty-three suckling kids, ninety-five sheep, three hundred suckling pigs in wine sauce, eleven score partridges, and six thousand pullets' (Eddy, 97–8).

Assignments upon: documents authorizing payment from.

upon his own Demesnes: on the income from the Crown lands.

Subsidies: taxes levied to meet special needs.

Lumos . . . Emposo: Pons (p. 227) points out that *pesso* and *Emposo* look like quasi-Spanish forms of *peace* and *Empire*, and interprets the other words as a mixture of Greek, Spanish, and French.

search me . . . Weapons: probably a satire on the activities of the Committee set up by the Whigs (1715) to investigate members of the previous Government, and to discover Jacobite intrigues. The confiscation of Gulliver's 'weapons' may parody the disarming of suspected Jacobites in Ireland: Gough (p. 350) refers to a story of a suspect who solemnly deposited his poker, tongs, and shovel in Dublin Castle, and was given a receipt for them. Case (p. 71) sees an allusion to the examination (1708) of William Gregg, a clerk in Harley's office who had been convicted of treasonable correspondence with France, by seven Whig lords, who failed to find any evidence against Harley himself.

20 IMPRIMIS: first of all (a legal term).

Quinbus Flestrin: Clark (p. 603) thinks that Gulliver has mistranslated his own title, which really means 'Dressed in Buff Skin'.

Foot-Cloth: carpet.

21 *Ranfu-Lo*: 'the place whence *Rain* (came) *from low*' (Clark, 603); Kelling (pp. 776–7) derives from Greek *ranis* (a drop) and *phullon* (leaf, i.e. fig-leaf).

red Metal: i.e. copper.

22 *Clefren Frelock, Marsi Frelock*: 'Meddler (or Maltreat) Traitor', 'Malice Traitor' (Clark, 604).

23 *Closeness*: i.e. the density and impermeability of its materials.

Perspective: telescope.

25 *Rope-Dancers*: a favourite turn in popular entertainments of the period. For the satirical application, cf. Swift's remark in a religious pamphlet (1708): 'Put the Case, that walking on the slack Rope were the only Talent required by Act of Parliament for making a Man a Bishop; no doubt when a Man had done his Feat of Activity in Form, he might sit in the House of Lords . . . but it requireth very little Christianity to believe this Tumbler to be one whit more a Bishop than he was before . . .' (*Prose*, ii. 75; E. W. Rosenheim, *PQ* xxxi (1952), 209).

Flimnap: 'Prime Knave' (Clark, 604), i.e. Sir Robert Walpole, who in 1715 and again in 1721 became Chancellor of the Exchequer and virtually Prime Minister. Swift attacks him especially as the man responsible for the impeachment of Oxford and Bolingbroke, and for the oppression of Ireland in the Wood affair (see note to p. 162).

26 *Summerset*: somersault.

Reldresal: variously identified, as the 1st Earl Stanhope, head of the Whig government 1717–21, but more kindly disposed to the Tories than Walpole (Williams, 462); Lord Carteret, Principal Secretary of State 1721–4, and a friend of Swift (Firth, 246); Lord Townshend, Secretary of State in the Whig cabinet and at first regarded by the Tory leaders as a friend at court, but later distrusted by them (Case, 78). See note to p. 58.

one of the King's cushions: doubtless the Duchess of Kendal, a mistress of George I. When Walpole had been forced to resign in 1717, her influence helped him to return to office (1721). She also used her influence, in return for a £10,000 bribe, to procure Wood's patent for supplying copper coins to Ireland (see note to p. 162).

26 *three fine silken Threads*: the ribbons of the Order of the Garter (blue), given to Walpole, May 1726; the Order of the Bath (red), revived by George I, May 1725; and the Order of the Thistle (green), revived by Queen Anne, 1703. Walpole was responsible for the revival of the Order of the Bath (Firth, 245). Motte evidently thought the satire too dangerous, for he changed the colours in the 1st edn. to purple, yellow, and white.

27 *nine of these Sticks*: a specialist in model-making (E. E. Calkins, *AM*, July 1952, p. 78) wonders how nine sticks can be arranged to form a quadrangle; and how four 2-ft. sticks can enclose an area $2\frac{1}{2}$ ft. square.

Twenty-four in Number: since the area of the stage is the equivalent of 30 sq. ft., each horse has $1\frac{1}{4}$ sq. ft. in which to manœuvre. Here Swift seems to have ignored his scale deliberately, either, as Case suggests (p. 58), for the sake of a picturesque incident or as an early hint to the reader that Gulliver's 'veracity' is not wholly to be relied on (cf. note to p. 284).

discovered: revealed, displayed.

close Chair: sedan chair.

28 *presently*: immediately.

29 *not in a very good Condition*: the incident was possibly suggested by a practical joke played on Swift in 1711, when a lady went off with his hat and put it on the railings five houses down the street (D. Taylor, *TSE* xii (1962), 13).

the Emperor: perhaps a satire on George I's passion for military display (Gough, 352).

Colossus: a 100-ft. statue traditionally believed to have stood astride the harbour entrance at Rhodes. The behaviour of the younger officers (ll. 29–31) seems to have been inspired by Shakespeare (*Julius Caesar*, I. ii. 133–5):

> Why, man, he doth bestride the narrow world
> Like a Colossus, and we petty men
> Walk under his huge legs, and peep about . . .

in a Breast: abreast.

Skyresh Bolgolam: 'Style 'im Mar'boro'—g(h)' (Clark, 604–5), i.e. the Duke of Marlborough, whom Swift had several times attacked (especially in the *Examiner*, 23 Nov. 1710) as chief representative of the Whig war policy. Firth (p. 242) identifies Bolgolam as the Earl of Nottingham, who had used his influence to prevent Swift from getting a bishopric. Though not an Admiral, Nottingham had been First Lord of the Admiralty (1680–4), and though totally ignorant of seamanship, had prided himself ever after on being a naval expert. Case (p. 72), who relates Gulliver's career in Lilliput not to Swift's biography but to the political fortunes of Oxford and Bolingbroke, accepts this identification, on the grounds that Nottingham was hostile to Oxford 'without any provocation' except that Oxford (then Harley) succeeded him in office (1704).

29 *a morose and sour Complection*: Swift had attacked Nottingham under the nickname of '*Dismal*, belike, by reason of his *dark* and *dismal* Countenance' (*Prose*, vi. 139). *Complection*: temperament; so texture and colour of skin, as symptomatic of temperament.

30 *Instrument*: legal document.

Delight . . . Universe: Mr J. C. Maxwell has suggested to me that this phrase may be derived from the first sentence of Suetonius's Life of the Emperor Titus, who is described as '*amor ac deliciae generis humani*' (the darling and delight of the human race).

Center: i.e. of the earth.

31 *Blefuscu*: Clark (p. 607) decodes: 'Bluff as you' or 'Brave as you', and finds that the name includes an anagram of *France* (which *Blefuscu* certainly represents). Kelling (p. 772) translates: 'Little-filthy' from French *bref* (short) and Latin *oscus* (filthy, unclean, barbarous), thus equating *Blefuscu* with *Lilliput* ('little-rotten', from Latin *putidus*).

32 *require as much Food*: a biological error (see note to p. 7).

33 *Mildendo*: Clark (p. 607) decodes the first six letters as 'Noldon', an anagram of *London* (and also finds a hint of *Mile End*).

sideling: sideways.

five Hundred Thousand: the population of London in 1700 has been estimated at 550,000.

34 *smile very graciously*: perhaps an allusion to Queen Anne's inclination towards the Tories (Case, 73).

anticipate the Reader: tell the reader beforehand what he can read later.

35 *pretend to some Merit in it*: claim some credit for it.

35 *above seventy Moons*: if Lilliputian 'moons' can indicate years, as Gough (p. 354) suggests, this implies that party strife originated in the Civil War, which ended 74 years before 1725 (when Swift was writing his final version of *GT*).

Tramecksan and Slamecksan: the High Church party (Tories) and Low Church party (Whigs). Clark (p. 607) decodes: 'Closet Man' and 'Low-set Man'; Kelling (pp. 766–7) reads the names backwards as pseudo-French: *Nas canard* (snub nose) and *nas camels* (camel nose).

his Majesty hath . . . Heels: George I favoured the Whigs.

36 *Tendency towards the High-Heels*: George II, when Prince of Wales, favoured the Tories.

six Thousand Moons: perhaps 6,000 years, the traditional age of the earth (Gough, 354).

six and thirty Moons: England was at war with France from 1689 (36 years before 1725) until 1697 (War of the League of Augsburg), and again in 1701–13 (War of the Spanish Succession).

Grand-father: presumably Henry VIII, who cut his finger (felt injured at not being allowed to marry Anne Boleyn) because he approached his egg (symbol of Easter, and so of Christianity) from the larger end (the Catholic Church). To soothe his childish irritation, his father (i.e. Henry himself in his adult capacity of King) commanded his subjects to approach their eggs from the smaller end (the Church of England). Thus Big-Endians are Catholics, Small-Endians Anglicans. Case (p. 74) interprets the great grandfather as Henry VIII, the small 'Boy' as Elizabeth, who was declared illegitimate by the Pope, the edict as Henry's proclamation of himself as head of the Church, and the egg as the Eucharist, the chief subject of theological controversy at the Reformation.

one Emperor: Charles I.

another: James II.

Blefuscu: France gave asylum and support to Royalists during the Commonwealth, and to Jacobites after 1688. Louis XIV declared the Pretender to be James III, King of England.

Books of the Big Endians . . . forbidden: i.e. by an Act of 1550, under which all Catholic literature was 'abolished, extinguished, and forbidden for ever to be used'.

rendred incapable by Law: by the Test Acts (1661, 1672, 1678).

37 *Alcoran*: the Koran.

Conscience . . . Magistrate: cf. *Sentiments of a Church-of-England Man* (1708): 'any great Separation from the established Worship, although to a new one that is more pure and perfect, may be an Occasion of endangering the publick Peace . . . For this Reason, *Plato* lays it down as a Maxim, that *Men ought to worship the Gods, according to the Laws of the Country* . . . So that, upon the whole, where *Sects* are tolerated in a State, it is fit they should enjoy a full Liberty of Conscience, and every other Privilege of free-born Subjects, *to which no Power is annexed*. And to preserve their Obedience upon all Emergencies, a Government cannot give them too much Ease, nor trust them with too little *Power*' (*Prose*, ii. 11–12). See also note to p. 119.

a bloody War: in *The Conduct of the Allies* (1711) Swift had argued against prolonging the war. There was, of course, no threat of a French invasion, but the imminent danger suggested in ll. 28–30 serves to depreciate Marlborough's victories, and imply that only the Tory government's peace negotiations had saved England (*Case*, 74).

39 *with great Ease*: another sidelight on Gulliver's 'veracity' (the largest Lilliputian warships were 9 ft. long). The capture of the Blefuscudian fleet doubtless represents the dismantling of the naval base at Dunkirk under the Treaty of Utrecht (1713).

40 *expecting*: awaiting.

a large Half-Moon: the formation in which the Spanish Armada approached England (1588).

Nardac: Clark (p. 608) decodes as 'Malgat', i.e. ill-begot, of ignoble birth; but 'malgat' would have more point if it meant 'ill-gotten'. It would then be a sarcastic reference to the great services (in ending the war) for which Oxford and Bolingbroke received their titles (1711, 1712), and for which they had been impeached by the Whigs.

reducing the whole Empire: the Whigs were unwilling to make peace with Louis, except on conditions that he could not accept, e.g. that he should send armies to expel his grandson Philip from the throne of Spain.

Topicks: general rules or maxims.

41 *by a Side-wind*: indirectly.

Visit in Form: formal visit.

42 *Mark of Disaffection*: Bolingbroke was similarly suspected

because of his visit to the French Court (1712), when he was thought to have had a secret interview with the Pretender (Ehrenpreis 3, 884).

42 *which*: the fact that many Blefuscudians could speak Lilliputian (see p. 61).

Adventure: chance.

43 *reading a Romance*: perhaps a hint that young ladies should not read romances. In *A Letter to a Young Lady* (1727) Swift referred to 'that ridiculous Passion which has no Being but in Play-Books and Romances' (*Prose*, ix. 89); and among MS notes headed *Hints: Education of Ladyes* he wrote: 'No French Romances, and few plays for young Ladyes' (*Prose*, xii. 308).

Glimigrim . . . Flunec: Clark (p. 608) decodes: 'Grimy grease' . . . 'Franec' (anagram of *France*) or 'Tranec' (anagram of *nectar*).

Fire was wholly extinguished: the method was probably suggested by a passage in Rabelais (p. 74), where Gargantua drowns 'two hundred and sixty thousand, four hundred and eighteen persons, not counting the women and small children'. Firth (p. 241) sees an allusion to *A Tale of a Tub* (1704), which so disgusted Queen Anne by its improprieties that she refused to give him a bishopric. Case (pp. 75–6) finds an allegory of the Tories' technically illegal (since secretly negotiated) but obviously beneficial peace with France. Ehrenpreis 3 (p. 883) supports this interpretation by quoting a similar image from a pamphlet written in 1714 with Swift's assistance: 'But the Quarreling with the Peace, because it is not exactly to our Mind, seems as if One that had put out a great Fire should be sued by the Neighbourhood for some lost Goods, or damag'd Houses; which happen'd (say they) by his making too much Haste' (*Prose*, viii. 194). D. Novarr (*ES* xlvii (1966), 341–54), who regards the whole chapter as a burlesque on Dryden's *Annus Mirabilis* (1667), points out the mock-heroic exaggeration of Gulliver's physical strength (see note to p. 39) and of his fluid capacity ('three minutes').

congratulate with: congratulate.

Capital: a capital crime.

45 *Of the Inhabitants*: this miniature Utopia, which interrupts the satirical narrative, is thought by Quintana (pp. 291–2) to date from 1714, by Eddy (p. 112) to be a late addition to *GT*. The disconcerting mixture of admirable and ludicrous features is

characteristic of the genre (e.g. the golden chamber-pots in *Utopia* (p. 86) are no more seriously recommended than the burial customs in Lilliput).

45 *between four and five Inches*: see note to p. 13.

an Inch and a half: though sheep at this period were probably taller than 18 in., they were much smaller than they are today. The bones of an extinct pygmy sheep have been found in southern England, comparable in size to a sub-breed confined to the Cameroons, which is only 19 in. high.

pulling: plucking.

clinched: clenched.

Manner of Writing: the prototype of this sentence appears in Sir William Temple's essay 'Of Heroick Virtue' of 1687 (M. L. Jarrell, *PQ* xxxvii (1958), 116–19); adapted versions, including diagonal lines, occur in J. Ovington, *A Voyage to Suratt* (1696), and the plagiarized (see note to p. 289) *A New Voyage to the East-Indies* (1715), by 'William Sympson' (R. W. Frantz, *HLQ* i (1938), 329–34). Swift has added two jokes, the non-existent 'Cascagians' and the reference to English ladies (cf. his letter to Mrs Howard, Introduction, p. xv).

46 *They bury their Dead . . . downwards*: possibly suggested by a picture in Herman Moll's Atlas (1709) showing Laplanders buried standing bolt upright (E. D. Leyburn, *Satiric Allegory* (1956), 74). Gough (p. 357) refers to a tradition that a man buried on Leith Hill, Surrey, chose the Lilliputian posture, for the reason given in the text. Swift's parody of literal-minded piety is in the tradition of satirical Utopian fiction (e.g. in Joseph Hall's *Mundus Alter et Idem* (*c.*1605), the inhabitants of Pious Fool-land habitually walk cross-legged: *Works of J. Hall* (1808), x. 205).

Charges he hath been at: expenses he has incurred.

largely: amply.

Fraud . . . Theft: legislation in *Utopia* (p. 105) is equally paradoxical; e.g. attempted crimes are punished no less severely than committed ones.

47 *different Nations . . . Customs*: a proverb recorded as early as 1100. In John Ray's *English Proverbs* (1670) it appears as 'So many countreys, so many customes'.

two Hinges: an image taken from Temple's 'Of Heroick Virtue' (1687): 'The two great Hinges of all Governments, Reward and Punishment' (*Works* (1770), iii. 331; M. L. Jarrell, *PQ* xxxvii (1958), 117).

47 *except that of Lilliput*: and also that of *Utopia*, where there are
'not only deterrents from crime, but also incentives to good
behaviour in the form of public honours' (pp. 105–6).

In chusing Persons: cf. *A Project for the Advancement of Religion*
(1709): 'if Piety and Virtue were once reckoned Qualifications
necessary to Preferment . . . Things would soon take a new Face,
and Religion receive a mighty Encouragement: Nor would the
publick Weal be less advanced; since of nine Offices in ten that
are ill executed, the Defect is not in Capacity or Understanding,
but in common Honesty' (*Prose*, ii. 48–9).

48 *Practices*: intrigues, manœuvres.

and had: and who had.

Disbelief . . . Station: so does it in *Utopia* (p. 115).

Grand-father: presumably (as on p. 36) Henry VIII, who was
particularly apt to promote or execute his ministers, according
to whether or not they advanced his current schemes. Wolsey
and Thomas Cromwell are among his famous victims, but in this
quasi-Utopian context Swift was probably thinking of More, who
was beheaded for refusing to acknowledge Henry as head of the
Church (cf. p. 196, l. 26).

Ingratitude . . . capital Crime: for the treatment of moral failings
as crimes in Utopian societies cf. Francis Godwin's *The Man in
the Moone* (1638): 'all Lying and falshood . . . is wont there to be
severely punished' (p. 77), and *Utopia* itself, where a second
conviction for adultery carries the death penalty (p. 100).

will never allow . . . World: the same point is made in Cyrano de
Bergerac's *Histoire comique de la lune* (1657): Eddy, 112–13.

49 *Parents are the last . . . Children*: in Plato's *Republic* (460b7 f.) and
in the historical Sparta (*Lycurgus*, xvi f.) the education of children was similarly taken out of the parent's hands.

Professors: teachers.

They are always employed: the basic principle of all social arrangements in *Utopia* (p. 84).

Professor . . . the like: Spartan nurses were similarly stern, not allowing the children to care about food, be afraid of the dark, or
cry (*Lycurgus*, xvi).

Pension: periodical payment.

50 *frightful or foolish Stories*: in Plato's *Republic* also (377b11 f.) the
state decides what stories are to be told to children by mothers
and nurses.

50 *despise . . . Ornaments*: in *Utopia* (pp. 87–8) only small children wear jewellery.

neither . . . any Difference: in the *Republic* (451e6–7) both sexes receive the same education.

cannot always be young: cf. *A Letter to a Young Lady* (1723): 'You have but a very few Years to be young and handsome in the Eyes of the World; and as few Months to be so in the Eyes of a Husband, who is not a Fool . . . You must, therefore, use all Endeavours to attain to some Degree of those Accomplishments which your Husband most values in other People . . . You must improve your Mind' (*Prose*, ix. 89–90).

twelve years old: the equivalent (see p. 49, l. 17) of nearly 17. In *Utopia* (p. 102) girls are allowed to marry at 18.

51 *Domestick*: domestic arrangements.

mechanically turned: with a turn for handicraft.

displayed: spread out.

52 *yields to ours*: is not so good as ours.

bits: bites, mouthfuls.

white Staff: symbol of the Lord High Treasurer's office.

53 *caressed*: treated with favour or kindness.

at great Discount: at a greatly reduced price. He had to borrow money by issuing government bonds ('Exchequer Bills') which nobody would buy except at a price reduced by at least 9 per cent; i.e. 100-Sprug bills were selling at 91 Sprugs.

under: at a discount of less than.

an excellent Lady: this episode may have been suggested by the love-affair between an equally ill-matched pair in the 16th-century Gaelic story 'Imtheachta Tuaithe Luchra agus Aidheadh Fhearghusa' (V. Mercier, *REL* iii (1962), 73–4). It has been explained (Firth, 245) as a satire on Walpole's notorious indifference to the infidelities of his first wife, Catherine Shorter.

54 *Clustril and Drunlo*: perhaps a reference to the spies Pancier and Neynoe employed by Walpole in the trial of Bishop Atterbury (1722): Case, 80.

ever came to me incognito: according to F. Brady (*Twentieth Century Interpretations of GT* (1968), 6) the reader is meant to see a contradiction between this statement and that on p. 54, l. 16, and infer that Gulliver is a liar; but he does not deny the fact, only the possibility of proving it.

54 *by one Degree*: an ironical understatement, if Gulliver represents the Tory leaders, since Oxford was an earl, Bolingbroke a viscount, and Walpole a mere knight.

55 *so remote a Country*: in *Utopia* (p. 108) More satirizes European diplomacy, by transferring it to the New World. In *Mundus Alter et idem* Hall locates in the New World caricatures of European follies. Swift employs a more subtle satiric technique, first implying in the quasi-Utopian Ch. 6 that Lilliput is morally superior to Europe, and then showing in the subsequent narrative that Lilliput is exactly like Europe, only worse. Thus the function of Ch. 6 is to increase the impact of the satire in Ch. 7.

a considerable Person: possibly Marlborough, who, when Bolingbroke asked him (1715), as an old friend, about rumours that the Whigs intended to impeach him, so played upon Bolingbroke's fears that he fled to France (Case, 77).

observing . . . enquiring: the subject of both hanging participles is *I*.

56 *Limtoc . . . Lalcon . . . Balmuff*: identified by Case (p. 77) as Whigs or independent Tories who either opposed the Oxford–Bolingbroke administration or investigated its conduct as members of the Committee of Secrecy (1715).

Articles of Impeachment: a burlesque of the actual charges made against Oxford and Bolingbroke (1715), referring to (1) their technically illegal peace negotiations with France: (2) their granting of easy terms to France: (3) their secret correspondence with the French diplomats; (4) Oxford's failure to procure a licence under the Great Seal to negotiate peace (Case, 77–8).

under Colour: on the pretext.

58 *Juice on your Shirts*: presumably suggested by the shirt, smeared with the poisoned blood of the Centaur Nessus, which made Hercules die in agony.

brought off: won over.

spare your Life . . . Eyes: perhaps a reference to the proposal by some Whigs that Oxford and Bolingbroke should not be charged with high treason (punishable by death), but only with 'high misdemeanours' (punishable by loss of titles and estates: Gough, 360). Firth (p. 246), who identifies Reldresal as Lord Carteret, sees an allusion to the occasion when,

as Lord-Lieutenant of Ireland, Carteret offered a reward of
£300 for the discovery of the author of the *Drapier's Letters*, i.e. of
his friend Swift (1724).

58 *no Impediment . . . Strength*: possibly suggested by the story of
Samson, blinded by the Philistines, and set to 'grind in the
prison house' (Judg. 16: 21).

greatest Princes do no more: a minister of the 'great King' of Persia
was called 'the king's eye' (Herodotus, i. 114; Gough, 360).

59 *Reasons of State*: political considerations. The phrase echoes the
Italian *ragioni di stato*, associated with the unscrupulous methods of government advocated by Machiavelli (see Bacon, iii.
271).

without the formal Proofs: perhaps an allusion to the trial of
Bishop Atterbury (1722). Since there was not enough evidence
against him to justify legal conviction, the Whigs had to bring in
a special bill of pains and penalties to give force to their moral
conviction of his guilt.

Censure: sentence.

60 *Encomiums . . . Mercy*: after the executions following on the
1715 rebellion, a proclamation was issued praising the king's
mercy. R. F. Kennedy (*NQ* ccxiv (1969), 340–1) suggests a
literary source in Suetonius: '*nunquam tristiorem sententiam sine
praefatione clementiae pronuntiavit, ut non aliud iam certius atrocis
exitus signum esset quam principii lenitas*' he never pronounced a
more than usually harsh sentence without first declaring his
clemency, so that a lenient beginning came to be the surest sign
of a horrible end: *Life of Domitian*, xi. 2).

61 *But having . . . Enemies*: an implied defence of Bolingbroke's
decision not to stand his trial. He said: 'I had certain and
repeated information . . . that a resolution was taken by those
who had power to execute it to pursue me to the
scaffold . . . nor could my innocence be any security, after it had
once been demanded from abroad, and resolved on at home,
that it was necessary to cut me off' (Firth, 244).

Youth: Gulliver was then at least 40. Bolingbroke was 37 when
he fled to France, but Swift had always been impressed by his
comparative youth (see Ehrenpreis 5, ii. 455).

pay my Attendance upon: make my formal visit to.

62 *suppose myself*: pretend to be.

Emperor would discover: Emperor (of Lilliput) would reveal.

64 *A Person of Quality*: England made frequent diplomatic protests to France about giving asylum to Jacobites.

65 *very glad*: when Bolingbroke arrived in France, he became Secretary of State to the Pretender. Louis XIV was sympathetic to the Jacobites, but when he died, 6 months later, the Duke of Orleans became regent, and resolved not to give the Jacobites any further help.

I was at the Pains: I had the laborious job.

66 *propagate the Breed*: cf. Gulliver's reactions to a similar plan of the King of Brobdingnag (p. 129).

67 *Antient*: ensign, flag.

North and South Seas: North and South Pacific.

my Veracity: since the reader cannot see the sheep and cattle, this proof of veracity is equivalent to Lucian's when, after telling some very tall stories about lunar society, he concludes: 'Well, that is what it was like on the Moon. If you don't believe me, go and see for yourself' (Lucian, 262). Until 20 July 1969 no one was in a position to refute him.

The Downs: a roadstead off the coast of Kent, where Dampier ended his voyage round the world (*Voyages*, i. 529).

68 *a considerable Profit*: cf. Gulliver's reactions to a similar commercial venture in Brobdingnag (p. 84).

Fineness of the Fleeces: in satirizing the fashionable taste for extra fine wool, Swift seems to echo More (*Utopia*, 89); but the real point of the satire is that Ireland then produced the best wool in Europe, but was forbidden, in the interests of the English wool trade, to export any. Cf. *Proposal for the Universal Use of Irish Manufacture* (1720): 'our *Neighbours* have done, and are doing all that in them lies to make our Wool a Drug to us, and a Monopoly to them' (*Prose*, ix. 15).

insatiable Desire . . . Countries: cf. Lucian's *Wanderlust*, which sends him off on a voyage across the Atlantic (Lucian, 250).

Black-Bull: the name of a real inn in Holborn, opposite Fetter Lane (Gough, 362).

towardly: apt to learn, promising.

Adventure: Quinlan (p. 413) points out that many real ships had this name, and that their commanders tended to get into trouble, e.g. Captain William Kidd, the pirate, who was hanged in 1701. See note to p. 213.

Part II. *A Voyage to Brobdingnag*

69 *Brobdingnag*: conceivably an anagram of *grand big noble* minus
    the last two letters (H. Morley, *GT* (1890), 18).

71 *carried*: not an early hint of the size of 'the Natives', since the
    word could then mean 'escorted' or 'led'.

    Gale: according to a nautical writer (1772) 'a common brisk
    gale is about 15 miles per hour'.

    Finding it was like to overblow: this whole paragraph, which par-
    odies the excessive use of nautical terms in travel-books, is
    copied almost verbatim from the instructions for the 'working
    of a Ship in all Weathers' in Samuel Sturmy's *Mariner's Magazine*
    (1669), 17–18 (quoted by Eddy, 143–4, and Williams,
    469–70). *like to overblow*: likely to blow too hard for topsails to
    be carried.

    Sprit-sail: sail attached to a yard slung under the bowsprit.

    hand: take in, furl.

    making: meeting with.

72 *looked the Guns were all fast*: made sure the guns were all secured
    (so that they would not roll about in the storm).

    Missen: mizen, a fore-and-aft sail set on the after side of the
    mizen-mast (the aftermost mast of a three-master).

    very broad off: heading well away from the wind.

    spooning: running.

    trying: lying to (i.e. setting the sails so as to keep a ship's bow to
    the sea, and prevent her rolling to windward in the trough of
    the sea).

    hulling: driving with all sails furled.

    Fore-sheet: the rope by which the lee corner of the foresail is kept
    in place.

    a Weather: towards the windward side.

    wore: came round.

    belay'd the Foredown-hall: made fast the rope used to pull down
    the foresail.

    hawl'd off upon the Lanniard of the Wipstaff: hauled away at the
    short rope attached to the tiller (so helping the steersman).

    wholesomer: steadier.

    brought the Ship to: brought her to a standstill.

    got the Star-board Tacks aboard: hauled the tacks (ropes used to
    secure to the ship's side the windward corners of the lower

square sails) into such a position as to trim the sails to a wind on the starboard side.

cast off our Weather-braces and Lifts: loosened on the windward side the braces (ropes attached to the yards to determine their angle to the ship's length) and the lifts (ropes reaching from the mast-head to the yard-arms to steady and support their ends).

set in the Lee-braces: shortened the braces on the lee side.

hawl'd forward by the Weather-bowlings: pulled forward the windward side of the square sails by the bowlines (ropes passing from the perpendicular edges of the sails to the port or starboard bow, to keep the edges of the sails steady).

kept her full and by as near as she would lye: kept her sailing close-hauled to the wind, and heading as near as possible to the direction from which the wind was blowing.

Great Tartary: the name given in Herman Moll's *Atlas Manuale* (1709) to a whole land mass north of China (roughly corresponding to Siberia). *North-west* seems to be a slip for *North-east*.

whether: which of the two.

73 *hollow*: shout.

walking after them in the Sea: perhaps suggested by a passage in Virgil (*Aeneid*, iii. 662 f.) where the Cyclops Polyphemus wades out into the sea after Aeneas's ship. This has just rescued a man who, like Gulliver, was left behind on the island, when his companions were escaping from the monster (iii. 616–18).

waded . . . Knees: cf. '*graditurque per aequor | iam medium, necdum fluctus latera ardua tinxit*' (he is already striding through the middle of the sea, but the wave has not yet wet his towering flanks: iii. 664–5).

74 *ten Yards at every Stride*: since the average pace is 30 in., this gives a 12 to 1 scale for Brobdingnag (Eddy, 136). Mogg (p. 52), who seems to regard the scale as 10 to 1, calls a 60-ft. man 'an engineering impossibility'. The skeleton would need considerable modification to support the weight (about 90 tons): shorter legs, smaller head, thicker neck, and larger trunk (to accommodate adequate internal organs to power such a huge machine).

75 *more Savage . . . Bulk*: the traditional view implied in Shakespeare's 'O! it is excellent | To have a giant's strength, but it is tyrannous | To use it like a giant' (*Measure for Measure*, II. ii.

107–9), and justified by the behaviour of the Giants and of the Cyclops in Greek mythology. Swift produces a surprise effect by making the Brobdingnagians the most humane and 'the least corrupted' of the nations described in *GT* (p. 284).

Philosophers: e.g. Bishop Berkeley, who in the first of *Three Dialogues between Hylas and Philonous* (1713) argues against the view that extension (size) is an inherent quality of external objects: 'A mite . . . must be supposed to see his own foot, and things equal or even less than it, as bodies of some considerable dimension; though at the same time they appear to you scarcely discernible . . . And to creatures less than the mite they will seem yet larger . . . Insomuch that what you can hardly discern, will to another extremely minute animal appear as some huge mountain . . . Can one and the same thing be at the same time in itself of different dimensions?' (*Works*, ed. G. N. Wright (1843), i. 166).

76 *Lappet*: lapel.

Pistoles: Spanish coins worth about 18*s*.

77 *articulate enough*: Brobdingnagian voices, vibrating at perhaps 3 cycles per second, though audible, 'would not merge into a continuous sound, but would seem like the sad undulations of a phonograph record dragging to a stop' (Mogg, 54).

about two Gallons: since a dram is $\frac{1}{8}$ fluid oz., the equivalent would be more like $1\frac{1}{3}$ gallons.

78 *surprize*: in the obsolete sense of 'alarm, terror, perplexity'.

arch: playful, mischievous.

Stocking-Weavers: stocking-frames (knitting machines of a type invented by the Revd William Lee in 1589).

79 *Mastiff . . . Elephants*: possibly inspired by the *Philopseudes* of Lucian (p. 209), where in one of several stories given as examples of fantastic lies, some hell-hounds are described as 'slightly larger than Indian elephants'.

80 *magnifying glass*: cf. 'The Virtues we must not let pass. | Of *Celia*'s magnifying Glass. | When frighted *Strephon* cast his Eye on't | It shew'd the Visage of a Gyant. | A Glass that can to Sight disclose | The smallest Worm in *Celia*'s Nose' ('The Lady's Dressing Room' (1730); *Poems*, ii. 527).

81 *Hanger*: short sword (originally hung from the belt).

82 *Sorrel*: the common variety is 1–2 ft. tall.

82 *my sole Design . . . World*: cf. Dampier's dedication of his *New Voyage*: 'I have not so much of the Vanity of a Traveller, as to be fond of telling Stories, especially of this kind . . . Yet dare I avow, according to my narrow sphere and poor abilities, a hearty Zeal for the promoting of useful Knowledge, and of any thing that may never so remotely tend to my Countries advantage' (*Voyages*, i. 17).

without affecting . . . Style: again modelled on Dampier: 'As to my Stile, it cannot be expected, that a Seaman should affect Politeness; for were I able to do it, yet I think I should be little sollicitous about it, in a work of this Nature . . . I am perswaded, that if what I say be intelligible, it matters not greatly in what words it is express'd' (*Voyages*, i. 20).

83 *towardly Parts*: promising abilities.

Baby: doll.

This young Girl . . . self: in *Histoire comique de la lune* (1657) Cyrano de Bergerac flies to the moon, which is inhabited by 18–22-ft. giants, and one of the Queen's maids falls in love with him. In the *Arabian Nights* (a French version of which was translated into English in 1724) Hassân al Bassri is captured by giants, and becomes the pet of a giant princess, who dresses and undresses him like a doll (Eddy, 128–30).

Grildrig: Clark (p. 610) decodes: 'Girl thing', i.e. doll. M. R. Grennan (*ELH* xii (1945), 201) derives from Irish *grileag* = 'any small matter', 'a small potato'. Kelling (pp. 774–5) derives from Latin *gryllus* (grasshopper), regarding *drig* as an invented diminutive suffix.

Nanunculus: a portmanteau word (from *nanus*, dwarf, and *homunculus*, manikin) invented like the proper names in *Utopia* (p. 8 n. 19) partly as a joke, partly to remind the reader not to believe everything he is told.

Homunceletino: a similar coinage, from homunculus with a quasi-Italian diminutive suffix.

Glumdalclitch: Clark (p. 610) decodes: 'grim doll clutch', since little girls are 'apt to clutch dolls grimly' (contradicted in this case by pp. 84–5). M. R. Grennan (*ELH* xii. (1945), 201) derives from Irish *glum* = 'large mouthful of liquid'. Kelling (p. 771), by letter substitutions based on the code used in Swift's *Journal to Stella*, produces: 'grand *altrix*' (Latin for 'nurse'), i.e. 'big nurse'. Ehrenpreis 2 (p. 715) suggests that Glumdalclitch's character is based on that of Stella.

84 *little Language*: Swift's name for the code in which he and Stella sometimes corresponded (*Journal*, i. pp. lv–lviii).

Reverence: bow.

85 *publick Spectacle*: Cyrano is also made to perform as a dwarf, in a lunar circus (Eddy, 21).

Monster: freak, monstrosity.

since the King . . . Distress: perhaps a hint that George I, as 'a perfect Stranger' in England, was also something of a freak.

In a Box: famous Swiss dwarf, John Wormberg (or Hans Worrenbergh), 31 in. high, was carried around in a box all over Europe (D. Taylor, *TSE* xii (1962), 31).

close: i.e. without any openings except the door and the gimlet-holes.

so careful to: so careful as to.

London to St Albans: 20 miles.

86 *I turned about*: Gulliver's performance is paralleled by several advertisements of contemporary shows, e.g. 'a little Marmoset . . . Exercises by Word of Command, he dances the Cheshire Rounds, he also dances with two Naked Swords'; 'A Noble Creature, which much resembles a Wild *Hairy Man* . . . pulls off his Hat, and pays his Respects to the Company'; 'A Man Teger' takes 'a Glass of Ale in his hand like a Christian, Drinks it, also plays at Quarter Staff'; 'A little Black Hairy Pigmey . . . two feet high, walks upright, drinks a Glass of Ale, or Wine.' (A. M. Taylor, *TSE* vii (1957), 31).

Fopperies: silly tricks.

unlucky: probably in the obsolete sense of 'mischievous, malicious'. Cyrano also has to dodge a huge nut thrown by a spectator (*Histoire*, 142; Eddy, 127–8).

Pumpion: Pumpkin.

Vehicle for me: container to carry me about in.

87 *Wednesday . . . is their Sabbath*: possibly implying that they worship Mercury (*mercredi*), the god of trade and theft, since the immediate object of satire is commercial greed.

Boy of the House: male domestic servant.

Lorbrulgrud: Clark (p. 611) decodes: 'Lonnoldon', i.e. London. Kelling (p. 771) finds an anagram of *L'urgul d'orb* (the pride of the world) or *L'orb d'urgul* (the world of pride), from French *orgueil* and Latin *orbis*.

88 *explain*: i.e. read and translate.

Sanson's Atlas: probably the *Atlas nouveau* (first published 1689), engraved by Guillaume and Adrien Sanson. It measured $20\frac{5}{8}$ by $20\frac{1}{2}$ in. (Williams, 471).

89 *Stomach*: appetite.

make as good a Hand of: make as much profit out of.

Slardral: Kelling (p. 764) refers to a cook in Rabelais (IV. xl) called Raslard ('smooth-shaven fat bacon'), and interprets the name as suggesting unctuousness and prosperity.

90 *that People*: i.e. courtiers.

91 *His Majesty*: modelled, according to Sir Walter Scott, on William III. Williams (p. 471) suggests that the King's character was meant as a flattering portrait of the Prince of Wales, since the Tories hoped for his support. Ehrenpreis 3 (pp. 885–9) thinks the character was inspired by Sir William Temple.

this Princess: possibly intended as a compliment to the Princess of Wales (Williams, 471) or as a portrait of Temple's wife, née Dorothy Osborne (Ehrenpreis 3, 886).

Scrutore: escritoire, writing-desk.

Clockwork . . . But when he heard my Voice . . .: conceivably a reflection of Descartes: 'if there were machines resembling our bodies, and imitating our actions as far as is morally possible, we should still have two means of telling that, all the same, they were not real men. First, they could never use words or other constructed signs as we do to declare our thoughts to others' (*Discourse on Method*, tr. L. J. Lafleur (1950), 36; Ehrenpreis 4, 28–9).

Artist: craftsman.

waiting: attendance at court.

92 *They all agreed . . . Nature*: Cyrano is similarly discussed by lunar philosophers, who agree that he must be a *lusus naturae* (*Histoire*, 117, 142; Eddy, 126–7).

Insects: 'formerly applied . . . to earthworms, snails, and even some small vertebrates, as frogs and tortoises' (*OED*).

evince: prove.

whose Professors: perhaps an oblique attack on Newton, who in the 2nd edn. of his *Optics* (1717) argued that modern science, with its 'general Laws of Nature' was much more useful than Aristotelianism, with its 'occult Qualities': 'Such occult Qualities put a stop to the improvement of natural Philosophy, and therefore of late Years have been rejected. To tell us that every Species of Things is endow'd with an occult specifick Quality by which it acts and produces manifest Effects, is to tell us nothing' (4th edn. (1730), 377). Swift replies that to explain a phenomenon as a *lusus naturae* (i.e. an exception to the 'general Laws of Nature') is just as much an evasion of the problem as a reference to 'occult Qualities'. Cf. p. 189.

92 *To this they only replied . . . contempt*: cf. the similar attitude of Gulliver's Houyhnhnm master (p. 227). In satirizing the ignorant dogmatism of scientists, Swift follows the Lucianic tradition: 'in spite of the difficulty of ascertaining the facts, they never put forward a theory as a tentative hypothesis. On the contrary, they struggled desperately to prove that no other theory could possibly be true' (*Icaromenippus*, Lucian, 115).

93 *Nice*: capable of fine, delicate work.

94 *Baby-house*: doll's house.

craunch: crunch.

Hogshead at a Draught: since a hogshead = half a pint (see note to p. 10), she sounds quite a heavy drinker, even by Brobdingnagian standards.

95 *a Whig or a Tory*: cf. *Sentiments of a Church-of-England Man* (1708): 'how has this Spirit of Faction . . . Broke all the Laws of Charity, Neighbourhood, Alliance and Hospitality; destroyed all Ties of Friendship, and divided Families against themselves? And no Wonder it should be so, when in order to find out the Character of a Person; instead of enquiring whether he be a Man of Virtue, Honour, Piety, Wit, good Sense, or Learning; the modern Question is only, Whether he be a *Whig* or a *Tory*' (*Prose*, ii. 24).

white Staff: see note to p. 52.

Royal Sovereign: Charles I's warship, *Sovereign of the Seas*, built 1637, and then 'the largest, most ornate, and most useless ship afloat' (M. Oppenheim, *History of the Royal Navy, 1509–1660* (1896), 252). Her main mast would have measured about 110 ft.

engage: bet.

Nests and Burrows . . . Cities: cf. *Icaromenippus*, where a town seen from the moon is compared to an ant-hill, 'with lots of ants crawling round it, some streaming off across country and some going back to town. One ant will be carrying out refuse, another racing in with a bean-pod or half a grain of corn. Then doubtless they have the ant-equivalents of architects, left-wing politicians, town councillors, literary men, and philosophers . . . the towns and the people in them looked exactly like that' (Lucian, 123). The contemptibility of 'human grandeur' when viewed from a great height is a theme that goes back to Cicero's *Somnium Scipionis* (viii), in which Scipio becomes a dream- astronaut and sees the whole Roman Empire reduced to a mere 'speck' (*punctum*).

95 *Birth-day Cloaths*: splendid clothes worn at court to celebrate royal birthdays.

96 *Queen's Dwarf*: Cyrano also meets a Queen's dwarf on the moon, who turns out to be Domingo Gonzales, the narrator of Godwin's *The Man in the Moone* of 1638 (Eddy, 21).

let me drop . . . Cream: in the 16th-century Irish story 'Aidedh Ferghusa', Esirt is picked up by the King's cupbearer and dropped into a wine goblet, where he is nearly drowned; he also slips into a porridge-bowl and gets stuck to his middle (cf. next paragraph, p. 100; A. C. L. Brown, *MLN* xix (1904), 46).

97 *raillied*: rallied, chaffed.

Dunstable Lark: larks for the London market were caught in large numbers on the downs round Dunstable (Gough, 370).

98 *Sashes*: see p. 93.

Gresham College: the home of the Royal Society 1661–6 and 1673–1710. The unpleasant picture of enormously magnified insects was possibly intended as a satire on such members of the Royal Society as Robert Hooke, whose *Micrographia* (1665) contained some striking micrographical illustrations of fleas and flies.

99 *The whole Extent*: J. R. Moore points out (*JEGP* xl (1941), 217–18) that at the latitude indicated, 6,000 miles would extend considerably more than a third of the way round the globe. Case (p. 58) notes that the dimensions of Brobdingnag, if divided by 12, are roughly those of the British Isles.

a Peninsula: as Utopia was, until a channel was cut through the isthmus (*Utopia*, 69).

100 *fifty-one Cities*: possibly an approximation, like the number of cities (54) in *Utopia* (p. 70), to the number of counties in England and Wales.

sufficient to describe Lorbrulgrud: cf. *Utopia* (pp. 71–2) where one town is described as representative of them all.

Glonglungs: apparently derived from English *long*, Italian *lungo*, plus the *g* (= great?) which seems as characteristic of Brobdingnagian as *h* is of Houyhnhnm-language.

100 *a Square of*: either a square equal to the area of (which Gough (p. 371) works out as 140 ft. sq.) or a square of the width of (68 ft.) or a square of the length of (290 ft.).

the Beggars: Firth (p. 248) suggests that Swift was thinking of the beggars in Dublin.

101 *Woolpacks*: large bags used for carrying fleeces or wool.

Louse through a Microscope: see note to p. 98.

Squares: rectangular sides (actually 12 by 10).

out of Order: unwell.

Officers: holders of high office.

102 *Field-Bed*: camp-bed.

Salisbury Steeple: 404 ft. high, the equivalent of 4,848 ft. in Brobdingnag.

measured a little Finger: cf. *True History*, where the travellers measure the footprints of Hercules and Dionysus, and find them 100 ft. and about 99 ft. long (Lucian, 251).

103 *Cupola at St Paul's*: 122 ft. in interior diameter and, like Salisbury steeple, 404 ft. in height (hence, perhaps, Swift's train of thought from the one building to the other). Gulliver arrived home from Brobdingnag in 1706; St Paul's was completed in 1710.

I should be hardly believed: a familiar formula in the mock-traveller's tale, e.g. 'I hardly like to tell you about their eyes, for fear you should think I am exaggerating, because it really does sound almost incredible' (*True History*, Lucian, 261); 'I hardly like to tell you how they do regard them [precious metals], for fear you shouldn't believe me' (*Utopia*, 85–6).

enlarged: exaggerated.

Travellers are often suspected to do: for an early statement of this 'suspicion' see Lucian (pp. 249–50), preface to *True History*.

diminutive: belittling.

fifty-four to sixty: see note to p. 13.

Battalia: battle-order.

104 *Allusion*: word-play, pun.

Bristol Barrel: barrel of the size used at Bristol (where Gulliver had started his voyage to Lilliput).

Lemmon Thyme: a creeping plant that normally rises only an inch or two off the ground.

105 *near Eighteen Hundred Times*: i.e: 1728 times (cf. p. 32).

Kindness: affection.

amazed: dazed, stupefied.

not be for: not be good for.

made a Stoop at: swooped down on.

106 *broke my right Shin*: possibly suggested by an occasion when Swift 'broke' (i.e. barked) his 'shin in the Strand over a tub of sand left just in the way' (*Journal*, i. 215; D. Taylor, *TSE* xii (1962), 13–14).

Birds . . . not afraid of me: Cyrano had the same experience on the sun (*Histoire*, 276; Eddy, 128–9).

Security: freedom from anxiety.

pick: peck.

The Maids of Honour: this passage 'grievously offended' the maids of honour at George I's court (*Corr.*, iii. 190), although the Brobdingnagian ladies behave much more decently than the giant princess in the *Arabian Nights* (see note to p. 83; Eddy, 130–1).

107 *Toylet*: dressing-table.

Motions: reactions, emotions.

three Tuns: equal to 12 hogsheads, or at least 1,200 wine-gallons. Ovid (*Remedia Amoris*, 437–40) suggests this type of spectacle as a possible remedy for love.

pleasant: humorous, jocular.

108 *great Jet d'Eau at Versailles*: the fountain in the Basin of Enceladus sent up a jet 75 ft. high.

upon a Pinch: in an emergency.

109 *Corking-pin*: 'a pin of the largest size' (Johnson's *Dictionary*).

110 *that Country Silk*: silk of that country.

clambered up to a Roof: this episode must have been written by June 1722, when Vanessa (Esther Vanhomrigh) wrote to Swift, describing some monkey-like 'Beaus' that she met at a party:

'one of these animals snatched my fan and was so pleased with me that . . . I apprehended nothing less than being carried up to the top of the House and served as a friend of yours was' (*Corr.* ii. 428).

112 *upon a Foot*: on an equal footing.

a Cow-dung: possibly suggested by *Iliad*, xxiii. 774 f., where Ajax, on the point of winning a foot-race, slips on some cow-dung and falls flat on his face in it.

113 *Levee*: a reception held by a king on getting up in the morning.

artificially: skilfully.

seasonable Supply: opportune replacement.

114 *Mechanical genius*: talent for handicraft.

decyphered: represented by a cipher or monogram.

Consorts: concerts.

Musick not disagreeable: Swift 'neither loved nor understood music' (Johnson, *Lives*, ed. G. B. Hill (1968), iii. 53), and once said: 'I know nothing of music; I would not give a farthing for all the music in the universe' (P. Delany, *Observations* (1754), 192).

116 *three mighty Kingdoms*: although, as Gough (p. 373) points out, Scotland was not finally united with England until 1707 (the year after Gulliver's return from Brobdingnag), William and Mary had become sovereigns of Scotland in 1689, and, after the Battle of the Boyne (1690), in fact as well as in name sovereigns of Ireland.

Plantations: colonies.

Temperature: temperateness.

extraordinary Care . . . Education: cf. *Intelligencer*, p. ix: 'Education is always the *worse* in Proportion to the *Wealth* and *Grandeur* of the Parents: Nor do I doubt in the least, that if the whole World were now under the Dominion of *one Monarch* . . . the only Son and Heir of that Monarch, would be the worst educated Mortal that ever was since the Creation' (*Prose*, xii. 46).

Counsellors born: hereditary advisers.

highest Court . . . Appeal: the House of Lords was the final court of appeal, an arrangement against which Swift protested in *A Short View . . . of Ireland* (1728): 'all Appeals for Justice . . . to another Country, are so many grievous Impoverishments' (*Prose*, xii. 6).

Conduct: leadership.

116 *never once known to degenerate*: the degeneracy of the aristocracy had been a familiar theme of satirists since Juvenal's Satire viii.

These were searched . . . : perhaps Swift was thinking of his own failure to become a bishop.

117 *sinister View*: dishonest consideration.

slavish prostitute Chaplains . . . Nobleman: possibly an allusion to the Earl of Wharton, whom Swift had alleged in *A Short Character* (1710) to have tried to make his subsidiary chaplain a bishop, as a reward for marrying one of the Earl's cast-off mistresses (*Prose*, iii. 182–3).

118 *Commoners*: members of the House of Commons.

How it came to pass: Ehrenpreis 3 (p. 888) suggests that this point is based on a passage written by Sir William Temple (*Works* (1770), iii. 42–3).

sifted: closely questioned.

Head: section (of my speech).

decreed for me: decided in my favour.

119 *Issues*: expenditure.

he was still at a Loss . . . Person: the King expresses the economic policy of the Tories, who opposed the principle of a permanent National Debt (Firth, 247). This had begun under the Whigs (1693), and been systematized by the foundation of the Bank of England (1694).

chargeable: expensive.

Wars . . . Kings: cf. *Conduct of the Allies* (1711): 'Ten glorious Campaigns are passed, and now at last, like the sick Man, we are just expiring with all sorts of good Symptoms. Did the Advisers of the War . . . think a Town taken for the *Dutch . . .* a sufficient Recompense to us for six Millions of Money? . . . all this brings no real solid Advantage to us . . . it hath no other End than . . . to increase the Fame and Wealth of our *General* [i.e. Marlborough]' (*Prose*, vi. 20).

mercenary standing Army: the argument against a standing army appears in *Utopia* (pp. 45–6), in Temple's essay on government (*Works* (1770), i. 45; Ehrenpreis 3, 888–9), and was a favourite theme of the Tories (Firth, 247).

odd Kind of Arithmetick: a satire on the dubious and devious methods of estimating population at this period. Cf. Martinus Scriblerus's calculation of 'The Number of Inhabitants of

London determin'd by the Reports of the Gold-finders [sewage collectors], and the Tonnage of their Carriages; with allowance for the extraordinary quantity of the *Ingesta and Egesta* [things carried in and out] of the people of England, and a deduction of what is left under dead walls, and dry ditches' (*Memoirs*, 167–8, 342).

119 *He knew no Reason*: cf. *Thoughts on Religion*: 'To say a man is bound to believe, is neither truth nor sense. You may force men, by interest or punishment, to say or swear they believe, and to act as if they believed: You can go no further. Every man, as a member of the commonwealth, ought to be content with the possession of his own opinion in private, without perplexing his neighbour or disturbing the public' (*Prose*, ix. 261). In *Utopia* (p. 120) the 'choice of creed' is left 'an open question', but atheists are forbidden to argue publicly in defence of their beliefs. See note to p. 37.

 Gaming: gambling (a 'stupid pleasure' rejected by the Utopians: *Utopia*, 95).

120 *Lines of an Institution*: traces of a system.

122 *could not consist*: was incompatible.

 Dionysius Halicarnassensis: a Greek writer (*fl. c.*25 BC) who lived at Rome and wrote a eulogistic account of Rome's early history. In ch. 3 of his *Letter to Pompeius* (774) he judges Thucydides inferior to Herodotus as a historian, because Thucydides showed 'a bitter and resentful attitude towards his country, for sending him into exile. Thus he very accurately lists all her wrongdoings, but when she does right, he either ignores it completely, or mentions it with obvious reluctance.'

123 *between three and four hundred Years ago*: gunpowder was said to have been invented by Berthold Schwarz in 1354; but guns are known to have been used in Florence as early as 1326, and an illustration of a gun appears in an Oxford MS of 1325.

 when linked . . . Chain: chain-shot (two balls or half-balls connected by a chain) was used chiefly in naval warfare.

124 *reduced Politicks into a Science*: for the history of this technical approach to politics, which goes back to Machiavelli's *The Prince* (1513), see E. B. Benjamin, *JHI* xviii (1957), 572–9.

 Topicks: commonplaces.

 he gave it for his Opinion: cf. *Drapier's Letters*: 'I once ventured to say to a great Man in *England*, that few *Politicians*, with all their

Schemes, are half so useful Members of a Commonwealth, as an *honest Farmer*, who, by skilfully draining, fencing, manuring and planting, hath increased the intrinsick Value of a Piece of Land; and thereby done a *perpetual Service* to his Country; which it is a great Controversy, whether any of the *former ever* did, since the Creation of the World; but no Controversy at all, that Ninety-nine in a Hundred, have done Abundance of Mischief' (*Prose*, x. 141). Williams (p. 474) points out that the Tories were united with the agricultural interest.

125 *what may be useful in Life*: cf. *Advancement of Learning* (1605), where the 'last or farthest end of knowledge' is 'the benefit and use of men' (Bacon, iii. 294).

Ideas: Plato's archetypal patterns, of which all individual objects are imperfect copies.

Entities: in scholastic philosophy, the essences or existences of things, as opposed to their qualities or relations.

Trancendentals: in Aristotelian philosophy, things transcending the bounds of any single category.

as to Ideas . . . Heads: for the attitude towards abstract technical terms and the satiric device of expressing wisdom as a form of unintelligence, cf. *Utopia*, 90: 'they're no match for the Moderns when it comes to logic . . . they've failed to invent a single one of those rules about Restrictions, Amplifications, and Suppositions . . . And so far from being equal to investigating Second Intentions, they're even blind to the existence of that notorious Universal, MAN.'

No Law: cf. *Utopia*, 106: 'They have very few laws . . . according to the Utopians, it's quite unjust for anyone to be bound by a legal code which is too long for an ordinary person to read right through, or too difficult for him to understand . . . the crudest interpretation is always assumed to be the right one.'

Mercurial: ingenious, quick-witted (here perhaps with a pejorative reference to Mercury's talent for theft and trickery).

Art of Printing: the Chinese printed the teachings of Confucius from wood-blocks in 932. The Utopians have to be taught this art by their visitor (*Utopia*, 101).

126 *Their Stile*: in *A Letter to a Young Gentleman* (1721) Swift warns against 'a quaint, terse, florid Stile, rounded into Periods and Cadencies, commonly without either Propriety or Meaning', and defines good style as 'Proper Words in Proper Places',

adding later: 'When a Man's Thoughts are clear, the properest Words will generally offer themselves first; and his own Judgment will direct him in what Order to place them, so as they may be best understood' (*Prose*, ix. 67, 65, 68).

Nature was degenerated: The idea that human beings used to be larger is as old as Homer (*Iliad*, xii. 447–9), but was particularly popular in the 17th century. A French dissertation (1718) argued that Adam was 123 ft. 9 in. high, Moses 13 ft., and Alexander a mere 6 ft. (Eddy, 123). Dr Thomas Molyneux, however, considered all giants purely fabulous (*PTRS* xxi (1700–1), 507–8; quoted by C. Kerby-Miller, *Memoirs*, 265).

126 *Tile falling*: a familiar illustration of the precariousness of human life, e.g. Juvenal, *Satires*, iii, 269–74; *Charon* (Lucian, 83): 'I'd heard a man invited . . . to a dinner-party. "I'll be there," he replied, and just as he said it, someone knocked a tile off a roof on to his head, and killed him. It made me laugh, because I didn't see how he was going to keep his appointment.'

127 *made up of Tradesmen*: cf. *Utopia* (p. 109), where all citizens of both sexes are given regular military training.

manner of Venice: the ballot was used in the election of the Great Council from 1297 onwards. Secret voting in Parliament was once proposed during the reign of Charles II, and in 1705 it was proposed again as part of a plan for the provisional government of Scotland in the event of Queen Anne's death.

the same Disease: cf. *A Discourse of the Contests and Dissentions* (1701), in which Swift states the necessity for a balance of power between the *'One'*, the *'Few'*, and the *'Many'*, and continues: 'The next next thing is to examine what Methods have been taken to break or overthrow this Balance; which every one of the three Parties have continually endeavour'd, as opportunities have served; which might appear from the Stories of most Ages and Countries' (*Prose*, i. 200–2). The argument was probably founded upon the writings of Temple (Ehrenpreis 3, 887).

128 *Composition*: agreement.

settled: established.

129 *Impulse*: feeling, presentiment.

Woman of my own Size: with the same object in view, Cyrano is married, by royal decree, to the (male) Spaniard, Gonzales (*Histoire*, 133; Eddy, 128).

like . . . Canary Birds: a simile with particularly disagreeable connotations, since in contemporary slang a 'Canary Bird' was 'a

Rogue or Whore taken, and clapp'd into the Cage or Round-house [lock-up]' (A. M. Taylor, *TSE* vii (1957), 52). Cyrano is kept literally in a cage (Eddy, 21). The King's wish to breed from Gulliver may have been suggested by recent marriages of court dwarfs (one at St Petersburg in 1710) and by several unsuccessful attempts to multiply the breed (A. M. Taylor, *TSE* v (1955), 99).

129 *even*: equal.

130 *wistful melancholy Look towards the Sea*: possibly a mock-heroic version of *Odyssey*, v. 151–8, where Odysseus sits weeping on the shore of Calypso's (= Glumdalclitch's) island, gazing out to sea and longing for home.

131 *some Eagle*: Cyrano is carried off in his cage by a roc (*Histoire*, 339; Eddy, 129).

like a Tortoise: Aeschylus was said to have been killed when an eagle mistook his bald head for a stone, and dropped a tortoise on to it.

Sign-post: i.e. a sign (e.g. of an inn) swinging on a post.

Squash: splash.

I was fallen into the Sea: possibly suggested by the fate of the dwarf John Wormberg, who was drowned at Rotterdam (1695) when the porter carrying his box fell into the river (A. M. Taylor, *TSE* vii (1957), 30).

133 *better*: more.

by all that was moving: as movingly as I could.

134 *into his Cabbin*: a touch admired by Thackeray (p. 36): 'he calls upon the crew to bring the box into the cabin, and put it on the table, the cabin being only a quarter the size of the box. It is the *veracity* of the blunder which is so admirable. Had a man come from such a country as Brobdingnag, he would have blundered so.'

to rights: completely.

Passages: incidents.

135 *make*: get to, arrive at.

discoursing: discussing.

138 *Phaeton*: son of Helios, the sun-god. He insisted on driving the chariot of the sun, lost control of the horses, nearly set fire to the earth, and was struck down by a thunderbolt from Zeus, falling into the river Eridanus. The Captain doubtless mentions

him as a familiar instance of pride going before a fall; hence Gulliver's cool reception of the joke.

138 *Tonquin*: Tongking, a province of Indochina, now forming the largest part of North Vietnam.

driven North Eastward: i.e. he had been blown directly out of his course for some thousands of miles (J. R. Moore, *JEGP* xl (1941), 221). Cf. *True History*, where the ship runs helplessly before a gale for 79 days (Lucian, 251).

Part III. *A Voyage to Laputa*

141 *Laputa*: Firth (p. 254) derives the name from Spanish *la puta* (the whore), referring to a proverb in Swift's Spanish dictionary: 'Beware of a whore, who leaves the purse empty', and seeing an allusion to England's impoverishment of Ireland. Cf. *A Short View ... of Ireland* (1728): 'One third part of the Rents of *Ireland*, is spent in *England*; which with the Profit of Employments, Pensions, Appeals, Journeys of Pleasure or Health, Education at the *Inns* of Court, and both Universities, Remittances at Pleasure, the Pay of all Superior Officers in the Army, and other Incidents, will amount to a full half of the Income of the whole Kingdom, all clear profit to *England*' (*Prose*, xi. 9). Since Laputa also satirizes scientists, academics, and intellectuals generally, it may at the same time be interpreted as 'the country of thinkers' from Latin *puto* (C. C. Seronsy, *NQ* cci (1957), 471).

143 *William Robinson ... Hopewell*: there are records of two ships named *Hopeful* in 1702; and in 1710 there is mention of an *Adventure* (the name of Gulliver's ship in Parts II and IV) captained by William Robinson (Quinlan, 413).

That: he said that.

Thirst ... seeing the World: cf. Raphael, who 'wanted to see the world'; 'travel ... was all he really cared about' (*Utopia*, 38–9). See note to p. 68.

proposed: anticipated.

Fort St George: the original nucleus of Madras, established by the East India Company (1640).

144 *be dispatched*: get his business done.

Pyrates: pirate ships.

strict Alliance: Though bitter commercial rivals, the English and the Dutch were members of the Grand Alliance (1701) against France.

145 *Longitude* 183: in Moll's maps (see p. 292, l. 24) longitude is usually reckoned up to 360° East of London, so this position is approximately 177° West (of Greenwich). Gulliver is somewhere in the Pacific east of Japan, south of the Aleutian Islands (Williams, 477).

Heath: heath plant, e.g. heather.

146 *vast Opake Body*: cf. the approach to the moon in the *True History* (Lucian, 253): 'On the eighth day we sighted what looked like a big island hanging in mid air, white and round and brilliantly illuminated.' The idea of using such an island for political satire may have been suggested by Defoe's *The Consolidator* (1705), in which the author flies to the moon in a chariot with mechanically flapped wings, and discovers lunar provinces representing Deists, High and Low Churchmen, Whigs and Tories, etc. (Eddy, 23–4).

shining very bright: possibly because 17th-century scientists used the word adamant (see p. 157) for diamond as well as for loadstone (*NM2*, 410–11).

Adventure: chance event.

147 *Island . . . as they pleased*: there was great interest during the 17th century in the construction of flying-machines. Thirty such machines were invented by Robert Hooke, secretary of the Royal Society (C. Kerby-Miller, *Memoirs*, 332–4).

polite: polished, refined.

149 *Humours*: eccentricities.

neither . . . Debt: I paid them back in their own coin (i.e. with equal astonishment).

Mortals so singular: the satiric device of putting unworldly intellectuals literally up in the air is as old as Aristophanes (*Clouds*, 218f.) who suspended Socrates in a basket. Ehrenpreis 3 (pp. 895–8) thinks that the Laputians are based on the character of Swift's absent-minded friend Thomas Sheridan, with whom Swift stayed at Quilca, Apr.–Sept. 1725, when completing and rewriting Part III.

Their Heads . . . Zenith: possibly suggested by an emblematic picture of 'Mathematica' in the *Icones Symbolicae* of C. Giarda (1626). She 'wears a tunic patterned with compasses, stars, numbers, and musical notations. She carries geometrical instruments, and ... the lid is closed over one eye, while the other looks directly upwards' (K. Williams, *NQ* ccviii (1963), 216).

149 *Taction*: touching, contact.

Climenole: Kelling (pp. 772–3) interprets as Latin *cieo* (rouse) interspersed with meaningless letters chosen for their 'smoothness' (see p. 147). The Flapper's function may be based on that of the King's Remembrancer (an official employed to collect the King's debts).

150 *so wrapped up*: a variation on the traditional story of Thales (one of the Seven Sages) falling into a well while star-gazing; but there may be a special reference to contemporary anecdotes about Newton's absent-mindedness and impracticality: e.g. that he once boiled his watch while holding an egg in his hand, and that he had two holes cut in his study door, a large one for the cat and a small one for the kitten (Gough, 382).

Kennel: gutter.

Before the Throne . . . Mathematical Instruments: though not much interested in mathematics, George I is reported to have expressed great satisfaction at having Newton as his subject in one country and Leibniz in another.

attended: waited.

151 *Hospitality to Strangers*: probably a reference to George I's appointments of Hanoverians to well-paid posts in England (Case, 85).

Terms of Art: technical terms.

152 *Floating Island*: a phrase applied by Temple to English foreign policy during the reign of Charles II: 'our counsels and conduct were like those of a floating island, driven one way or t'other, according to the winds or tides' (*Works* (1770), ii. 454; Firth, 253).

the true Etymology: a parody of Richard Bentley's philological conjectures. Cf. his lengthy discussion of Boyle's statement 'That the word Tragedy may signifie Comedy', which concludes: 'If I may have leave to talk without proof, as well as some others, I should rather suspect that κωμωδία was the old and common name both for Tragedy and Comedy . . . But when men understood the difference between the two Sorts, and a distinct Prize was appointed to *Thespis*'s, it was natural to give each sort a particular Name taken from the several Prizes; and the one was called τραγωδία from the Goat and the other τρυγῳδία from the Cask of Wine. But I only propose it as a Guess, to set against the Conjecture of the Author of the *Etymologicon*; and perhaps it may be accounted as probable as his' (*Dissertation upon the Epistles of Phalaris* (1699), 303, 308, 309). The paragraph also serves to stress the political satire, since 'a high governor' is said to have been corrupted into 'a whore' (see note to p. 141)

152 *happening to mistake a Figure*: a satire on recent attempts to determine the altitude of the sun, moon, stars, and mountains, both lunar and terrestrial, by quadrants and other instruments (*NM1*, 120), perhaps with special reference to a mistake made by Newton's printer in adding an extra nought to the distance of the earth from the sun.

North-East and by East: a point midway between north-east and east-north-east.

Lagado: Clark (p. 613) decodes as 'Lonnod', an anagram of *London*.

King . . . Musical Instruments: a satire on George I, who had given Handel a pension of £600 p.a., an contributed £1,000 towards the establishment of the Royal Academy of Music (1720), an organization created to produce Handel's operas; on the fashionable enthusiasm for music, of which Gay wrote to Swift (3 Feb. 1723): 'As for the reigning Amusement of the town, tis entirely Musick. real fiddles, Bass Viols and Haut boys not poetical Harps, Lyres and reeds' (*Corr.*, ii. 447; Firth, 255); and on such members of the Royal Society as Dr John Wallis, who had contributed several papers on the analogies between music and mathematics (*NM1*, 120–3).

153 *stunned with the Noise . . . Musick of the Spheres*: a burlesque of Cicero's *Somnium Scipionis* (x–xi), where Scipio, taken up to the Milky Way, hears 'a great sweet sound', and is told that it is a seven-note harmony formed by the revolution of the planets. The ears of ordinary mortals are so deafened by the noise that they cease to hear it. The Laputians, as virtual planet-dwellers, actually contribute to this harmony.

Packthreads were let down: the system seems to be modelled on a passage in the *Icaromenippus* (Lucian, 127–8) where Zeus removes the lids from a row of holes in his palace floor, and after listening to the prayers that come up through one, enjoys the scent of sacrifice (corresponding to the 'Wine and Victuals') that rises through another.

153 *bevil*: not at right angles.

Intellectuals: mental capacities.

154 *Opposition . . . right Opinion*: i.e. they will contradict any view, except a wrong one.

judicial Astrology: astrology in the modern sense of the word (which could then mean practical astronomy). In *Utopia* (p. 90) there is a contemptuous reference to astrology. In 1708 Swift posed as an astrologer, calling himself Isaac Bickerstaff, and predicted the death at a certain hour of a popular astrologer, John Partridge. When the time came, Swift published a circumstantial account of Partridge's death, while his victim protested in vain that he was still alive (*Prose*, ii. 139–70).

Disposition . . . Politicks: cf. Patrick observes that 'the rabble here [London] are much more inquisitive in politicks than in Ireland' (*Journal*, i. 14): 'It is a common topick of Satyr' that there is 'a pragmatical disposition to politicks in the very nature and genius of the [English] People' (*Prose*, v. 79; Firth, 255).

same Disposition . . . Mathematicians: mathematicians tended to be Whigs. Newton was a close friend of the Whig Chancellor of the Exchequer Charles Montagu (originator of the permanent National Debt policy), and backed up Walpole in the Wood affair (see Introduction, p. xii, and note to p. 162). The German mathematician Leibniz actively supported the Grand Alliance (Gough, 384–5).

conceited: opinionated.

that the Earth . . . swallowed up: Newton's analysis of planetary motion (*Principia Mathematica* (1687), bk. I, sect. vii–viii) had shown that there must be a delicate balance between the speed at which the earth is falling towards the sun and the tangential speed at right angles to that fall. If the latter speed were reduced in relation to the former, the earth would move gradually nearer to the sun, and eventually fall into it (*NM1*, 125).

That the Face . . . Effluvia: William Derham had suggested (*PTA* IV. i. 238) that sunspots were caused by the eruption of solar volcanos; from which it seemed to follow that the surface of the sun might become encrusted with lava (*NM1*, 125–7).

the last Comet: Halley's comet of 1682. Edmund Halley had actually predicted its return in 1758 (32, not 31, years after 1726); but he had calculated 'the mean period' as $75\frac{1}{2}$ years from which the layman would expect a return in, 1757 (*NM1*, 127–9).

154 *will probably destroy us*: William Whiston, in his *Sacred Theory of the Earth* (1696), had suggested (pp. 126–56) and in *The Cause of the Deluge Demonstrated* (1716), that the biblical Flood had been caused by a comet. In *A True and Faithful Narrative of What Passed in London* (1732), a satire formerly attributed to Swift, but now to Pope, Whiston is reported as announcing that, owing to a comet, 'on Friday next the World shall be no more', and the comet duly appeared on the Wednesday morning 'at three Minutes after five' (Scott, iv. 276, 278). In 1724 Halley read a paper about Noah's Flood to the Royal Society (*PTA* VI. ii. 1–5), vividly describing the chaos that collision with a comet could have produced (*NM1*, 129–32).

155 *That the Sun . . . annihilated*: Robert Hooke (*Posthumous Works* (1705), 94) had indicated the possibility that the sun was gradually burning itself up (*NM1*, 126–7).

from it: i.e. from the sun.

want the same Endowments: have not the same intellectual capacity as the Laputians.

Husband . . . Implements: conceivably a punning allusion to Juvenal's phrase for an unjealous husband: '*doctus spectare lacunar*' (trained to stare at the ceiling: *Satires*, i. 56), *doctus* being made in this context to carry the additional sense of 'erudite'.

156 *married to the prime Minister*: presumably another jibe at Walpole and Catherine Shorter (see note to p. 53); but C. H. Firth (*RES* ii (1926), 340–1) has detected also a special reference to a lawsuit (1715) in which a certain John Dormer sued his footman Thomas Jones for beating and otherwise ill-using his master's wife, with whom he had committed adultery.

tolerable Proficiency: reasonable progress.

157 *A Phænomenon solved*: i.e. scientifically explained (in the style of a Royal Society paper).

its Diameter: the island appears to be modelled on the *terrella* (little earth) described in William Gilbert's *De Magnete* (1600), a loadstone ground to spherical form and used for experiments designed to investigate the magnetic action of the earth. Among the exhibits of the Royal Society was a *terrella* about $4\frac{1}{2}$ in. in diameter; hence Laputa's diameter of $4\frac{1}{2}$ miles. The figure 7,837 seems to refer to contemporary estimates of the diameter of the earth, Newton, e.g., had estimated the semi-diameter as 3,923 miles (*NM2*, 415–17).

Adamant: see note to p. 146.

in their usual Order: cf. John Strachey (*PTRS* xxx (1719), 973): 'The Hills . . . seem also to observe a regular Course in the Strata of Stone and Earth found in their Bowels' (*NM*2, 408).

as Naturalists agree: modern 'naturalists' would agree that *cirrus* can rise to a height of over 8 miles; but in 1729 J. T. Desaguliers gave 2 miles as the maximum height at which 'Vapour raised by the Heat . . . will settle' (*PTA* VI. ii. 68).

Astronomers Cave: probably suggested by the 'very deep Cave, having an hundred threescore and ten steps of descent' at the Royal Observatory in Paris (*PTRS* vi (1671), 2217; *NM*2, 409).

158 *a Loadstone*: apparently a magnification and adaptation of Gilbert's dipping-needle (a magnetized needle capable of turning in a vertical plane about a horizontal axis, to indicate the direction of the earth's magnetism: *NM*2, 413).

Weaver's Shuttle: Corolini's *Key* (1726) suggests an allusion to 'the *British* Linen and Woollen Manufactures' (p. 15). This may not be wholly irrelevant, since Laputa later satirizes England's oppression of Ireland, which was partly in the interests of the English wool trade (see note to p. 68). There may also be an allusion to Job 7: 6: 'My days are swifter than a weaver's shuttle', hopefully implying that the Whigs will not be in power for ever.

over: across.

turned round: i.e. in a horizontal plane so that a course can be steered towards any point of the compass.

Sides: ends, poles.

in this Magnet . . . Direction: in a normal magnet the lines of force radiate from the poles in all directions.

159 *When the Stone*: R. C. Merton (*JHI* xxvii (1966), 275–7) argues that the equal upward and downward forces acting on the opposite ends of the stone would actually make it rotate until the attracting end pointed downwards and the island fell. But both he and Swift seem to have forgotten p. 165, ll. 35–6, which imply that when the magnet is horizontal, there are no vertical lines of force whatever (in which case it is not clear what keeps the island airborne).

161 *For, although . . . Clearness*: this sentence does not appear in the 1st edn., but was inserted by Ford, with 'an hundred Yards' in place of 'a Hundred', in the copy of the 1st edn. in the Victoria

& Albert Museum (see note to p. xxxii). No contemporary telescope measured 100 yds., but in 1722 James Bradley, Professor of Astronomy at Oxford, had measured the diameter of Venus with a tubeless telescope 212 ft. long. Faulkner's realistic emendation of 'an hundred Yards' to read 'a Hundred [i.e. feet]' may be evidence that Swift himself supervised the production of the 1735 text (H. Williams, *The Text of GT* (1952), 53–5). There is probably a reference to the recently developed refracting telescope, e.g. that made by J. Hadley, only 6 ft. long but magnifying up to 230 times (*PTA* VI. i. 1723, 133–5; Gough, 388; *NMI*, 123 n. 28).

161 *Catalogue . . . Stars*: John Flamsteed's *British Catalogue of Stars* (1725) listed 2,935 stars. He had annoyed Swift's friend Arbuthnot (a member of the Royal Society committee appointed to superintend the publication of the *Catalogue*) by his uncooperative behaviour (C. Kerby-Miller, *Memoirs*, 329).

two . . . Satellites: the satellites of Mars, Phobos and Deimos, whose movements agree very closely with this description, were not discovered until 1877; but Swift's successful prediction was apparently a fluke. He probably chose *two* moons on the theory, advanced by Kepler, that each planet should have twice as many moons as the planet immediately preceding it in order of distance from the sun (the earth had one, Jupiter was known to have four, so Mars, between them, should have two). The periods of revolution of Swift's satellites were perhaps intended to contradict an accepted law that a satellite's period of revolution is far greater than its primary planet's period of rotation. The relation of periods and distances was based on Kepler's Third Law, that the square of the period of revolution varies as the cube of the distance. Otherwise the figures seem to have been chosen at random (S. H. Gould, *JHI* vi (1945), 91–101).

observed Ninety-three . . . Comets: in 1704 Halley calculated the orbits of twenty-four comets.

deprive . . . Benefit . . . Sun: cf. *True History* (Lucian, 258) where the Sun-people make the Moon-people come to terms by building a thick wall of cloud in mid-air and thus cutting off the moon from sunlight. For the political significance, cf. *Drapier's Letters* (*Prose*, x. 141): 'we are so strangely limited in every Branch of Trade that can be of Advantage to us; and utterly deprived of those, which are of the greatest Importance . . . we are denied the *Benefits* which *God* and *Nature* intended to us' (Firth, 253).

162 *Adamantine Bottom*: interpreted by Firth (p. 257) as 'the English interest in Ireland', i.e. the colony of English descent on which the English rule in Ireland was founded; by M. Price (Swift's *Rhetorical Art* (1953), 83) as 'the royal prerogative'; but the general sense seems clear: if the English government is too oppressive, it will fall.

About three Years: this passage allegorizing the anti-Wood campaign (which began 'about three Years' before 1726, with the publication of James Maculla's pamphlet *Ireland's Consternation* in Aug. 1723) was among Ford's MS additions to the 1st edn. in the Victoria & Albert Museum (see note to p. xxxii). Presumably it was included in Swift's original MS, but neither Motte nor Faulkner (if indeed Faulkner received a copy of it from Ford) thought it safe to print it. On 12 July 1722 William Wood was given a patent (he had bribed the Duchess of Kendal £10,000 to procure it) authorizing him to supply £100,800-worth of copper coins for Ireland. The Irish Parliament, which had not been consulted, protested in vain that the importation of the new coins would be disastrous for Ireland's economy, and Swift wrote his anonymous *Drapier's Letters* to mobilize Irish resistance to the scheme. Eventually (Aug. 1725) the patent was withdrawn. For details of the affair see H. Davis's edition of *Drapier's Letters* (1935), pp. ix–lxvii.

Lindalino: Clark (p. 613) decodes: 'double lin', i.e. Dublin. Kelling (p. 776) detects the same pun, pointing out that the *da* between the two *lins* is an Irish word for *two*.

163 *four large Towers*: the four chief agencies of Irish local government: the Privy Council, the Grand Jury, and the two houses of the Irish Parliament (Case, 84).

strong pointed Rock: the Irish Church, centred on St Patrick's Cathedral, of which Swift was dean (Case, 84).

most combustible Fewel: e.g. the resolutions of the Irish Parliament and Swift's inflammatory pamphlets (Firth, 256).

It was eight Months: in Apr. 1724, 8 months after Maculla's pamphlet, the Duke of Grafton, Lord-Lieutenant of Ireland, was recalled to London, where he doubtless reported to the King on the Irish situation.

Immunitys: i.e. from prosecution, presumably a reference to the refusal of the Grand Jury (Nov. 1724) to present a Bill of indictment against John Harding, the printer of the Drapier's 'Fourth Letter'.

163 *Choice of their own Governor*: in his 'Fourth Letter' (*Prose*, x. 62–3) the Drapier had acknowledged the jurisdiction of the English King only because the Irish Parliament had accepted him as King of Ireland: 'For in *Reason*, all *Government* without the Consent of the *Governed* is the *very Definition of Slavery*.'

164 *a fundamental Law*: under the Act of Settlement (1701) the King was forbidden to leave England without special permission from Parliament, but George I had persuaded Parliament to repeal this provision in 1716. His visits to Hanover had caused much resentment (Case, 85).

165 *very desirous . . . heartily weary . . .*: cf. Lucian's reaction to a 20-month stay in another 'floating island', the whale of the *True History*: 'After a while I got rather bored with life inside the whale, and started trying to think of some method of escape' (Lucian, 271). He had just watched a battle between two fleets of floating islands (p. 270).

Countenance: favour, encouragement.

166 *Munodi*: variously identified as Bolingbroke (Scott, viii. 181); as Lord Middleton, who (though a Whig) had, as Lord Chancellor of Ireland, opposed the Wood project (Firth, 257–8); as Oxford (Case, 87–9); and as Temple (R. C. Steensma, *NQ* ccx (1965), 216–17). Kelling (p. 770) interprets the name as an anagram of *dominus*, appropriate enough for a Lord and an ex-Lord Mayor; Case (p. 87) reads it as short for *mundum odi* (I hate the world), an allusion to Oxford's withdrawal from public life (1717).

167 *I never knew a Soil . . . Want*: Firth (p. 254) suggests that Swift is thinking of Dublin (where in 1724 he found 1,500 houses empty and falling into ruin) and of the decline of Irish agriculture, due to the conversion of arable land into pasture. There may be a specific reference to conditions at Quilca, where Swift stayed with his friend Sheridan (Ehrenpreis 3, 897).

Insufficiency: incompetence.

polite: elegant.

168 *about Forty Years ago*: the Royal Society received its 1st charter in 1662, its 2nd in 1663, 45 years before the supposed date of this conversation (or 44 by the 'Old Style' calendar, which counted Feb. 1708 as part of 1707; see note to p. 275).

Volatile . . . Airy: the primary meaning of *volatile* is 'flying'.

169 *PROJECTORS*: a word applied to the inventors of political, social, and financial, as well as scientific, schemes. In its scientific aspect, the Academy is based not only on the Royal Society, but also on such literary models as the House of Solomon in Bacon's *New Atlantis* and the Kingdom of the Quintessence (V. xxi–xxii) in Rabelais (pp. 649–53).

All the Fruits . . . chuse: cf. *New Atlantis*: 'And we make (by art) . . . trees and flowers to come earlier or later than their seasons; and to come up and bear more speedily than by their natural course they do' (Bacon, iii. 158).

ill Commonwealthsmen: people without public spirit.

prevent: anticipate.

a ruined Building: the hydraulic elements in this story may have been suggested by the experiments of Francis Hawksbee and James Jurin, to investigate the ascent of water in capillary tubes and the force of running water at various altitudes (*PTA* IV. i. 423–41; *NM1*, 150–1). There is possibly an allusion to the South Sea Bubble (1720), for which Oxford had been much criticized, since he had given the South Sea Company its charter in 1712. The implied defence is that he had been the unwilling victim of such 'projectors' as Defoe, who had persuaded him to replace the old mill (the traditional English financial system) by the new one (a speculative venture far away, which was supposed to produce the same income with half the capital: Case, 88–9).

170 *not very well with*: not in great favour at. Queen Anne disliked Oxford's personal behaviour.

putting others upon: urging others to make.

171 *largely*: at length, in detail.

Continuation of several Houses: i.e. several separate houses linked together. In 1710 the Royal Society moved into two houses in Crane Court, Fleet St., and by 1724 had acquired several more pieces of property, including two houses in Coleman St. (*NM1*, 137 n. 52).

growing waste: falling empty.

could not be: could not have been.

five Hundred Rooms: possibly a satire on the Royal Society's ambitions for greatly expanded accommodation (*NM1*, 137).

extracting Sun-Beams out of Cucumbers: perhaps suggested by the recent investigations of John Hales into the action of sunlight in promoting the respiration of plants. For the system of bottling, cf. Thomas Shadwell's *The Virtuoso* (1676), where Sir Nicholas Gimcrack employs 'men all over England . . . who bottle up air . . . sealing the bottles hermetically' (IV. iii. 256–8; *NM1*, 146–8).

171 *Practice of begging*: an ironical inversion of the practice in Solomon's House, where the visitor is the one who receives 'a bounty' of 2,000 ducats (*New Atlantis*; Bacon, iii. 166).

a horrible Stink: cf. Rabelais (V. xxii; p. 651): 'an archasdarpenim fermenting a great tub of human urine in horse-dung, with plenty of Christian shit . . . He told us . . . that he watered kings and great princes with this holy distillation, and thereby lengthened their lives by a good six or nine feet.'

172 *Malleability of Fire*: cf. Rabelais (V. xxii; p. 652): 'Others were cutting fire with a knife, and drawing up water in a net.'

a man born blind: doubtless based on Robert Boyle's account of 'a blind man at Maestricht . . . who at certain times could distinguish colours by the touch with his fingers'. Boyle suspected that it was really done by smelling, since different-coloured dyes had different scents (*Philosophical Works*, ed. P. Shaw (1725), ii. 10–12; *NM1*, 140–2). Cf. Scriblerus, *Memoirs*, 167: 'He it was, that first found out the *Palpability* of *Colours*; and by the delicacy of his Touch, could distinguish the different Vibrations of the heterogeneous Rays of Light.'

plowing the Ground with Hogs: cf. Rabelais (V. xxii; p. 651): 'Others were ploughing the sandy shore with three pairs of foxes in a yoke, and losing none of their seed.' A paper on the cultivation of tobacco in Ceylon (1702) describes how buffaloes are shut up in a small patch of ground, to manure the soil with their dung (*PTA* IV. ii. 313; *NM1*, 149).

Maste: beech-nuts, chestnuts, etc., used as food for pigs.

173 *the Artist*: apparently modelled on a Frenchman, M. Bon, who wrote a paper on the 'Silk of Spiders', and presented the Royal Society with some stockings and gloves woven out of spiders' webs. He claimed that his 'silk' was 'no way inferiour in Beauty to common Silk. It easily takes all sorts of Colours' (*PTA* V. i. 20–4). The proposed method of colouring was perhaps suggested by Dr Wall's account (*PTA* V. ii. 275–8) of ants that feed on the sap of certain plants, with the result that their excreta become coloured and can be used as dyes (*NM1*, 143–5).

173   *place a Sun-Dial . . . Weather-Cock*: Sir Christopher Wren had constructed an automatic wind recorder by attaching a clock to a
weathercock (1663), and J. Williamson had written a paper
(1719) about clocks that he had made 'to agree with the Sun's
apparent Motion' (*PTA* IV. i. 394–6; *NM1*, 139–40). Swift's
contribution is to replace Wren's clock by a sundial, and instead
of adjusting the timepiece, like Williamson, to adjust the actual
movements of the Earth and Sun.

Town-House: town hall.

large Pair of Bellows: cf. Rabelais, V. xxii; p. 651: 'I saw one young
calcinator artificially extracting farts from a dead donkey, and
selling them at fivepence a yard.' Sprat's *History of the Royal
Society* (1667) (p. 232), records a famous experiment by Robert
Hooke (1667) in which artificial respiration was induced in a
dog by blowing into its windpipe with a pair of bellows.
Shadwell's *The Virtuoso* (II. ii. 102–7) satirizes the experiment,
and adds the idea of 'blowing wind in the breech', which was
also used by Swift in *A Tale of a Tub (Prose*, i. 96) when mocking
the windy oratory of Nonconformist preachers.

175   *the universal Artist*: possibly Robert Boyle, who was a specialist
on the nature of the air, on petrifaction, on marble, on agriculture, and on the breeding of sheep (*NM1*, 151).

sow Land with Chaff: cf. the traditional images for wasted labour
in Rabelais (V. xxii; p. 651): 'Others were ploughing the sandy
shore . . . Others were shearing asses . . . Others were gathering
grapes from thornbushes, and figs from thistles. Others were
milking he-goats.'

true seminal Virtue: cf. S. Moreland, *PTA* IV. ii. 305: 'Dr
[Nehemiah] Grew . . . has observ'd that the *Farina* . . . doth
some way perform the office of Male Sperm . . . this *Farina* is *a
Congeries* of Seminal Plants, one of which must be convey'd into
every *Ovum*, before it can become prolifick' (*NM1*, 149–50).

propagate the Breed of naked Sheep . . . : the animal-breeding pro-
gramme at Solomon's House includes some equally futile
projects: 'we make them greater or taller than their kind is; and
contrariwise dwarf them, and stay their growth; we make them
more fruitful and bearing than their kind is; and contrariwise
barren and not generative. Also we make them differ in colour,
shape, activity, many ways' (*New Atlantis*, Bacon, iii. 159).

a Frame: this thinking-machine may be intended to illustrate an
argument which goes back to Cicero, and which Swift thought

sufficiently commonplace to include in his *Tritical Essay* (*c.*1707): 'how can the *Epicureans* Opinion be true, that the Universe was formed by a fortuitous Concourse of Atoms; which I will no more believe, than that the accidental Jumbling of the Letters in the Alphabet, could fall by Chance into a most ingenious and learned Treatise of Philosophy' (*Prose* i. 246–7; Ehrenpreis 1, 98–100).

176 *the most ignorant Person*: for the satire on short cuts to learning and authorship, cf. *A Tale of a Tub*: 'we of this Age have discovered a shorter, and more prudent Method, to become *Scholars* and *Wits*, without the Fatigue of *Reading* or of *Thinking*. The most accomplisht Way of using Books at present, is . . . to get a thorough Insight into the *Index*' (*Prose*, i. 91).

broken Sentences . . . Sciences: cf. the mass production of oracles by the pseudo-prophet Alexander (Lucian, 243): 'Most of these answers were . . . extremely muddled and obscure . . . he . . . just scribbled down the first thing that came into his head . . . There was also an interpretation department, which charged a high fee for trying to make sense of these responses.'

177 *Custom . . . to steal Inventions . . .*: doubtless a reference to the controversy between Newton and Leibniz as to which of them had discovered the differential and integral calculus. It began (1699) with a suggestion by Fatio de Duillier that Leibniz had plagiarized Newton, which was virtually the conclusion of the Royal Society committee appointed to investigate the question (1712). It now appears that Newton had priority, but that Leibniz made his discovery independently.

School of Languages: in his *History of the Royal Society*, Sprat (pp. 40–2) had recommended the establishment of an English academy, which 'would take the whole Mass of our Language into their hands', and 'make a great Reformation in the manner of our Speaking, and Writing'.

shorten Discourse: cf. *Polite Conversation* (1738): 'The only Invention of late Years, which hath any Way contributed to advance Politeness in Discourse, is that of abbreviating or reducing Words of many Syllables into one, by lopping off the rest' (*Prose*, iv. 106). George Orwell's 'Newspeak' employs the same principle (*1984* (1949), 306–9).

Nouns: i.e. names (see note after next).

Diminution of our Lungs: cf. the argument of Lucretius (*DRN* iv. 526–41) that sound must be composed of physical particles, since much speaking 'scrapes the throat' and is physically exhausting.

Words are only Names for Things: cf. Bacon, i. 451–2: '*quid . . . aliud sunt verba quam imagines rerum*' (what are words but images of things?); Hobbes, *Leviathan* (1651), ed. Waller (1935), 13: 'But the most noble and profitable invention of all other, was that of SPEECH, consisting of *Names or Appellations*, and their Connexion'; and Sprat, *History of the Royal Society*, 113, where he speaks of the Society's 'constant Resolution . . . to return back to the primitive purity, and shortness, when men deliver'd so many *things* almost in an equal number of *words*'. A. C. Howell (*ELH* xiii (1946), 131–42) traces the idea back to Cicero and Quintilian.

the Subject: the subjects of the realm, the whole population.

only this Inconvenience: cf. the 'inconvenience' of Wood's copper currency: 'If a *Squire* has a mind to come to Town to buy Cloaths and Wine and Spices for himself and Family . . . ; he must bring with him five or six Horses loaden with *Sacks* as the *Farmers* bring their Corn' (*Drapier's Letters*; *Prose*, x. 6).

178 *an universal Language*: an allusion to such works as George Dalgarno's *Ars Signorum, vulgo Character Universalis, et Lingua Philosophica* (1661) and Bishop John Wilkins's *Essay Towards a Real Character and a Philosophical Language* (1668). Each constructed a logical language by assigning symbols or letters to categories of things and ideas, and illustrated it with a translation of the Lord's Prayer. It began: 'Pagel lalla lul tim bred Nammi' (Dalgarno) and 'Ηαι coba . . . a ril dad' (Wilkins).

was at: visited.

Cephalick Tincture: medicine for the head.

Quantum: quantity (a reference to the formula used in prescriptions: *quantum sufficit* = a sufficient quantity).

179 *Professors . . . out of their Senses*: cf. *A Tale of a Tub*, where Swift recommends the appointment of 'Commissioners to inspect into *Bedlam* . . . to examine into the Merits and Qualifications of every Student and Professor' (*Prose*, i. 111).

Resemblance . . . Body: the parallel is developed at length in Shakespeare's *Coriolanus* (I. i. 95–154).

180 *redundant . . . Humours*: according to an old theory of medicine,

health depended on maintaining the correct balance between four humours or fluids in the body: blood, phlegm, choler, and black bile. *ebullient*: causing heat or agitation.

180 *peccant*: morbid.

the Right: i.e. the hand that takes bribes and grasps at profit.

Flatus: wind; i.e. inflated oratory.

Ructations: belches. Cf. *A Tale of a Tub*, where inspired preachers are satirized as Aeolists, who 'affirm the Gift of BELCHING, to be the noblest Act of a Rational Creature' (*Prose*, i. 96).

Canine Appetites: 'morbid hunger, chiefly occurring in idiots and maniacs' (*OED*).

Crudeness of Digestion: indigestion.

Lenitives . . . required: *Lenitives*: soothing drugs. *Aperitives*: aperients. *Abstersives*: purgatives. *Corrosives*: caustics. *Restringents*: drugs to restrain the action of the bowels. *Cephalalgicks*: remedies for headache. *Ictericks*: remedies for jaundice. *Apophlegmaticks*: phlegm-removers (to make politicians less dull and sluggish). *Acousticks*: cures for deafness.

181 *When Parties . . . are violent*: see note to p. 95.

182 *take a strict View . . . Excrements . . .*: the whole passage seems to refer to the use at the trial of Bishop Atterbury (1722) of correspondence found in his close-stool (*Case*, 91).

Conjunctions: circumstances.

Trial: experiment.

183 *Tribnia*: an anagram of *Britain*.

Langden: an anagram of *England*.

Evidences: witnesses.

Instruments: tools.

The Plots in that Kingdom: the Tories took the line that Jacobite plots were largely invented by the Whigs.

Forfeitures: the estates of the leaders of the 1715 rebellion were confiscated by the government.

Opinion of publick Credit: i.e. the price of government bonds.

a lame Dog, an invader: references in Atterbury's correspondence to a small spotted dog called Harlequin, which he received as a present from France, and which had its leg broken on the journey, were used at his trial as evidence against him. cf.

Swift's poem (1722) 'Upon the horrid Plot discovered by Harlequin the B—— of R——'s French Dog' (ll. 47–56; *Poems*, i.
300):

> His name is *Harlequin*, I wot,
> And that's a Name in ev'ry *Plot*:
> Resolv'd to save the *British* Nation,
> Though *French* by Birth and Education:
> His Correspondence plainly dated,
> Was all *decypher'd* and *translated*.
> His Answers were exceeding pretty
> Before the secret wise Committee;
> Confess't as plain as he could bark;
> Then with his Fore-foot set his *Mark*.

Harlequin helped to identify Atterbury with the 'T. Illington'
who figured in correspondence with the Earl of Mar, since a
paper found at the house of a Mrs Barnes, with whom the Earl's
messenger lodged, mentioned a lame dog called Harlequin as
having been dispatched from France to Illington, and Mrs
Barnes innocently admitted, when questioned, that she had
looked after such a dog for the Bishop of Rochester (H.
Williams, *Poems*, i. 300 n. 47).

183 *the Plague*: before these words, Ford's MS corrections give 'a
Codshead a ——'. Since the blank should probably be filled
with *king*, and the first word means 'blockhead', neither Motte
nor Faulkner would have considered it safe to print.

Buzard: a useless kind of hawk, hence a stupid or ignorant
fellow.

Gout, a High Priest: possibly a reference to William King, Archbishop of Dublin, who had suffered from gout for 30 years
(Gough, 397). In a letter to King (18 May 1727) Swift wrote:
'from the very moment of the Queen's death, your Grace hath
thought fit to take every opportunity of giving me all sorts of
uneasiness, without ever giving me, in my whole life, one single
mark of your favour, beyond common civilities. And, if it were
not below a man of spirit to make complaints, I could date them
from six and twenty years past' (*Corr.*, iii. 210).

Sieve: i.e. someone who cannot keep a secret.

Employment: a position in the public service. Gough (p. 398)
suggests that Swift is expressing his sense of being trapped and
thwarted by his ecclesiastical appointment. He may rather be

recalling *Hamlet* (III. ii. 249–53), where 'The Mouse-trap' is described as 'a knavish piece of work', and so commenting on other holders of government posts.

183 *Sink a C——t*: cesspool, a court.

184 *Our Brother . . . Piles*: Faulkner's edn. (1735) reads 'hath'. This spoils the anagram, which is perfect if one reads 'has' (as in Motte's 1st edn., 1726) and counts 'j' as a form of 'i' (Case, 44–5).

The Tour: the signature of the message. During part of his exile in France, Bolingbroke asked his friends to address him as 'M. La Tour' (Case, 91).

185 *Maldonada*: Clark (p. 615) decodes the first six letters as 'Noldon', an anagram of *London*.

Glubbdubdrib: Clark (p. 615) decodes as 'Dub-bul-lin', i.e. Dublin.

Luggnagg: Clark (p. 615) decodes the first six letters (by reading them backwards) as 'Anggul', i.e. Angle (for Angleland, England).

North-West: the map on p. 142 shows Luggnagg as south-west of Balnibarbi.

Maldonada: the map on p. 160 shows 'Malonada' at the southeast corner of Balnibarbi, which is probably where it belongs; but the map on p. 142 has dumped 'Maldoneda' in the sea south-west of Luggnagg.

to the South-West: presumably of Maldonada (though the map on p. 142 shows 'Glubdrubdrib' south-west of Luggnagg).

186 *antick*: grotesque, bizarre.

187 *call up whatever Persons . . .*: these interviews with famous dead people seem to have been suggested by Lucian's *True History*, in which Lucian meets such celebrities as Socrates, Plato, and Homer in the Elysian fields. cf. also 'Menippus goes to Hell', in which the Persian magician Mithrobarzanes arranges for Menippus to visit the underworld, where he sees Xerxes, Darius, and Philip of Macedon (Lucian, 278–81, 103–8).

Battle of Arbela: the Battle of Gaugamela, at which Alexander finally defeated Darius (331 BC).

188 *not poisoned, but . . . Drinking*: in his *Life of Alexander* (lxxvii) Plutarch mentions the story that Alexander was poisoned, on the advice of Aristotle, but says that it is generally thought to be

entirely fictitious. His own account is that Alexander died of a fever after drinking all one night and the following day; but he quotes Aristobulus to the effect that the excessive drinking was itself caused by a fever, which had made Alexander desperately thirsty (lxxv).

188 *not a Drop of Vinegar* . . . : an allusion to Livy's story (XXI. xxxvii. 2–3) that when Hannibal was crossing the Alps, he softened obstructing rocks by lighting bonfires on them and then pouring on vinegar.

just ready to engage: i.e. just before the Battle of Pharsalia (48 BC), at which Pompey was defeated.

last great Triumph: after his victory at Munda (45 BC) over the sons of Pompey.

in counterview: as a contrasting picture.

Brutus: Marcus Junius Brutus, one of the conspirators who assassinated Julius Caesar (44 BC). Swift's view of Brutus, like Shakespeare's, was somewhat idealized: he was, e.g., quite ruthless in the pursuit of financial profit.

in good Intelligence: on good terms.

Junius: Lucius Junius Brutus, who, after the rape of Lucretia, led the rising against the Tarquins, and expelled them from Rome.

Socrates: the Athenian philosopher (469–399 BC).

Epaminondas: a Theban general and statesman (c.420–362 BC).

Cato the Younger: Marcius Porcius Cato (95–46 BC), Stoic moralist and chief defender of the Roman Republic against Julius Caesar.

Sir Thomas More: the author of *Utopia* (1516), but here included as a martyr for his convictions, executed for refusing to acknowledge Henry VIII as head of the English Church.

Sextumvirate: group of six men. Four of them (Socrates, Epaminondas, Cato, More) are included in Swift's list of 'those who have made great FIGURES in some particular Action or Circumstance of their Lives' (*Prose*, v. 83–4).

189 *I proposed that Homer*: cf. *True History*, where Lucian questions Homer about his poems, and hears his opinion of his editors and critics (Lucian, 280–1).

his Eyes . . . piercing: Homer was traditionally blind. cf. *True History*: 'There was no need to ask if he was really blind, for I could see for myself that he was nothing of the sort' (Lucian, 281).

189 *a Ghost*: possibly Sir William Temple, whose views on classical scholarship Swift had defended against the 'commentator', Bentley, in *The Battle of the Books* of 1704 (Case, 92).

Didymus: an Alexandrian scholar (*c*.65 BC–AD 10), nicknamed 'brazen-guts' because of his enormous industry, who wrote a commentary on Homer.

Eustathius: Archbishop of Thessalonica (died *c*.1194) and author of a *Commentary on the Iliad and Odyssey*.

they wanted a Genius . . . Poet: cf. Homer's remark in Lucian (p. 281): 'The trouble about these wretched editors is that they've got no taste.'

Scotus: Duns Scotus (*c*.1265–*c*.1308), scholastic philosopher, author of a commentary on Aristotle (and the origin of the word *dunce*).

Ramus: Pierre la Ramée (1515–72), Professor of Philosophy at the Collège de France and a famous opponent of the Aristotelian system.

Descartes: René Descartes (1596–1650), French philosopher and mathematician, here mentioned for his theory that the heavenly bodies were carried round in 'vortices' or whirlpools of material particles. cf. *Battle of the Books* (*Prose*, i. 156), where he is hit by an arrow fired by Aristotle, which 'went in at his Right Eye. The Torture of the Pain, whirled the valiant *Bow-man* round, till Death, like a Star of superior Influence, drew him into his own *Vortex*.'

190 *Gassendi*: Pierre Gassendi (1592–1655), French mathematician, astronomer, and philosopher. He opposed the systems of Aristotle and Descartes, and tried to revive the atomic physics of Epicurus, while rejecting his anti-religious philosophy.

Attraction: Newton's theory of gravitation, which superseded the vortex theory of Descartes.

even those . . . Mathematical Principles: i.e. Newton, who expounded his theory in a book called *Philosophiae Naturalis Principia Mathematica* (1687).

determined: ended.

Eliogabalus: Varius Avitus Bassianus, Roman Emperor (218–22) under the name of Marcus Aurelius Antoninus. He was notorious for extravagant luxury. According to Gibbon (*Decline and Fall of the Roman Empire*, ed. J. B. Bury (1909), i. 159

n. 68), 'The invention of a new sauce was liberally rewarded: but if it was not relished, the inventor was confined to eat of nothing else, till he had discovered another more agreeable to the Imperial Palate.'

190 *Helot*: a member of the slave race at Sparta.

Agesilaus: King of Sparta (*c.*398–61 BC).

Spartan Broth: a black broth served at the communal meals in Sparta. A king of Pontus once hired a Spartan cook to make him some, and found it quite revolting (*Lycurgus*, xii). Martinus Scriblerus is almost killed by a dose of it as a baby (*Memoirs*, 106).

instead of a long Train . . . Cardinals: cf. Rabelais, I. i; p. 41: 'I think there are many today among the Emperors, Kings, Dukes, Princes, and Popes of this world whose ancestors were mere pedlars of pardons and firewood; as, on the contrary, there are many almshouse beggars . . . who are descended from the blood and lineage of great Kings and Emperors' (Williams, 482).

Polydore Virgil: an Italian who became Archdeacon of Wells (1508–54). The quotation has not been found in his works (which include a 26-vol. history of England), and may be Swift's own invention, based on the epitaph of Margaret Cavendish, Duchess of Newcastle: 'All the brothers were valiant, and all the sisters virtuous' (Case, 92).

Nec . . . Casta: not a man (was) brave, nor a woman chaste.

191 *Pox*: syphilis.

prostitute Writers: cf. Lucian's *How to Write History* (vii), where historians are criticized for not realizing the vital distinction between history and panegyric.

practising . . . upon: taking advantage of.

contemptible Accidents . . .: cf. *A Tale of a Tub* (*Prose*, i. 103–4), where the campaigns of Henry IV of France are attributed to an unsuccessful love-affair, and those of Louis XIV to an anal fistula.

secret History: cf. Swift's 'Short Remarks' on Bishop Gilbert Burnet's *History of My Own Times* (1724–34): 'The author is in most particulars the worst qualified for an historian that I ever met with . . . His Secret History is generally made up of coffee-house scandals, or at best from reports at the third, fourth, or fifth hand. The account of the Pretender's birth, would only become an old woman in a chimney-corner' (*Prose*, v. 183).

191 *ill Conduct*: bad leadership or strategy.

an Admiral: probably Admiral Edward Russell, Earl of Orford (1653–1727), who, while negotiating with the exiled James II, tried to avoid a naval action with the French, but defeated them at La Hogue (1692) because their commander voluntarily engaged the allied fleet, not realizing its numerical superiority (82 to 45).

192 *Three Kings*: identified by Sir Walter Scott (*Works of Swift*, xii. 258) as Charles II, James II, and William III.

grating upon: being derogatory to.

Infirmities: weaknesses.

193 *one Person whose Case*...: possibly an allegory of the Whigs' ingratitude towards Swift's friend Charles Mordaunt, 3rd Earl of Peterborough. After some brilliant successes in the Peninsular campaign of 1706, he was recalled to England, and replaced in his command by the young and inexperienced Emperor Charles. On the voyage home (1707) he was attacked by the enemy, and his son, who was commanding a convoying ship, received severe wounds which may have contributed to his death some time later (*Case*, 92–3).

Actium: the naval battle (31 BC) at which Antony and Cleopatra were defeated by Octavian (later Augustus).

sole Cause of Antony's Flight: according to Plutarch (*Life of Antonius*, lxvi) the real cause was that Cleopatra suddenly sailed away with her sixty ships, and Antony followed her.

Libertina: a freedwoman, i.e. a member of the class to which prostitutes normally belonged (cf. Horace, *Satires*, I. ii. 47–8).

Publicola: L. Gellius Publicola, who with Antony led the right wing of Antony's fleet at Actium (Plutarch, *Life of Antonius*, lxv–lxvi). The satirical point is that a protégé of a defeated enemy commander is more generously treated by Augustus than the man to whom Augustus owes his victory.

Agrippa: Marcus Vipsanius Agrippa (c.62–12 BC), who in 37 BC superintended the training of Octavian's fleet, and was primarily responsible for its success at Actium.

whole Praise... *chief Commander*: doubtless aimed at Marlborough (see note to p. 119).

194 *How the Pox* ... *rancid*: cf. 'the Representation, which on

occasion of one distemper which was become almost epidemical [Martinus Scriblerus] thought himself oblig'd to lay before both Houses of Parliament, intitled *A Proposal for a General Flux* [i.e. for medical treatment of the whole population with mercury] to exterminate at one blow the P——x out of this Kingdom' (*Memoirs*, 130).

194 *managing*: influencing by bribery, flattery, etc.

195 *Dutch ... that Kingdom*: after suppressing the Christian revolt of Shimabara in 1638, the Japanese government closed the country to all Europeans except the Dutch, who had earned this privilege by bringing up twenty big guns and bombarding Christian rebels for 15 days in the castle of Hara.

196 *Convenience*: convenient method.

Traldragdubb or Trildrogdrib: Kelling (p. 773) interprets as 'slaves of the evil dirt (or snare)' from Irish *traill* (slave, *droc* (evil), and *drib* (dirt or snare).

lick the Dust: the image is Hebraic (cf. Isa. 49: 23: 'they shall bow down to thee with their face toward the earth, and lick up the dust of thy feet'); but the translation into literal fact may have been suggested by the description of the audience chamber of the Berklam of Siam in E. Kaempfer's *History of Japan*, i. 17: 'It is white within and full of Dust and Cobwebs.' Cf. also Kaempfer (ii. 531), where an audience given by the Emperor of Japan involves crawling on hands and knees. See note to p. 207.

197 *maliciously*: mischievously.

198 *Fluft ... Friend*: cf. Kaempfer's reference (i. 343) to the Japanese *Tsjuunsj or Tsjuunsi Sju*: 'a *through mouth* or a *through mouth people*, whereby must be understood persons through whose mouth things must be dispatch'd'.

I stayed three Months in this Country: a statement that cannot be reconciled with pp. 195 and 207 (Case, 66).

199 *Struldbrugs*: Clark (p. 616) decodes as 'Stir dull blood'. R. P. Fitzgerald (*SP* lxv (1968), 657–76) suggests a satirical reference to the members of the French Academy, who were called 'the Immortals'. For the general theme of the chapter, cf. the myth of Tithonus (who suffered from immortality without perpetual youth); Juvenal, *Satires*, x, 188–288 (where the folly of praying for a long life is proved by an account of the miseries of old age); Swift's *Thoughts on Various Subjects* (*Prose*, iv. 246): 'Every Man desires to live long: but no Man would be old'; and

Thoughts on Religion (*Prose*, ix. 263): 'It is impossible that any thing so natural, so necessary, and so universal as death, should ever have been designed by providence as an evil to mankind.' There was great contemporary interest in longevity, exemplified by Dr Cotton Mather's account of 'Long-Liv'd *Persons*' in New England (*PTA* V. ii. 165; *NM1*, 116) and by Harcouet de Longeville's *Histoire des personnes qui ont vécu plusieurs siècles* (1716), translated into English as *Long Livers* by 'Philalethes' (Robert Samber) in 1722. Throughout this book long life was assumed to be a blessing (J. L. Barroll, *PMLA* lxxiii (1958), 43–50; S. Klima, *PQ* xlii (1963), 566–9).

200 *Happy . . . Happy . . . happiest*: an ironical echo of Virgil, *Aeneid*, i. 94–6: 'O thrice and four times happy were those whose fate it was to die before their parents' eyes beneath the high walls of Troy!'

201 *the Publick*: the state.

never marry after Threescore: cf. *Resolutions when I Come to be Old* (*Prose*, i, p. xxxvii): 'Not to marry a young Woman.'

202 *Memorials*: memoirs, records.

lower and upper World: earth and sky.

antient Cities . . . Famous Rivers . . .: for the theme of the mortality of famous towns and rivers, cf. *Charon* (Lucian, 95–6).

Discovery of the Longitude: i.e. of a method of determining the longitude at sea. In 1714 Parliament had offered a £20,000 reward for the invention of a satisfactory method, and William Whiston and Humphrey Ditton had proposed a plan which involved anchoring ships with huge cannons and rockets at each degree of the meridian. Martinus Scriblerus had a better idea: 'to build *Two Poles* to the *Meridian*, with immense Lighthouses on the top of them; to supply the defect of Nature, and to make the Longitude as easy to be calculated as the Latitude' (*Memoirs*, 168, 334–5, 343).

perpetual Motion: a favourite subject of scientific research in the 17th century, which was seriously discussed as late as 1721 by Desaguliers (*PTRS* xxxi, 234–9; C. Kerby-Miller, *Memoirs*, 332).

the universal Medicine: the *panacea* or *catholicon*, a supposed cure for all diseases, which would prolong life indefinitely. *Long Livers* (see 1st note to this chapter) ends with detailed instructions on 'How to prepare the Universal Medicine'; 'The Dose is 5 or 6 Drops in Wine or Broth, according to the Indisposition'

(p. 191; S. Klima, *PQ* xlii (1963), 567; L. D. Peterson, *ELN* i (1964) 265–7).

203 *Imbecility*: weakness.

hard to believe: slow to believe, hard to convince.

unjust: inappropriate.

204 *of Course*: as a matter of course.

Courtesy of Kingdom: a customary legal right (comparable to 'Courtesy of England', which entitled a widower to hold certain types of property inherited by his wife).

205 *Meers*: boundaries or landmarks.

At Ninety: the list of disabilities corresponds with that in Juvenal, *Satires*, x: loss of teeth, hair, taste, and appetite (ll. 199–204); miscellaneous diseases (ll. 218–19); loss of memory (ll. 232–6).

upon the Flux: in a state of flux.

ominous: i.e. a bad omen.

206 *Consequent*: consequence.

207 *I do not remember . . . Travels*: cases of unusual longevity were actually quite common in travellers' tales, from those incorporated in Pliny's *Natural History* (1st century AD) onwards; hence the parody in the *True History*: 'When Moon-people grow old, they do not die. They just vanish into thin air, like smoke' (Lucian, 260). Swift's remark is equally ironic, although the unpleasantness of his account of longevity was certainly without precedent, except perhaps in Juvenal.

I hope the Dutch: possibly an allusion to the *History of Japan*, written in German by Englebrecht Kaempfer (1651–1716), physician to the Dutch Embassy at the Emperor's court in Japan. The MS may have been available in England from 1716 onwards, and J. G. Scheuchzer's English translation, though not published until 1727, may have been completed as early as 1722. Swift could have heard of it through his friend Carteret, who was among the subscribers to the 1727 edn. In an interview with the Emperor, Kaempfer is asked whether 'European Physicians did not search after some Medicine to render people immortal, as the Chinese Physicians had done for many hundred years?' (Kaempfer, ii. 534; J. L. Barroll, *PQ* xxxvi (1957), 504–8).

red Diamond: like green, blue, and black diamonds, a rarity.

208 *Yedo*: renamed Tokyo in 1868.

    A King lifting up a lame Beggar . . . : R. P. Fitzgerald, who identifies Luggnagg as France, sees a reference to the fact that Louis XIV put his illegitimate (and lame) son, the Duc de Maine, in the line of succession (*SP* lxv (1968), 660).

    Low-Dutch: Dutch (as opposed to High-Dutch = German).

    Nangasac: Nagasaki, near which the Dutch traders were virtually imprisoned on the tiny island of Deshima.

    trampling upon the Crucifix: a test used on Japanese suspected of being Christians, but not apparently applied to the Dutch. From a cliff called Takaboko near the entrance to Nagasaki harbour thousands of Christians were said to have been thrown during the 17th century for refusing to trample on the crucifix.

    I was the first . . . CHRISTIAN: Kaempfer (i. 325) describes how the Dutch, for commercial reasons, had accepted the Japanese prohibition of all outward signs of Christianity, and mentions the story (i. 357) that when asked by the Japanese if they were Christians, they replied 'No, not Christians, but Dutchmen' (J. A. Dussinger, *NQ* ccxi (1966), 210–11).

209 *Amboyna*: a name chosen to arouse further anti-Dutch feeling. Amboyna was a spice-island in the East Indies, controlled by the Dutch. Under three treaties the English had been given trading rights there; but in 1623 ten Englishmen were tortured by the Dutch into contradictory confessions of plotting to overthrow the Dutch garrison, paraded through the streets, and executed (W. J. Brown, *ELN* i (1964), 262–4).

    Theodorus Vangrult: in the context the choice of Christian name ('Gift of God') must be ironical; the surname seems to have no significance in Dutch, but may conceivably be derived from the Greek *grulos* or *grullos* (pig).

    Skipper: seaman.

Part IV. *A Voyage to the Country of the Houyhnhnms*

211 *HOUYHNHNMS*: probably to be pronounced 'Whinnims', suggesting the word *whinny* and the sound of whinnying. Kelling (p. 769), by reading *Houyhnhnm* backwards, omitting two *h*'s, and counting the third as a guttural *c*, produces *mnny* (*manni*) voc = 'horses voice', i.e. 'speaking horses', from Latin *mannus* (horse), *vox* (voice). Buckley (pp. 272–4) decodes the name as 'Who inhuman', implying that the Houyhnhnms are

subhuman, not superhuman.

The idea of an intellectually superior horse goes back to Chiron, the Centaur in Greek mythology, who was wise, just, an expert in medicine and music, and the educator of Jason and Achilles. The argument that animals behave more sensibly and morally than human beings was first developed by Plutarch (*Moralia*, 985d–992) in a dialogue between Gryllus and Odysseus, entitled 'About the use of reason by irrational animals' (Gryllus has been turned into a pig by Circe, and has no wish to become a man again).

The traditional view (recently defended by G. Sherburn, *MP* lvi (1958), 92–7, and C. Peake, *MLR* lv (1960), 177–80) is that the Houyhnhnms are meant to be wholly admirable; but a modern interpretation takes them as objects of satire, on various grounds: e.g. that they partially represent Deists and Stoics, of whom Swift disapproved (Ehrenpreis 3, 889–92; K. Williams, *Jonathan Swift and the Age of Compromise* (1968), 180–92), that they lack some characteristic human virtues (Buckley, 270–2), and that they are inherently ridiculous (E. Stone, *MLQ* x (1949), 367–76). The most satisfactory conclusion seems to be that the Houyhnhnms represent a largely false ideal, and that Gulliver, in coming under the spell of these horses, becomes a figure of fun. Cf. the last episode of the *True History* (Lucian, 293–4), where the travellers are nearly killed and eaten by some seductive young witches, who turn out to have donkey's hooves beneath their skirts. For the whole question of the interpretation of Part IV, see *A Casebook on Gulliver among the Houyhnhnms*, ed. M. P. Foster (1961).

213 *Yahoos*: Clark (pp. 621–2) suggests that this name is also derived from *whinny*, by transposing the syllables (*y-whinn*), dropping the *nn* (*y-whi*), rewriting the *whi* as *houy*, and dropping the *y* (y-hou). Buckley (p. 270) translates *Yahoo* as 'Ye who (behave thus)', an indictment of the readers. J. R. Moore (*NQ* cxcv (1950), 182–5) connects the name with some degraded Semitic tribes in Africa named in travel-books *Yahoodees* or *Yahoos*, F. Kermode (*NQ* cxcv (1950), 317–18) with the *Yaios* of Guiana. The simplest derivation of the name is from two exclamations of disgust: 'yah!' and 'ugh!' (Morley, *GT* (1890), 15, 20).

The Yahoos may be intended to pose a question of definition (see Introduction, p. xxv). Manuals of logic defined man as *animal rationale* (a rational animal), and often illustrated the term *animal irrationale* (irrational animal) by *equus* (horse); but if men behave like Yahoos and horses like Houyhnhnms, the nature of man must be defined differently (R. S. Crane, *Reason and the Imagination*, ed. J. A. Mazzeo (1962), 243–53). The Yahoos also seem to represent, in traditional Christian imagery, the sin and corruption of fallen man; they thus refute optimistic philosophies like those of Shaftesbury (1671–1713), which stressed the natural goodness of man, and reassert the doctrine of Original Sin (E. Tuveson, *UTQ* xxii (1953), 368–75). Finally, Swift's picture of the Yahoos may refer obliquely to the condition of the 'savage old Irish', who lived, he said, 'in the utmost Ignorance, Barbarity, and Poverty; giving themselves wholly up to Idleness, Nastyness, and Thievery' (*Corr.*, v. 58; *Prose*, x. 139; Firth, 250).

213 *Adventure*: a name possibly chosen to associate Gulliver with Captain William Kidd, the pirate, who also sailed on two different ships called the *Adventure* (see p. 71), and who stated at his trial (1701) that his men had mutinied and deserted him to join a group of pirates (cf. p. 214; Quinlan, 414–16). By relating Gulliver to Kidd, who was originally appointed to bring pirates to justice, and then turned pirate himself, Swift may be hinting at a deterioration in Gulliver's moral character.

Purefoy: i.e. 'Pure faith'. Cf. 'Sermon upon the Martyrdom of K. Charles I' (1726): 'These people called themselves *Puritans* as pretending to a purer faith than those of the church established' (*Prose*, ix. 221). This new association of Gulliver with 'Those wicked Puritans' (ibid. 225) seems to give another hint that Gulliver's self-righteousness is going to destroy his humanity.

Captain Pocock: probably modelled on Dampier, who spent three years with the logwood-cutters around the Bay of Campeche, and whose dogmatism had involved him in a violent feud with his lieutenant, which led to a court martial (Bonner, 8, 165).

Logwood: the central wood of an American tree (*Haematoxylon Campechianum*), used for making a dye.

a little too positive in his own Opinions: this strikes the keynote of Gulliver's development in Part IV: his obsessive positiveness in maintaining the Houyhnhnm system of values converts him into a psychopathic misanthrope.

Calentures: fevers contracted by sailors in the tropics.

These Rogues: conceivably an allegory of the political events of 1714–15, when the Whigs ousted the Tories from control of the ship of state, and imprisoned their 'captain' Oxford in the Tower (A. Schlösser, *ZAA* xv (1967), 375).

214 *Piece*: firearm.

Madagascar: a well-known meeting-place for pirates. There Captain Kidd (see 3rd note to this chapter) joined another famous pirate called Robert Culliford (in some accounts spelled *Cullever*: Guinlan, 416).

215 *Toys*: trinkets.

Animals in a Field: the description of the Yahoos seems to have been partly suggested by accounts in travel-books of savage tribes, especially Hottentots, and of monkeys (Frantz). Cf. Dampier on Australian aborigines (*Voyages*, i. 453): 'The Inhabitants of this Country are the miserablest People in the world. The Hodmadods [Hottentots] of Monomatapa, though a nasty People, yet for Wealth are Gentlemen to these; who have no Houses, and skin Garments . . . as the Hodmadods have; And setting aside their Humane Shape, they differ but little from Brutes.'

Claws . . . hooked: quoted by Thomas Sheridan (*Life of Swift* (1784), 505) to prove that the Yahoos were not intended to represent human beings: 'Now it is well known, that the human nails, when suffered to grow to any considerable length, never assume that shape, and unless pared, disable the hands from discharging their office'; but these claws are probably meant to symbolize human aggressiveness.

Their Dugs . . . walked: cf. 'The [African] women give suck, the Uberous dugg stretched over her naked shoulder'; 'their breasts hang down below their navells, so that when they stoop at their common work of weeding, they hang almost to the ground, that at a distance, you would think they had six legs' (Thomas Herbert, *Some Yeares Travels* (1638), 18; Richard Ligon, *A True and Exact History* (1657), 51; Frantz, 54).

Cabbin: hovel, hut.

216 *Excrements on my Head*: in *A New Voyage and Description of the Isthmus of America* (1699), a book owned by Swift, Lionel Wafer mentions monkeys that skipped 'from Bough to Bough . . . chattering, and, if they had opportunity, pissing

down purposely on our Heads' (p. 108). Cf. Dampier's monkeys in Panama: 'They were a great Company dancing from Tree to Tree, over my Head; chattering and making a terrible Noise; and a great many grim Faces, and shewing antick Gestures. Some broke down dry Sticks and threw at me; others scattered their Urine and Dung about my Ears' (*Voyages*, ii. 161; Frantz, 52).

217 *applying himself to*: approaching, accosting.

expect: await.

218 *Philosopher*: scientist.

Magicians . . . metamorphosed: possibly suggested by the *Metamorphoses* or *Golden Ass* of Apuleius, the hero of which turns himself by magic into a donkey. The same story is told in Lucian's *Lucius or The Ass.*

Climate: region.

Conjurers: magicians.

Passions: feelings, emotions.

imitating . . . surprized: perhaps an ironic comment on Aristotle's statement (*Poetics*, 1448b6–7) that 'man differs from the other animals in being the most imitative'.

220 *Vista*: an open corridor or long passage through a large building.

221 *occurred*: presented themselves.

Asses . . . Dogs . . . Cow dead . . . Disease: the diet of the Yahoos (asses, dogs, cats, cows that have died, corrupted flesh of animals, weasels, rats: see pp. 253–4; p. 263; and p. 258) is described in Leviticus (11: 3, 27, 39–40, 29) as polluting; which seems to confirm that the Yahoos represent, among other things, the theological concept of Original Sin (R. M. Frye, *JHI* xv (1954), 216).

Wyths: halters made of tough, flexible branches of willow or osier.

222 *carrying them on their Backs*: see note to p. 215.

whereof they had no Conception: in spite of their devotion to 'Reason' (see p. 272, l. 37), the Houyhnhnms are not very intelligent. The 'Master Grey' has already seen Gulliver take off his hat and put it on again (p. 227, l. 37).

223 *complaisant*: courteous.

224 *how easily Nature is satisfied*: an Epicurean sentiment (cf. Lucretius, *DRN* ii. 16–19; Horace, *Satires*, I. ii. 111–16). Praise of a simple diet was a stock theme of ancient satire: e.g. Horace, *Satires*, II. ii., which was imitated by Pope. Swift seems to be making fun of this satirical commonplace.

reconciled the: reconciled me to the.

225 *Provocative to Drink*: this nonsensical theory warns the reader that Gulliver's judgement is now quite unreliable.

no Animal . . . but Man: nonsense again; cattle, for instance, are fond of salt, and graze better and produce better milk if they have it. Salt is also an essential element in human economy. Gulliver's rejection of salt implies a rejection of human society, since Pliny had written: '*Vita humanior sine sale non quit degere*' (civilized life is impossible without salt: *Natural History*, XXXI. xli. 88; p. Bruckmann, *SN* i (1963), 7–8). Cf. de Lahontan, *Dialogues curieux* (1703), ed. G. Chinard (1931), 97, 128, where North American savages are said to hate salt, and to consider it the cause of all diseases among civilized nations.

fare: Swift seems to be punning on the two meanings of the word, 'get on' and 'feed'.

226 *significant*: expressive.

almost the same Observation: he was supposed to have said that he would address his God in Spanish, his mistress in Italian, and his horse in German. Perhaps Swift had this saying in mind when he made the language of 'La Puta' sound like Italian (p. 147).

227 *not the least Idea of Books or Literature*: quoted by Buckley (p. 271) as evidence that the Houyhnhnms lack creativity; but they do have oral poetry (see p. 266), and for rejecting written literature they have the authority of Socrates, who in Plato's *Phaedrus* (274d–278b) argued that written books were far less valuable than oral teaching.

He knew it was impossible: thus Houyhnhnm 'reason' is compatible with ignorant dogmatism like that of the scientists in Brobdingnag (p. 92); but there may also be some satire on rationalism in religion (cf. Swift's sermon 'on the Trinity', *Prose*, ix. 164–6: 'It is an old and true Distinction, that Things may be above our Reason without being contrary to it . . . If an ignorant Person were told that a Loadstone would draw Iron at a

Distance, he might say it was a Thing contrary to his Reason . . . It would be well, if People would not lay so much Weight on their own Reason in Matters of Religion, as to think everything impossible and absurd which they cannot conceive').

227 *The Word . . . Perfection of Nature*: here the Houyhnhnms seem to represent not a human ideal, but a human failing, pride.

228 *right*: real, genuine.

because . . . a different Covering: i.e. they possess 'that Wisdom, which converses about the Surface', and which Swift ironically calls preferable to 'that pretended Philosophy which enters into the Depth of Things', that 'Reason' which comes 'officiously with Tools for cutting, and opening, and mangling, and piercing, offering to demonstrate, that they are not of the same consistence quite thro'' (*Tale of a Tub*; *Prose*, i. 109).

from the Hides of Yahoos: perhaps an indication of Gulliver's increasing inhumanity. Cf. *A Modest Proposal* (1729), where it is suggested that the skins of poor Irish children 'will make admirable *Gloves for Ladies*, and *Summer Boots for fine Gentlemen*' (*Prose*, xii. 112).

229 *those Parts that Nature . . . had given*: cited (Ehrenpreis 3, 889–90) as evidence that the Houyhnhnms represent the Deists, since 'It was not nature that taught us to conceal our genitalia; it was a supernatural moral law'. J. J. McManmon, however, points out (*JHI* xxvii (1966), 61) that such sexual modesty was not a response to a supernaturally revealed code, but was an instinctive reaction of fallen human nature (Gen. 3: 7).

All this . . . consented to: i.e. he agreed to a *suppressio veri* and to a *suggestio falsi*. Though the Houyhnhnms have no word for lying, they perfectly understand the concept. Cf. their insincere behaviour on p. 230 (J. H. White, *ELN* iii (1966), 188).

232 *Nature of Manhood*: human nature.

233 *Houyhnhnms are your Masters*: possibly a satire on the English passion for horses. Cf. Pope's reference ('Epistle to Miss Blount, on her leaving the Town', ll. 29–30) to the country squire

> Whose laughs are hearty, tho' his jests are coarse,
> And loves you best of all things—but his horse.

their Bodies . . . Prey: a paraphrase of *Iliad*, i. 4–5. Swift's tone, though not Gulliver's, is subtly mock-heroic.

234 *Wants and Passions are fewer*: a link between the Houyhnhnms and the Stoics. Cf. *Thoughts on Various Subjects* (*Prose*, i. 244): 'The Stoical Scheme of supplying our Wants, by lopping off our Desires; is like cutting off our Feet when we want Shoes.'

As to my fore Feet: this criticism of the human hand should be read in the light of p. 266.

235 *resemble*: compare.

I left it to get Riches: not the motive given for two of his voyages (see p. 68; p. 143). He can no longer take an objective view of travelling, or of sailors (see p. 236).

236 *flying from their Colours*: deserting from the army.

237 *our barbarous English*: barbarous, presumably, because it 'abounds in Variety of Words' (cf. p. 234).

Revolution: that of 1688.

long War: that of the League of Augsburg (1689–97), soon followed by the War of the Spanish Succession (1701–13). For Swift's and the Tories' attitude towards this war, see note to p. 119.

238 *Ambition . . . to govern*: cf. *Utopia* (p. 58): 'I advise the King [of France, who is planning a war to annex Italy] to forget about Italy and stay at home. I tell him that France is already almost too big for one man to govern properly, so he really needn't worry about acquiring extra territory.'

Difference in Opinions: for this contemptuous view of religious controversies, cf. pp. 36–7 and *A Tale of a Tub*.

Whether Flesh be Bread . . . : a reference to the doctrine of transubstantiation, burlesqued in *A Tale of a Tub* (*Prose*, i. 173), where Peter (the Roman Catholic Church) serves up bread at dinner to his brothers Martin and Jack (Anglicans and Dissenters), assuring them that '*it is true, good, natural Mutton as any in* Leaden-hall *Market; and G——confound you both eternally, if you offer to believe otherwise*'.

Whether Whistling . . . : under the influence of the Presbyterians and the Independents during the Commonwealth (1649–60), organs and choirs were removed from the churches, and in Scotland organs continued to be thought sinful until the mid-19th century.

Post: i.e. an image or crucifix, veneration of which was condemned by Calvinists and Puritans. Gough (p. 415) quotes a

Wycliffite saying that images had at least one use: 'thai myghtten warme a mans body in colde, if thaie were sette upon a fire.'

238 *What is the best Colour for a Coat*: probably an allusion to disputes between Dominicans, Carmelites, Trinitarians, and Franciscans, known respectively, from the colour of their habits, as Black, White, Red, and Grey Friars; and in general to controversies about the correct colour and form of vestments.

indifferent: of no consequence either way. The Greek word for 'things indifferent', *adiaphora*, was a technical term used by theologians to mean 'non-essential points upon which the Church has given no decision'.

Sometimes the Quarrel . . . Right: cf. *Utopia*, 58: 'A fifth [adviser of the French King] thinks it might be wise for him to improve relations with the King of Aragon, and as a peace-offering hand over the kingdom of Navarre—which doesn't belong to him anyway.'

reduce: convert.

239 *many Northern Parts of Europe*: Ford's correction to the 1st edn. (so probably Swift's original MS) reads: 'Germany and other *Northern* Parts of Europe'. Presumably both Motte and Ford felt that this made too dangerously obvious the satire on George I, who employed German mercenaries to defend Hanover.

Culverins: large cannons, very long in proportion to their bore.

Carabines: fire-arms, shorter than muskets, used by cavalry.

Undermines: excavations under the walls (e.g. of a fortress).

Countermines: excavations made by the defenders of a fortress, to intercept those made by the besiegers.

240 *he no more blamed . . . Hoof*: cf. Swift's letter to Pope, 26 Nov. 1725: 'I am no more angry with ―― [probably Walpole] Then I was with the Kite that last week flew away with one of my Chickins' (*Corr.*, iii. 118).

Nature and Reason were sufficient Guides . . .: a remark that, together with that on p. 251, suggests a connection between the Houyhnhnms and the Deists. Cf. Swift's sermon 'On the Testimony of Conscience': 'there is no solid, firm Foundation of Virtue, but in a Conscience directed by the Principles of Religion . . . Suppose a Man thinks it his duty to obey his Parents, because Reason tells him so . . . if he stops here, his Parents can have no lasting Security' (*Prose*, ix. 154; Ehrenpreis 3, 893–4).

240 *wherein . . . conversed*: that I had not had much to do with.

241 *I said there was a Society . . .*: this long satire on lawyers was considerably softened by Motte in the 1st edn.; e.g., his version stated that only a section of the legal profession was being criticized, not the whole of it. What Swift had chiefly in mind was probably the behaviour of Lord Chief Justice Whitshed, who, when Edward Waters was prosecuted for printing Swift's *Proposal for the Universal Use of Irish Manufactures* (1720), refused to accept a verdict of not guilty, sent the jury back nine times, and kept them for 11 hours; and who in 1724 dissolved the Grand Jury, because they refused to present Swift's *Seasonable Advice* as a seditious paper.

speak for himself: cf. *Utopia*, 106: 'They think it better for each man to plead his own cause, and tell the judge the same story as he'd otherwise tell his lawyer.'

Practice: there is probably a play on the two senses: 'professional work' and 'machinations'.

Faculty: profession.

242 *sound the Disposition . . .*: cf. the account in *Utopia* (pp. 60–1) of how a king can always ensure 'a verdict for the Crown'.

Generation: breed, species.

243 *under Queen Anne*: Ford's correction reads simply: 'A Continuation of the State of England. The Character of a first Minister'. The reference to Queen Anne and to European Courts was doubtless inserted by Motte to conceal the satire on England under George I. See note to p. xxxii.

Use of Money . . .: cf. the ironical accounts of the power of gold in *Charon* (Lucian, 86–7) and in *Utopia* (p. 89).

the Rich man . . . plentifully: one of the themes of *Utopia* (p. 129).

to seek: at a loss, unable to understand.

especially those . . . rest: i.e. especially the ruling species (in Houyhnhnm-land the horses, elsewhere human beings).

244 *this whole Globe . . .*: Swift was probably thinking of the effect on the Irish economy of the import of luxury goods, among which he included 'those detestable Extravagancies of . . . Tea, Coffee, Chocolate, China-ware' (*Answer to Several Letters; Prose*, xii. 79).

Stargazing: see note to p. 154.

That, Wine was not . . . short: not the attitude of Swift, who enjoyed wine and whose letters include many references to buying

it (D. Taylor, *TSE* xii (1962), 59). In 1736 he wrote: 'I will make
Mr Hall . . . who deals in Spanish wine, to bring me over as large
a cargo as I can afford, of wines as like French claret as he can
get. For my disorders, with the help of years, make wine absolutely necessary to support me' (*Corr.*, iv. 469).

245 *I carry on my Body* . . . : for the protest against the waste of labour
on luxury trades, cf. *Utopia*, 77.

But that Nature . . . impossible: in a letter of 6 Oct. 1714 (*Corr.*, ii.
135) Swift wrote: 'My stable is a very hospital for sick horses';
but he seemed to think that all illness in horses was attributable
to the inefficiency of his grooms.

Mystery: trade secret.

246 *a Vomit*: probably an allusion to Dr John Woodward (1665–
1728). Professor of Physic at Gresham College, who believed
that the sovereign remedy for disease was to evacuate the
'biliose salts' from the stomach by long and severe 'courses of
vomits' (C. Kerby-Miller, *Memoirs*, 274).

Clyster: enema.

approve their Sagacity . . . Dose: cf. 'Verses on the Death of Dr
Swift', ll. 131–2 (*Poems*, ii. 557):

> He'd rather chuse that I should dye,
> Than his Prediction prove a Lye.

For the homicidal tendencies of doctors, cf. Juvenal, *Satires*, x.
221.

247 *I told him* . . . : see note to p. xxxii.

Mind: real meaning or intention.

forlorn: lost, doomed to destruction.

Act of Indemnity: such as the Act of Indemnity and Oblivion
(1660), which pardoned all who had taken part in the rebellion
or the subsequent republican governments, except some fifty
named individuals (thus providing, according to the Cavaliers,
'Indemnity for the King's enemies and Oblivion for the King's
friends').

248 *Wench*: mistress.

Tunnels: i.e. secret passages (perhaps referring to Juvenal's
optima via processus (best avenue of advancement): *Satires*, i.
38–9).

Graces: favours. See note to p. 26. Her Grace the Duchess of
Kendal was a firm ally of Walpole, until Bolingbroke (according

to Walpole) paid her £11,000 for her support (Firth, 245).

248 *in the last Resort*: as a court from which there is no appeal (a legal expression; hence the italics).

match: mate, marry.

249 *Without the . . . Appeal*: one of Ford's corrections to the 1st edn., first published in 1735. The use of the word 'Body' is awkward after the different use only two lines above; and, for other reasons, H. C. Hutchins suggested (*RES* iii (1927), 471–2) that the sentence should really have been inserted after 'Legislature is committed' (p. 116). Since it refers to the House of Lords, however, it would not make much sense after a sentence concerned with both Houses of Parliament ('these two Bodies' (p. 116).

250 *managing*: treating carefully, sparing.

Truth appeared so amiable . . .: possibly modelled on the remark attributed to Aristotle: 'I'm fond of Plato, and I'm fond of Socrates, but I'm even fonder of Truth.'

251 *Reason*: see note to p. 240.

we had no Pretence to challenge: we had no right to claim, i.e. we did not live up to the definition *animal rationale* (see note to p. 213).

253 *this unnatural Appetite*: cf. *Utopia*, 94, where people with 'a passion for jewels' are classified as 'illusory pleasure-addicts'.

That he had once . . .: the 'experiment' may have been suggested by Defoe's *Colonel Jack* (1722), where young Jack hides some money, wrapped in 'a foul Clout', in a hollow tree, cries and roars with despair when it drops out of reach, and goes wild with joy when he finds it again: 'I . . . snatch'd it up, hug'd and kiss'd the dirty Ragg a hundred Times; then danc'd and jump'd about' (ed. S. H. Monk (1965), 23–6).

sordid: possibly used in one sense of the Latin *sordidus*: 'miserly, avaricious'.

take the Advantage: seize the opportunity.

Courts of Equity: courts (e.g. that of Chancery) designed to decide, on general principles of justice, cases not adequately covered by the common law.

their undistinguishing Appetite: cf. the Hottentots: 'a People that will eat any thing that is foul: If the *Hollanders* kill a Beast, they will get the Guts and squeeze the Excrements out, and then without washing or scraping, lay them upon the Coals, and before they are well hot through, will take them and eat them' (Captain Cowley, *Voyage round the Globe*, 35–6, in William Hacke's *A Collection of Original Voyages* (1699); Frantz, 53).

254 *their Language*: the Houyhnhnms'.

255 *had their Females in common*: the system in Plato's *Republic* (457c10–d1). It is an ironical touch to imply that this 'Utopian' arrangement is normally practised in European society.

256 *Spleen*: nervous depression, a fashionable ailment of the period.

a Female Yahoo: traditional female tactics in literary pastoral, e.g. Virgil, *Eclogues*, iii. 64–5: 'Galatea throws an apple at me, the naughty girl, and then runs off towards the willows, hoping to be seen before she gets there.'

might refine a little: might have been a little over-ingenious.

these politer Pleasures: for the idea that sexual perversions are the product of civilization, cf. Juvenal, *Satires*, ii. 162–70.

258 *the Red-haired . . . the rest*: a medieval theory doubtless connected with the fact that Judas (who according to legend committed incest with his mother) had red hair.

present: immediate.

Luhimuhs: Kelling (p. 768) derives the word from Irish *luć* (mouse or rat) and Latin *mus* (mouse).

Kennels: a word used elsewhere for the holes or lairs of foxes.

259 *softly*: slowly.

a young Female Yahoo: the setting may have been ironically adapted from the 'Adam and Eve's pools' in *New Atlantis* (Bacon, iii. 154) where prospective husbands and wives bathe, so that they can be inspected in the nude before marriage by a representative of their intended mates.

Eleven Years old: the extreme disparity in age suggests that there may be an allusion to Vanessa (Esther Vanhomrigh), who, though nearly 25 years his junior, fell in love with Swift, and wrote to him in 1720: 'I was born with violent passions which terminate all in one that unexpressible passion I have for you' (*Corr.*, ii. 364). Gulliver's experience in the river seems almost like a grotesque parody of Vanessa's pursuit of Swift to Ireland (1714) and his discouragement of her sexual advances.

their grand Maxim: in a letter to Swift in defence of Deism (12 Sept. 1724) Bolingbroke had written: 'the faculty of distinguishing between right & wrong, true & false, which we call Reason or common Sence . . . is the light of the mind, and ought to guide all the operations of it' (*Corr.*, iii. 28; Ehrenpreis 3, 893–4).

259 *strikes you with immediate Conviction*: cf. Descartes's 'principle, that all the things which we very clearly and distinctly conceive are true' (*Discourse on Method* (1637), pt. IV, tr. J. Veitch (1957), 27); and Locke's '*intuitive knowledge*' in which 'the mind is at no pains of proving or examining, but perceives the truth as the eye doth light, only by being directed towards it . . . This part of knowledge is irresistible, and, like bright sunshine, forces itself immediately to be perceived, as soon as ever the mind turns its view that way' (*Essay Concerning Human Understanding* (1690), bk. IV, ch. ii, ed. A. C. Fraser (1958), ii. 176–7).

260 *Reason taught . . . either*: a principle clearly transgressed by Gulliver's master (p. 227).

Sentiments of Socrates: i.e. that it was a waste of time trying to investigate the physical universe, about which certain knowledge was impossible, and that ethics was the only useful subject of enquiry (see Plato, *Apology*, 19c–d; Xenophon, *Memorabilia*, I. i. 11 f.; IV. vii. 6). Cf. Plato, *Republic* (475e3–480a13), where those who study the eternal 'Ideas', e.g. of Beauty or Justice, are said to achieve *episteme* (knowledge), but those who study the world of sense perception can only attain to *doxa* (opinion or belief).

Friendship and Benevolence: favourite words with Shaftesbury (1671–1713), who held that human beings have instinctive social affections (E. Tuveson, *UTQ* xxii (1953), 373), and with Bolingbroke, who wrote to Swift (Aug. 1723): 'I know no Vows so solemn as those of Friendship' (*Corr.*, ii. 462), and in a published essay: 'Sociability is the great instinct, and benevolence the great law, of human nature' (*Philosophical Works* (1754), iv. 256; Ehrenpreis 3, 892–3).

where-ever he goes . . . at home: cf. *Utopia*, 84: 'wherever you go [in Utopia] you'll be equally at home, and able to get everything you want.'

ignorant of Ceremony: so are the Utopians (*Utopia*, 106).

Fondness: foolish affection.

same Affection . . . his own: in Plato's *Republic* (461d) men call all children born 7–10 months after their own mating their children.

260 *Nature . . . love the whole Species*: the Utopians 'say treaties make people regard one another as natural enemies . . . They think . . . Human nature constitutes a treaty in itself' (*Utopia*, 108–9).

Reason only . . . Virtue: a principle incorporated in the ethical system of William Godwin (a great admirer of the Houyhnhnms) and illustrated by the imaginary case of being able to save only one person from a burning building: 'that life ought to be preferred which will be most conducive to the general good', even if it means leaving one's own 'brother, father, or benefactor' to die in the flames (*Political Justice* (1793), ed. F. E. L. Priestley (1946), i. 126–8).

When the Matron . . . Consorts: cf. *Hakluytus Posthumus* (1625; Glasgow, 1905), i. 240–1, where the 'Brachmans' of the Ganges consort with their wives during limited periods only, and 'when a woman hath a child or two, her Husband forbeareth her altogether' (F. Kermode, *NQ* cxcv (1950), 318).

prevent . . . Numbers: the Houyhnhnms cannot, like the Utopians (*Utopia*, 79), export their excess population, since they know it is 'impossible that there could be a Country beyond the Sea'.

261 *In their Marriages*: in Plato's *Republic* (458d–461e) all mating is state-controlled, on eugenic principles.

merely because . . . reasonable Being: cf. *A Letter to a Young Lady* (written 1723): 'I have always born an entire Friendship to your Father and Mother; and the Person they have chosen for your Husband, hath been . . . my particular Favourite . . . yours was a match of Prudence and common Good-liking, without any Mixture of that ridiculous Passion which has no Being, but in Play-Books and Romances' (*Prose*, ix. 87, 89).

Violation . . . never heard of: cf. Godwin's *The Man in the Moone*, 1638, p. 103: 'Againe their Females are all of a absolute Beauty: and I know not how it commeth to passe by a secret disposition of nature there, that a man having once knowne a Woman, never desireth any other.'

which: i.e. a rule which.

thought it monstrous . . .: in Plato's *Republic* (451e6–7) and in *Utopia* (p. 89) both sexes receive the same education. In his unfinished essay, 'Of the Education of Ladies' (*c.*1728) Swift complains that only half as many women as men are properly educated, which means that about a thousand nobles and gentlemen must either stay single or marry women 'for whom they can possibly have no esteem' (*Prose*, iv. 228).

262 *Representative Council . . .*: in *Utopia* (p. 84) an annual parliament deals with similar questions.

263 *Whether . . . exterminated*: this example of Houyhnhnm 'benevolence' may have been suggested by the *krupteia* (a system for massacring Helots) at Sparta (*Lycurgus*, xxviii; W. H. Halewood, *PQ* xliv (1965), 191).

indocile: unteachable.

a Mountain: presumably a reference to the 'steep savage Hill' or 'Mountain' on which Milton places the Garden of Eden (*Paradise Lost*, iv. 172, 226).

produced by the Heat . . . Sea: apparently an allusion to Lucretius, *DRN* v. 791–8, where all living creatures are said to have risen out of the earth, since they cannot have fallen from the sky, nor emerged from the sea: 'And even now many animals arise from the earth, formed by rain and the warmth of the sun.' By contrasting the Epicurean with the biblical theory of creation, Swift probably means to remind his readers that human beings, however degraded, are of divine origin.

264 *Ylnhiamshy*: by reading the word backwards, and transposing and supplying certain letters, Kelling (p. 770) deciphers as Latin *ex mannis nullis* (born of no horses).

cultivate . . . Asses: possibly suggested by the recent introduction of donkeys into Ireland (Firth, 250); but the comparison of human beings to asses was, of course, an ancient joke that Swift had used frequently in *A Tale of a Tub* and *The Battle of the Books*.

Composure: composition.

265 *exhorted*: perhaps a satirical allusion to the Quakers, the rulings of whose meetings were always circulated in the form of advice. See p. 272.

he was pleased to conceal: see note to p. 229.

have no Letters . . . traditional: see note to p. 227.

In Poetry . . . Mortals: the idea of horse-poetry is, no doubt intentionally, comic; and the description of it seems to be expressed in the bland critical clichés of the day, so should not be taken too seriously (R. A. Greenberg, *Exp.*, xvi (1957), item 2).

266 *and usually contain . . . Exercises*: cf. Spartan poetry, which largely consisted of 'the praises of those who had died for Sparta' (*Lycurgus*, xxi); and the type of poetry approved of in Plato's

Republic (390d1–3): 'describing feats of endurance by famous men'. The chief surviving works of Pindar (*c.*522–422 BC) celebrate victories in races or other forms of athletics, and Swift's earliest attempts at poetry were 'Pindaric Odes' (1690–2).

266 *neither Joy nor Grief*: a Stoical attitude; see note to p. 234. Contrast that of the Utopians who, 'when a person dies in a cheerful and optimistic mood', 'sing for joy at his funeral' (*Utopia*, 121).

upon returning: just about to return. Cf. Cornelius Nepos, *Life of Atticus*, xxii. 1–2: 'all this he said with so steady a voice and countenance, that he seemed to be passing, not out of life, but merely from one house to another.'

267 *For Instance . . . Yahoo*: Buckley (pp. 276–7) deciphers the four terms as 'Houyhnhnm Yahoo', 'Wee Houyhnhnm Yahoo', 'You-know-well-home-in-a-while-may Yahoo', and 'In-home-Houyhnhnm-roll-now Yahoo'.

268 *Skins of Yahoos*: see note to p. 228.

Honey . . . mingled with Water: a Utopian beverage (*Utopia*, 71).

Nature . . . satisfied: see note to p. 224.

I enjoyed . . . Mind: cf. Lucretius, *DRN* ii. 16–19: 'Don't you see that nature demands nothing but a body free from pain, a mind capable of enjoying pleasant sensations, free from anxiety and fear?'

269 *Controvertists*: controversialists.

Virtuoso's: scientists (or more frequently, dabblers in science, like Shadwell's *Virtuoso*, Sir Nicholas Gimcrack).

Mechanicks: manual workers.

descend: condescend.

expressed in the fewest . . . Words: cf. the 'laconic' speech of the Spartans (*Lycurgus*, xix).

Their Subjects: for a similar list see Horace, *Satires*, II. vi. 70–6 (in Pope's imitation, 141–52). For the opposite extreme see Swift's *Polite Conversation* (1738), a parody of the futile conversations heard in fashionable society, which he started to write not later than 1704.

271 *When I happened . . . Lake or Fountain . . .*: an ironical adaptation of a stock passage in pastoral love-poetry (Theocritus, vi. 34–8; Virgil, *Eclogues*, ii. 25–6; Pope, *Pastorals*, ii. 27–30) where the unsuccessful lover (Polyphemus, Corydon, 'A Shepherd's Boy')

looks at himself (in the sea, a 'crystal spring') to check that he is not really so very unattractive. Gulliver has fallen in love with the Houyhnhnms, but feels a Cyclops to their Galatea.

271 *ravenous*: plundering.

    doubted: feared.

272 *contrive some Sort of Vehicle*: there seems to be a near-parody of *Odyssey*, v. 105–261, where Calypso receives orders from Olympus to send Odysseus away, and help him to build a boat. See note to p. 130.

    Urgency: earnest entreaty.

    consist with Reason: be compatible with Reason.

    Temper: equanimity.

273 *renowned*: Swift's choice of epithet is ironical, since, like the Tall-storians (Polyleritans) in *Utopia* (p. 51), the Houyhnhnms are 'not exactly famous or glorious—for, apart from their immediate neighbours, I doubt if anyone has ever heard of them'.

    Wattles: rods, sticks.

274 *Skins of Yahoos . . . youngest I could get*: see note to p. 228.

    stanch: watertight.

    Kindness: affection.

    But as I was going . . .: Thackeray (pp. 36–9) called this incident 'the best stroke of humour' in the book; 'it is truth topsy-turvy, entirely logical and absurd.' It serves a serious purpose in alerting the reader to the absurdity of Gulliver's final misanthropy.

275 *171⁴⁄₅*: until 1752 the legal year in England still began on 25 Mar. so to avoid confusion in dates between 1 Jan. and 24 Mar. both years were given; i.e. the voyage began in 1714 ('Old Style'), 1715 ('New Style').

276 *I arrived . . . South-East Point of New-Holland*: J. R. Moore comments (*JEGP* xl (1941), 220): 'If the land of the Houyhnhnms was where Gulliver *seemed* to place it, west of the southwestern extremity of Australia, he was able, in leaving the country, to travel 1,500 or 2,000 nautical miles eastward in a canoe of stitched Yahoo skins, *in an actual sailing time of sixteen hours at a speed which he estimated at no more than a league and a half an hour*'. Scott (vii. 295) suggests emending to '*South-West* Point'. Case (pp. 60–1) defends the text, explaining that Gulliver is meant to have reached the southern point of Tasmania, so that Houyhnhnm-land lies a short distance due west of the southern tip of Tasmania (about 44°S., 140°E.).

276 *Maps and Charts . . . really is*: possibly modelled on *Voyages*, ii.
430–1, 432–3), where Dampier indicates that he found New
Holland further west than Tasman's chart indicated (Bonner,
174).

Mr Herman Moll: a Dutch geographer (died 1732) who came to
London *c.*1680, and whose atlas, *A New and Correct Map of the
Whole World* (1719), was probably the basis of the geography of
GT (Case, 51–2).

Authors: authorities.

277 *stood to*: steered towards.

278 *about five Years ago*: Case (p. 63) calculates that Gulliver had
been away from England exactly 4 years, 6 months, and 18 days.

delivering: pronouncing.

279 *five*: the 1st edn. correctly reads 'three' (cf. p. 259). Faulkner
emended it to 'five', apparently wishing to reconcile Gulliver's
statement to Don Pedro with his previous statement to the
seamen (p. 278), but forgetting to allow for the voyage out,
which lasted over 9 months (Case, 63).

of my Veracity: in the 1st edn. the sentence continues: 'and the
rather, because he confessed, he met with a *Dutch* Skipper, who
pretended to have landed with Five others of his Crew upon a
certain Island or Continent *South of New-Holland*, where they
went for fresh Water, and observed a Horse driving before him
several Animals exactly resembling those I described under the
Name of *Yahoos*, with some other Particulars, which the Captain
said he had forgot; because he then concluded them all to be
Lies'. These words were omitted by Faulkner in 1735, presumably to avoid a contradiction with p. 303: 'That no *European* did
ever visit these Countries before me.' Both passages, however,
are highly significant. The first virtually equates Gulliver's 'veracity' with that of the Dutch, whose dishonesty he has often
stressed; and the second expresses not a fact, but a statement
that Gulliver is prepared to make on oath, and also raises a
doubt in the reader's mind about the veracity of the
Houyhnhnms themselves ('if the Inhabitants ought to be
believed').

Accident: incident.

280 *backwards*: at the back of the house.

imprisoned, or burnt . . .: either because his story contradicted
Gen. 1: 28, which gave man 'dominion . . . over every living
thing that moveth upon the earth'; or because it implied that he

had been associating with magicians (see p. 218). Cf. Godwin's
The Man in the Moone (p. 120), where Gonzales, on landing from
the moon in China, is accused of being a magician.

280 *almost of my Size*: perhaps a hint that Don Pedro's charitable
philosophy is to be seen as an alternative to Gulliver's misanthropy (see Introduction, p. xxvi).

281 *put it upon me*: urged it on me.

Commerce: dealings, intercourse.

I fell in a Swoon . . . : this incident has been seriously interpreted
by Lord Brain (*Irish Journal of Medical Science*, 6th ser., 1952, p.
342) as evidence of Swift's own emotional immaturity; but
'Mary Gulliver to Captain Lemuel Gulliver', a poem parodying
the theme of Ovid's *Heroides* (first published with *GT* in 1727,
and possibly written in collaboration by Swift, Pope, Gay, and
Arbuthnot) shows that the author and his friends saw the incident as comic; e.g.:

> Welcome, thrice welcome to thy native Place!
> What, touch me not? what, shun a Wife's Embrace?
> Not touch me! never Neighbour call'd me Slut!
> Was *Flimnap*'s Dame more sweet in *Lilliput*?
> I've no red Hair to breathe an odious Fume;
> At least thy Consort's cleaner than thy *Groom*.
> Why then that dirty Stable-boy thy Care?
> What mean those Visits to the *Sorrel Mare*?
> Forth in the Street I rush with frantick Cries:
> The Windows open; all the Neighbours rise;
> *Where sleeps my* Gulliver? *O tell me where?*
> The Neighbours answer, *With the Sorrel Mare.*

(ll. 1–2, 25–30, 45–8; G. Sherburn, *TSLL* iii (1961), 4; T. G.
Wilson, *FL*, 25–7).

282 *suffer . . . presume . . . Bread . . . Cup . . . Hand*: cf. Mark 10: 14:
'Suffer the little children to come unto me, and forbid them
not: for of such is the kingdom of God'; *Book of Common Prayer*
(Facsimile of Original Manuscript, Signed 1661, 1891, pp. 240,
244): 'Saint Paul exhorteth all persons diligently to try and
examine themselves, before they presume to eat of that Bread
and drink of that Cup . . . We do not presume to come to this
thy Table (O mercifull Lord) trusting in our own righteousness,
but in thy manifold, and great mercyes'; Mark 9: 27: 'Jesus took

him [the man possessed by 'a dumb spirit'] by the hand' (the same phrase is frequently used in connection with miracles of healing, e.g. Mark 1: 31; 5: 41; 8: 23). The allusions to the Gospels and the Communion service (first pointed out by H. Davis, *Irony in Defoe and Swift* (1966), 55) serve to emphasize the un-Christian quality of Gulliver's final attitude, and his appalling self-righteousness.

282 *Stone-Horses*: stallions.

283 GENTLE *Reader*: presumably ironical, since addressed to English Yahoos.

faithful History: i.e. a *True History* (see Introduction, p. xvii).

wonderful Animals . . . Places: cf. *Utopia*, 40: 'We did not ask him if he had seen any monsters, for monsters have ceased to be news. There is never any shortage of horrible creatures . . . but examples of wise social planning are not so easy to find. Of course, he saw much to condemn in the New World, but he also discovered several regulations which suggested possible methods of reforming European society.'

284 *Nec si miserum . . . finget*: nor, if cruel Fortune has made Sinon miserable, shall she also make him false and deceitful (Virgil, *Aeneid*, ii. 79–80). The words are spoken by the Greek Sinon, as a preface to a wholly untrue story, designed to persuade the Trojans to take the wooden horse within their walls, and so bring about their own destruction. The quotation implies that Gulliver's gospel of the Rational Horse is as dangerous, hollow, and false as the Trojan Horse (C. Winton, *SR* lxviii (1960), 32).

Writings which require . . . Journal: cf. *Utopia*, 29: 'in this work I didn't have the problem of finding my own subject-matter and puzzling out a suitable form—all I had to do was repeat what Raphael told us.'

my sole Intention . . . PUBLICK GOOD: see note to p. 82.

can possibly meet with no: cannot possibly meet with any.

285 *against whom the Tribes . . . Talents*: cf. p. 285.

Ferdinando Cortez: Hernando Cortes (1485–1547), the Spaniard who, by terrorizing the inhabitants, conquered Mexico in less than 2½ years (4 Mar. 1519 to 13 Aug. 1521).

missive Weapons: missiles.

Mummy: pulp. The sadistic fantasy is symptomatic of Gulliver's psychological state.

286 *Yerks*: kicks.

Recalcitrat undique tutus: he kicks back, protected on every side (Horace, *Satires*, II. i. 20). Gulliver means simply that the Houyhnhnms are, like Augustus, majestic and well able to protect themselves; but Swift implies a reference to the context of the quotation. Horace is explaining why he writes satire, instead of writing a eulogy of Augustus: for one thing, he says, Augustus rejects unseasonable flattery, and is like a horse that lashes out if you stroke it the wrong way. The suggestion is that Gulliver's praise of the Houyhnhnms is excessive and dangerous, and that Swift is really writing satire (on Gulliver's attitude), not eulogy (of the Houyhnhnms).

distributive: concerned with the determination of rights (here the rights of the natives as against those of their exploiters).

A Crew of Pyrates: the earliest Spanish colonizers of America were adventurers chiefly interested in finding gold, and notoriously cruel to the aborigines.

their Princes tortured . . . Gold: Montezuma II of Mexico was kept in chains by Cortes (1519) until he handed over £400,000 worth of pure gold and an immense quantity of precious stones; Atahuallpa, the last Inca of Peru, was murdered by Pizarro (1533) in spite of having paid a vast ransom in silver and gold.

convert: Atahuallpa was sentenced to be burnt alive, but earned the privilege of being strangled instead by allowing himself to be converted to Christianity at the stake.

But this Description: for the heavy irony cf. the praise of European diplomacy in *Utopia* (pp. 107–8).

liberal Endowments: cf. Swift's letter of 4 Sept. 1724, to Carteret, supporting George Berkeley's 'Notion of founding an University at Bermudas' (*Corr.*, iii. 31–2).

287 *believed*: the 1st edn. continued: 'unless a Dispute may arise about the two *Yahoos*, said to have been seen many Ages ago on a Mountain in Houyhnhnm-land, from whence the Opinion is, that the Race of those Brutes hath descended; and these, for any thing I know, may have been *English*, which indeed I was apt to suspect from the Lineaments of their Posterity's Countenances, although very much defaced. But, how far that will go to make out a Title, I leave to the Learned in Colony-Law.' Faulkner omitted this passage, possibly because the insult to the English closely following apparent praise of the British seemed danger-

ous to publish in Ireland; or else because he took 'British' and 'English' as synonymous, and felt that the juxtaposition of the two passages made it impossible to believe in Gulliver's consistency (A. Easthope, *SoR* ii (1967), 265).

287 *docible*: teachable.

Intellectuals: intellects.

288 *Evidence*: witness.

and therefore . . . Sight: like *Utopia* (p. 131), *GT* ends with a sermon against Pride; but the last sentence shows that the prime example of 'this absurd Vice' is Gulliver himself.

A SELECTION OF OXFORD WORLD'S CLASSICS

JAMES BOSWELL — Boswell's Life of Johnson

FRANCES BURNEY — Cecilia
Evelina

JOHN CLELAND — Memoirs of a Woman of Pleasure

DANIEL DEFOE — A Journal of the Plague Year
Moll Flanders
Robinson Crusoe

HENRY FIELDING — Joseph Andrews and Shamela
Tom Jones

WILLIAM GODWIN — Caleb Williams

OLIVER GOLDSMITH — The Vicar of Wakefield

ELIZABETH INCHBALD — A Simple Story

SAMUEL JOHNSON — The History of Rasselas

ANN RADCLIFFE — The Italian
The Mysteries of Udolpho

TOBIAS SMOLLETT — The Adventures of Roderick Random
The Expedition of Humphry Clinker

LAURENCE STERNE — The Life and Opinions of Tristram
Shandy, Gentleman
A Sentimental Journey

JONATHAN SWIFT — Gulliver's Travels
A Tale of a Tub and Other Works

HORACE WALPOLE — The Castle of Otranto

GILBERT WHITE — The Natural History of Selborne

MARY WOLLSTONECRAFT — Mary and The Wrongs of Woman

A SELECTION OF   OXFORD WORLD'S CLASSICS

JANE AUSTEN	Emma
	Persuasion
	Pride and Prejudice
	Sense and Sensibility
ANNE BRONTË	The Tenant of Wildfell Hall
CHARLOTTE BRONTË	Jane Eyre
EMILY BRONTË	Wuthering Heights
WILKIE COLLINS	The Woman in White
JOSEPH CONRAD	Heart of Darkness
	Nostromo
CHARLES DARWIN	The Origin of Species
CHARLES DICKENS	Bleak House
	David Copperfield
	Great Expectations
	Hard Times
GEORGE ELIOT	Middlemarch
	The Mill on the Floss
ELIZABETH GASKELL	Cranford
THOMAS HARDY	Jude the Obscure
WALTER SCOTT	Ivanhoe
MARY SHELLEY	Frankenstein
ROBERT LOUIS STEVENSON	Treasure Island
BRAM STOKER	Dracula
WILLIAM MAKEPEACE THACKERAY	Vanity Fair
OSCAR WILDE	The Picture of Dorian Gray

American Literature

British and Irish Literature

Children's Literature

Classics and Ancient Literature

Colonial Literature

Eastern Literature

European Literature

History

Medieval Literature

Oxford English Drama

Poetry

Philosophy

Politics

Religion

The Oxford Shakespeare

A complete list of Oxford Paperbacks, including Oxford World's Classics, OPUS, Past Masters, Oxford Authors, Oxford Shakespeare, Oxford Drama, and Oxford Paperback Reference, is available in the UK from the Academic Division Publicity Department, Oxford University Press, Great Clarendon Street, Oxford OX2 6DP.

In the USA, complete lists are available from the Paperbacks Marketing Manager, Oxford University Press, 198 Madison Avenue, New York, NY 10016.

Oxford Paperbacks are available from all good bookshops. In case of difficulty, customers in the UK can order direct from Oxford University Press Bookshop, Freepost, 116 High Street, Oxford OX1 4BR, enclosing full payment. Please add 10 per cent of published price for postage and packing.

An Anthology of Elizabethan Prose Fiction

An Anthology of Seventeenth-Century
Fiction

APHRA BEHN   Oroonoko and Other Writings

JOHN BUNYAN   Grace Abounding
                     The Pilgrim's Progress

SIR PHILIP SIDNEY   The Old Arcadia

IZAAK WALTON   The Compleat Angler